American Dream Houses

American Dream Houses

Presented by
Concept House Plans GmbH

KÖNEMANN

© Concept Home Plans GmbH

© 2000 Könemann Verlagsgesellschaft mbH
Bonner Strasse 126, D-50968 Cologne

© 2000 for this English edition
Könemann Verlagsgesellschaft mbH

Translation from German: Sally Schreiber
Editing: Tammi Reichel
Typesetting: APE, Overath
Lithography: Typografik, Cologne
Production: Mark Voges
Printing and binding: EuroGrafica, Marano Vicenza
Printed in Italy

ISBN 3-8290-4845-9
10 9 8 7 6 5 4 3 2 1

American Dream Houses

The architecture of the United States of America is as diverse and as varied as the country itself. *American Dream Houses* contains a selection of the finest house designs by some of the most renowned architects in America, and gives the reader insight into a wide spectrum of regional styles.

So choose your personal dream house from the chapters:

Introduction

The incomparable variety of American architectural styles is rooted in the Colonial period of the 16th and 17th centuries, when the first European pioneers settled in the New World. Their simple log cabins represent the original form of the American country style. Built with materials available in their new homeland, the early immigrants' cabins reflect the traditions and customs of their countries of origin. Logically, the main building material was native wood from the heavily forested north and the southern Atlantic coast. The need for simplicity, functionality, and permanence determined the architectural style, with the most important requirement being protection from harsh weather conditions. The first modest homes already exhibited both traditional craftsmanship and regional differences.

Thus, between 1620 and 1700 the early New England style became the first American architectural style. A typical New England house was

simple two-story wooden structure with a gable—or occasionally hip—roof. Some of these homes still stand today. One of the striking characteristics of this epoch is the protruding second story that offered protection from wind

and precipitation. To conserve heat during the long winters, the latticed windows were small and few in number, and the fireplace was placed in the middle of the house. The architecture of the northeastern Atlantic coast was chiefly determined by English settlers. Based on the one-room stone cottage typical of the British Isles, the settlers developed smaller New World versions in the form of one-story houses constructed of light-colored cedar. Both roof and facade were sheathed with shingles, and on the north side the roof was usually drawn deeply downward to protect from icy winds. Because of their shape, these came to be known as "saltbox" houses. The facades sported only two win-

main house balanced by dormers and gables adorning the side buildings.

In the southern states, architecture took a different tack. Here, instead of defending from the raw northern climate, houses had to protect inhabitants from the intense heat of summer. Extended eaves, covered porches, and pillared

dows, with the simple entry to the extreme right or left of the house. In the interior, a central chimney heated a large living room, while the bedrooms were located under the sloping roof. This so-called half-house is classified as a Cape Cod house—a term that also includes the larger three-quarters Cape and full Cape, with two windows to the left and right of the door.

Beginning around 1700, Puritanical simplicity gave way to Georgian charm. New England was booming commercially, and the prosperity was reflected not only in increasingly splendid interiors, but also in facades that reflected the newly improved standards of living. Houses increased in size and magnificence, with the elaborate ornamentation of the entry of the

verandas proved a good solution against the southern sun and heat. In its architectural symmetry, the southern style resembled that of the north, but houses in the south tended to be built of masonry. In place of the traditional central chimney found in the north, the southern country style typically has a pair of large side chimneys placed on the gable ends of the house.

By the end of the 18th century, Southern architecture felt the wind of a new design trend. Arched windows decorated with lattice work made their appearance, inspired by the Italian architect Andrea Palladio, who had also exerted a strong influence in the English motherland.

Between 1820 and 1840, Romanticism began to have an impact on architecture, and styles developed that would eventually culminate in what is now known as the Victorian style.

The modern single-family house of the 20th century distinguishes itself through its high standard of comfort. Classical farmhouses, typically found in the suburbs, often contain a living area of around 2,500 square feet. Characteristic of traditional farmhouses is a large, live-in kitchen. As a matter of course, this country design features a spacious master suite with a private luxury bath and adjoining dressing rooms, all of which form an independent unit within the house. The facade often sports a deep front porch over the entry. In wealthier suburbs, the elegant ambiance of modern European-style country houses is also a source of inspiration. The playful treatment of bays, generous window areas, and an elegant brick facade are characteristic of this design trend.

The sun-bathed regions of America have developed a look of their own. Known as the sunbelt style, this architecture, which is found chiefly along the coast of the southern states, calls up images of elegant single-family houses and cottages. Wide hip roofs, staggered bays in the entry area, and floor-to-ceiling windows mark the facades of these one-story villas.

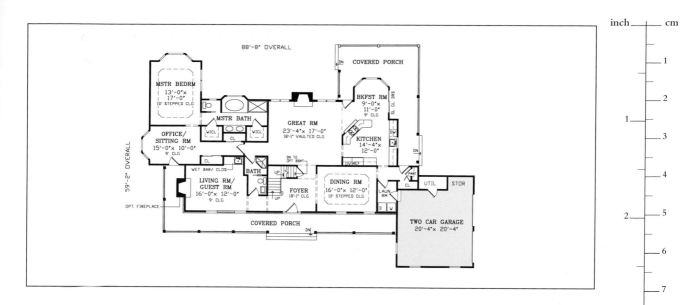

CONVERSION TABLE

1 inch	2,54 cm
1 square inch	0,000645 m²
1 feet	30,48 cm
1 square feet	0,092903 m²
10 square feet	0,92903 m²
100 square feet	9,290304 m²
1000 square feet	92,90304 m²

SAMPLE CALCULATION

The measurements for a garage:

20-4 x 20-4   oder   (20^4 x 20^4)

20 feet x 20 feet	=	400 square feet
4 inch x 4 inch	=	16 square inch
400 sq. feet : 10,7641	=	37,16056 m²
16 square inch	=	0,010323 m²
		37,17088 m²

inch ___ cm

1

2

1

3

4

5

6

7

3

8

9

10

4

11

12

5

13

14

15

6

16

17

18

7

19

20

EARLY NEW ENGLAND STYLE

Early New England Style 11

The hallmark of this house design is its simple elegance. Based on authentic New England models dating from the early 17th century, the classic wood exterior is kept simple, without trim or decorations, except for the traditional cupola on the garage roof. Also typical for early New England style houses is the placement of the chimney in the center of the building. The balance of the design is continued in the clear arrangement of rooms in the interior. Located to the left and right of the entrance, are the formal living areas, including the dining room and the living room with fireplace, from which one can progress directly into the study. To the rear of the house is a cozy family room (or "keeping room") with a cathedral ceiling and fireplace, which in turn opens into the eat-in kitchen. A laundry room and pantry are located outside the main body of the house and share a roof with the two-car garage.

Design 5127 – Homes for Today
© Augustus Suglia, Architect

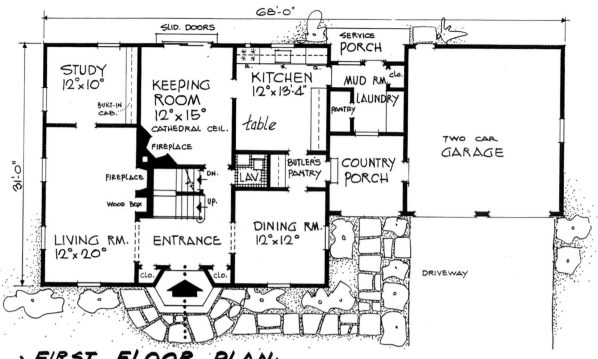

68'-0"

31'-0"

SLID. DOORS

SERVICE PORCH

STUDY
12°×10°

KEEPING
ROOM
12°×15°
CATHEDRAL CEIL.

BUILT-IN CAB.

FIREPLACE

KITCHEN
12°×13'-4"

table

MUD RM.
LAUNDRY
PANTRY

TWO CAR
GARAGE

FIREPLACE

DN.

UP.

LAV.

BUTLER'S PANTRY

COUNTRY
PORCH

WOOD BOX

LIVING RM.
12°×20°

ENTRANCE

DINING RM.
12°×12°

CLO.

CLO.

DRIVEWAY

· FIRST FLOOR PLAN ·

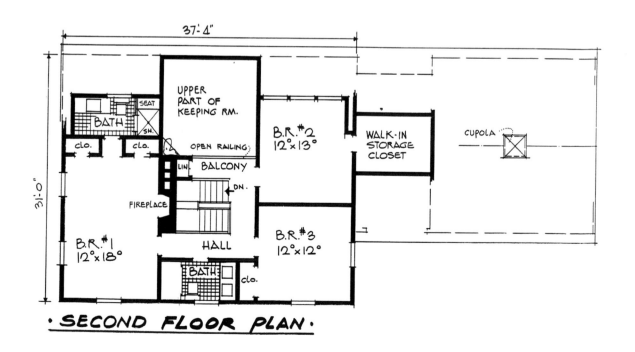

37'-4"

31'-0"

SEAT

BATH

SH.

CLO.

CLO.

UPPER
PART OF
KEEPING RM.

OPEN RAILING

LIN.

B.R. #2
12°×13°

WALK-IN
STORAGE
CLOSET

CUPOLA

BALCONY

FIREPLACE

DN.

B.R. #1
12°×18°

HALL

B.R. #3
12°×12°

BATH

CLO.

· SECOND FLOOR PLAN ·

Early New England Style 13

The design of this country-style house effectively incorporates the essential characteristics of early New England architecture. The striking overhang of the second story gives an unmistakable historical accent to the exterior of this classic design. The effective use of various building materials in the facade lends further emphasis to this detail. The ground floor and the two gable ends of the house are clad in classic clapboards, whereas the second-story overhang is covered with wooden shingles. The extended roof on the garage, including a cupola, completes the authentic appearance. The floorplan of the interior of the house is essentially symmetrical. The 1,184-square-foot ground floor is divided into a living room with fireplace, a dining room, a family room, a country kitchen, and a study or guest room. Other features include a mud room and a butler's pantry. The three bedrooms are located in the 807-square-foot second story.

Design 5135 – Homes for Today
© Augustus Suglia, Architect

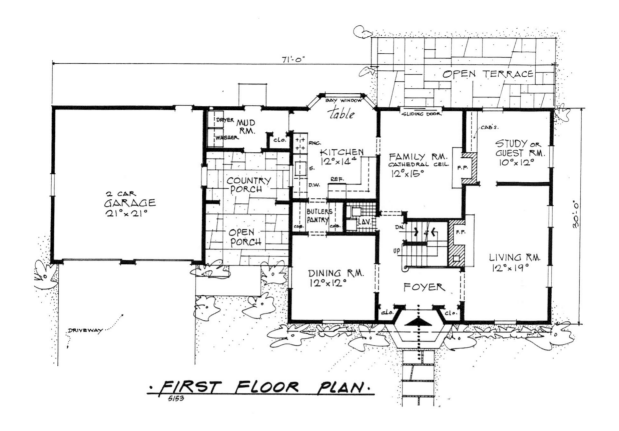

· FIRST FLOOR PLAN ·
5153

2 CAR GARAGE 21⁰×21⁰

DRIVEWAY

DRYER WASHER

MUD RM.

CLO.

COUNTRY PORCH

OPEN PORCH

BUTLERS PANTRY

CAB.

RNG.

S.

D.W.

REF.

LAV.

KITCHEN 12⁰×14⁴

BAY WINDOW table

DINING RM. 12⁰×12⁰

FAMILY RM. CATHEDRAL CEIL. 12⁰×16⁰

SLIDING DOOR

OPEN TERRACE

CAB'S.

STUDY or GUEST RM. 10⁰×12⁰

F.P.

DN.

UP

F.P.

LIVING RM. 12⁰×19⁰

FOYER

CLO.

CLO.

71'-0"

30'-0"

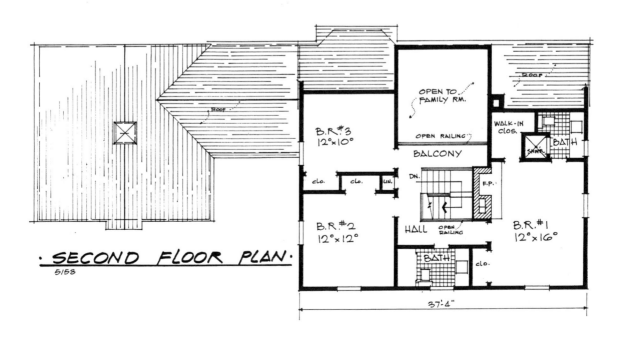

· SECOND FLOOR PLAN ·
5153

ROOF

ROOF

B.R.#3 12⁰×10⁰

OPEN TO FAMILY RM.

OPEN RAILING

BALCONY

WALK-IN CLOS.

SHWR.

BATH

CLO.

CLO.

LIN.

DN.

F.P.

B.R.#2 12⁰×12⁰

HALL

OPEN RAILING

B.R.#1 12⁰×16⁰

BATH

CLO.

37'-4"

This house is sure to appeal to anyone who appreciates authentic colonial-style houses, because numerous elements characteristic of the colonial period have been worked into the design. Today, of course, the wing attached to the main house is no longer used as a barn, but a two-car garage, which the designers have fitted with a gable and a door over the center garage as an important visual reminder of the colonial period. As a result, the house gives viewers the impression of an old house with a hay barn. The 2,013-square-foot interior is divided into two stories. With its 1,203 square feet, the ground floor features a foyer, living room, country kitchen with eating area, dining room, and family room (or "harvest room"). As in all early colonial-style houses, the bedrooms are located on the second story; three bedrooms and two bathrooms are incorporated into this design. The area above the garage offers additional space for expansion.

Design 5135 – Homes for Today
© Augustus Suglia, Architect

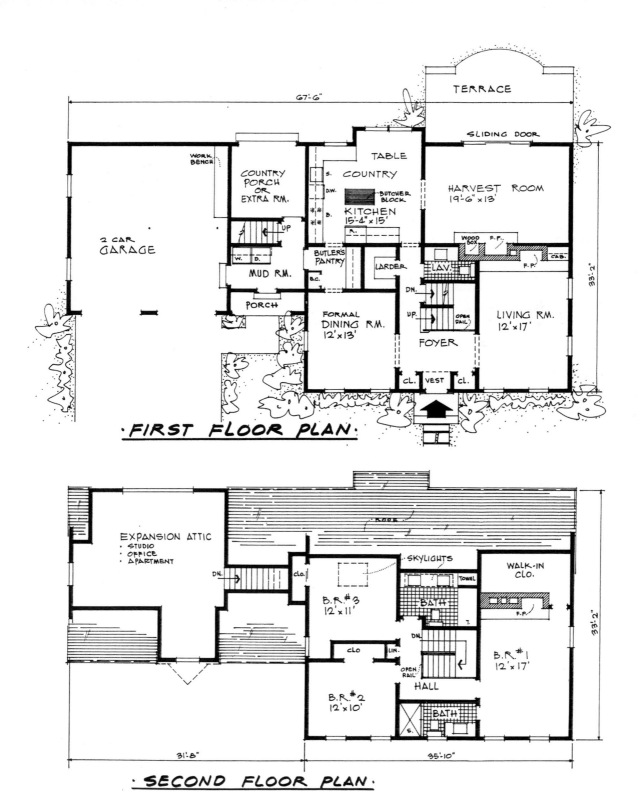

FIRST FLOOR PLAN

67'-6"

33'-2"

2 CAR GARAGE

WORK BENCH

COUNTRY PORCH OR EXTRA RM.

UP

W. D.

MUD RM.

B.C.

BUTLERS PANTRY

PORCH

TABLE

S.
D.W.
BUTCHER BLOCK
B.

COUNTRY KITCHEN 15'-4" x 15'

R.

LARDER

FORMAL DINING RM. 12' x 13'

TERRACE

SLIDING DOOR

HARVEST ROOM 19'-6" x 13'

WOOD BOX   F.P.

F.P.   CAB.

LAV.

DN.

UP

OPEN RAIL

LIVING RM. 12' x 17'

FOYER

CL.   VEST   CL.

SECOND FLOOR PLAN

EXPANSION ATTIC
• STUDIO
• OFFICE
• APARTMENT

DN.

CLO.

ROOF

SKYLIGHTS

TOWEL

WALK-IN CLO.

B.R.#3 12' x 11'

BATH

T.

F.P.

CLO

CLO   LIN.

DN

OPEN RAIL

B.R.#1 12' x 17'

HALL

B.R.#2 12' x 10'

BATH

S.

33'-2"

31'-8"

35'-10"

Early New England Style 17

This classic American "salt box" has a chimney at each of the gable ends. The symmetrical arrangement of the latticed windows with their wide shutters lend the house its harmonious exterior impression, while elegant wooden framing emphasizes the front door. Inside the house, a living room and a family room, each with a fireplace, flank the central foyer. To the rear, the living room leads directly to the dining room, while the family room connects to the large country kitchen with a glass bay that provides a well-lighted sitting area. The kitchen allows direct entry into the mud room and an adjoining terrace, as well as a spacious pantry. The second story houses three bedrooms and two baths. Special mention must be given to the detailed design of the various closets, including a walk-in closet in the upstairs hallway. With a total area of 1,991 square feet, this design offers ideal living space for a family.

Design 5173 – Homes for Today
© Augustus Suglia, Architect

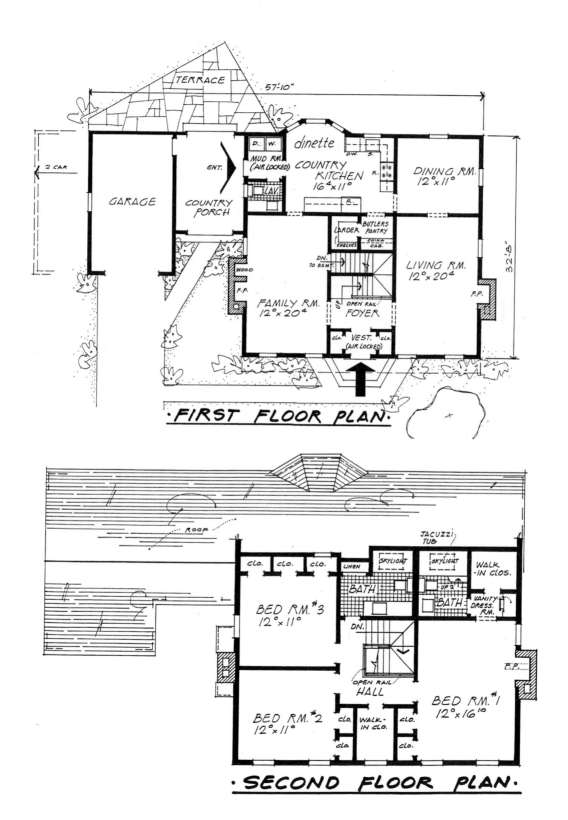

· FIRST FLOOR PLAN ·

· SECOND FLOOR PLAN ·

Early New England Style 19

The general impression of the exterior of this Georgian-style colonial design is one of simplicity, allowing the contrastingly elaborate entry area to stand out all the more strikingly. The heart of this 1,776-square-foot house is its generously proportioned country kitchen, which offers enough room for a large round table. To the left of the foyer is a room with direct access to a bathroom with shower that can be used either as a study or as a bedroom. The keeping room with fireplace boasts a cathedral ceiling and entry to both the covered porch and a utility room with a back entrance to the house. The generous, high windows in the keeping room provide a wonderful view into the garden. On the second floor are two bedrooms that share a full bath. Numerous windows flood these rooms with light, and the interior walls that border the bathroom are ideal for built-in closets. The second-floor gallery offers an open view into the keeping room.

Design 5181 – Homes for Today
© Augustus Suglia, Architect

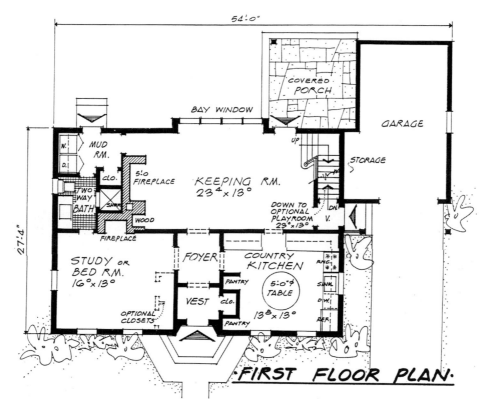

54'-0"

27'-4"

BAY WINDOW

COVERED PORCH

GARAGE

MUD RM.

N.
D.

CLO.

5'-0
FIREPLACE

TWO WAY BATH

WOOD

FIREPLACE

STUDY OR BED RM.
16⁰ x 13⁰

FOYER

VEST

OPTIONAL CLOSETS

PANTRY

CLO.

PANTRY

KEEPING RM.
23⁴ x 13⁰

UP

STORAGE

DOWN TO OPTIONAL PLAYROOM
23⁰ x 13⁰

DN.

V.

COUNTRY KITCHEN

5'-0"ø TABLE

13⁸ x 13⁰

RNG.

SINK.

D.W.

REF.

FIRST FLOOR PLAN.

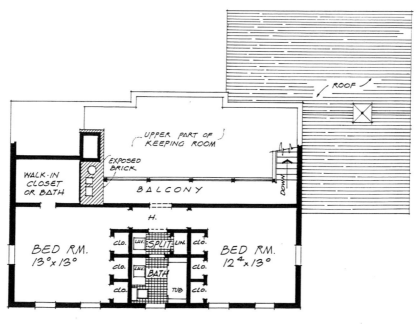

ROOF

UPPER PART OF KEEPING ROOM

EXPOSED BRICK

WALK-IN CLOSET OR BATH

BALCONY

DOWN

H.

BED RM.
13⁰ x 13⁰

CLO.

LAV.

SPLIT

LIN.

CLO.

CLO.

BATH

CLO.

CLO.

LAV.

CLO.

TUB

CLO.

BED RM.
12⁴ x 13⁰

· SECOND FLOOR PLAN ·

Early New England Style 21

The design of this house in the true early New England tradition combines all the architectural characteristics typical of the era. The steep roof, the large and centrally located chimney, the classical paneled wooden facade, and the symmetrically arranged windows are all features of the authentic "salt box" style. The ground floor, with 1,130 square feet, is entirely devoted to the activities of daily living. The solid chimney in the center of the house contains two fireplaces which can be used to heat the living and dining rooms, as can the barbecue grill in the large country kitchen. Upstairs, the 741 square foot area is divided into three bedrooms. The largest bedroom features its own bath and dressing room, as well as another fireplace. The plans for this authentically designed colonial house also include a two-car garage and a full basement.

Design 2113 – Homes for Today
© Augustus Suglia, Architect

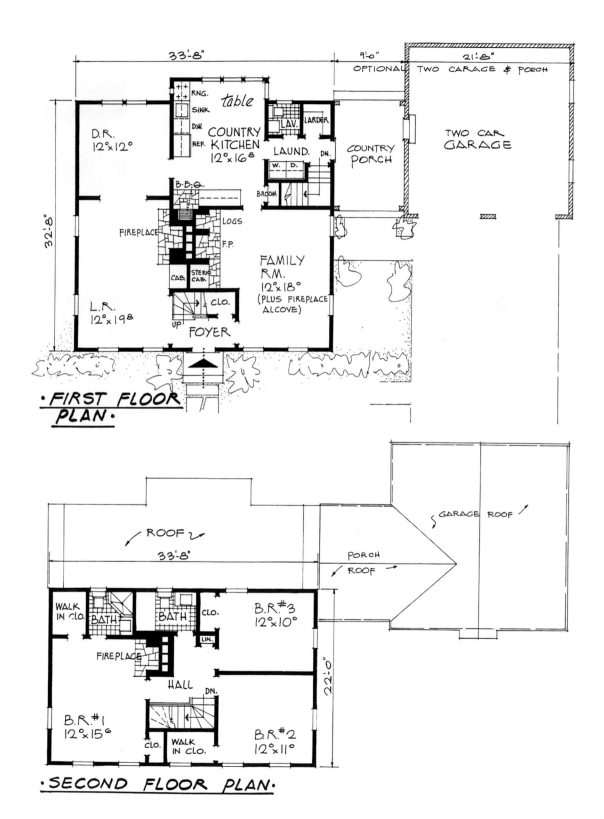

·FIRST FLOOR PLAN·

33'-8"

9'-0"   21'-8"

OPTIONAL TWO CARAGE & PORCH

RNG.
SINK   table
D.W.   COUNTRY   LAV.   LARDER
REF.   KITCHEN
        12⁰×16⁸   LAUND.   DN.

TWO CAR GARAGE

D.R.
12⁰×12⁰

32'-8"

B·B·Q.   W.   D.
FIREPLACE   LOGS   BROOM
        F.P.

COUNTRY PORCH

CAB.   STEREO CAB.   FAMILY RM.
                12⁰×18⁰
            (PLUS FIREPLACE ALCOVE)

L.R.
12⁰×19⁸   CLO.

UP   FOYER

·SECOND FLOOR PLAN·

ROOF   33'-8"   GARAGE ROOF

PORCH ROOF

WALK IN CLO.   BATH   BATH   CLO.   B.R.#3
                            12⁰×10⁰
            LIN.
FIREPLACE

22'-0"

HALL   DN.

B.R.#1
12⁰×15⁶   CLO.   WALK IN CLO.   B.R.#2
                            12⁰×11⁰

Early New England Style 23

Architect William Poole designed the "Hollyhock Cottage" with its total floor area of 2,433 square feet in the Cape Cod tradition. The facade is accentuated by the symmetrical arrangement of the latticed windows and the three roof dormers directly above them. On the rear of the house is a porch facing toward the garden and opening directly onto the terrace. Inside, the spacious great room with fireplace is located to the right of the entry, and the central area of the house is formed by the kitchen, which offers direct entry to the formal dining room and a laundry room. Upstairs there are three bedrooms. The master bedroom features its own bath and walk-in closet, and the two others share a full bath.

Design Hollyhock Cottage
by William Poole

Ground floor 1,344 sq. ft.
Second floor 1,088 sq. ft.
Total 2,433 sq. ft.

Two Car Garage

STOR.

Laun.

PORCH

DRY WASH

BRM CLST

DECK

Dining

OVEN

BAR ISLAND

Breakfast Room

Porch

Kitchen

D/W SINK REFG

P'DR. ROOM

PANTRY

Living Room

W.C.

ARCHED OPENING

FOYER 10'0"X10'7"

Great Room

Fireplace

Porch

ROOF AREA

CEILING BREAK LINE

Bonus RM

DOWN

ROOF AREA

W.C.

WHIRLPOOL TUB

LINEN

SHLV

HIS/HER WARDROBE

Bed Room 2

SHOWER

Master Bath

VANITY

SEAT

Bed Room 3

CEILING BREAK LINE

STOR

LIN

WALK IN CLOSET

SHLV

Bath

Master Suite

TUB/SHWR

VANITY

DOWN

W.C.

CEILING BREAK LINE

© by William Poole

Early New England Style 25

COLONIAL STYLE

Photo © Mark Englund / HomeStyles

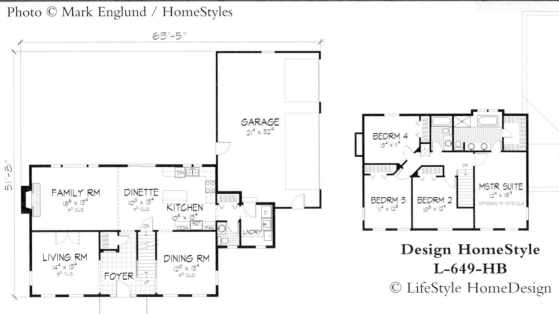

63'-5"

51'-8"

GARAGE
21⁴ x 32⁴

FAMILY RM
18⁶ x 13⁴
9⁰ CLG

DINETTE
10⁰ x 13⁴
9⁰ CLG

KITCHEN
10⁶ x 13⁴

DW

DESK REF FAN

LNDRY

D W

LIVING RM
14⁴ x 13⁴
9⁰ CLG

FOYER

DN

UP

DINING RM
12⁰ x 13⁴
9⁰ CLG

BEDRM 4
13⁴ x 11⁴

BEDRM 3
11⁴ x 12⁸

BEDRM 2
10⁸ x 12⁴

DN

MSTR SUITE
12⁴ x 18⁴
OPTIONAL 11' VLTD CLG

Design HomeStyle
L-649-HB
© LifeStyle HomeDesign

Photo © Mark Englund / HomeStyles

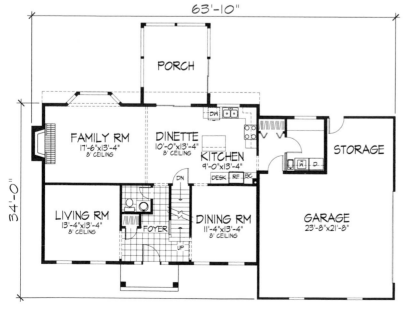

63'-10"

34'-0"

PORCH

FAMILY RM
17'-6"x13'-4"
8' CEILING

DINETTE
10'-0"x13'-4"
8' CEILING

KITCHEN
9'-0"x13'-4"

DESK RE BC

DN

STORAGE

LIVING RM
13'-4"x13'-4"
8' CEILING

FOYER

DINING RM
11'-4"x13'-4"
8' CEILING

UP

GARAGE
23'-8"x21'-8"

BEDRM 4
12'-8"x10'-4"
8' CEILING

BEDRM 3
10'-4"x12'-4"
8' CEILING

MSTR SUITE
15'-4"x13'-4"
8' CEILING

DN

BEDRM 2
11'-4"x14'-0"
8' CEILING

**Design HomeStyle
LS-97806-RE**
© LifeStyle HomeDesign

Colonial Style 29

The exterior of this elegant colonial-style house is marked by a high portico. The lines of its wide gable, supported by four pillars, are echoed again by the roof of the double garage. The front door is ornamented with a richly detailed frame. The interior of the house, with a living area of 3,270 square feet, is notable for its classical floor plan. To the left and right of the spacious foyer are the living room and family room, each with a beautifully designed fireplace. Upstairs there is room for four bedrooms, each with its own walk-in closet.

**Design HomeStyle
H-1410-1**
© LifeStyle HomeDesign

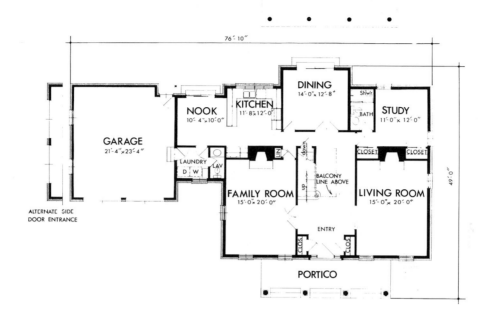

76'-10"

DINING
14'-0" x 12'-8"

NOOK
10'-4" x 10'-0"

KITCHEN
11'-8" x 12'-0"

Shwr

BATH

STUDY
11'-0" x 12'-0"

GARAGE
21'-4" x 23'-4"

CLOSET   CLOSET

49'-0"

LAUNDRY

D   W   LAV

FAMILY ROOM
15'-0" x 20'-0"

BALCONY
LINE ABOVE

up

down

LIVING ROOM
15'-0" x 20'-0"

ALTERNATE SIDE
DOOR ENTRANCE

CLOS   CLOS

ENTRY

PORTICO

BEDROOM
15'-0" x 12'-0"

BATH

CLOSET

BEDROOM
12'-7" x 12'-0"

LINEN

HALL

WALK-IN
CLOSET

WALK-IN
CLOSET

CLOS

down

OPEN TO
ENTRANCE
HALL

HALL

WALK-IN
CLOSET

WALK-IN
CLOSET

BEDROOM
15'-8" x 17'-8"

BEDROOM
15'-0" x 17'-0"

Shwr

LIN
TOWELS

BATH

Colonial Style 31

The design of this splendid country manor house takes its reference from the Georgian period. The full splendor and elegance of days gone by has been carried over into the design. The brick exterior is in perfect harmony with the gable architecture of the roof with its stucco cornices, while the imposing entry raises curiosity about the interior of the house. The house offers a 2,680-square-foot interior, with a detailed floor plan of generous proportions distributed over two stories.

**Design HomeStyle
FB-2680**
© Frank Betz Associates, Inc.

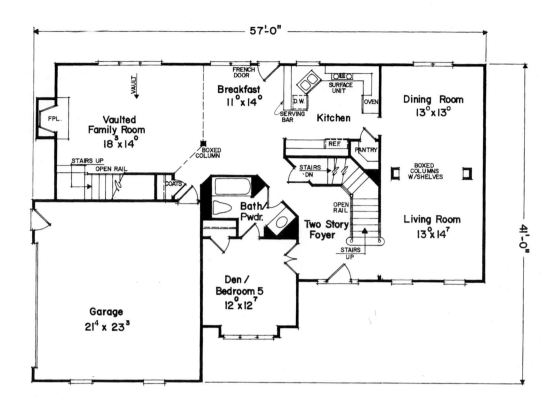

57'-0"

41'-0"

Vaulted Family Room 18³ x 14⁰

FPL.

VAULT

STAIRS UP
OPEN RAIL
COATS

BOXED COLUMN

Breakfast 11⁰ x 14⁰

FRENCH DOOR

D.W.
SERVING BAR

SURFACE UNIT

Kitchen

OVEN

Dining Room 13⁰ x 13⁰

REF.
PANTRY

BOXED COLUMNS W/SHELVES

STAIRS DN

Bath/ Pwdr.

Two Story Foyer

OPEN RAIL

STAIRS UP

Living Room 13⁰ x 14⁷

Garage 21⁴ x 23³

Den / Bedroom 5 12⁰ x 12⁷

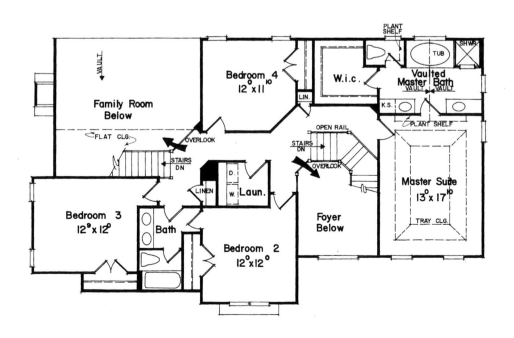

VAULT

Family Room Below

FLAT CLG.
OVERLOOK

STAIRS DN

Bedroom 4 12⁰ x 11¹⁰

LIN.

W.i.c.

PLANT SHELF

Vaulted Master Bath
VAULT   VAULT
K.S.
PLANT SHELF

TUB   SHWR.

OPEN RAIL
STAIRS DN
OVERLOOK

Bedroom 3 12⁹ x 12⁰

Bath

LINEN
D.
W.
Laun.

Bedroom 2 12⁰ x 12⁰

Foyer Below

Master Suite 13⁰ x 17¹⁰

TRAY CLG.

Colonial Style 33

Photo © Mark Englund / HomeStyles

The exterior of this manor house is clearly reminiscent of the beloved Georgian style. The elegant stylistic details that were characteristic of this epoch have been adopted in full by this modern design. The finely finished brick facade ideally sets off the beautiful plaster work decorating the entry, the windows, and the gables. The living area, distributed over two complete stories, consists of an impressive 3,219 square feet.

**Design HomeStyle
FB-5347-Hast**
© Frank Betz Associates, Inc.

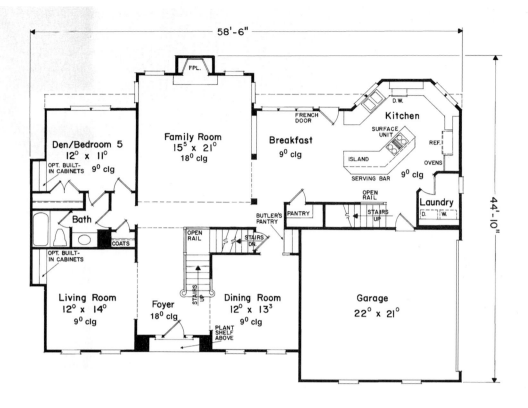

58'-6"

44'-10"

Den/Bedroom 5
12⁰ x 11⁰

OPT. BUILT-
IN CABINETS   9⁰ clg

Family Room
15⁵ x 21⁰
18⁰ clg

FPL.

Breakfast
9⁰ clg

FRENCH
DOOR

Kitchen

D.W.

SURFACE
UNIT

REF.

OVENS

ISLAND

SERVING BAR   9⁰ clg

Laundry

D.   W.

Bath

COATS

OPT. BUILT-
IN CABINETS

OPEN
RAIL

BUTLER'S
PANTRY

PANTRY

OPEN
RAIL

STAIRS
UP

Living Room
12⁰ x 14⁰
9⁰ clg

Foyer
18⁰ clg

STAIRS
DN.

STAIRS
UP

Dining Room
12⁰ x 13³
9⁰ clg

Garage
22⁰ x 21⁰

PLANT
SHELF
ABOVE

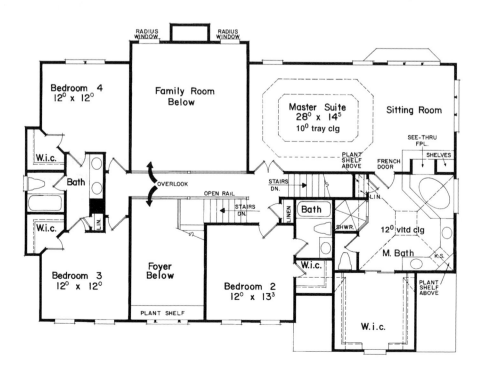

RADIUS
WINDOW

RADIUS
WINDOW

Bedroom 4
12⁰ x 12⁰

Family Room
Below

Master Suite
28⁰ x 14⁵
10⁰ tray clg

Sitting Room

SEE-THRU
FPL.

SHELVES

W.i.c.

Bath

PLANT
SHELF
ABOVE

FRENCH
DOOR

OVERLOOK

OPEN RAIL

STAIRS
DN.

LIN.

W.i.c.

LIN.

STAIRS
DN.

LINEN

Bath

12⁰ vltd clg

SHWR.

Bedroom 3
12⁰ x 12⁰

Foyer
Below

STAIRS
DN.

W.i.c.

M. Bath

K.S.

Bedroom 2
12⁰ x 13³

PLANT
SHELF
ABOVE

PLANT SHELF

W.i.c.

Colonial Style 35

Photo © Mark Englund / HomeStyles

The design of this house is determined by the typically straight, clean lines of the colonial style. Symmetrically arranged windows with shutters contribute to the harmonious impression of the facade, which is given a particular accent by the elegant entrance. Inside, the two-storied house presents a generous array of rooms, with a large space for additional expansion above the two-car garage.

**Design HomeStyle
CDG-2012**
© Columbia Design Group

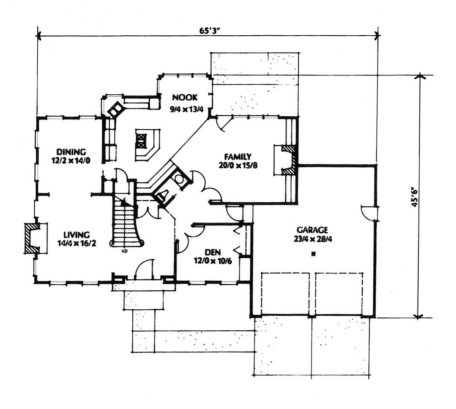

65'3"

45'6'

DINING
12/2 × 14/0

NOOK
9/4 × 13/4

FAMILY
20/0 × 15/8

LIVING
14/4 × 16/2

up

DEN
12/0 × 10/6

GARGE
23/4 × 28/4

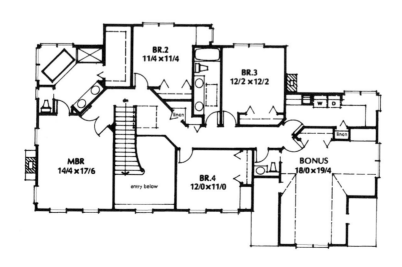

BR.2
11/4 × 11/4

BR.3
12/2 × 12/2

linen

w D

linen

MBR
14/4 × 17/6

entry below

BR.4
12/0 × 11/0

BONUS
18/0 × 19/4

Colonial Style 37

Photo © Mark Englund / HomeStyles

The princely dimensions of the entrance to this impressive house magically draw the viewer's attention. The rich stucco on the gable and window frames signal style and good taste. The living area of 2,416 square feet, distributed over two stories, is generous and conveniently organized. A large unfinished space above the three-car garage could easily be converted into additional living area.

**Design HomeStyle
B-92016**
© LifeStyle HomeDesign

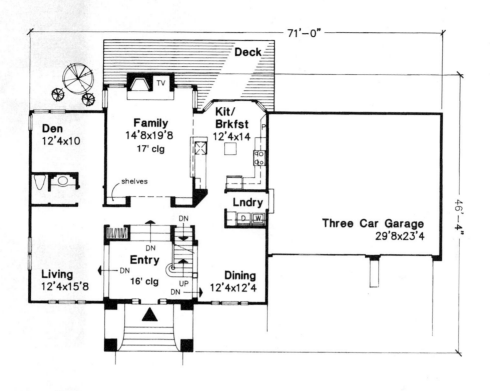

Deck

71'-0"

Den
12'4x10

Family
14'8x19'8
17' clg

TV

shelves

**Kit/
Brkfst**
12'4x14

P

Lndry

D   W

Three Car Garage
29'8x23'4

46'-4"

DN

DN

DN

Entry
16' clg

UP

DN

Living
12'4x15'8

Dining
12'4x12'4

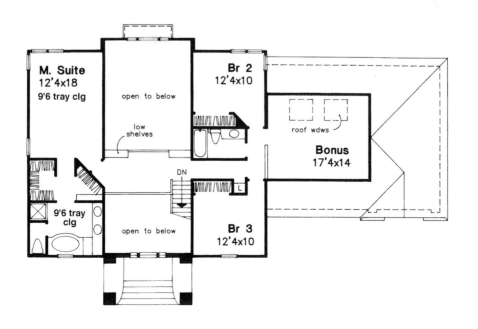

M. Suite
12'4x18
9'6 tray clg

open to below

low
shelves

Br 2
12'4x10

roof wdws

Bonus
17'4x14

9'6 tray
clg

DN

open to below

Br 3
12'4x10

L

Colonial Style 39

Photo © Mark Englund / HomeStyles

This classically designed colonial style house catches the eye with its straight, clean lines. A broad, covered porch stretches across the front of this 2,359-square-foot house. The interior is also marked by its clear floor plan. The ground floor includes areas for formal and informal living areas, while the bedrooms are located on the second floor.

**Design HomeStyle
AX-94337**
© Jerold Axelrod & Associates, P.C.

56'-8" OVERALL

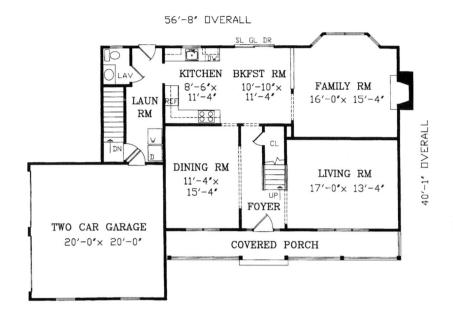

SL GL DR

KITCHEN
8'-6"x
11'-4"

BKFST RM
10'-10"x
11'-4"

FAMILY RM
16'-0"x 15'-4"

LAV

LAUN
RM

REF

W
D

DINING RM
11'-4"x
15'-4"

CL

LIVING RM
17'-0"x 13'-4"

DN

UP

FOYER

40'-1" OVERALL

TWO CAR GARAGE
20'-0"x 20'-0"

COVERED PORCH

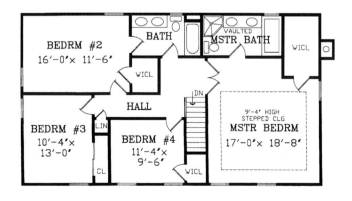

BEDRM #2
16'-0"x 11'-6"

BATH

VAULTED
MSTR BATH

WICL

WICL

HALL

DN

BEDRM #3
10'-4"x
13'-0"

LIN

BEDRM #4
11'-4"x
9'-6"

CL

WICL

9'-4" HIGH
STEPPED CLG
MSTR BEDRM
17'-0"x 18'-8"

Colonial Style 41

Photo © Mark Englund / HomeStyles

This house, with its classic design, offers space enough for a large family. Its living area of 3,046 square feet features a generous assortment of rooms. On the second floor are three bedrooms and a master suite with its own sitting area, and additional space for expansion above the three-car garage.

Design HomeStyle
AX–91310
© Jerold Axelrod & Associates, P.C.

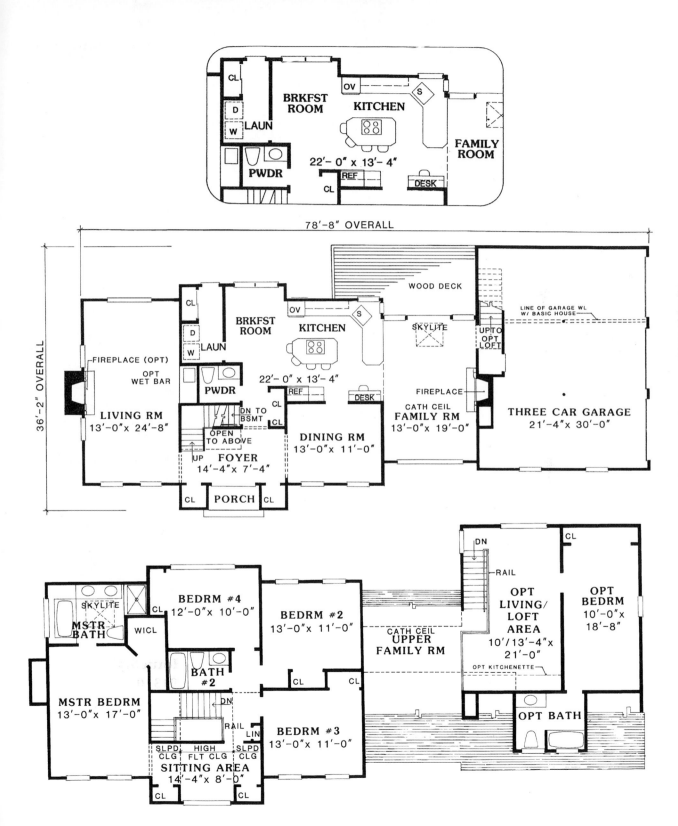

CL

BRKFST
ROOM

KITCHEN

OV

S

FAMILY
ROOM

D
W LAUN

PWDR

22'-0" x 13'-4"

REF

CL

DESK

78'-8" OVERALL

36'-2" OVERALL

WOOD DECK

CL

BRKFST
ROOM

OV

KITCHEN

S

SKYLITE

LINE OF GARAGE WL
W/ BASIC HOUSE

UP TO
OPT
LOFT

FIREPLACE (OPT)

OPT
WET BAR

D
W LAUN

PWDR

22'-0" x 13'-4"

REF

CL

FIREPLACE

THREE CAR GARAGE
21'-4"x 30'-0"

DESK

CL

LIVING RM
13'-0"x 24'-8"

DN TO
BSMT

CATH CEIL
FAMILY RM
13'-0"x 19'-0"

OPEN
TO ABOVE

DINING RM
13'-0"x 11'-0"

UP

FOYER
14'-4"x 7'-4"

CL

PORCH

CL

DN

CL

SKYLITE

BEDRM #4
12'-0"x 10'-0"

CL

BEDRM #2
13'-0"x 11'-0"

RAIL

OPT
LIVING/
LOFT
AREA
10'/13'-4"x
21'-0"

OPT
BEDRM
10'-0"x
18'-8"

MSTR
BATH

WICL

CATH CEIL
UPPER
FAMILY RM

BATH
#2

CL

CL

OPT KITCHENETTE

MSTR BEDRM
13'-0"x 17'-0"

DN

RAIL

BEDRM #3
13'-0"x 11'-0"

OPT BATH

SLPD
CLG

HIGH
FLT CLG

LIN

SLPD
CLG

SITTING AREA
14'-4"x 8'-0"

CL

CL

Colonial Style 43

Photo © Mark Englund / HomeStyles

This stately colonial-style house offers a living area of almost 2,550 square feet The clearly arranged ground floor features a formal living room, a den, a dining room, an eat-in kitchen, and a large family room with fireplace. Upstairs are four bedrooms and two baths, with additional space for expansion above the two-car garage.

Design HomeStyle
A-2283
Design © Carini Engineering Designs, P.C.

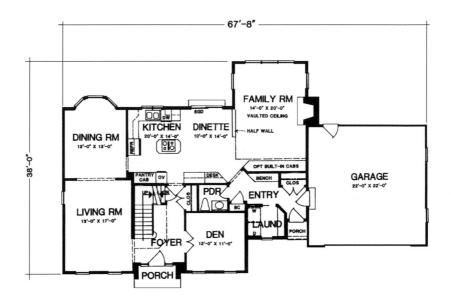
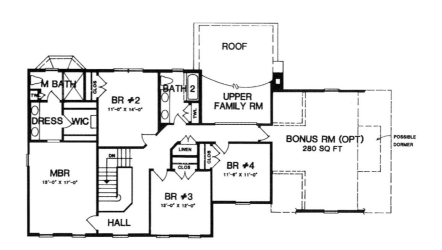

Colonial Style 45

Photo © Mark Englund / HomeStyles

This large and beautiful colonial style house offers approximately 5,060 square feet of space spread over two full stories. Imposing columns support the porch roof that shelters the entry area. The bay windows on the front are roofed with copper.

**Design HomeStyle
AX-91017**
© Jerold Axelrod & Associates, P.C.

46 Colonial Style

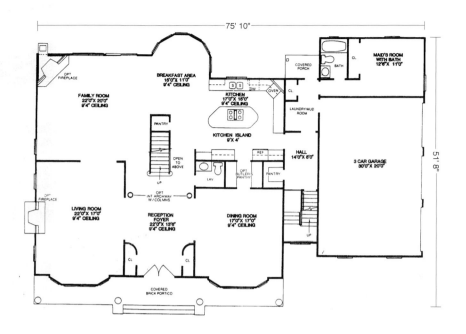

75' 10"

51' 8"

OPT
FIREPLACE

FAMILY ROOM
22'0"X 20'0"
9'4" CEILING

BREAKFAST AREA
15'0"X 11'0"
9'4" CEILING

KITCHEN
17'0" X 16'0"
9'4" CEILING

COVERED
PORCH

BATH

MAID'S ROOM
WITH BATH
12'6"X 11'0"

PANTRY

KITCHEN ISLAND
9'X 4'

DW

OVEN

CL

LAUNDRY/MUD
ROOM

OPEN
TO ABOVE

REF

HALL
14'0"X 8'0"

3 CAR GARAGE
30'0"X 20'0"

UP

LAV

OPT
BUTLER'S
PANTRY

PANTRY

OPT
FIREPLACE

OPT. INT ARCHWAY
W / COLMNS

LIVING ROOM
22'0"X 17'0"
9'4" CEILING

RECEPTION
FOYER
22'0"X 13'6"
9'4" CEILING

DINING ROOM
17'0"X 17'0"
9'4" CEILING

UP

CL

CL

COVERED
BRICK PORTICO

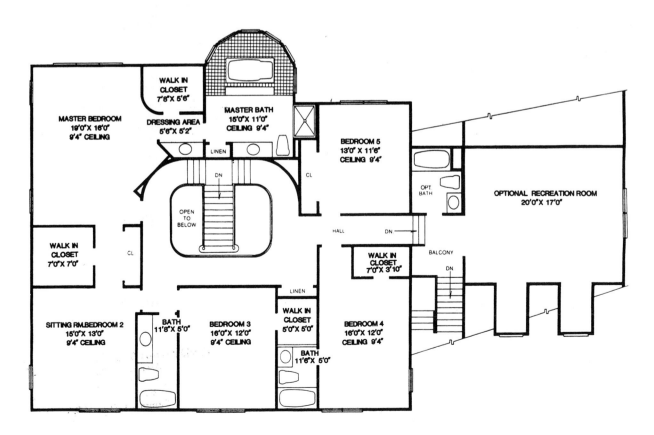

MASTER BEDROOM
19'0"X 16'0"
9'4" CEILING

WALK IN
CLOSET
7'8"X 5'6"

DRESSING AREA
5'6"X 5'2"

MASTER BATH
15'0" X 11'0"
CEILING 9'4"

BEDROOM 5
13'0" X 11'6"
CEILING 9'4"

OPTIONAL RECREATION ROOM
20'0"X 17'0"

LINEN

DN

CL

OPT.
BATH

WALK IN
CLOSET
7'0" X 7'0"

CL

OPEN
TO
BELOW

HALL

DN

BALCONY

WALK IN
CLOSET
7'0"X 3'10"

DN

LINEN

SITTING RM
15'0"X 13'0"
9'4" CEILING

BEDROOM 2

BATH
11'8"X 5'0"

BEDROOM 3
16'0"X 12'0"
9'4" CEILING

WALK IN
CLOSET
5'0"X 5'0"

BEDROOM 4
16'0"X 12'0"
CEILING 9'4"

BATH
11'6"X 5'0"

Colonial Style 47

The exterior of this attractive colonial-style house features an elegant front entry flanked by two bay windows. The intelligent placement of the garage creates a covered walk-through area connecting it with the house, while the small cupola on the roof of the garage lends the finishing touch to the historically accurate design. This house plan offers 2,800 square feet of living area distributed over two stories. The ground floor features a dining room, a kitchen with breakfast nook, a family room, and an impressive formal living room. Four bedrooms are located in the second story.

**Design HomeStyle
AX-2801**
©Jerold Axelrod & Associates, Inc.

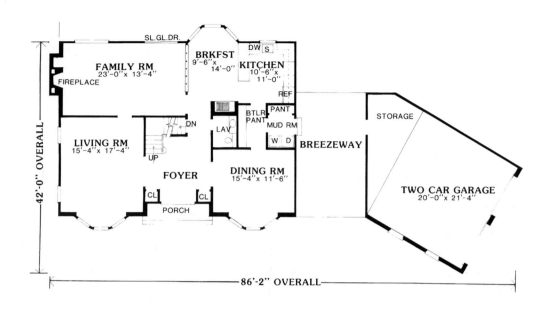

FAMILY RM.
23'-0" x 13'-4"

FIREPLACE

SL.GL.DR.

BRKFST
9'-6" x 14'-0"

DW S

KITCHEN
10'-6" x 11'-0"

REF

PANT

BTLR PANT

MUD RM

W D

BREEZEWAY

STORAGE

DN

LIVING RM.
15'-4" x 17'-4"

LAV

UP

FOYER

DINING RM.
15'-4" x 11'-6"

CL

CL

PORCH

TWO CAR GARAGE
20'-0" x 21'-4"

42'-0" OVERALL

86'-2" OVERALL

DRSG

BATH #1

BATH #2

BEDRM #2
14'-0" x 13'-4"

WARDROBE

LIN

WICL

WICL

UPPER HALL

CL

CL

MASTER BEDRM
15'-4" x 17'-4"

DN

OPEN

CL

BEDRM #4
13'-0" x 11'-4"

BEDRM #3
12'-0" x 15'-0"

CL

Colonial Style 49

Photo © Mark Englund / HomeStyles

The characteristic feature of this colonial-style house is its protruding gabled front element and stylistically accurate entryway. Symmetrically arranged windows with shutters lend the facade a harmonious appearance. The design offers a total living area of 3,285 square feet, equally divided between the two stories.

**Design HomeStyle
AX-87105**
© Jerold Axelrod & Associates, Inc.

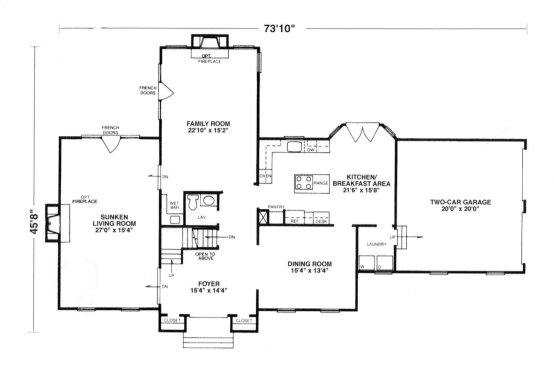

73'10"

45'8"

OPT.
FIREPLACE

FRENCH
DOORS

FAMILY ROOM
22'10" x 15'2"

FRENCH
DOORS

DW

OVEN

RANGE

KITCHEN/
BREAKFAST AREA
21'6" x 15'8"

TWO-CAR GARAGE
20'0" x 20'0"

OPT.
FIREPLACE

SUNKEN
LIVING ROOM
27'0" x 15'4"

DN

WET
BAR

LAV

PANTRY

REF

DESK

UP

OPEN TO
ABOVE

UP

DN

LAUNDRY

W

D

DN

FOYER
15'4" x 14'4"

DINING ROOM
15'4" x 13'4"

CLOSET

CLOSET

SKYLIGHT

MASTER BATH
15'4" x 10'8"
12' CATHEDRAL CEILING

WALK IN
CLOSET

BATH

SITTING AREA
11'0" x 9'4"

WALK IN
CLOSET

DRESSING
AREA

OPT.
VANITY

LINEN
CAB

CL

BEDROOM 2
13'4" x 13'0"

OPT.
FIREPLACE

MASTER BEDROOM
18'8" x 15'4"

DN

BALCONY

BEDROOM 4
15'0" x 10'10"
12' CATHEDRAL CEILING

CL

CL

BEDROOM 3
13'4" x 13'0"

Colonial Style 51

Photo © Mark Englund / HomeStyles

This decorative colonial-style house features an elegantly designed entry. The bright central gable provides an interesting contrast to the mottled brick facade, and wide, latticed windows framed with shutters underscore the balance of the design. The straight lines of the exterior are continued in the floor plan of the house, bending only for the large bay window in the breakfast nook that offers a view into the garden. The total living area provided by the house amounts to 2,899 square feet.

**Design HomeStyle
DD-2928-A**
© Danze & Davis Architects, Inc.

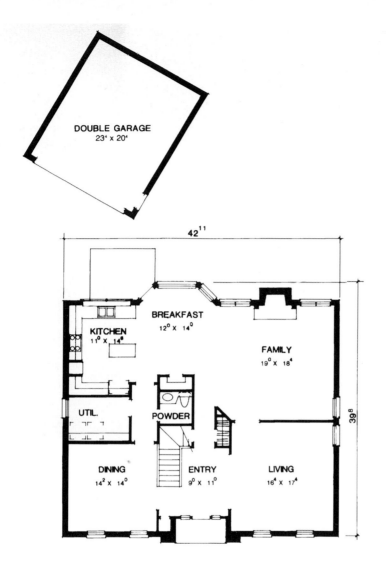

DOUBLE GARAGE
23⁴ x 20⁴

42¹¹

BREAKFAST
12⁰ x 14⁰

KITCHEN
11⁰ x 14⁸

FAMILY
19⁰ x 18⁴

UTIL.

POWDER

39⁸

DINING
14² x 14⁰

ENTRY
9⁰ x 11⁰

LIVING
16⁴ x 17⁴

M. BATH

BEDROOM 4
11³ x 13⁸

BEDROOM 3
11⁴ x 17⁰

BATH 3

HALL

MASTER BEDROOM
14² x 20⁶

OPEN

BEDROOM 2
16⁴ x 11⁴

Colonial Style 53

A richly detailed gable, symmetrically arranged windows, and a broad front porch are the hallmarks of the front of this magnificent country manor. The classically simple wooden facade stands in contrast to the decorative columns of the porch with its decorative railing. The house features a total living area of 3,272 square feet apportioned between the two stories. The open foyer is flanked by the formal living room and dining room, while the great room, kitchen and breakfast room compose a unit that looks out onto the garden. The house contains four bedrooms altogether, three of which are located on the second floor.

Design Woodbridge
by William Poole

Ground floor 1,876 sq. ft.
Second floor 1,396 sq. ft.
Total 3,272 sq. ft.

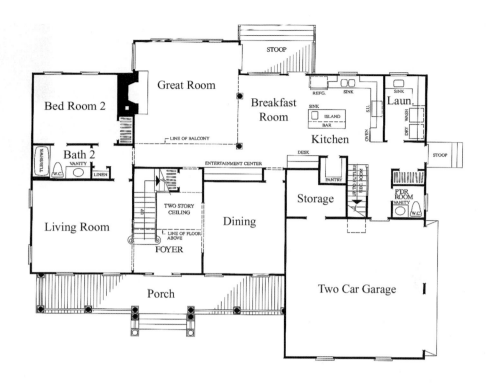

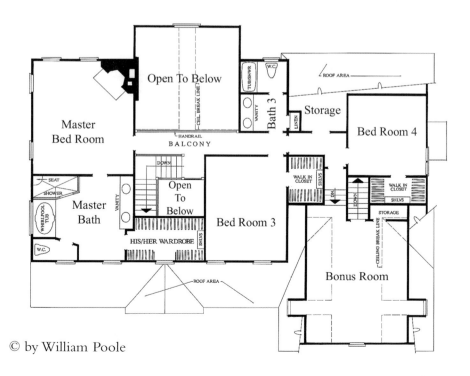

© by William Poole

Photo © Mark Englund / HomeStyles

This colonial-style house is an exact replica of a historical model—with a modern interior arrangement, of course. The floor plan of the 2,982-square-foot house is classic in design, featuring a formal living area on the ground floor consisting of the dining room and living room to either side of the foyer, along with a country kitchen and family room. On the second floor are four bedrooms, with a large space above the garage for expansion.

Design HomeStyle
S-71091
© Suntel Home Design, Inc.

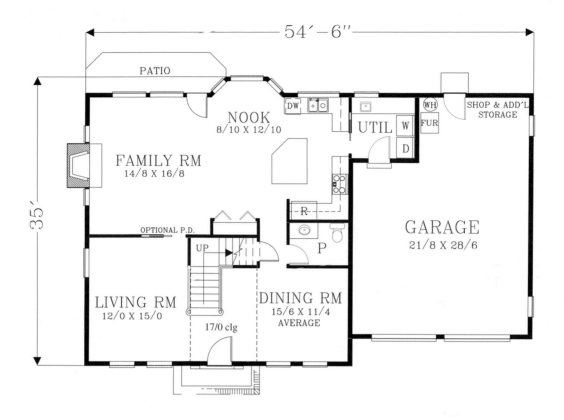

PATIO

54'−6"

35'

NOOK
8/10 X 12/10

FAMILY RM
14/8 X 16/8

UTIL

W   FUR

WH

SHOP & ADD'L STORAGE

DW

GARAGE
21/8 X 28/6

R

OPTIONAL P.D.

UP

P

LIVING RM
12/0 X 15/0

DINING RM
15/6 X 11/4
AVERAGE

17/0 clg

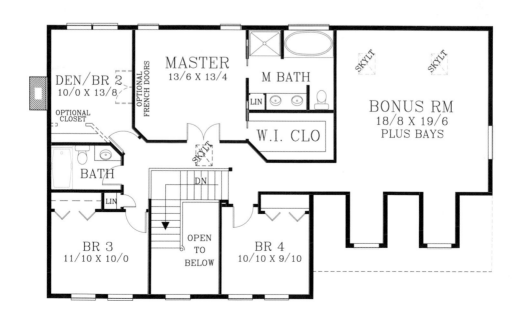

DEN/BR 2
10/0 X 13/8

OPTIONAL FRENCH DOORS

MASTER
13/6 X 13/4

M BATH

LIN

SKYLT   SKYLT

BONUS RM
18/8 X 19/6
PLUS BAYS

OPTIONAL CLOSET

BATH

LIN

W.I. CLO

SKYLT

DN

BR 3
11/10 X 10/0

OPEN
TO
BELOW

BR 4
10/10 X 9/10

Colonial Style 57

Large latticed windows accent the front of this imposing Georgian-style house. On the interior, 3,197 square feet of living space are designed in a classic floor plan appropriate to the style of the house throughout both stories.

**Design HomeStyle
KLF–9213**
© Estate Creations, Inc.

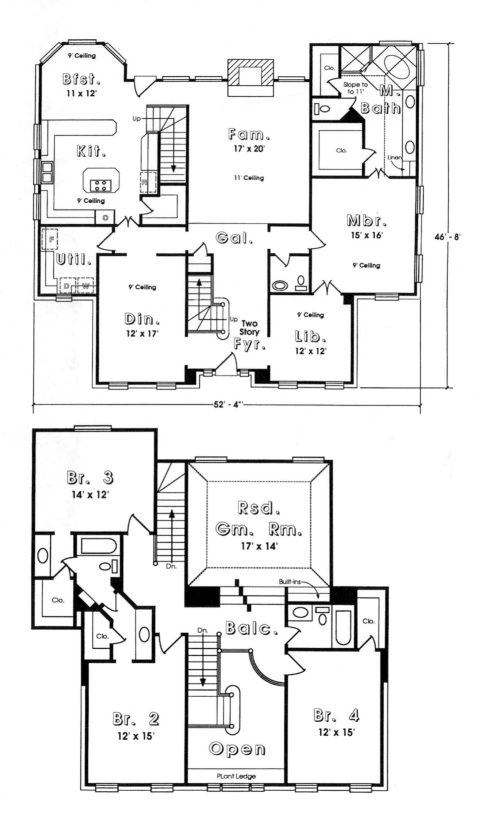

9' Ceiling

Bfst.
11 x 12'

Kit.
9' Ceiling

Up

Fam.
17' x 20'

11' Ceiling

Clo.

Slope to
to 11'

M.
Bath

Clo.

Linen

F

Util.

D   W

Din.
9' Ceiling
12' x 17'

Gal.

Up   Two
Story
Fyr.

Lib.
9' Ceiling
12' x 12'

Mbr.
15' x 16'

9' Ceiling

9' Ceiling

46' - 8'

52' - 4"

Br. 3
14' x 12'

Rsd.
Gm. Rm.
17' x 14'

Clo.

Built-ins

Dn.

Clo.

Clo.

Balc.

Clo.

Dn.

Br. 2
12' x 15'

Open

Br. 4
12' x 15'

PLant Ledge

Colonial Style 59

This design by William Poole will appeal to admirers of two-story houses. The classical wooden shingle facade provides a particularly effective contrast to the snow-white latticed windows with shutters, the striking columns on the front porch, and the delicate railing on the balcony above the porch. The elegant styling is continued on the interior. The formal living room and the dining room opposite it are both visible from the two-story-high foyer. A family room with fireplace and the kitchen with its generous breakfast area form a separate area of the house. Also on the ground floor is a master suite with its own bath. The spacious floor plan of the second story features three additional large bedrooms, three full bathrooms, and a generous space for future expansion.

Design Chesapeake
by William Poole

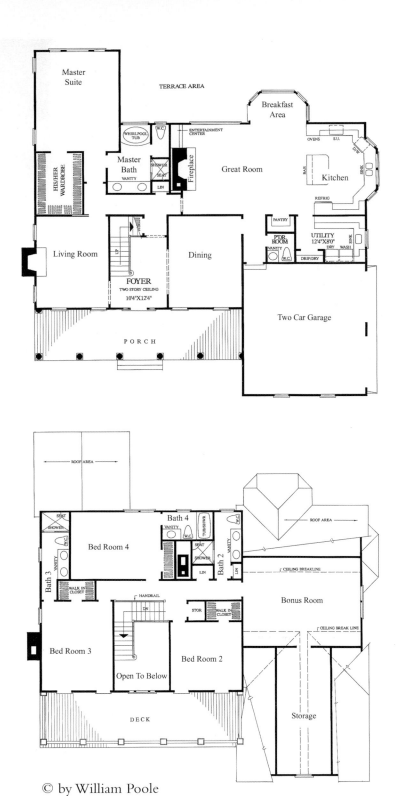

Master
Suite

TERRACE AREA

Breakfast
Area

WHIRLPOOL
TUB

W.C.

ENTERTAINMENT
CENTER

OVENS   S.U.

D/W

Master
Bath

SHOWER
SEAT

Fireplace

Great Room

BAR

Kitchen

SINK

VANITY

LIN

HIS/HER
WARDROBE

REFRIG

PANTRY

Living Room

FOYER
TWO STORY CEILING
10'4"X12'4"

Dining

PDR.
ROOM

VANITY

W.C.

UTILITY
12'4"X8'0"

DRY   WASH.

SINK

DRIP/DRY

Two Car Garage

PORCH

ROOF AREA

ROOF AREA

SEAT

SHOWER

W.C.

VANITY

Bath 4

W.C.

TUB/SHWR

Bed Room 4

SEAT

SHOWER

CEILING BREAKLINE

Bath 2

W.C.

Bath 3

VANITY

LIN

LIN

VANITY

WALK IN
CLOSET

Bonus Room

HANDRAIL

DN

STOR

WALK IN
CLOSET

CEILING BREAK LINE

Bed Room 3

Open To Below

Bed Room 2

Storage

DECK

© by William Poole

Colonial Style 61

The exterior of this house is particularly rich in historical details typical of the style. The balustrade, the pilasters, and the decorative trim delineate the facade, whose individual architectural elements—such as the door and the windows—are especially emphasized by the steep roof, the segmented gable ends, and the profiled framing elements. Inside, a two-story-high foyer provides entry into the dining room, the formal living room, and the well-lit family room. The family room opens into the kitchen with breakfast area, located at the back of the house. The master suite features a luxurious bath with space for a whirlpool tub and a shower, and enormous walk-in closets. The second floor of this two-story house offers three bedrooms and two full baths, with the option to expand further.

Design Cape Charles
by William Poole

Ground floor 2,306.5 sq. ft.
Second floor 925.5 sq. ft.
Total 3,232 sq. ft

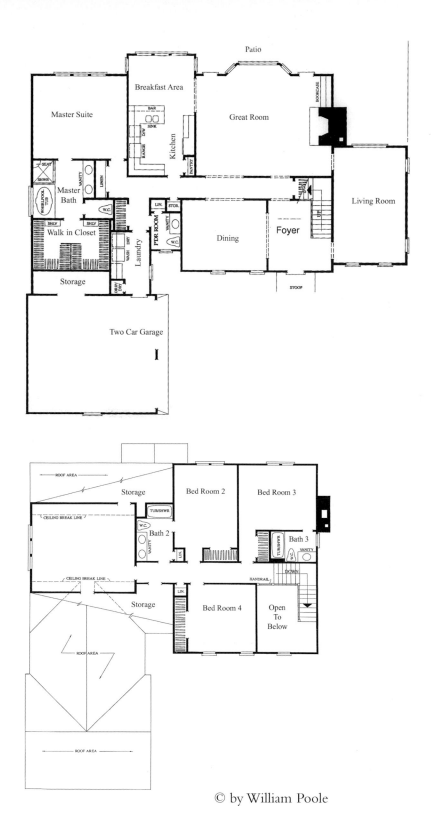

Patio

Breakfast Area

Great Room

BOOKCASE

Master Suite

BAR

DW

SINK

RANGE

Kitchen

PANTRY

Living Room

SEAT

SHWR

VANITY

LINEN

Master Bath

WHIRLPOOL TUB

W.C.

LIN.

STOR.

UP

SHLV

SHLV

PDR ROOM

VANITY

Dining

Foyer

Walk in Closet

WASH DRY

Laundry

W.C.

Storage

DRAIN/ DRY

STOOP

Two Car Garage

ROOF AREA

CEILING BREAK LINE

Storage

TUB/SHWR

Bed Room 2

Bed Room 3

W.C.

Bath 2

VANITY

LIN.

TUB/SHWR

Bath 3

W.C.

VANITY

CEILING BREAK LINE

DOWN

HANDRAIL

Storage

LIN.

Bed Room 4

Open To Below

ROOF AREA

ROOF AREA

© by William Poole

Colonial Style 63

The colonial-style "Cumberland" design by William Poole offers a living area of 2,105 square feet, distributed over two full stories. A roofed porch over the front entrance welcomes visitors. The layout of the ground floor is arranged in a formal unit with dining room and living room, and a family area composed of a great room with fireplace, kitchen, and breakfast room opening onto the garden deck. On the second floor are three bedrooms. The master suite features a generous separate bath, while the other two bedrooms share a full bath. In addition, there is a large room above the garage that can be used for various purposes.

Design Cumberland
by William Poole

Ground floor 1,083 sq. ft.
Second floor 1,022 sq. ft.
Total 2,105 sq. ft.

DECK

Breakfast Room

Great Room

Two Car Garage

SINK

D.W.

RANGE

Kitchen

REFG.

P'DR ROOM

W.C.

Livingroom

Dining

UP

Porch

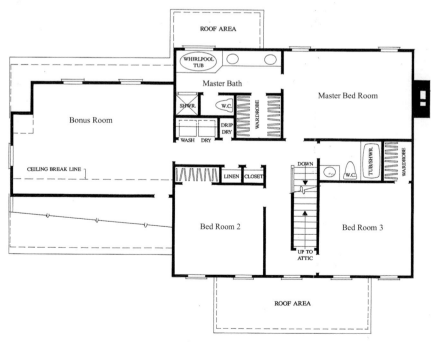

ROOF AREA

WHIRLPOOL TUB

Master Bath

Master Bed Room

Bonus Room

SHWR.

W.C.

WARDROBE

DRIP DRY

WASH   DRY

DOWN

W.C

TUB/SHWR.

WARDROBE

CEILING BREAK LINE

LINEN   CLOSET

Bed Room 2

Bed Room 3

UP TO ATTIC

ROOF AREA

© by William Poole

Photo © Mark Englund / HomeStyles

This stately colonial-style house features a living area of 2,870 square feet distributed over two stories. The striking front gable corresponds to the portico that graces the front entrance.

**Design HomeStyle
HDS-99-306**
© James Zirkel Home Designers, Inc.

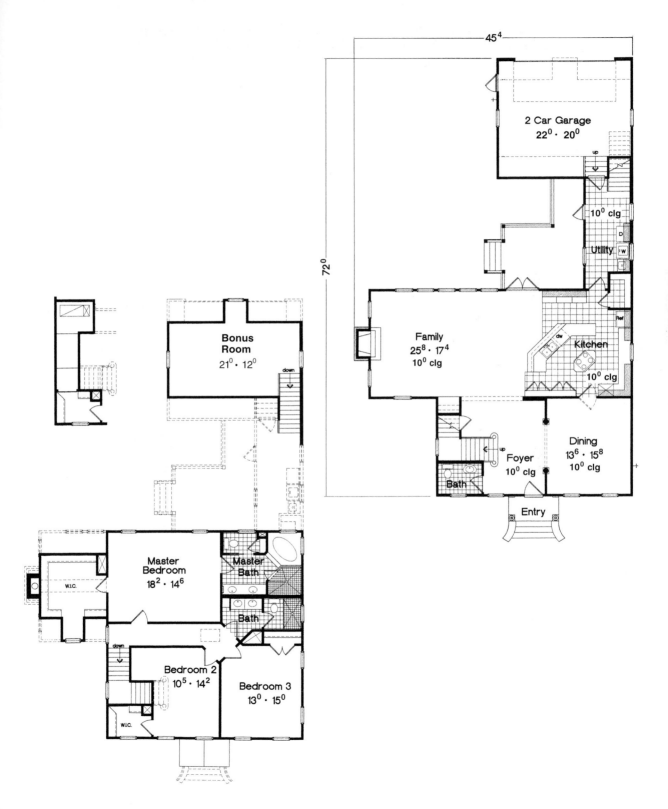

2 Car Garage
$22^0 \cdot 20^0$

10^0 clg

Utility

Family
$25^8 \cdot 17^4$
10^0 clg

Kitchen
10^0 clg

Bonus Room
$21^0 \cdot 12^0$

down

up

Dining
$13^6 \cdot 15^8$
10^0 clg

Foyer
10^0 clg

Bath

Entry

Master Bedroom
$18^2 \cdot 14^6$

W.I.C.

Master Bath

Bath

down

Bedroom 2
$10^5 \cdot 14^2$

W.I.C.

Bedroom 3
$13^0 \cdot 15^0$

45^4

72^0

Colonial Style 67

SOUTHERN COUNTRY STYLE

This variation of a southern country-style design features a hipped roof, which allows for a wide, wrap-around porch that offers the inhabitants a sheltered place in the open air. The massive chimneys and two dormer windows have a marked effect on the appearance of the design. A generous assortment of rooms providing a total living area of 3,180 square feet offers enough space for even a large family.

**Design HomeStyle
L-182**

© Larry W. Garnett Associates, Inc.

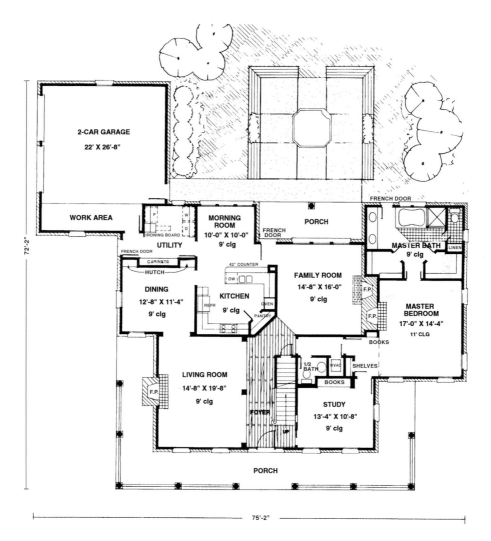

2-CAR GARAGE
22' X 26'-8"

72'-2"

WORK AREA

UTILITY

IRONING BOARD

F W
D

MORNING ROOM
10'-0" X 10'-0"
9' clg

FRENCH DOOR

PORCH

FRENCH DOOR

MASTER BATH
9' clg

LINEN

FRENCH DOOR

CABINETS
HUTCH

DINING
12'-8" X 11'-4"
9' clg

42" COUNTER

DW

KITCHEN
9' clg

REFR

OVEN
PANTRY

FAMILY ROOM
14'-8" X 16'-0"
9' clg

F.P.

F.P.

BOOKS

MASTER BEDROOM
17'-0" X 14'-4"
11' CLG

LIVING ROOM
14'-8" X 19'-8"
9' clg

F.P.

FOYER

1/2 BATH

HVAC

SHELVES

BOOKS

STUDY
13'-4" X 10'-8"
9' clg

PORCH

75'-2"

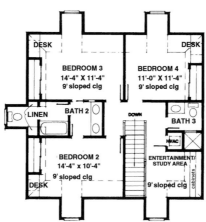

DESK

DESK

BEDROOM 3
14'-4" X 11'-4"
9' sloped clg

BEDROOM 4
11'-0" X 11'-4"
9' sloped clg

LINEN

BATH 2

DOWN

BATH 3

BEDROOM 2
14'-4" x 10'-4"
9' sloped clg

HVAC

ENTERTAINMENT/
STUDY AREA

DESK

9' sloped clg

cabinets

Southern Country Style 71

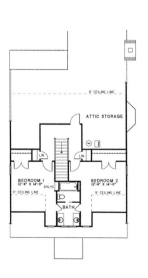

**Design
HomeStyle
NBV-10496**
© Nelson Design
Group, L.L.C.

Photo ©Mark Englund / HomeStyles

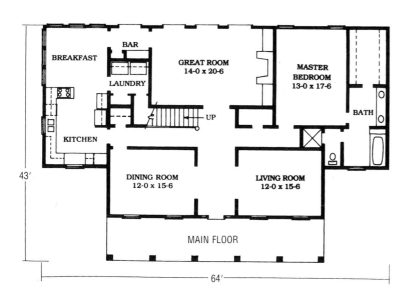

BREAKFAST

BAR

GREAT ROOM
14-0 x 20-6

MASTER
BEDROOM
13-0 x 17-6

LAUNDRY

BATH

KITCHEN

UP

DINING ROOM
12-0 x 15-6

LIVING ROOM
12-0 x 15-6

43'

MAIN FLOOR

64'

BEDROOM
10-0 x 13-0

BATH

DOWN

BATH

BEDROOM
12-0 x 12-6

BEDROOM
12-0 x 14-0

Design HomeStyle
V-2848
© Historical Replications, Inc.

Southern Country Style 73

A rough facade and two massive chimneys lend this 1 1/2-story colonial variation designed by Larry W. Garrett its rustic appearance. The stucco decoration of the dormer windows and the imposing and beautifully designed entry contribute to the perfection of the total impression. The house boasts a total living area of 4,158 square feet spread over two stories.

**Design HomeStyle
L-160-HD**

©Larry W. Garnett & Associates, Inc.

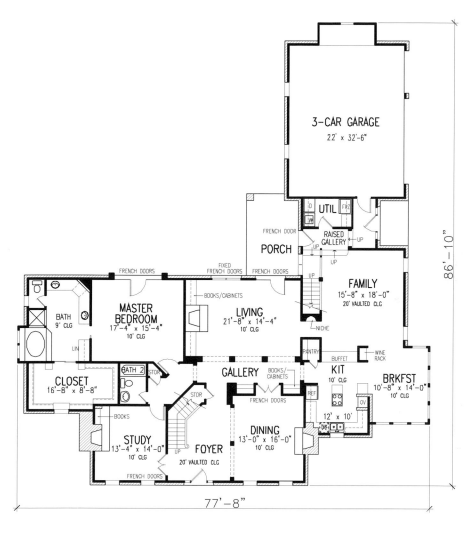

3-CAR GARAGE
22' x 32'-6"

86'-10"

UTIL
FRZ
D
W

FRENCH DOOR

RAISED GALLERY
UP

PORCH

UP
UP

FAMILY
15'-8" x 18'-0"
20' VAULTED CLG

FRENCH DOORS
FIXED FRENCH DOORS
FRENCH DOORS

BOOKS/CABINETS

BATH
9' CLG

MASTER BEDROOM
17'-4" x 15'-4"
10' CLG

LIVING
21'-8" x 14'-4"
10' CLG

UP

NICHE

PANTRY

BUFFET

WINE RACK

LIN

BATH 2

STOR

GALLERY

BOOKS/CABINETS

KIT
10' CLG

BRKFST
10'-8" x 14'-0"
10' CLG

CLOSET
16'-8" x 8'-8"

STOR

REF

OV

BOOKS

FRENCH DOORS

12' x 10'

STUDY
13'-4" x 14'-0"
10' CLG

UP

FOYER
20' VAULTED CLG

DINING
13'-0" x 16'-0"
10' CLG

FRENCH DOORS

77'-8"

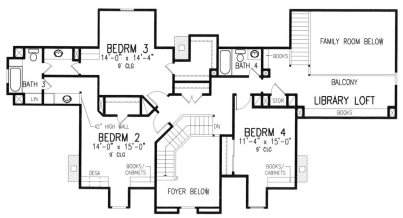

BEDRM 3
14'-0" x 14'-4"
9' CLG

FAMILY ROOM BELOW

BOOKS

BATH 4

BATH 3

BALCONY

LIN

LIBRARY LOFT

BOOKS

42" HIGH WALL

STOR

DN

BEDRM 2
14'-0" x 15'-0"
9' CLG

FOYER BELOW

BEDRM 4
11'-4" x 15'-0"
9' CLG

DESK

BOOKS/CABINETS

BOOKS/CABINETS

Southern Country Style 75

64-4

STORAGE
20-2 x 4-9

GARAGE
20-2 x 22-9

PORCH
21-4 x 11-8

77-6

MASTER
BATH
17-3 x 11-3

MASTER
BEDROOM
17-2 x 17-6

LIVING
16-8 x 17-2

UTIL.
8-7 x 12-0

KITCHEN
12-10 x 12-11

BEDROOM
11-5 x 12-11

BEDROOM
11-0 x 16-5

FOYER
5-8 x 16-9

DINING
11-1 x 16-5

BREAKFAST
12-10 x 11-8

PORCH
30-0 x 6-0

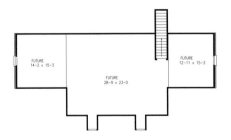

FUTURE
14-2 x 15-3

FUTURE
28-9 x 23-0

FUTURE
12-11 x 15-3

Design HomeStyle
J-90010
©Larry James & Associates, Inc.

Photo © Mark Englund / HomeStyles

Design HomeStyle
E-3400
© Breland & Farmer Designers, Inc.

Floor plan labels:

GARAGE 22' x 22'
POOL STORAGE 10' x 12'
STORAGE 8' x 12'
GUEST ROOM 14' x 16'
PORCH 2
DECK
SUN ROOM
BATH 2
EATING
PORCH 3 6' x 8'
BATH 1
UTILITY
KITCHEN
HERS
HIS
LIVING 18' x 20'
MASTER SUITE 15' x 21'
STOR.
ENTRY 11' x 15'
SITTING 4' x 11'
DINING 12' x 14'
PORCH 1

68'
64'

Beautiful stucco trim, white columns, and the low railing of the front porch stand in clear contrast to the dark brick facade of this elegant variation of a southern country manor. The beautifully designed windows, the richly decorated dormers, and the exceptional entryway complete the exterior of this southern dream house, which offers a total living area of 3,188 square feet distributed over two stories.

**Design HomeStyle
DD-3052**
© Danze & Davis Architects, Inc.

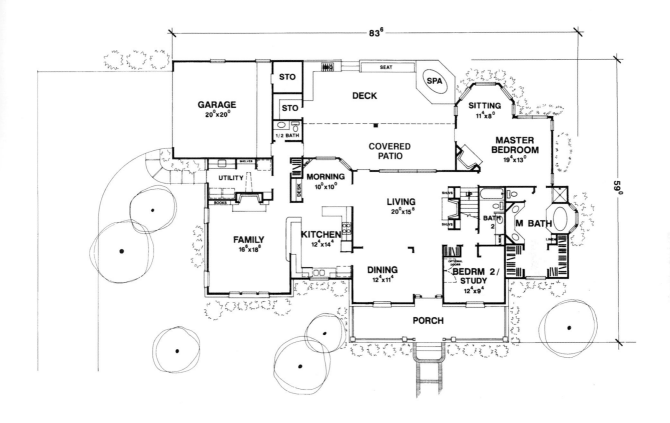

83⁶

59⁰

GARAGE
20⁰x20⁰

STO

STO

1/2 BATH

DECK

SEAT

SPA

SITTING
11⁴x8⁰

COVERED
PATIO

MASTER
BEDROOM
19⁴x13⁰

UTILITY

SHELVES

BOOKS

DESK

MORNING
10⁰x10⁰

LIVING
20⁰x15⁸

SHLVS

SHLVS

UP

BATH
2

M BATH

LINEN

FAMILY
16⁶x18⁸

KITCHEN
12⁴x14⁴

DINING
12⁴x11⁴

OPTIONAL
DOORS

BEDRM 2/
STUDY
12⁴x9⁴

PORCH

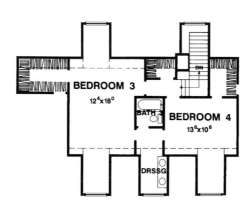

BEDROOM 3
12⁴x18⁰

DN

BATH

BEDROOM 4
13⁶x10⁸

DRSSG

Southern Country Style 79

One striking feature of this southern country-style house is the three dormer windows jutting like small towers from the steep gabled roof, which are echoed by the small gable over the window in the garage. White columns support the roof over the entrance, and the absence of a railing allows a clear view of the beautiful front windows. The interior plan of the 2,480-square-foot house offers a generous array of rooms. The ground floor is divided into a formal area and a family area. The plan includes three bedrooms, with additional room for expansion above the garage.

**Design HomeStyle
DD-2480**
© Danze & Davis Architects, Inc.

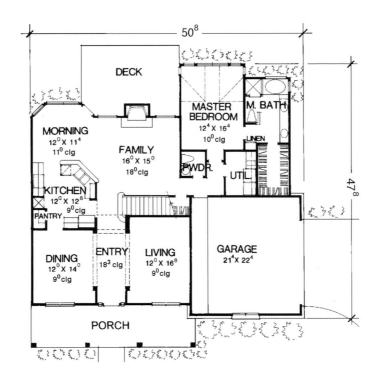

50⁸

DECK

MORNING
12⁰ X 11⁴
11⁰ clg

FAMILY
16⁰ X 15⁰
18⁰ clg

MASTER
BEDROOM
12⁴ X 16⁴
10⁰ clg

M. BATH

PWDR.

LINEN

KITCHEN
12⁰ X 12⁸
9⁰ clg

PANTRY

UTIL.

47⁸

DINING
12⁰ X 14⁰
9⁰ clg

ENTRY
18³ clg

LIVING
12⁰ X 16⁸
9⁰ clg

GARAGE
21⁴ X 22⁴

PORCH

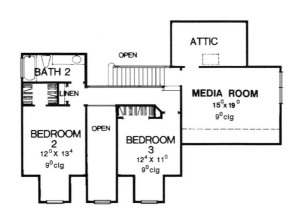

ATTIC

OPEN

BATH 2

LINEN

MEDIA ROOM
15⁰ x 19⁰
9⁰ clg

BEDROOM
2
12⁰ X 13⁴
9⁰ clg

OPEN

BEDROOM
3
12⁴ X 11⁰
9⁰ clg

Southern Country Style 81

This classical design in the southern country tradition offers 3,133 square feet of living area on one level. The exterior suggests that there are rooms on the second floor, but in fact the open design of the house does away with the ceiling, allowing the light from the dormer windows to fall directly into the rooms below.

Design HomeStyle
DD-1914
© Danze & Davis Architects, Inc.

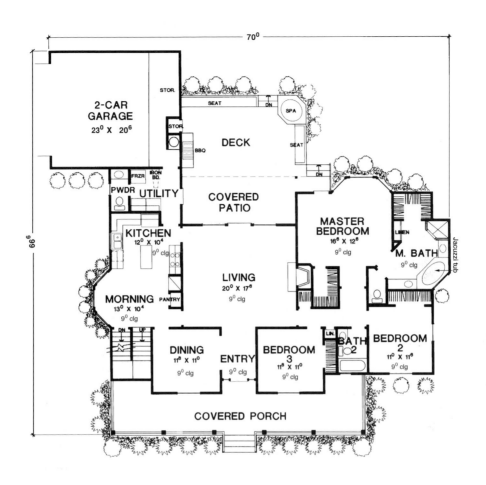

70⁰

2-CAR
GARAGE
23⁰ X 20⁶

STOR.

SEAT

DN

SPA

STOR.

DECK

SEAT

BBQ

FRZR

IRON BD.

DN

PWDR

UTILITY

COVERED
PATIO

MASTER
BEDROOM
16⁶ X 12⁶
9⁰ clg

LINEN

M. BATH
9⁰ clg

Jacuzzi tub

KITCHEN
12⁰ X 10⁴

LIVING
20⁰ X 17⁶
9⁰ clg

66⁹

MORNING
13⁰ X 10⁴
9⁰ clg

PANTRY

DN

UP

DINING
11⁸ X 11⁰
9⁰ clg

ENTRY
9⁰ clg

BEDROOM
3
11⁸ X 11⁰
9⁰ clg

LIN.

BATH
2

LIN.

BEDROOM
2
11⁰ X 11⁶
9⁰ clg

COVERED PORCH

9⁰ clg

9⁰ clg

BONUS SPACE
44⁰ X 24⁰

1216 SQ. FT.
8⁰ clg

DN

9⁰ clg

9⁰ clg

Southern Country Style 83

This variation of a classic southern country house combines all the important architectural details of the genre. The exterior makes a nostalgic impression, while the interior surprises the visitor with its smart, modern floor plan. The unusual high ceiling construction in the breakfast room, the family room and the master suite contribute to the generous proportions of the design.

**Design HomeStyle
AX–3305**
© Jerold Axelrod & Associates, Inc.

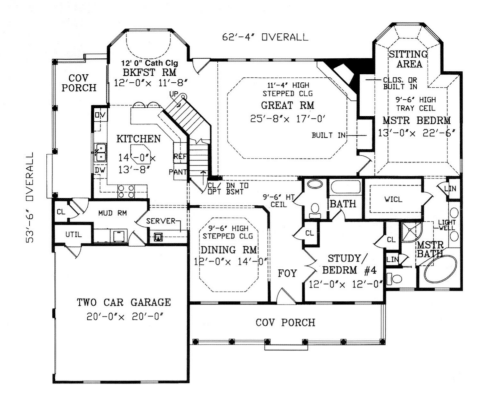

62'-4" OVERALL

COV PORCH

12' 0" Cath Clg
BKFST RM
12'-0" x 11'-8"

11'-4" HIGH
STEPPED CLG
GREAT RM
25'-8" x 17'-0"

BUILT IN

SITTING AREA

CLOS. OR BUILT IN

9'-6" HIGH
TRAY CEIL
MSTR BEDRM
13'-0" x 22'-6"

KITCHEN
14'-0" x 13'-8"

REF

PANT

CL/ DN TO
OPT BSMT

9'-6" HT CEIL

BATH

WICL

LIN

LIGHT WELL

MSTR BATH

CL

MUD RM

SERVER

UTIL

9'-6" HIGH
STEPPED CLG
DINING RM
12'-0" x 14'-0"

FOY

STUDY/ BEDRM #4
12'-0" x 12'-0"

CL

LIN

53'-6" OVERALL

TWO CAR GARAGE
20'-0" x 20'-0"

COV PORCH

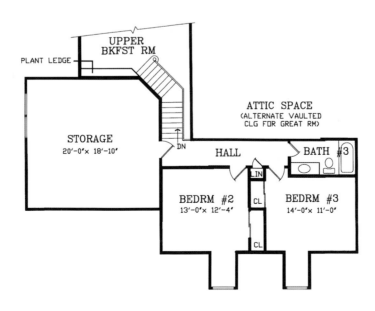

PLANT LEDGE

UPPER BKFST RM

ATTIC SPACE
(ALTERNATE VAULTED
CLG FOR GREAT RM)

STORAGE
20'-0" x 18'-10"

DN

HALL

BATH #3

LIN

BEDRM #2
13'-0" x 12'-4"

CL

BEDRM #3
14'-0" x 11'-0"

CL

Southern Country Style 85

This design in typical southern country style is a distinct option for building on a sloped lot. The floor plan features a large, light-flooded family room that opens into the kitchen with breakfast nook. The first floor also includes a dining room and an office. The master suite with integrated bath is on the same level, in an adjacent wing. Upstairs are two additional bedrooms, a full bathroom and a loft.

Design HomeStyle
APS-2315
© Atlanta Plan Source, Inc

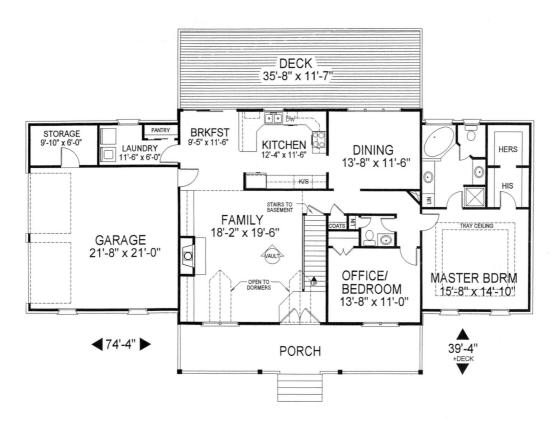

DECK
35'-8" x 11'-7"

STORAGE
9'-10" x 6'-0"

PANTRY

LAUNDRY
11'-6" x 6'-0"

BRKFST
9'-5" x 11'-6"

DW

KITCHEN
12'-4" x 11'-6"

DINING
13'-8" x 11'-6"

HERS

HIS

LIN

GARAGE
21'-8" x 21'-0"

FAMILY
18'-2" x 19'-6"

K/S

STAIRS TO BASEMENT

COATS

VAULT

OPEN TO DORMERS

UP

OFFICE/
BEDROOM
13'-8" x 11'-0"

TRAY CEILING

MASTER BDRM
15'-8" x 14'-10"

74'-4"

PORCH

39'-4"
+DECK

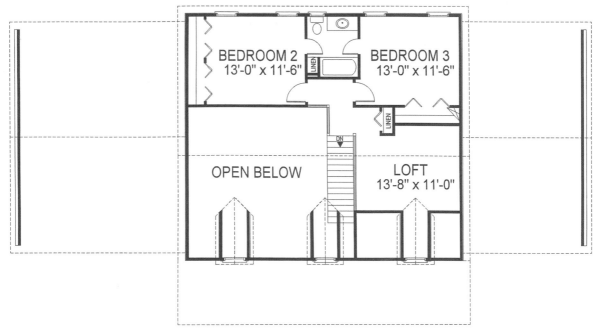

BEDROOM 2
13'-0" x 11'-6"

LINEN

BEDROOM 3
13'-0" x 11'-6"

LINEN

DN

OPEN BELOW

LOFT
13'-8" x 11'-0"

Southern Country Style 87

American Home Plans designed this attractive variation on a southern country-style house for ideal family life. The broad, covered front porch, the tastefully designed arched windows and the elegant entry form a beautiful ensemble. The interior of the 2,705-square-foot house is dominated by clear lines. At the center of the house, the great room features two French doors that allow direct entry into the garden.

**Design HomeStyle
AHP-9360**
© American Home Plans

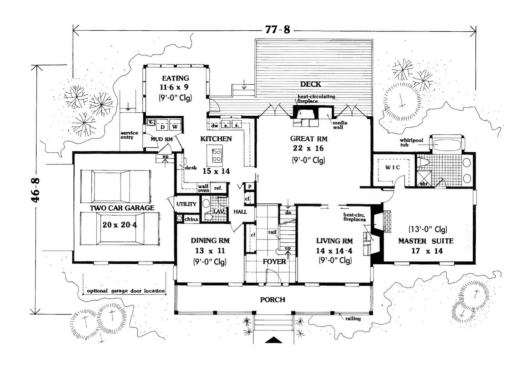

77-8

46-8

EATING
11-6 x 9
(9'-0" Clg)

DECK

heat-circulating
fireplace

service
entry

MUD RM

KITCHEN

GREAT RM
22 x 16
(9'-0" Clg)

media
wall

whirlpool
tub

WIC

desk

KITCHEN
15 x 14

shr

TWO CAR GARAGE
20 x 20-4

wall
oven

ref.

UTILITY

LAV.

china

HALL

p

cl

dn

DINING RM
13 x 11
(9'-0" Clg)

rail

FOYER

up

LIVING RM
14 x 14-4
(9'-0" Clg)

heat-circ.
fireplaces

MASTER SUITE
17 x 14

(13'-0" Clg)

optional garage door location

cl

PORCH

railing

whirlpool tub

shelves

BED RM - 2
15 x 14

sloping ceiling

cl

cl

BED RM-5
10-4 x 14-6

cl

skylight

HALL

dn

BED RM - 3
15 x 11

lin

open to
below

BED RM - 4
14 x 10-6

cl

cl

cl

cl

Southern Country Style 89

An inviting front porch and beautiful arched windows lend this southern country house a nostalgic note. The roof features striking white dormers that rise like small towers from the roof, and two stately chimneys flank the main body of the house. The two single-story wings house the master suite on one side and a two-car garage on the other. The clearly delineated floor plan offers 2,473 square feet of living space distributed over two stories. With five bedrooms, this house provides room enough even for large families.

**Design HomeStyle
AHP-9397**
© American Home Plans

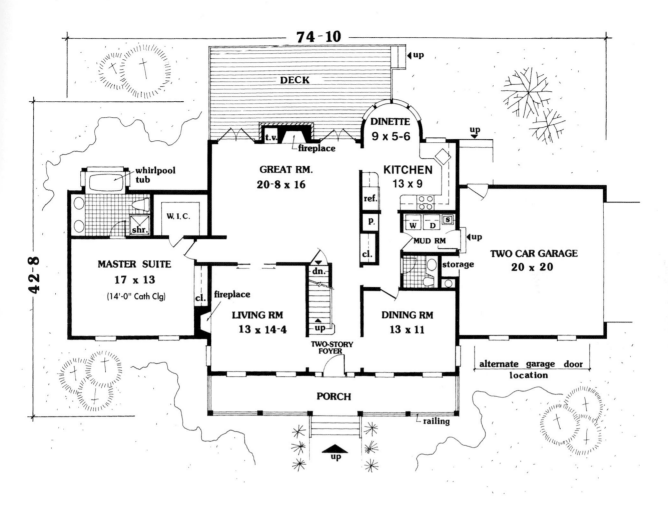

74-10

DECK

↑up

DINETTE
9 x 5-6

↑up

t.v.

fireplace

GREAT RM.
20-8 x 16

KITCHEN
13 x 9

whirlpool
tub

ref.

W. I. C.

p.

shr.

cl.

W   D

S

MUD RM

↓up

TWO CAR GARAGE
20 x 20

42-8

MASTER SUITE
17 x 13
(14'-0" Cath Clg)

cl.   fireplace

cl.

storage

LIVING RM
13 x 14-4

dn.

DINING RM
13 x 11

up

**TWO-STORY
FOYER**

alternate garage door
location

PORCH

up

railing

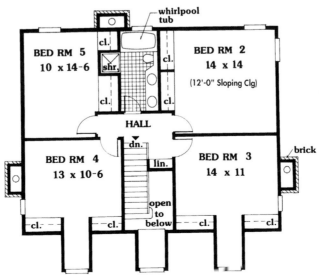

whirlpool
tub

BED RM 5
10 x 14-6

cl.

cl.

BED RM 2
14 x 14
(12'-0" Sloping Clg)

shr.

cl.

cl.

cl.

HALL

dn.

brick

BED RM 4
13 x 10-6

lin.

BED RM 3
14 x 11

cl.

cl.

open
to
below

cl.

cl.

Southern Country Style 91

With this one-story country-style house in the southern tradition, Atlanta Plan Source presents a design that is suitable for sloped terrain. The facades of both the main house and the wings feature white wooden siding, beautifully accented by red shutters. On the lower level, which houses two bedrooms, generous storage space and potential building reserves, the exterior walls are clad in rustic natural stone. Located on the upper level are the kitchen with breakfast nook, dining room, family room, master suite, and an office.

Design HomeStyle
APS-2315
© Atlanta Plan Source, Inc.

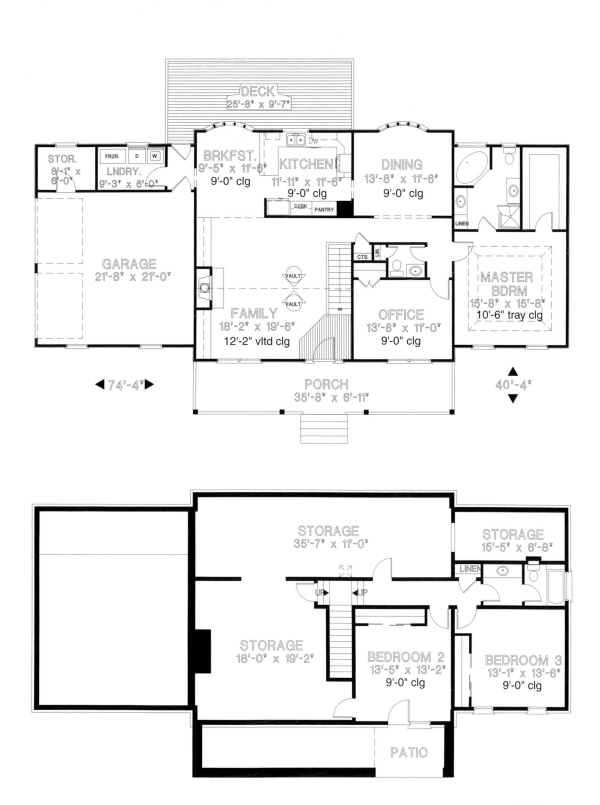

DECK
25'-8" x 9'-7"

STOR.
8'-1" x 6'-0"

LNDRY.
9'-3" x 6'-0"

FRZR. D W

BRKFST.
9'-5" x 11'-6"
9'-0" clg

KITCHEN
11'-11" x 11'-6"
9'-0" clg

DW

DESK PANTRY

DINING
13'-8" x 11'-6"
9'-0" clg

LINEN

GARAGE
21'-8" x 21'-0"

VAULT

VAULT

FAMILY
18'-2" x 19'-6"
12'-2" vltd clg

DN

CTS.

LIN.

OFFICE
13'-8" x 11'-0"
9'-0" clg

MASTER
BDRM
15'-8" x 15'-8"
10'-6" tray clg

◄ 74'-4" ►

PORCH
35'-8" x 6'-11"

40'-4"

STORAGE
35'-7" x 11'-0"

STORAGE
15'-5" x 6'-8"

LINEN

UP   UP

STORAGE
18'-0" x 19'-2"

BEDROOM 2
13'-5" x 13'-2"
9'-0" clg

BEDROOM 3
13'-1" x 13'-6"
9'-0" clg

PATIO

Southern Country Style 93

Photo © Mark Englund / HomeStyles

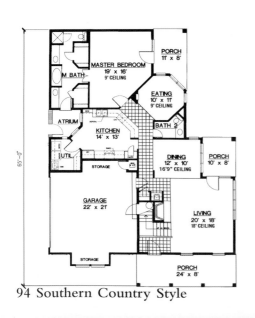

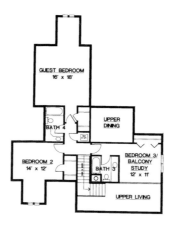

Design HomeStyle
E-2504

© Breland & Farmer
Designers, Inc.

94 Southern Country Style

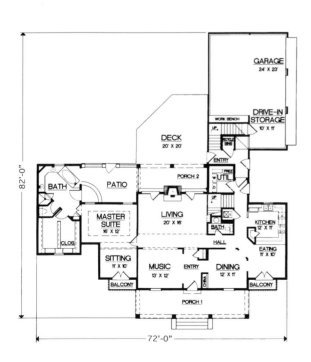

GARAGE
24' X 23'

DRIVE-IN STORAGE
10' X 11'

WORK BENCH

DECK
20' X 20'

ENTRY

UTIL

PORCH 2

BATH

PATIO

LIVING
20' X 16'

KITCHEN
12' X 11'

BATH

MASTER SUITE
16' X 12'

HALL

EATING
11' X 10'

CLOS

SITTING
11' X 10'

MUSIC
13' X 12'

ENTRY

DINING
12' X 11'

CHINA

BALCONY

BALCONY

PORCH 1

82'-0"

72'-0"

FUTURE ROOM
26' X 14'

DOWN

CLO.

OPEN TO LIVING ROOM BELOW

DOWN

BATH

CLO.

BALCONY

BEDROOM
12' X 11'

BEDROOM
12' X 12'

BATH

BEDROOM
12' X 12'

Design HomeStyle
E-2607
© Breland & Farmer Designers, Inc.

Southern Country Style 95

The design of this house in the southern country style incorporates the garage into the building, yielding space for two additional bedrooms above it. The 3,223-square-foot living area offered by this plan makes it a favorite with families.

**Design HomeStyle
DD-3272**
© Danze & Davis Architects, Inc.

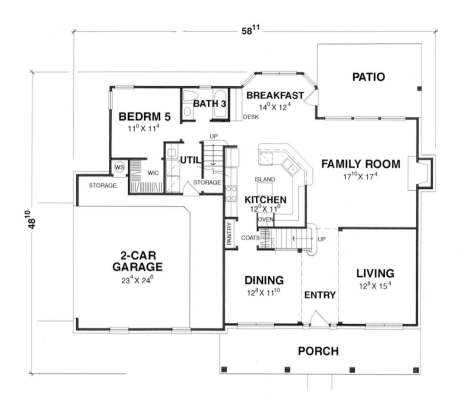

58¹¹

48¹⁰

BEDRM 5
11⁰ X 11⁴

BATH 3

BREAKFAST
14⁰ X 12⁴

DESK

PATIO

FAMILY ROOM
17¹⁰ X 17⁴

UP

UTIL

WS

WIC

STORAGE

STORAGE

ISLAND

KITCHEN
12⁰ X 11⁰

OVEN

PANTRY

COATS

UP

2-CAR GARAGE
23⁴ X 24⁶

DINING
12⁸ X 11¹⁰

ENTRY

LIVING
12⁸ X 15⁴

PORCH

50¹⁰

44⁰

BEDRM 2
14⁶ X 11⁸

GAME ROOM
18⁴ X 22⁴

DECK

SHLVS

WIC

M BATH

SHLVS

LINEN

BATH 2

LIN

DWN

DWN

BEDRM 3
13⁸ X 11⁸

BEDRM 4
12⁴ X 11¹⁰

OPEN TO BELOW

MASTER BEDROOM
12⁴ X 13⁴

Southern Country Style 97

An imposing portico above the entryway is the hallmark of this design. Bay windows on the ground floor and arched windows on the second decorate the two protruding gable elements. Delicate stucco trim perfects the exclusive exterior design. The interior, with a living area of 4,767 square feet, offers a generous and intelligently planned arrangement of rooms.

**Design HomeStyle
DD-4767**
© Danze & Davis Architects, Inc.

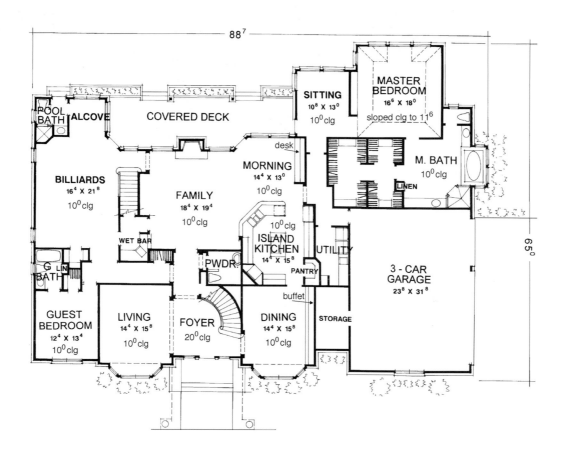

88⁷

POOL BATH

ALCOVE

COVERED DECK

SITTING
10^8 X 13^0
10^0clg

MASTER BEDROOM
16^6 X 18^0
sloped clg to 11^6

BILLIARDS
16^4 X 21^8
10^0clg

FAMILY
18^4 X 19^4
10^0clg

desk

MORNING
14^4 X 13^0
10^0clg

M. BATH
10^0clg

LINEN

65⁰

WET BAR

ISLAND KITCHEN
14^4 X 15^8
10^0clg

UTILITY

G LIN
BATH

PWDR.

PANTRY

3 - CAR GARAGE
23^8 X 31^8

GUEST BEDROOM
12^4 X 13^4
10^0clg

LIVING
14^4 X 15^8
10^0clg

FOYER
20^0clg

buffet

DINING
14^4 X 15^8
10^0clg

STORAGE

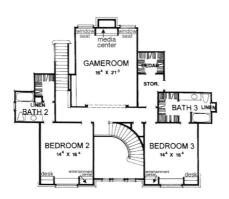

window seat

media center

window seat

GAMEROOM
16^4 X 21^0

CEDAR

STOR.

LINEN
BATH 2

BATH 3 LINEN

BEDROOM 2
14^4 X 16^4

BEDROOM 3
14^4 X 16^4

desk

entertainment center

entertainment center

desk

Southern Country Style 99

Photo © Mark Englund / HomeStyles

This house features all the essential details that define the southern country-style tradition. Along with the broad, covered porch, the three gabled dormer windows and beautifully designed arched windows adorning the front of the house catch the viewer's eye. The delicate porch railing is repeated as a decorative trim above the side window bays. The white elements stand in strong contrast to the brick facade. The same attention to detail is also evident in the interior of the house.

**Design HomeStyle
E–3000**

© Breland & Farmer Designers, Inc..

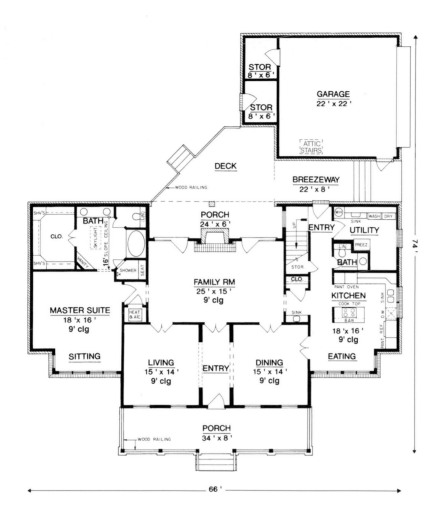

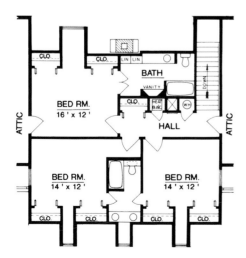

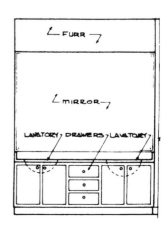

Southern Country Style 101

Photo © Mark Englund / HomeStyles

The combination of a beautiful exterior and a generous 3,468 square feet of living area make this design an impressive family house. The interior offers an intelligent floor plan that lives up to the promise of the exterior. The ground floor includes the living and dining rooms as well as an eat-in kitchen with direct access to the utility room. The large family room with fireplace is at the heart of the house and allows entry into the garden.

Design HomeStyle
E–3501
© Breland & Farmer Designers, Inc.

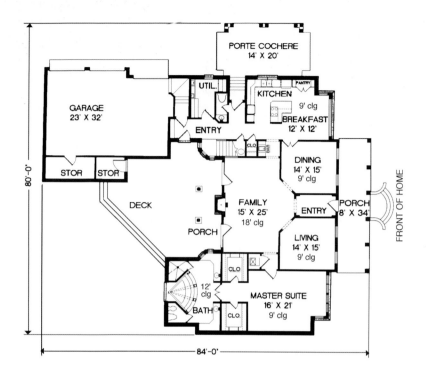

PORTE COCHERE
14' X 20'

GARAGE
23' X 32'

UTIL.

KITCHEN
9' clg

PANTRY

BREAKFAST
12' X 12'

ENTRY

CLO
BAR

DINING
14' X 15'
9' clg

STOR   STOR

DECK

FAMILY
15' X 25'
18' clg

ENTRY

PORCH
8' X 34'

FRONT OF HOME

PORCH

LIVING
14' X 15'
9' clg

CLO

12'
clg

BATH

CLO

CLO

MASTER SUITE
16' X 21'
9' clg

80'-0"

84'-0"

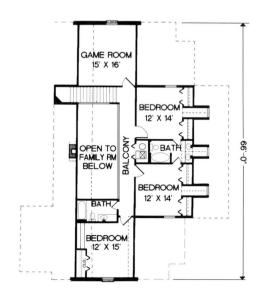

GAME ROOM
15' X 16'

BEDROOM
12' X 14'

OPEN TO
FAMILY RM
BELOW

BALCONY

BATH

BEDROOM
12' X 14'

BATH

BEDROOM
12' X 15'

CLO

66'-0"

Southern Country Style 103

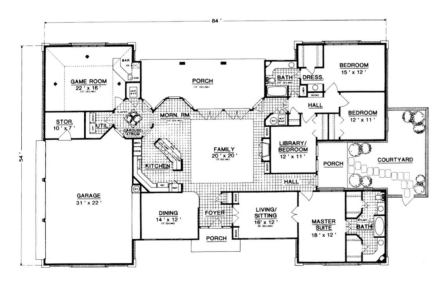

This unusual design offers approximately 2,700 square feet of living area on a single level, arranged in an equally fascinating floor plan.

**Design HomeStyle
E-2704**
© Breland & Farmer
Designers, Inc..

Design HomeStyle
DD-3152
© Danze & Davis Architects, Inc.

This historical replica of a farmhouse reflects the ideal of life in the country. The combination of stone and wood lends the house its rustic charm, while the deep porch roof provides for a spacious porch. The ground floor plan features a roomy foyer with a view into the living room to the side. The heart of the house is the great room with a cathedral ceiling, naturally illuminated by skylights, and the adjacent kitchen is complemented by a breakfast room. The master suite with its own bath completes the ground floor design. Two bedrooms and a full bath are located on the second floor.

**Design HomeStyle
GA-9601**
© Genesis Architecture and Planning

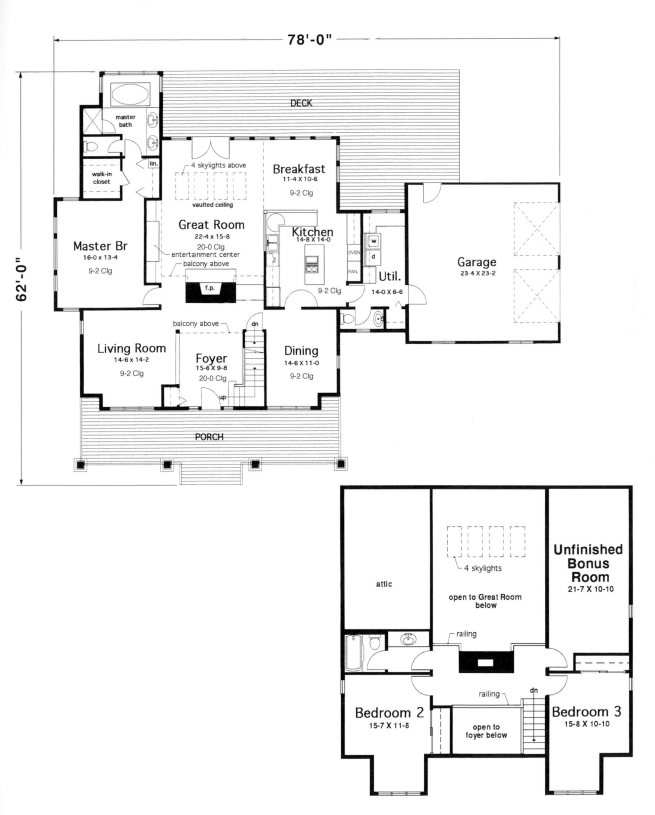

78'-0"

62'-0"

DECK

master
bath

walk-in
closet

4 skylights above

lin.

vaulted ceiling

Breakfast
11-4 X 10-6

9-2 Clg

Great Room
22-4 x 15-8
20-0 Clg
entertainment center
balcony above

Kitchen
14-8 X 14-0

OVEN

PAN.

w

d

Util.
14-0 X 6-6

Garage
23-4 X 23-2

Master Br
16-0 x 13-4

9-2 Clg

f.p.

9-2 Clg

balcony above

dn

Living Room
14-6 x 14-2

9-2 Clg

Foyer
15-6 X 9-8

20-0 Clg

up

Dining
14-6 X 11-0

9-2 Clg

PORCH

attic

4 skylights

open to Great Room
below

railing

**Unfinished
Bonus
Room**
21-7 X 10-10

Bedroom 2
15-7 X 11-8

railing

dn

open to
foyer below

Bedroom 3
15-8 X 10-10

Southern Country Style 107

A beautiful front with generous, over-sized windows is the hallmark of this southern country-style house of 2,962 square feet. As is typical in the South, the house also features a broad, covered front porch. Richly decorated dormers with arched windows underline the elegance of the design. On the ground floor are the dining room and living room, a large kitchen with a breakfast room in the bay, and a luxurious master suite with its own sitting room and bath. Upstairs are three additional bedrooms and two full baths.

**Design HomeStyle
DD-2912**
© Danze & Davis Architects, Inc.

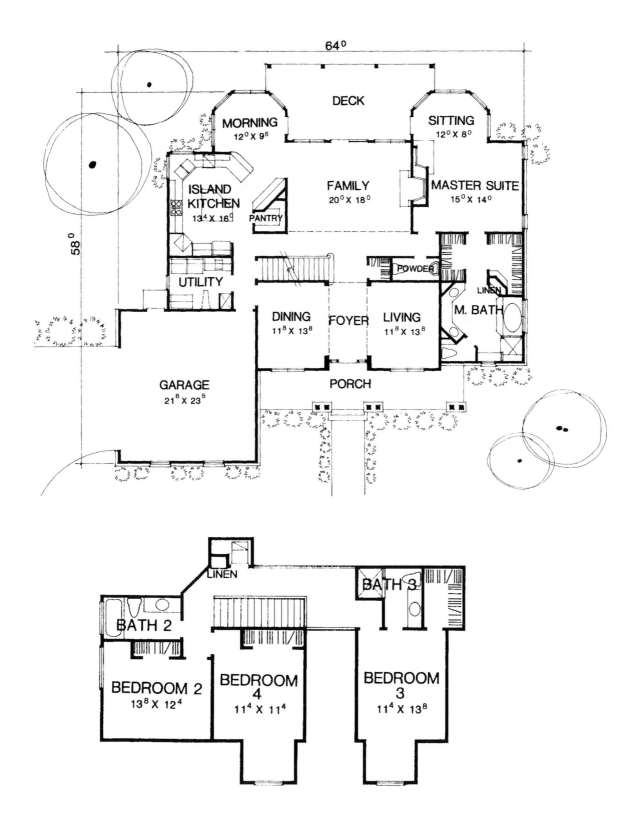

64⁰

58⁰

DECK

MORNING
12⁰ X 9⁶

SITTING
12⁰ X 8⁰

ISLAND
KITCHEN
13⁴ X 16⁹

FAMILY
20⁰ X 18⁰

MASTER SUITE
15⁰ X 14⁰

PANTRY

UTILITY

DINING
11⁸ X 13⁸

FOYER

LIVING
11⁸ X 13⁸

POWDER

LINEN

M. BATH

GARAGE
21⁸ X 23⁸

PORCH

LINEN

BATH 3

BATH 2

BEDROOM 2
13⁸ X 12⁴

BEDROOM
4
11⁴ X 11⁴

BEDROOM
3
11⁴ X 13⁸

Southern Country Style 109

The facade of this house is characterized by a successful combination of brick and clapboard. A broad covered porch protects the entry to the house. The 2,617 square feet of living space are distributed over two floors. To the front of the house are a dining room and study (or additional bedroom), while the great room, kitchen, and breakfast room offer a large living area for the family. This design features four bedrooms.

Design HomeStyle
NBV-11196
© Nelson Design Group, L.L.C.

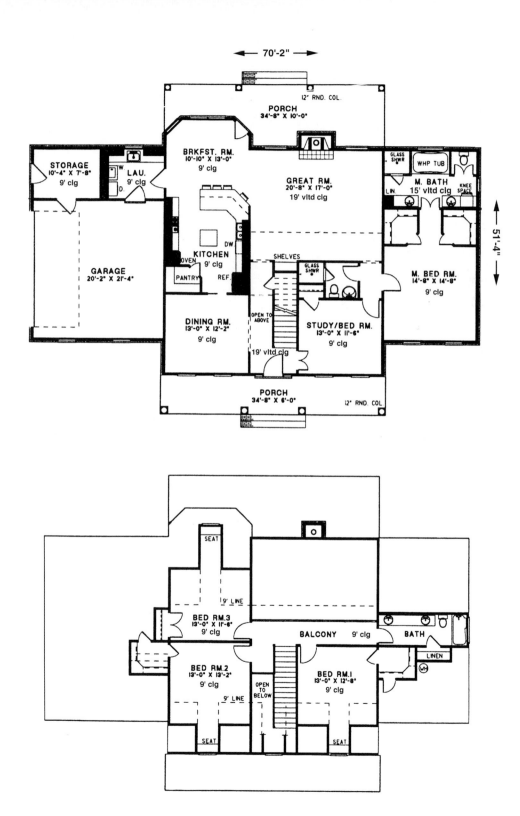

Southern Country Style 111

Photo © Mark Englund / HomeStyles

This southern-country-style house features a singe-story layout. Spread over 2,840 square feet, the interior has an open floor plan with high ceilings that add to the sense of spaciousness.

Design HomeStyle
J-90019
© Larry James & Associates, Inc.

Floor plan labels:

64' 4"

GARAGE
20' 4" X 23' 4"

DECK
20' 0" X 14' 0"

STORAGE
12' 8" X 5' 8"

PORCH OR SUNROOM
21' 6" X 12' 2"

MASTER BEDROOM
11' 8" X 16' 8"

UTILITY

LIVING
21' 9" X 17' 2"
10' CLG

KITCHEN

BEDROOM
11' 0" X 12' 0"

BEDROOM
11' 0" X 13' 6"

FOYER

DINING
11' 0" X 16' 4"
10' CLG

BREAKFAST
12' 9" X 11' 6"

PORCH
29' 8" X 6' 2"

77' 6"

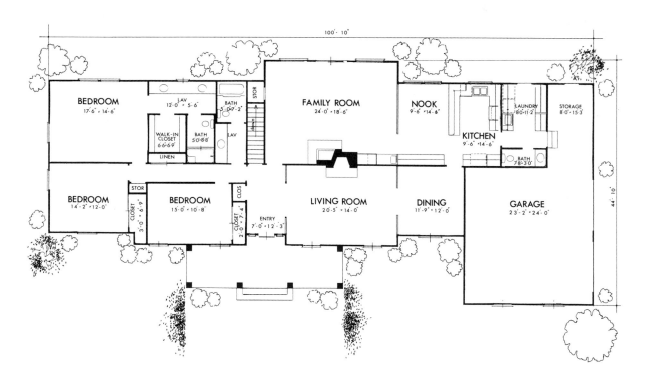

This country house offers 2,695 square feet of comfortable living on a single level.

Design HomeStyle
H 1419
© LifeStyle HomeDesign

Southern Country Style 113

Photo © Mark Englund / HomeStyles

An impressive, broad covered porch marks this design in typical southern country style. The two-story floor plan offers 2,840 square feet of living area. To the rear, between the house and the garage, is a sun room with direct access to the garden.

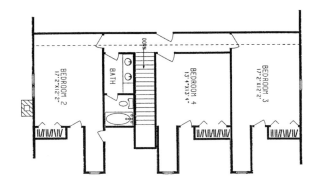

**Design HomeStyle
J-91068**
© Larry James & Associates, Inc.

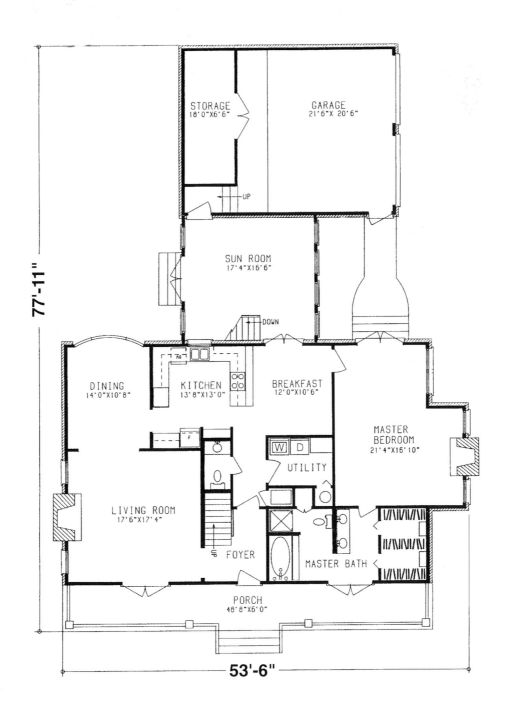

STORAGE
18'0"X6'6"

GARAGE
21'6"X 20'6"

UP

77'-11"

SUN ROOM
17'4"X16'6"

DOWN

DINING
14'0"X10'8"

KITCHEN
13'8"X13'0"

BREAKFAST
12'0"X10'6"

MASTER
BEDROOM
21'4"X16'10"

W D

UTILITY

LIVING ROOM
17'6"X17'4"

FOYER

MASTER BATH

UP

PORCH
48'8"X6'0"

53'-6"

Photo © Breland & Farmer Designers, Inc.

GARAGE & STOR.
36' X 22'

PORCH
36' X 10'

WH

UTIL.
12' X 8'
D | W | FRZ.

SEWING | PANTRY

REF

KITCHEN
12' X 12'
DW

OVEN

CT

BATH

UP

DEN
22' X 21'

SHWR.

CLO.

BATH

A/C

EATING
16' X 12'

CHINA

DINING
14' X 12'

ENTRY

LIVING
14' X 12'

MASTER SUITE
23' X 16'

PORCH
46' X 8'

80'-0"

62'-0"

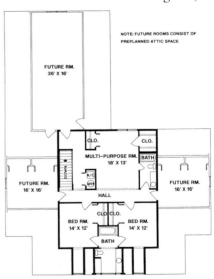

NOTE: FUTURE ROOMS CONSIST OF
PREPLANNED ATTIC SPACE

FUTURE RM.
36' X 16'

CLO.

CLO.

MULTI–PURPOSE RM.
18' X 13'

BATH

FUTURE RM.
16' X 16'

DOWN

A/C

WH

FUTURE RM.
16' X 16'

HALL

BED RM.
14' X 12'

CLO CLO.

BED RM.
14' X 12'

BATH

Design HomeStyle
THD-330-0
© Breland & Farmer Designers, Inc.

116 Southern Country Style

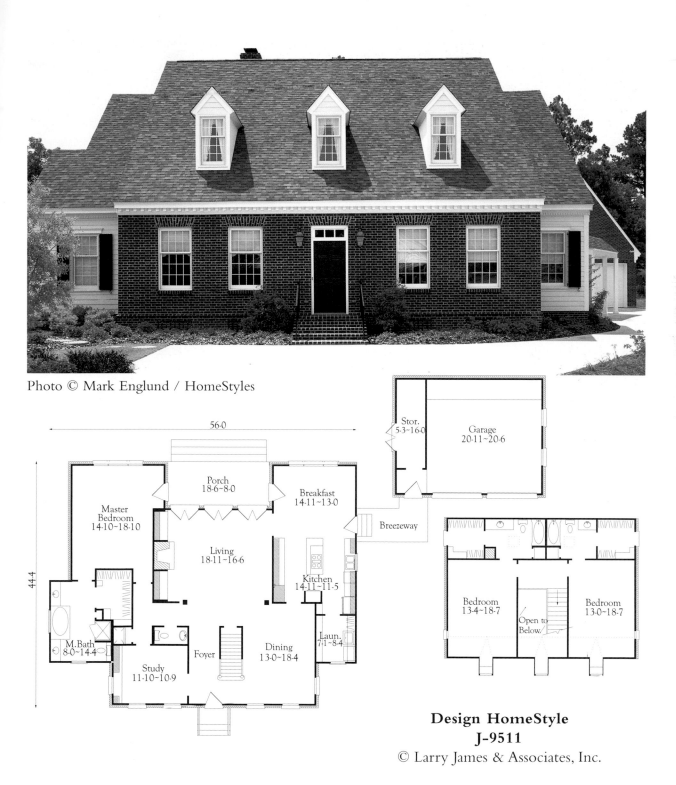

Photo © Mark Englund / HomeStyles

56-0

Porch
18-6~8-0

Breakfast
14-11~13-0

Master
Bedroom
14-10~18-10

Living
18-11~16-6

Kitchen
14-11~11-5

M. Bath
8-0~14-4

Study
11-10~10-9

Foyer

Dining
13-0~18-4

Laun.
7-1~8-4

44-4

Stor.
5-3~16-0

Garage
20-11~20-6

Breezeway

Bedroom
13-4~18-7

Open to
Below

Bedroom
13-0~18-7

Design HomeStyle
J-9511
© Larry James & Associates, Inc.

Southern Country Style 117

Photo © Historical Replications, Inc.

The architects from Historical Replication, Inc. know how to combine the charm of historical architecture with modern living needs. The imposing white columns and covered porch set the scene for this historically accurate southern design, and stucco decorations on the dormers underline the charm of the exterior. The interior of the house offers a classically designed living area of 4,566 square feet.

Design HomeStyle
V–3822
© Historical Replications, Inc.

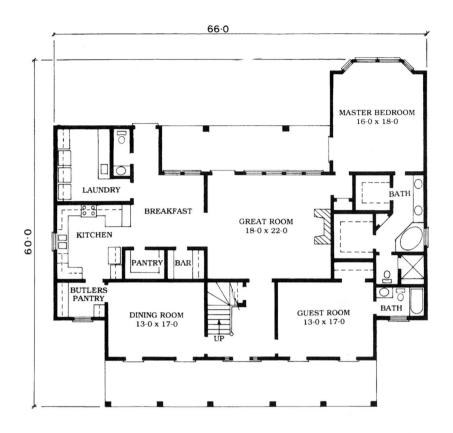

66·0

60·0

MASTER BEDROOM
16-0 x 18-0

LAUNDRY

BREAKFAST

BATH

KITCHEN

GREAT ROOM
18-0 x 22-0

PANTRY   BAR

BUTLERS
PANTRY

DINING ROOM
13-0 x 17-0

GUEST ROOM
13-0 x 17-0

BATH

UP

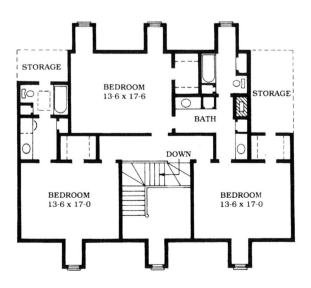

STORAGE

BEDROOM
13-6 x 17-6

STORAGE

BATH

DOWN

BEDROOM
13-6 x 17-0

BEDROOM
13-6 x 17-0

Southern Country Style 119

Known for his architecturally accurate southern designs, Larry James here presents an ideal family home. The front features a wide covered porch and three dormers, which are typical of the style. The interior offers 2,597 square feet of living area on one floor, with the possibility to expand by finishing the up-stairs. The dormer windows provide natural light and emphasize the open floor plan.

**Design HomeStyle
J-9506**
© Larry James & Associates, Inc.

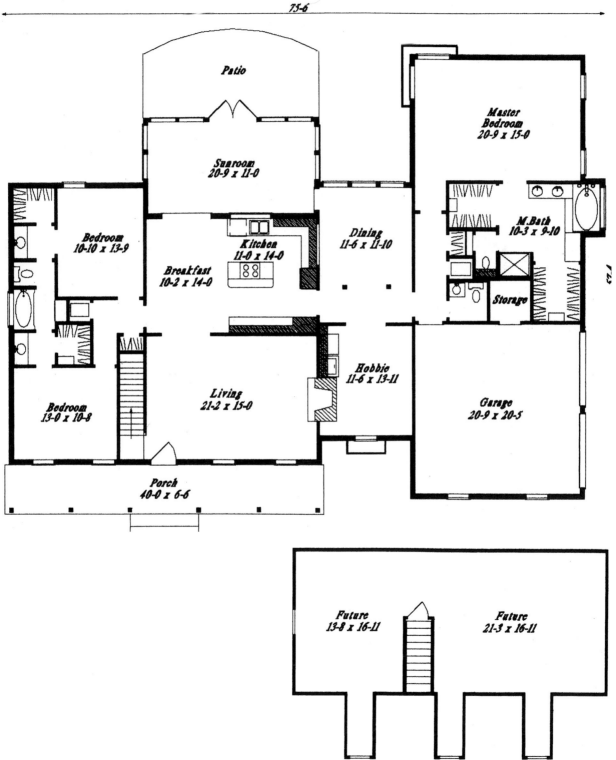

75-6

Patio

Sunroom
20-9 x 11-0

Master
Bedroom
20-9 x 15-0

M.Bath
10-3 x 9-10

Bedroom
10-10 x 13-9

Dining
11-6 x 11-10

Kitchen
11-0 x 14-0

Breakfast
10-2 x 14-0

Storage

Hobbie
11-6 x 13-11

Bedroom
13-0 x 10-8

Living
21-2 x 15-0

Garage
20-9 x 20-5

Porch
40-0 x 6-6

Future
13-8 x 16-11

Future
21-3 x 16-11

Southern Country Style 121

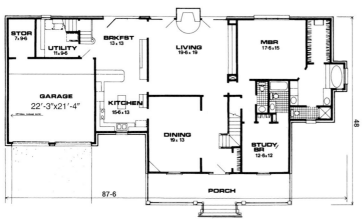

**Design HomeStyle
J-8688**

© Larry James &
Associates, Inc.

STOR
7x 9-6

UTILITY
11x 9-6

BRKFST
13 x 13

LIVING
19-6 x 19

MBR
17-6 x 15

GARAGE
22'-3"x21'-4"

OPTIONAL GARAGE ENTRY

KITCHEN
15-6 x 13

DINING
19 x 13

STUDY/
BR
12-6 x 12

48

87-6

PORCH

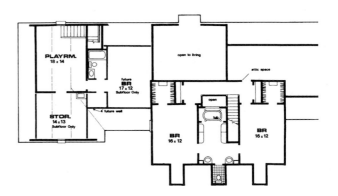

PLAYRM.
18 x 14

open to living

attic space

future
BR
17 x 12
Subfloor Only

STOR.
14 x 13
Subfloor Only

future wall

open

BR
16 x 12

BR
16 x 12

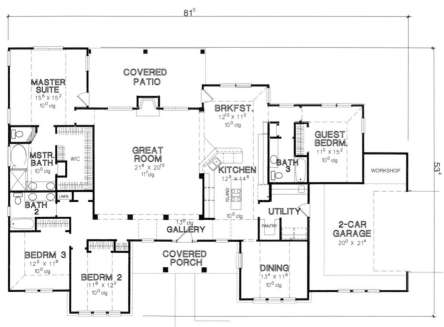

MASTER SUITE 15⁶ X 15²
10⁰ clg

COVERED PATIO

BRKFST. 12⁰ X 11⁰
10⁰ clg

GUEST BEDRM. 11⁰ X 15²
10⁰ clg

MSTR. BATH 10⁰ clg

WIC

GREAT ROOM 21⁸ X 20⁰
11⁷clg

KITCHEN 12⁹ X 14⁶

ISLAND

BATH 3

WORKSHOP

BATH 2

LINEN

UTILITY

PANTRY

2-CAR GARAGE 20⁰ X 21⁴

GALLERY 13⁰ clg

10⁰ clg

BEDRM 3 12⁰ X 11⁸
10⁰ clg

BEDRM 2 11⁸ X 12⁰
10⁰ clg

COVERED PORCH

DINING 13⁴ X 11⁶
10⁰ clg

81⁰

53⁴

This single-story estate features a living area of 2,541 square feet. The striking design of the windows harmonizes perfectly with the stone facade.

**Design HomeStyle
DD-2541**
© Danze & Davis
Architects, Inc.

Southern Country Style 123

This 1 1/2-story country-style house in typical southern tradition features a magnificent broad covered porch. A clear floor plan sets the tone on the interior. From the foyer, one looks directly into the dining room to the right, which opens into the kitchen with breakfast room and adjacent utility room. The large living room with fireplace is placed in the center of the house. Also on the ground floor is the master suite with its own bath. In the second story are two additional bedrooms and a full bath.

Design HomeStyle
J-86113
© Larry James & Associates, Inc.

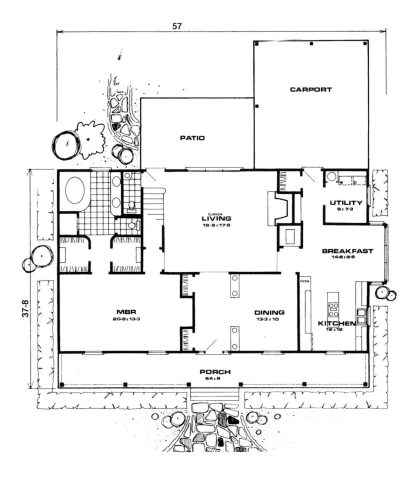

57

CARPORT

PATIO

UTILITY
9 x 7-3

SUNKEN
LIVING
19-8 x 17-8

BREAKFAST
14-8 x 9-8

37-8

MBR
20-8 x 13-3

DINING
13-3 x 10

OVEN

KITCHEN
12 x 12

PORCH
54 x 8

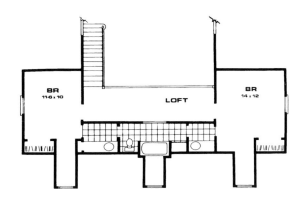

BR
11-6 x 10

LOFT

BR
14 x 12

Southern Country Style 125

Photo © Mark Englund / HomeStyles

The entry porch of this architecturally accurate southern villa is supported by solid
columns, while the delicate stucco trim
underlines the elegance of the front facade.
The wide entry is fitted above with an elegant
arched window that allows natural light into
the foyer. The interior of the house, with
4,566 square feet of living area, is arranged
according to a clearly delineated floor plan.

**Design HomeStyle
V–4566**
© Historical Replications, Inc.

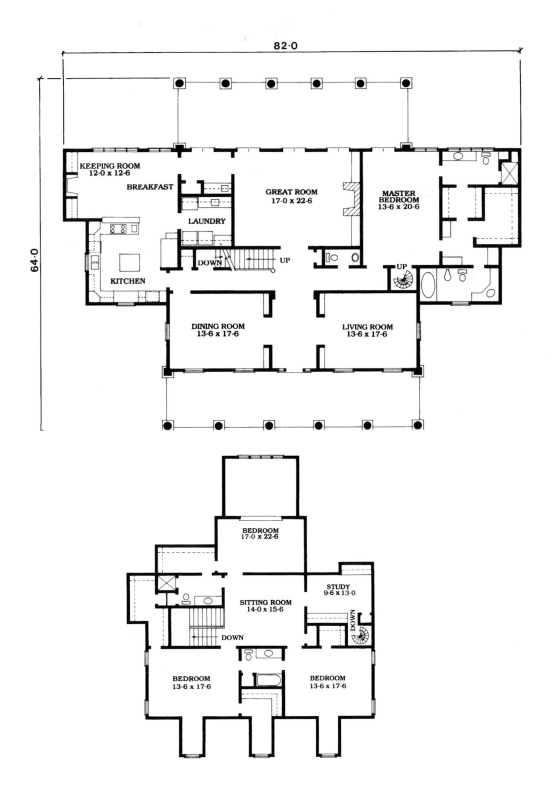

KEEPING ROOM
12-0 x 12-6

BREAKFAST

GREAT ROOM
17-0 x 22-6

MASTER
BEDROOM
13-6 x 20-6

LAUNDRY

KITCHEN

DOWN   UP

UP

DINING ROOM
13-6 x 17-6

LIVING ROOM
13-6 x 17-6

BEDROOM
17-0 x 22-6

STUDY
9-6 x 13-0

SITTING ROOM
14-0 x 15-6

DOWN

DOWN

BEDROOM
13-6 x 17-6

BEDROOM
13-6 x 17-6

82·0

64·0

Southern Country Style 127

An inviting front porch and beautiful arched windows lend this southern country house a nostalgic note. The roof features striking white dormers that rise like small towers from the roof, and two stately chimneys flank the main body of the house. The two single-story wings house the master suite on one side and a two-car garage on the other. The clearly delineated floor plan offers 2,473 square feet of living space distributed over two stories. With five bedrooms, this house provides room enough even for large families.

Design HomeStyle
AHP-9397
© American Home Plans

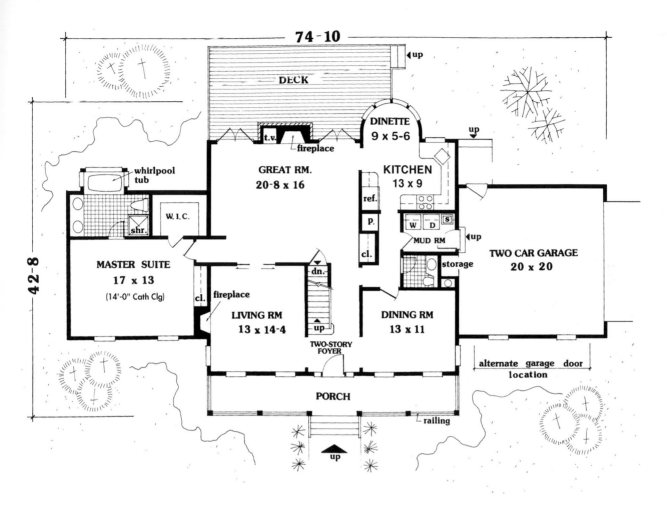

74-10

DECK

↿up

t.v.   fireplace

DINETTE
9 x 5-6

↿up

whirlpool
tub

GREAT RM.
20-8 x 16

KITCHEN
13 x 9

42-8

MASTER SUITE
17 x 13
(14'-0" Cath Clg)

W. I. C.

shr.

ref.

p.

cl.

W   D   s

MUD RM

↿up

TWO CAR GARAGE
20 x 20

cl.   fireplace

LIVING RM
13 x 14-4

dn.

up

storage

DINING RM
13 x 11

TWO-STORY
FOYER

alternate garage door
location

PORCH

railing

up

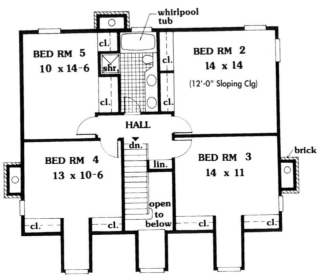

whirlpool
tub

cl.

BED RM 5
10 x 14-6

shr.

cl.

cl.

BED RM 2
14 x 14
(12'-0" Sloping Clg)

cl.

HALL

dn.

BED RM 4
13 x 10-6

lin.

brick

BED RM 3
14 x 11

cl.   cl.

open
to
below

cl.   cl.

Southern Country Style 129

This lovely southern-style estate impresses the viewer with its welcoming exterior. The symmetrically arranged dormer windows set into the steep gabled roof emphasize the balance of the design. The roof extends over a broad front porch that invites visitors to linger. The use of varied materials in the facade optically relaxes the long line of the house. The total living area is 3,383 square feet.

**Design HomeStyle
C-8915**
© Corley Plan Service, Inc.

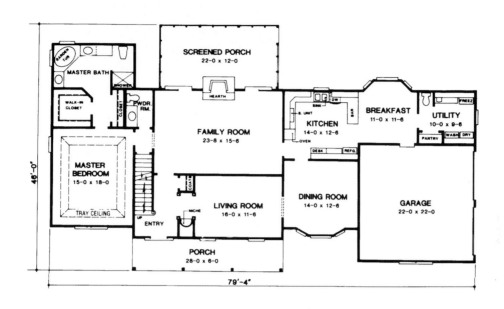

SCREENED PORCH
22-0 x 12-0

MASTER BATH

WALK-IN CLOSET

PWDR. RM.

HEARTH

FAMILY ROOM
23-8 x 15-6

KITCHEN
14-0 x 12-6

S. UNIT

SINK

BAR

BREAKFAST
11-0 x 11-6

UTILITY
10-0 x 9-6

FREEZ.

PANTRY

WASH

DRY

OVEN

DESK

REFG.

46'-0"

MASTER BEDROOM
15-0 x 18-0

TRAY CEILING

UP

ENTRY

COAT

NICHE

LIVING ROOM
16-0 x 11-6

DINING ROOM
14-0 x 12-6

GARAGE
22-0 x 22-0

PORCH
28-0 x 6-0

79'-4"

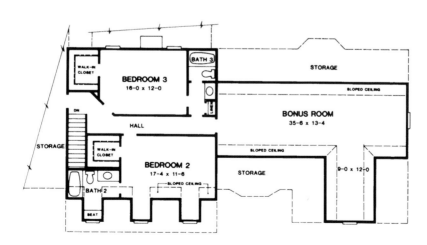

WALK-IN CLOSET

BEDROOM 3
16-0 x 12-0

BATH 3

STORAGE

SLOPED CEILING

DN

HALL

BONUS ROOM
35-6 x 13-4

STORAGE

WALK-IN CLOSET

BEDROOM 2
17-4 x 11-6

SLOPED CEILING

STORAGE

9-0 x 12-0

BATH 2

SLOPED CEILING

SEAT

Southern Country Style 131

Photo © Mark Englund / HomeStyles

The inviting porch and three dormer windows rising from a steep gabled roof characterize this southern-style country estate house. At first glance, one does not suspect that the house offers a proud 3,308 square feet of living space. The unusual ceiling design on the first floor gives this home an air of distinction.

Design HomeStyle
CDG-4002
© Columbia Design Group

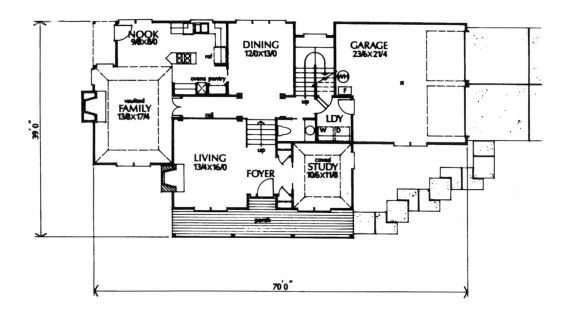

NOOK
9/6x8/0

DINING
12/0x13/0

GARAGE
23/6x21/4

ovens pantry

vaulted
FAMILY
13/8x17/4

LDY
W D

LIVING
13/4x16/0

FOYER

coved
STUDY
10/6x11/8

up

up

rail

porch

39'0"

70'0"

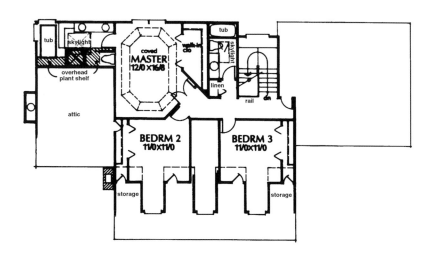

tub

skylight

tub

skylight

coved
MASTER
12/0x16/8

walk-in
clo

overhead
plant shelf

linen

rail
dn

attic

BEDRM 2
11/0x11/0

BEDRM 3
11/0x11/0

storage

storage

Numerous dormers and a broad covered porch distinguish the exterior of this southern-style country house. Its two stories provide living area of 2,695 square feet. The master suite on the ground floor includes a luxurious bath, while three additional bedrooms are located on the second floor.

**Design HomeStyle
CH-445-A**
© Caddhomes

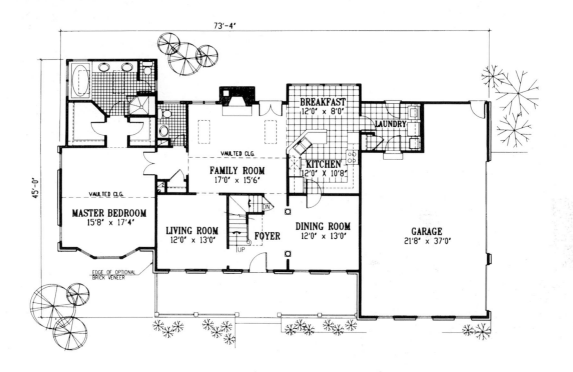

73'-4'

45'-0'

BREAKFAST
12'0' x 8'0'

LAUNDRY

VAULTED CLG.

FAMILY ROOM
17'0' x 15'6'

KITCHEN
12'0' x 10'8'

VAULTED CLG.

MASTER BEDROOM
15'8' x 17'4'

LIVING ROOM
12'0' x 13'0'

FOYER

DINING ROOM
12'0' x 13'0'

GARAGE
21'8' x 37'0'

DN

UP

EDGE OF OPTIONAL
BRICK VENEER

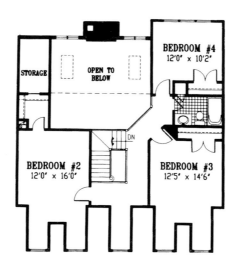

STORAGE

OPEN TO
BELOW

BEDROOM #4
12'0' x 10'2'

BEDROOM #2
12'0' x 16'0'

DN

BEDROOM #3
12'5' x 14'6'

Southern Country Style 135

Photo © Mark Englund / HomeStyles

This beautiful house in the southern country tradition wins approval at first glance with its bright and friendly entry porch, which stands in stark contrast to the brick facing of the side wing. The two high, pointed dormer windows are also authentic characteristics of the style. The house provides 3,079 square feet of floor space distributed over two levels, and with its clear, straight lines the floor plan offers a room arrangement ideal for a young family.

Design HomeStyle
J-8601
© Larry James & Associates, Inc.

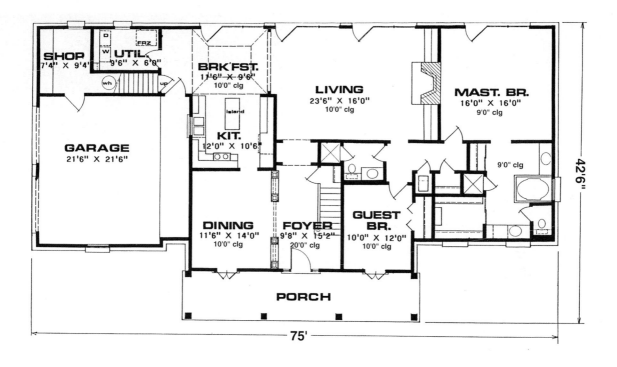

SHOP
7'4" X 9'4"

UTIL.
9'6" X 6'0"

BRK'FST.
11'6" X 9'6"
10'0" clg

LIVING
23'6" X 16'0"
10'0" clg

MAST. BR.
16'0" X 16'0"
9'0" clg

9'0" clg

GARAGE
21'6" X 21'6"

KIT.
12'0" X 10'6"

island

DINING
11'6" X 14'0"
10'0" clg

FOYER
9'8" X 15'2"
20'0" clg

GUEST BR.
10'0" X 12'0"
10'0" clg

PORCH

42'6"

75'

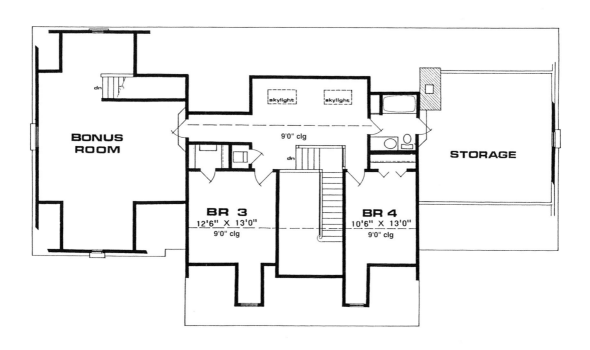

BONUS ROOM

dn

skylight   skylight

9'0" clg

dn

STORAGE

BR 3
12'6" X 13'0"
9'0" clg

BR 4
10'6" X 13'0"
9'0" clg

Southern Country Style 137

Photo © Tom Gibbs Photographics

Characteristic of this southern design is the wide covered porch adorning the front of the house. White paneled dormers and the beautifully turned woodwork on the porch create an appealing contrast to the dark brick facade. The large French doors to the dining room located to one side of the foyer allow the entrance of natural light. The two-storied house with a total of 2,669 square feet offers sufficient room for the needs of a family.

Design HomeStyle
J-90012
© Larry James & Associates, Inc.

PATIO

73'-0"

44'-0"

MASTER
BEDROOM
16-0 X 15-4
9-4 clg

LIVING ROOM
21-8 X 16-0
9-4 clg

BREAKFAST
12-0 X 12-0
9-4 clg

UTILITY
9-4 X 9-4

STORAGE
9-4 X 7-6

MASTER
BATH
9-4 clg

1/2 B.

KITCHEN
12-0 X 10-4

GARAGE
21-4 X 20-2

CLO.

BEDROOM 2
10-0 X 9-10
9-4 clg

17-6
vltd
clg

FOYER

DINING
13-8 X 11-10
9-4 clg

PORCH
33-0 X 8-0

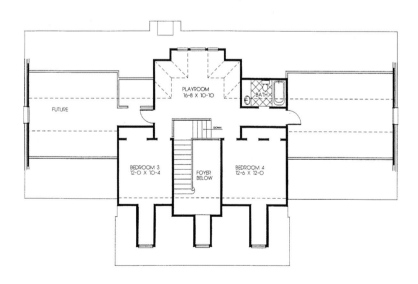

PLAYROOM
16-8 X 10-10

BATH

FUTURE

DOWN

BEDROOM 3
12-0 X 10-4

FOYER
BELOW

BEDROOM 4
12-6 X 12-0

Southern Country Style 139

Photo © Mark Englund / HomeStyles

The offset roofs and extended porches both
on the front and the rear characterize this
southern estate house. Its 2,836 square feet
make it a good candidate for a family home.
The design provides two bedrooms with baths
on the ground floor, and the second floor can
be finished to provide two additional bedrooms, another bathroom and a playroom.

**Design HomeStyle
J-91096**
© Larry James & Associates, Inc.

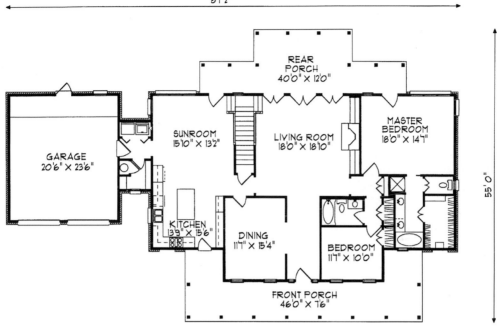

87' 2"

55' 0"

REAR
PORCH
40'0" X 12'0"

GARAGE
20'6" X 23'6"

SUNROOM
15'10" X 13'2"

LIVING ROOM
18'0" X 18'10"

MASTER
BEDROOM
18'0" X 14'7"

KITCHEN
13'9" X 15'6"

DINING
11'7" X 15'4"

BEDROOM
11'7" X 10'0"

FRONT PORCH
46'0" X 7'6"

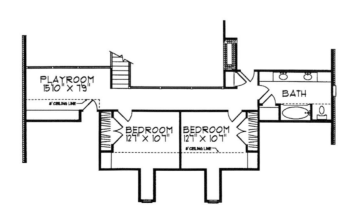

PLAYROOM
15'10" X 7'9"

BATH

BEDROOM
12'7" X 10'7"

BEDROOM
12'7" X 10'7"

8' CEILING LINE

8' CEILING LINE

Southern Country Style 141

The tasteful details of this beautifully designed house grace the exterior with a special charm. The interior offers a generous amount of living space, and the room arrangement of the ground floor alone would be suitable for many families. In addition to the master suite, there are two further bedrooms, a dining room, a kitchen with a pantry and large breakfast room, and a living room. If desired, two additional rooms can be finished on the second floor, with even more potential for expansion above the garage.

Design HomeStyle
J-9303
© Larry James & Associates, Inc.

M.Bath

Master
Bedroom
15-0~14-0
11-9 clg.

Porch
15-0~8-0

Den/Brkfst
15-0~17-9
11-9 clg.

Comp.
Desk

Storage

Bedroom
11-4~11-0
9-0 clg.

Living
15-10~17-7
11-9 clg.

Garage
21-10~21-6

Kitchen
15-0~13-5
9-0 clg.

Bath

Laun.

Bedroom
11-8~12-2
9-0 clg.

Foyer

Dining
13-6~12-2
11-9 clg.

Pantry

Storage

Porch

Porch
36-4~6-0

64-2

77-0

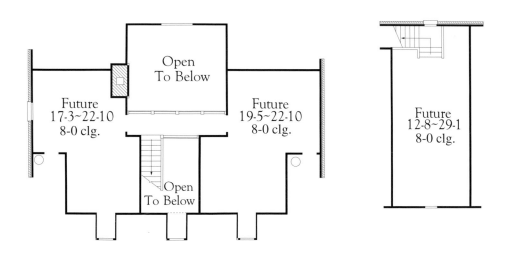

Open
To Below

Future
17-3~22-10
8-0 clg.

Future
19-5~22-10
8-0 clg.

Future
12-8~29-1
8-0 clg.

Open
To Below

Southern Country Style 143

Photo © Mark Englund / HomeStyles

The exterior of this southern country-style house is marked by an elaborate gable design, which emphasizes the elegant entryway. The large, half-round window above the door provides natural light to the open foyer inside the house. Wide, curving stairs hint at the elegance of the interior. The ground floor houses the large formal dining room and the open, country-style kitchen with breakfast room in the right hall of the house. The center is dominated by the great room, which has a fireplace and a cathedral ceiling. The left wing of the house contains the generously proportioned master suite and two additional bedrooms, each with their own bath. The second floor can be expanded as desired.

Design HomeStyle
J-9307
© Larry James & Associates, Inc.

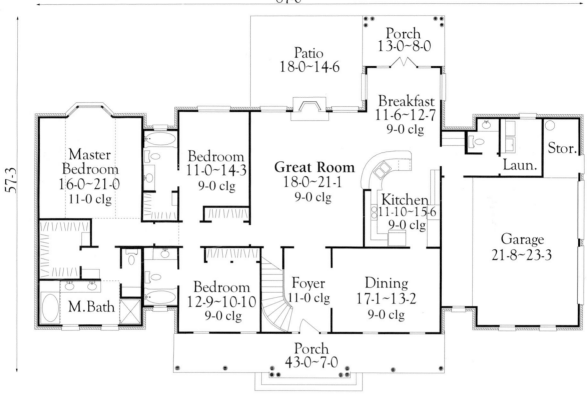

87-0

57-3

Patio
18-0~14-6

Porch
13-0~8-0

Breakfast
11-6~12-7
9-0 clg

Master
Bedroom
16-0~21-0
11-0 clg

Bedroom
11-0~14-3
9-0 clg

Great Room
18-0~21-1
9-0 clg

Kitchen
11-10~15-6
9-0 clg

Laun.

Stor.

M.Bath

Bedroom
12-9~10-10
9-0 clg

Foyer
11-0 clg

Dining
17-1~13-2
9-0 clg

Garage
21-8~23-3

Porch
43-0~7-0

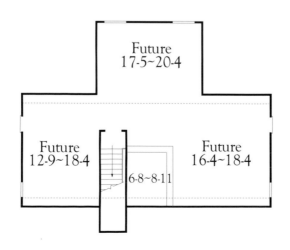

Future
17-5~20-4

Future
12-9~18-4

6-8~8-11

Future
16-4~18-4

Southern Country Style 145

Photo © Mark Englund / HomeStyles

Beautiful arched windows correspond perfectly to the extravagant entrance of this southern country-style house. The high front door gives access to an open foyer, which in turn offers a view into the living room and the dining room, located to the side. The spacious kitchen includes a generous breakfast room with large windows. At the center of this house is the vaulted living room with fireplace. The ground floor also features three bedrooms, with space on the second floor for later expansion. The total living area of the house comprises 2,378 square feet.

Design HomeStyle
J-9320
© Larry James & Associates, Inc.

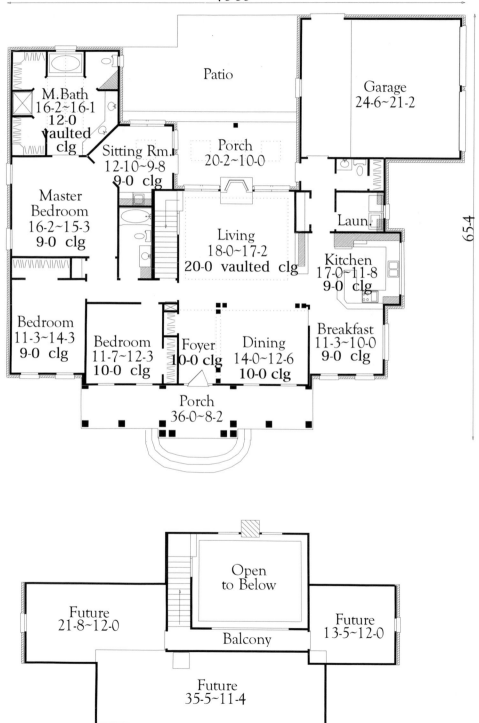

70-10

65-4

Patio

Garage
24-6~21-2

M.Bath
16-2~16-1
12-0
vaulted
clg

Sitting Rm.
12-10~9-8
9-0 clg

Porch
20-2~10-0

Master
Bedroom
16-2~15-3
9-0 clg

Living
18-0~17-2
20-0 vaulted clg

Laun.

Kitchen
17-0~11-8
9-0 clg

Bedroom
11-3~14-3
9-0 clg

Bedroom
11-7~12-3
10-0 clg

Foyer
10-0 clg

Dining
14-0~12-6
10-0 clg

Breakfast
11-3~10-0
9-0 clg

Porch
36-0~8-2

Open
to Below

Future
21-8~12-0

Balcony

Future
13-5~12-0

Future
35-5~11-4

Southern Country Style 147

With porches gracing both its front and garden sides, William Poole's "Back Bay Cottage" promises a great enjoyment of the outdoors. The interior of the house continues the generous design principles. The foyer and the great room with fireplace directly behind it feature cathedral ceilings. The kitchen occupies a central place between the formal dining room and the breakfast room with its large windows facing the garden. The first-floor master suite has its own luxurious bath, a walk-in closet, and direct access to the garden porch. In the second story are two further bedrooms, each with a full bath, and a gallery offering a view of the great room. Space for further expansion is available above the garage.

Design Back Bay Cottage
by William Poole

Ground floor 1,712 sq. ft.
Second floor 885 sq. ft.
Total 2,597 sq. ft.

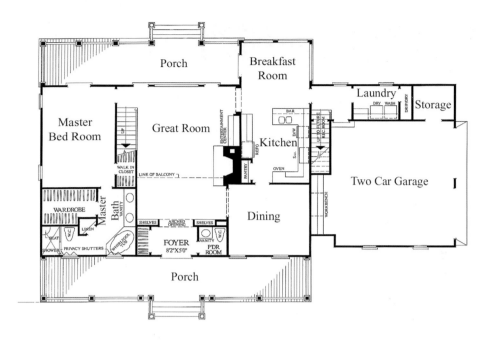

Porch

Breakfast Room

Laundry

DRY WASH

DRAPERY

Storage

Master Bed Room

UP

WALK IN CLOSET

Great Room

ENTERTAINMENT CENTER

LINE OF BALCONY

BAR

Kitchen

REFG

D/W

S.O.

UP TO FUTURE REC ROOM

PANTRY

OVEN

WORK BENCH

Two Car Garage

WARDROBE

Master

Bath

VANITY

SHELVES

ARCHED OPENING

SHELVES

Dining

LINEN

WHIRLPOOL TUB

FOYER 8'2"X5'0"

VANITY

P'DR ROOM

W.C.

SEAT

W.C.

SHOWER   PRIVACY SHUTTERS

Porch

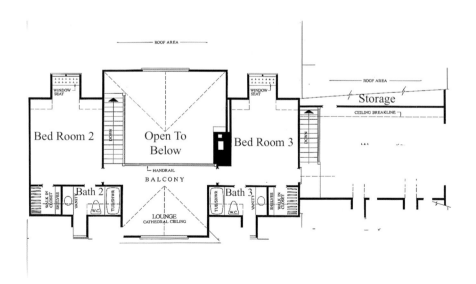

ROOF AREA

ROOF AREA

WINDOW SEAT

DOWN

Open To Below

Storage

CEILING BREAKLINE

Bed Room 2

WINDOW SEAT

Bed Room 3

DOWN

HANDRAIL

B A L C O N Y

WALK IN CLOSET

SHELVES

VANITY

Bath 2

W.C.

TUB/SHWR

TUB/SHWR

Bath 3

W.C.

VANITY

SHELVES

WALK IN CLOSET

LOUNGE
CATHEDRAL CEILING

© by William Poole

The design "Appomatox" by William Poole boasts a living area of 3,493 square feet. The exterior is marked by five symmetrically arranged dormers that suggest well-lit and generous rooms in the 1,117-square-foot upper story, which houses three large bedrooms, each with a full bath, and storage spaces. On the ground floor are a large, open kitchen and a breakfast room with several windows. In the center of the house is the great room, while a separate living room with fireplace and a master bedroom with bath and walk-in closet form the left wing of the house. Above the attached two-car garage, which is connected to the laundry room, there is space that may be finished to suit the owners' needs.

Design Appomattox
by William Poole
Ground floor 2,376 sq. ft.
Second floor 1,117 sq. ft.
Total 3,493 sq. ft.

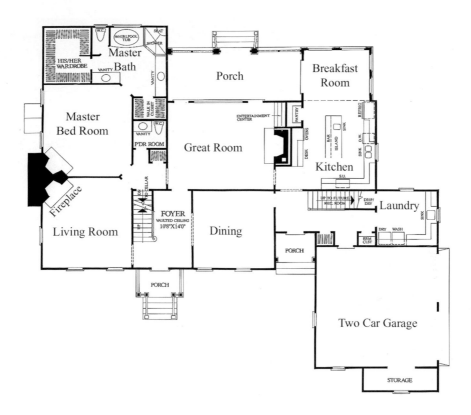

Master Bath

W.C.
WHIRLPOOL TUB
SEAT
SHOWER
HIS/HER WARDROBE
VANITY

Master Bed Room

WALK IN CLOSET
W.C.
VANITY
PDR ROOM

Porch

Breakfast Room

REFRIG
BAR ISLAND
SINK
D.W.
PANTRY
DESK
OVENS
SINK

Great Room

ENTERTAINMENT CENTER

Kitchen

S.U.

Fireplace

Living Room

DN TO CELLAR
UP

FOYER
VAULTED CEILING
10'8"X14'0"

Dining

UP TO FUTURE REC. ROOM
DRIP/DRY

Laundry

SINK
DRY WASH
BRM CLST

PORCH

PORCH

Two Car Garage

STORAGE

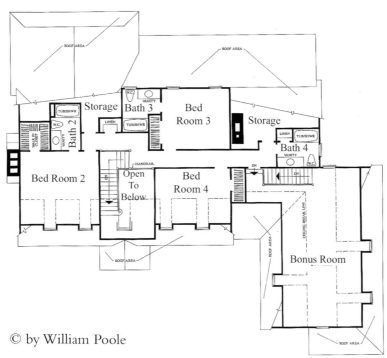

ROOF AREA

ROOF AREA

W.C.
VANITY
Bath 3
TUB/SHWR
W.C.

Storage

Bed Room 3

LINEN
TUB/SHWR

Storage

LINEN
TUB/SHWR
Bath 4
VANITY
W.C.

WALK IN CLOSET
W.C.
VANITY
Bath 2

Bed Room 2

Open To Below

HANDRAIL

Bed Room 4

DN
ON

CEILING BREAK LINE

ROOF AREA

Bonus Room

ROOF AREA

ROOF AREA

© by William Poole

In the one-story design of the "Somerset," William Poole presents an elegant variation of the typical southern country-style house. Both the gables on the front of the house as well as those on the narrower sides are finished in white stucco and, together with the white windows and the entry porch, form a striking contrast to the brick facade. Behind the roomy two-car garage, which also features a gable in keeping with the style of the house, is the private master suite with its own bath. Typically for a house in the country, the kitchen has a central island and an adjacent breakfast room, and offers access to the formal dining room, the laundry room, and the open great room with fireplace. On the right side of the house are two bedrooms, each with a full bath. The living room can be reached through both the foyer and the dining room. With its 2,394 square feet of living area, the Somerset offers sufficient room for many families.

Design Somerset
by William Poole

Total 2,394 sq. ft.

BRICK PLANTER

DOWN

W.C.

Master
Bath

JACUZZI/WHIRL
TUB

Master
Bed Room

ENTERTAINMENT
CENTER

Bed Room 2

SHOWER

LINEN

SINK   D.W.   REFG.

WARDROBE

S.L.L.

ISLAND   SINK

Breakfast
Room

Great Room

Bath 3

WARDROBE

FOLD
DN.
LB.

Laundry

Kitchen

W.C.

DRY   WASH   SINK

OVENS

DESK

LINEN

TUB/SHWR.

WARDROBE

BROOM

PANTRY

TUB/SHWR

Two Car Garage

Dining

Living Room

Bed Room 3

Bath 2

W.C.

FOYER

Porch

© by William Poole

With two porches, imposing columns, a classic white paneled facade, latticed windows and dormers, and a cupola on the garage roof, the exterior design of the "Shenandoah" by William Poole proves to be a faithful reproduction of traditional colonial architectural style. In contrast to the exterior appearance, which is elegantly based on nostalgic notions, the interior of the house features a modern floor plan and a wealth of comforts one expects from a house today. In addition to the master suite, the Shenandoah offers two additional bedrooms, an open great room, a formal dining room, and a country kitchen with a large breakfast room. There is additional space for expansion above the two-car garage as well.

Design Shenandoah
by William Poole

Ground floor 2,038 sq. ft.
Second floor 667 sq. ft.
Total 2,705 sq. ft.

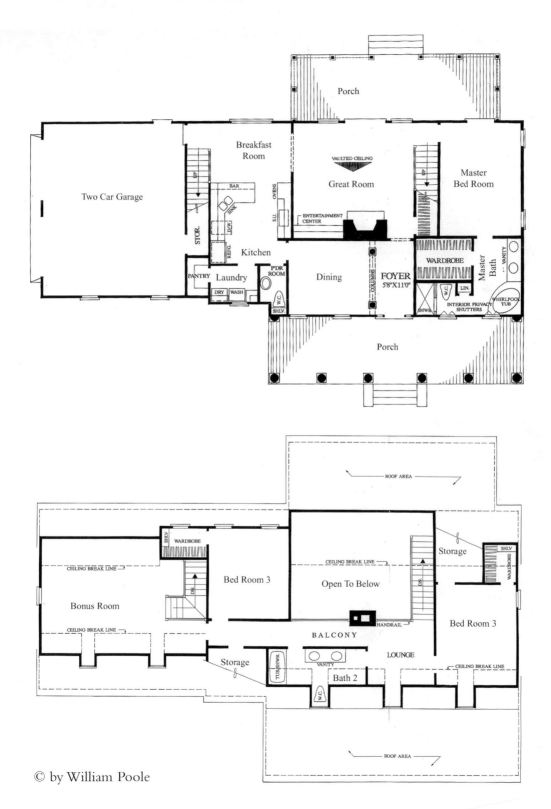

Porch

Breakfast
Room

VAULTED CEILING

Great Room

Master
Bed Room

Two Car Garage

UP

BAR

SINK

D/W

STOR.

ENTERTAINMENT
CENTER

WARDROBE

Master
Bath

VANITY

OVENS

S.U.

UP

Kitchen

REFG.

PANTRY

Laundry

DRY

WASH

P'DR
ROOM

Dining

COLUMNS

FOYER
5'8"X11'0"

W.C.

LIN.

WHIRLPOOL
TUB

W.C.

SHLV.

SHWR.

INTERIOR PRIVACY
SHUTTERS

Porch

ROOF AREA

Bonus Room

CEILING BREAK LINE

CEILING BREAK LINE

SHLV

WARDROBE

DN.

Bed Room 3

Open To Below

CEILING BREAK LINE

Storage

DN.

SHLV

WARDROBE

HANDRAIL

Bed Room 3

BALCONY

Storage

TUB/SHWR.

VANITY

Bath 2

LOUNGE

CEILING BREAK LINE

W.C.

ROOF AREA

© by William Poole

Southern Country Style 155

Upwards is the direction taken by William Poole's design for the "Port Royal"—the area for daily living lies on the second floor of this house, which is accentuated with wide covered porches that border both the front and rear sides of the building. On this floor are found the dining room, kitchen with breakfast room, the master suite with bath and walk-in closet, as well as an open great room with fireplace and cathedral ceiling. From the great room, stairs lead up to the attic, which houses two bedrooms and a bath. On the ground level are a fourth bedroom, a hobby room, and a double garage.

Design Port Royal
by William Poole

First floor 1,376 sq. ft.
Second floor 694 sq. ft.
Total 2,070 sq. ft.

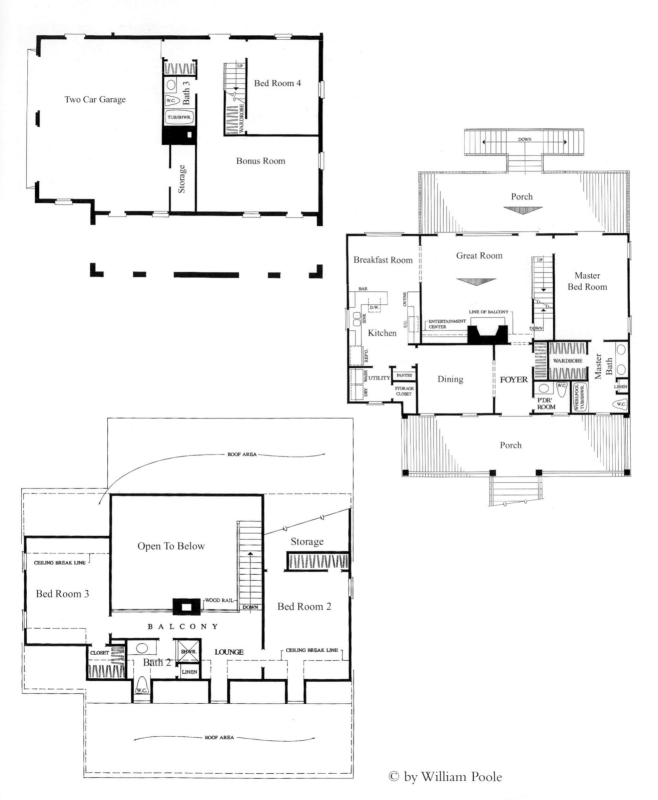

Two Car Garage

Bath 3

W.C.

TUB/SHWR.

Storage

UP

Bed Room 4

WARDROBE

Bonus Room

DOWN

Porch

Breakfast Room

Great Room

UP

Master Bed Room

BAR

D.W.

SINK

OVENS

S.U.

LINE OF BALCONY

ENTERTAINMENT CENTER

DOWN

Kitchen

WARDROBE

Master Bath

REF'G.

DRY WASH

UTILITY

PANTRY

STORAGE CLOSET

Dining

FOYER

W.C.

LINEN

P'DR' ROOM

WHIRLPOOL TUB/SHWR.

W.C.

Porch

ROOF AREA

Open To Below

Storage

CEILING BREAK LINE

Bed Room 3

UP

WOOD RAIL

DOWN

Bed Room 2

B A L C O N Y

CLOSET

SHWR.

LOUNGE

CEILING BREAK LINE

Bath 2

LINEN

W.C.

ROOF AREA

© by William Poole

Southern Country Style 157

The "Palmetto" by William Poole recreates the image of an authentic southern estate, largely due to the two-story porch that dominates the front of the house. The elaborate formal principles are continued on the interior. The living and dining rooms on the ground floor, and two of the upstairs bedrooms, are located at the front of the house and feature floor-to-ceiling bay windows. The master bedroom is located in a side wing to the back of the house. Like the master bedroom, the rooms opening onto the garden, including the great room with fireplace and the country kitchen with breakfast room, have direct access to the large rear deck. On the second floor are three bedrooms and two full baths as well as a balcony with a view into the kitchen below.

Design Palmetto
by William Poole

Ground floor 1,995 sq. ft.
Second floor 1,062 sq. ft.
Total 3,059 sq. ft.

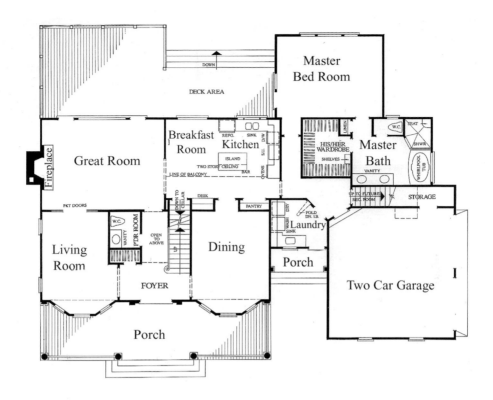

Great Room

Fireplace

Living Room

P'DR ROOM
W.C.
VANITY

FOYER

PKT DOORS

Breakfast Room

Kitchen
REFG.
SINK
D/W
TLT.
ISLAND
TWO STORY CEILING
BAR
OVENS

DESK

DOWN TO CELLAR

OPEN TO ABOVE

Dining

PANTRY

WASH DRY
SINK
Laundry

FOLD DN. LB.

Porch

DECK AREA

DOWN

Master Bed Room

HIS/HER WARDROBE
SHELVES
LINEN

W.C.
SEAT
SHWR

Master Bath
VANITY
WHIRLPOOL TUB

UP TO FUTURE REC. ROOM
STORAGE

Two Car Garage

Porch

LINE OF BALCONY

© by William Poole

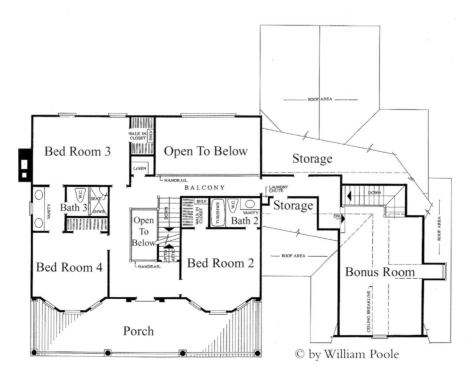

Bed Room 3

WALK IN CLOSET
SHLV
LINEN

Open To Below

Storage

ROOF AREA

Bath 3
W.C.
SEAT
SHWR
VANITY

HANDRAIL
BALCONY

Open To Below
DN
UP TO ATTIC
HANDRAIL

WALK IN CLOSET
SHLV
TUB/SHWR
W.C.
VANITY
Bath 2

LAUNDRY CHUTE

Storage

DOWN
DN

ROOF AREA

Bed Room 4

Bed Room 2

ROOF AREA

Bonus Room

CEILING BREAKLINE

Porch

Southern Country Style 159

In typical southern country style, "La Petit Natchez" features a chimney on both gable sides of the house. The arched dormer windows find resonance with the elegant glazing of the entrance. The interior of the house also consciously pursues the country theme. The path to the house leads across a wide porch into a large foyer that offers a view into the rooms on either side of it, planned as a formal living room and library. To the rear are an open country kitchen with spacious breakfast room and the formal dining room. The master suite with its own luxurious bath, designed for exacting tastes, is situated between the deck and its own small, private garden.

Design La Petit Natchez
by William Poole

Ground floor 2,091 sq. ft.
Second floor 1,044 sq. ft.
Total 3,135 sq. ft.

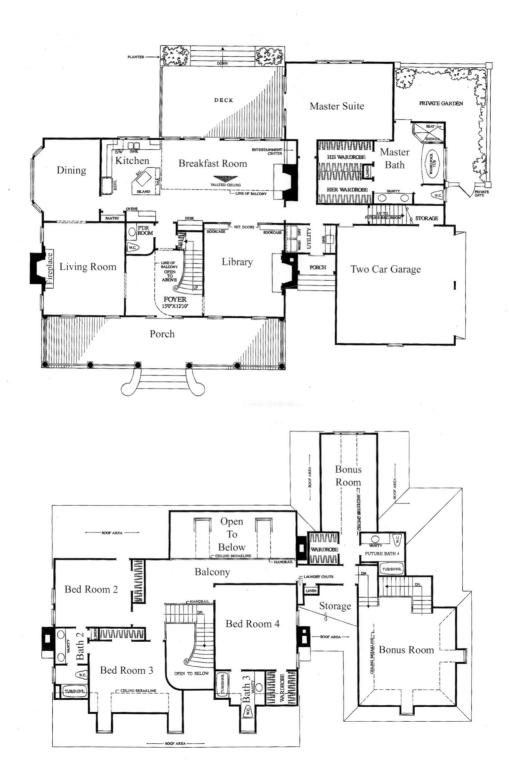

PLANTER

DOWN

DECK

Master Suite

PRIVATE GARDEN

Dining

Kitchen

SINK

D.W.

REFR.

BAR

ISLAND

Breakfast Room

ENTERTAINMENT CENTER

VAULTED CEILING

LINE OF BALCONY

HIS WARDROBE

HER WARDROBE

LINEN

WHIRLPOOL TUB

SEAT

SHOWER

Master Bath

VANITY

W.C.

PRIVATE GATE

OVENS

PANTRY

P'DR ROOM

W.C.

DESK

BOOKCASE

PKT. DOORS

BOOKCASE

WASH

DRY

UTILITY

SINK

UP TO FUTURE REC ROOM

STORAGE

Living Room

Fireplace

LINE OF BALCONY OPEN TO ABOVE

UP

FOYER
15'0"X12'10"

Library

PORCH

Two Car Garage

Porch

ROOF AREA

Bonus Room

ROOF AREA

CEILING BREAKLINE

Open To Below

CEILING BREAKLINE

WARDROBE

HANDRAIL

VANITY

W.C.

FUTURE BATH 4

Balcony

LAUNDRY CHUTE

LINEN

TUB/SHWR.

Bed Room 2

HANDRAIL

Storage

DN.

DN.

Bath 2

VANITY

LINEN

Bed Room 4

ROOF AREA

Bed Room 3

OPEN TO BELOW

STAIR

DN.

TUB/SHWR.

TUB/SHWR.

Bath 3

WARDROBE

W.C.

CEILING BREAKLINE

W.C.

CEILING BREAKLINE

Bonus Room

ROOF AREA

ROOF AREA

The finely detailed design gives the "Melrose" by William Poole its distinctive character and makes clear at first glance that this house belongs to the highest class. The elegance of the exterior is continued inside the house, with a total living area of 3,200 square feet distributed over a generously conceived floor plan. The ground floor includes a dining room, a kitchen with breakfast room, an open great room, a formal living room/library combination and a master suite with its own bath and wardrobe. From the second floor balcony, one can look down onto the foyer and the great room opposite. On the upper floor are three bedrooms and two baths.

Design Melrose
by William Poole

Ground floor 2,199 sq. ft.
Second floor 1,001 sq. ft.
Total 3,200 sq. ft.

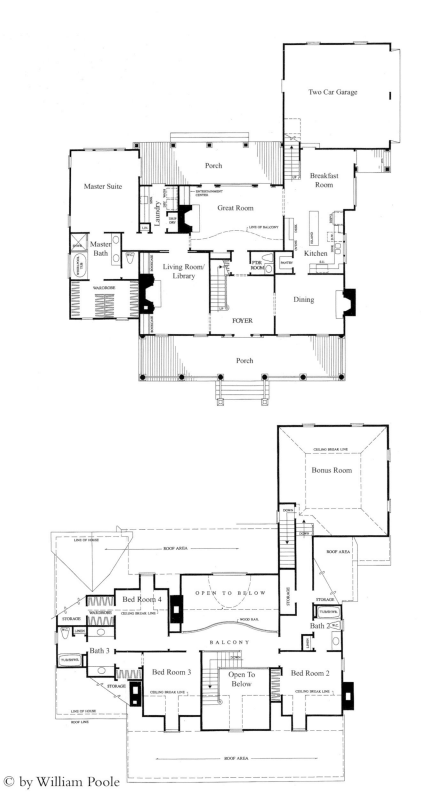

Two Car Garage

Master Suite

Porch

Breakfast Room

Laundry

Great Room

ENTERTAINMENT CENTER

LINE OF BALCONY

Master Bath

WHIRLPOOL TUB

W.C.

WARDROBE

BOOKCASE

Living Room/ Library

UP

PDR ROOM

PANTRY

Kitchen

S.U.

Dining

FOYER

Porch

Bonus Room

CEILING BREAK LINE

DOWN

DOWN

ROOF AREA

LINE OF HOUSE

ROOF AREA

Bed Room 4

WARDROBE

STORAGE

W.C.

LINEN

CEILING BREAK LINE

O P E N   T O   B E L O W

STORAGE

STORAGE

TUB/SHWR.

W.C.

Bath 2

LINEN

Bath 3

TUB/SHWR.

STORAGE

Bed Room 3

CEILING BREAK LINE

Open To Below

DOWN

B A L C O N Y

WOOD RAIL

Bed Room 2

CEILING BREAK LINE

LINE OF HOUSE

ROOF LINE

ROOF AREA

© by William Poole

Southern Country Style 163

A particularly attractive example of authentic southern architecture, designed by the leading architect for this style, is the "Currituck Cottage." This design is especially appealing for those who are fond of fresh air, and invites you to slow down and take advantage of the wide, wrap-around porch. The interior of the house offers a large country kitchen with adjacent breakfast room. Behind the dining room is the great room with fireplace, which offers access to the garden. The master suite features a large bath with shower and whirlpool. On the second floor, beneath the roof, are two more bedrooms that share a full bath.

A fourth bedroom with full bath, a hobby room, and the two-car garage are located in the basement.

Design Currituck Cottage
by William Poole

Ground floor 1,554 sq. ft.
Second floor 755 sq. ft.
Total 2,309 sq. ft.

Storage

Bonus Room

Storage

Two Car Garage

TUB/SHWR.

W.C.

WARDROBE

Bed Room 4

UP

DECK

Breakfast
Room

Great Room

WARDROBE

WHIRLPOOL
TUB

SEAT

SHOWER

Master
Bath

BAR

OVEN

DESK

ENTERTAINMENT
CENTER

W.C.

LINEN CABINET

PDR.
ROOM

W.C.

Kitchen

D.W.

SINK

PANTRY

REFG.

FOLD
DN LR.

DRIP
DRY

SINK

DRY

WASH

Dining

FOYER

DOWN

UP

Master Suite

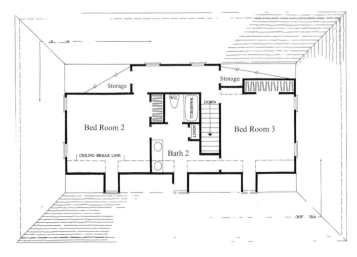

Storage

W.C.

Storage

Bed Room 2

TUB/SHWR.

DOWN

LINEN

Bed Room 3

CEILING BREAK LINE

Bath 2

ROOF AREA

© by William Poole

Southern Country Style 165

The design for "Belle Grove" by William Poole conveys the full charm of the southern country style. Typical elements such as the covered front porch with columns and the cupola on the two-car garage underline the stylistic purity of the design. The interior of the house foresees four large bedrooms, three of which are located on the second floor. The master suite, with its generous bath and wardrobe, is located on the ground floor with a door to the back yard. Adjacent to the large great room with fireplace is the country kitchen with direct access to the dining room and the laundry room. With its wide bay windows, the breakfast room offers a bright place to enjoy meals with a view into the yard.

Design Belle Grove
by William Poole

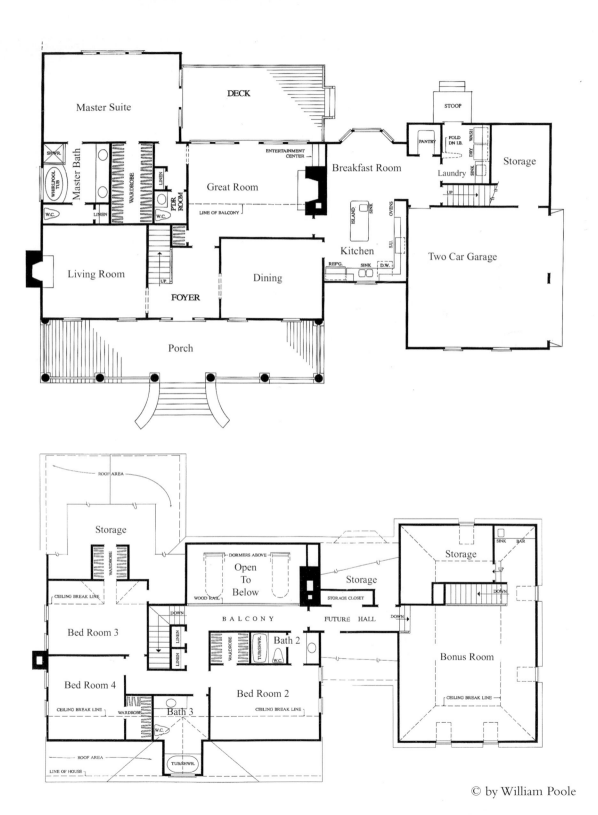

© by William Poole

Southern Country Style 167

The "Bowling Green" design by William Poole is distinguished by a clear division between the areas for active living and for sleeping. The floor plan places all three bedrooms on the ground floor. The master bedroom has its own bath, while the other two bedrooms share a full bath located between them. The highlight of the design is the spacious, open living area. Beneath its high ceiling construction, the kitchen forms the center point around which a living room with fireplace, a light-flooded great room with large windows, and a breakfast bay are located. The second floor offers room for expansion either in the dormer area alone (as shown), or above the ground floor bedrooms, as well.

Design Bowling Green
by William Poole

Ground floor 2,777 sq. ft.
Second floor 818 sq. ft.
Total 3,595 sq. ft.

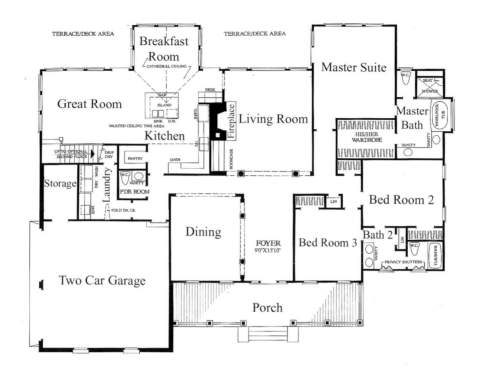

Breakfast Room
CATHEDRAL CEILING

TERRACE/DECK AREA

TERRACE/DECK AREA

Master Suite

W.C.

SEAT
SHOWER

Great Room

BAR
ISLAND
SINK   D.W.
VAULTED CEILING THIS AREA

DESK

Fireplace

Living Room

Master Bath

WHIRLPOOL TUB

VANITY

Kitchen

REFG.

BOOKCASE

HIS/HER WARDROBE

VANITY

UP TO OPTIONAL
SECOND FLOOR

DRIP
DRY

PANTRY

OVEN

Storage

DRY WASH

W.C.
VANITY

P'DR ROOM

SINK

FOLD DN. I.B.

Laundry

LIN

Bed Room 2

Dining

FOYER
9'0"X15'10"

Bed Room 3

Bath 2

VANITY

LIN

W.C.

TUB/SHWR

PRIVACY SHUTTERS

Two Car Garage

Porch

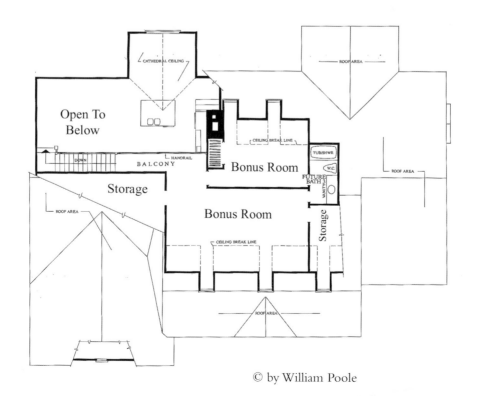

CATHEDRAL CEILING

ROOF AREA

Open To Below

CEILING BREAK LINE

TUB/SHWR

W.C.

DOWN

HANDRAIL

BALCONY

Bonus Room

FUTURE BATH

VANITY

ROOF AREA

Storage

ROOF AREA

Bonus Room

Storage

CEILING BREAK LINE

ROOF AREA

© by William Poole

Southern Country Style 169

This magnificent country cottage designed by William Poole offers a total living area of 2,936 square feet. On the ground floor are a master suite and two additional bedrooms. The kitchen features a pantry and a comfortable breakfast area with a large bay window. Adjoining the kitchen is the great room with fireplace. With its open design and high ceiling, the room can also be viewed from the gallery on the second floor. In addition, the upper story provides a fourth bedroom and a large area for expansion. Finally, there is ample storage room under the roof joists.

Design Country Cottage
by William Poole

Ground floor 2,151 sq. ft.
Second floor 786 sq. ft.
Total 2,936 sq. ft.

Balcony

Bed Room 3

BOOKCASE

Great Room

Breakfast Area

Master Suite

BOOKCASE

BAR

SINK

OVEN

SHLV

WALK IN CLOSET

UP TO OPTIONAL SECOND FLOOR

TUB/SHWR

LINEN

Bath 2

VANITY

W.C

Gallery

Kitchen

D.W

S.U.

REFG.

PANTRY

Master Bath

VANITY

SEAT

SHOWER

WHIRLPOOL TUB

Bed Room 2

Foyer

Dining

Laundry

SINK

WASH

DRY

DRIP/DRY

LIN.

Walk in Closet

LINEN

W.C

Porch

Two Car Garage

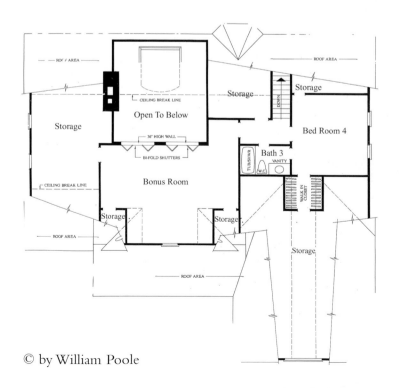

ROOF AREA

ROOF AREA

CEILING BREAK LINE

Storage

Storage

DOWN

Storage

Open To Below

36" HIGH WALL

BI-FOLD SHUTTERS

Bonus Room

Bed Room 4

CEILING BREAK LINE

TUB/SHWR

W.C

Bath 3

VANITY

WALK IN CLOSET

Storage

Storage

Storage

ROOF AREA

Storage

ROOF AREA

© by William Poole

The characteristic feature of this southern country house is the covered porch gracing its front. Three dormers rise tower-like from the dark gabled roof, while high windows framed by shutters harmonize with the elegant entry, which is fitted with an exclusive arched window. The interior is arranged according to a clear floor plan. The ground floor provides a dining room, a study, a kitchen with breakfast room, a large great room with fireplace, and the master suite with bath. On the second floor are three further bedrooms, as well as room for expansion above the two-car garage.

Design Biloxi
by William Poole

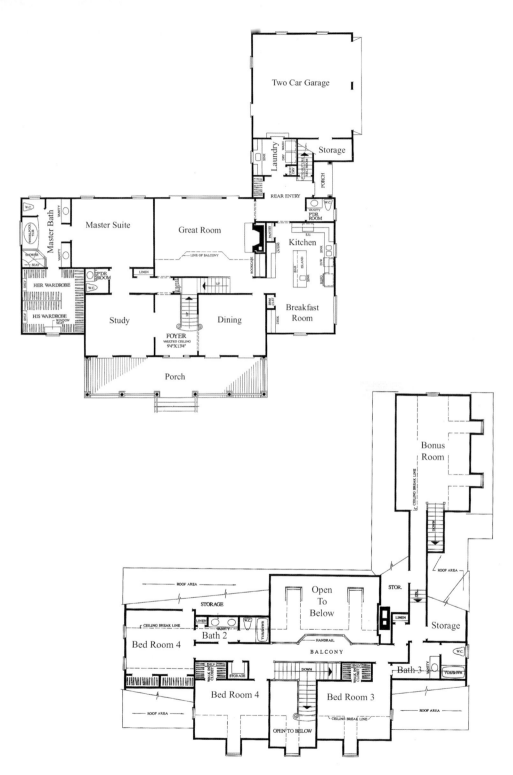

Two Car Garage

Laundry

Storage

REAR ENTRY

PORCH

Master Bath

W.C.

WHIRLPOOL TUB

VANITY

VANITY

SHOWER

SEAT

Master Suite

Great Room

PANTRY

OVENS

BOOKCASE

LINE OF BALCONY

VANITY

PTDR ROOM

W.C.

Kitchen

S.U.

BAR

ISLAND

D.W.

SINK

REF.

SINK

HER WARDROBE

HIS WARDROBE

WINDOW SEAT

P'TDR ROOM

W.C.

LINEN

Study

Dining

FOYER
VAULTED CEILING
9'4"X13'4"

Breakfast
Room

DESK

BRM CLST.

UP

Porch

Bonus
Room

CEILING BREAK LINE

DOWN

ROOF AREA

ROOF AREA

STORAGE

CEILING BREAK LINE

LINEN

W.C.

VANITY

WARDROBE

STOR.

UP

LINEN

Storage

W.C.

Open
To
Below

Bed Room 4

Bath 2

HANDRAIL

BALCONY

SHLV

WALK IN
CLOSET

STORAGE

DOWN

SHLV

WALK IN
CLOSET

Bath 3

VANITY

TUB/SHWR

Bed Room 4

Bed Room 3

ROOF AREA

OPEN TO BELOW

CEILING BREAK LINE

ROOF AREA

© by William Poole

Southern Country Style 173

This variation of the stately country house designed in the southern tradition shares many exterior features with the house described on the preceding two pages. The interior of this home features formal living and dining rooms to either side of the foyer, a great room with fireplace, a kitchen with breakfast area, and a master suite with all the trimmings, all on the 2,190-square-foot ground floor. Three additional bedrooms and two full baths are located on the 1,220-square-foot second floor, with additional room for expansion above the two-car garage.

Design Biloxi
by William Poole

Total 3,410 sq. ft.

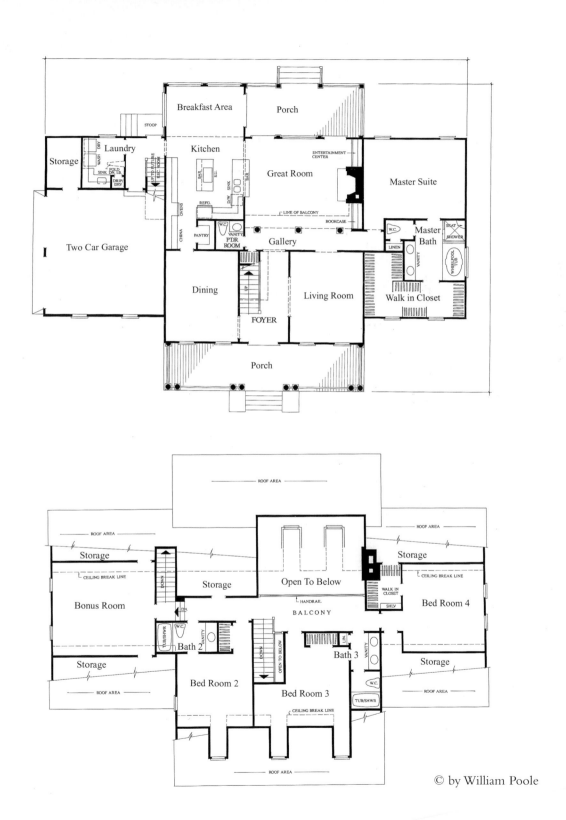

Breakfast Area

Porch

Storage

Laundry

Kitchen

Great Room

Master Suite

ENTERTAINMENT CENTER

LINE OF BALCONY

BOOKCASE

Two Car Garage

CHINA

PANTRY

P'DR. ROOM

Gallery

Master Bath

W.C.

LINEN

VANITY

WHIRLPOOL TUB

SEAT SHOWER

Dining

FOYER

Living Room

Walk in Closet

Porch

ROOF AREA

Storage

CEILING BREAK LINE

ROOF AREA

Storage

ROOF AREA

Storage

Open To Below

Storage

CEILING BREAK LINE

Bonus Room

HANDRAIL

BALCONY

WALK IN CLOSET

SHLV.

Bed Room 4

Bath 2

TUB/SHWR

W.C.

VANITY

Bed Room 2

OPEN TO BELOW

Bath 3

LIN.

VANITY

Storage

ROOF AREA

Storage

ROOF AREA

Bed Room 3

W.C.

TUB/SHWR

CEILING BREAK LINE

ROOF AREA

© by William Poole

Southern Country Style 175

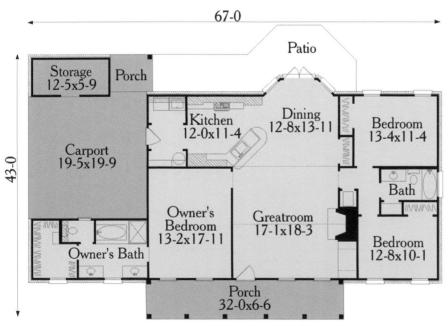

Storage 12-5x5-9	Porch	Patio
Carport 19-5x19-9	Kitchen 12-0x11-4	Dining 12-8x13-11

67-0

43-0

Patio

Storage
12-5x5-9

Porch

Kitchen
12-0x11-4

Dining
12-8x13-11

Bedroom
13-4x11-4

Carport
19-5x19-9

Bath

Owner's
Bedroom
13-2x17-11

Greatroom
17-1x18-3

Owner's Bath

Bedroom
12-8x10-1

Porch
32-0x6-6

Design 9527
Allason

© Larry James

Living area 1,689 sq. ft.
Total 2,414 sq. ft.

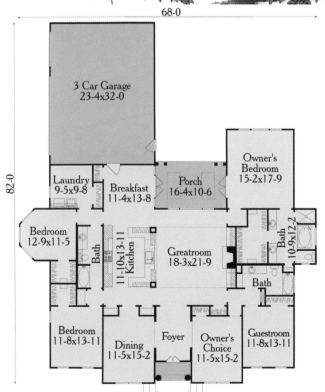

3 Car Garage
23-4x32-0

82-0

68-0

Laundry
9-5x9-8

Breakfast
11-4x13-8

Porch
16-4x10-6

Owner's
Bedroom
15-2x17-9

Bedroom
12-9x11-5

Bath

11-10x13-11
Kitchen

Greatroom
18-3x21-9

Bath
10-9x12-2

Bath

Bedroom
11-8x13-11

Dining
11-5x15-2

Foyer

Owner's
Choice
11-5x15-2

Guestroom
11-8x13-11

Design 9530
Camberley
© Larry James

Living area 2,773 sq. ft.
Total 3,754 sq. ft.

Southern Country Style 177

71-9

3 Car Garage
22-3x33-6

79-3

1/2 Bath

Laun.

Porch
25-0x8-6

Bath

Owner's
Bedroom
14-7x26-2

Kitchen
12-0x17-11

Breakfast/Greatroom
26-6x17-11

Bath

Bedroom
11-9x12-3

Butler's
Pantry

Dining
13-3x12-4

Foyer

Owner's
Choice
13-3x12-4

Bedroom
11-9x12-1

Stoop

Design 9602
Leighton
© Larry James

Living area 2,519 sq. ft.
Total 3,743 sq. ft.

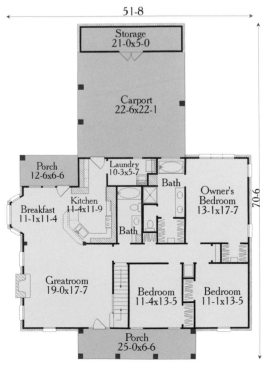

Storage
21-0x5-0

Carport
22-6x22-1

51-8

70-6

Porch
12-6x6-6

Laundry
10-3x5-7

Bath

Kitchen
11-4x11-9

Breakfast
11-1x11-4

Bath

Owner's
Bedroom
13-1x17-7

Greatroom
19-0x17-7

Bedroom
11-4x13-5

Bedroom
11-1x13-5

Porch
25-0x6-6

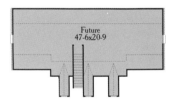

Future
47-6x20-9

Design 9607
Hillcrest
© Larry James

Living area 1,726 sq. ft.
Total 2,599 sq. ft.

Southern Country Style 179

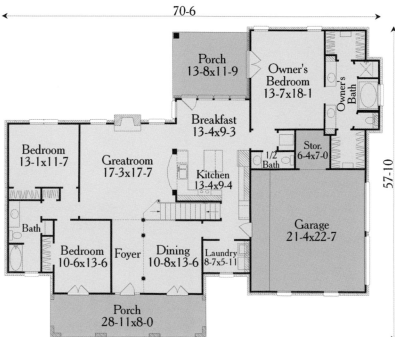

Porch
13-8x11-9

Owner's
Bedroom
13-7x18-1

Owner's
Bath

Breakfast
13-4x9-3

Bedroom
13-1x11-7

Greatroom
17-3x17-7

Kitchen
13-4x9-4

1/2
Bath

Stor.
6-4x7-0

70-6

57-10

Bath

Bedroom
10-6x13-6

Foyer

Dining
10-8x13-6

Laundry
8-7x5-11

Garage
21-4x22-7

Porch
28-11x8-0

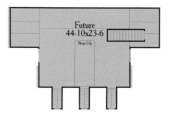

Future
44-10x23-6

Step-Up

Design 9608
Lansing
© Larry James

Living area 2,082 sq. ft.
Total 3,039 sq. ft.

180 Southern Country Style

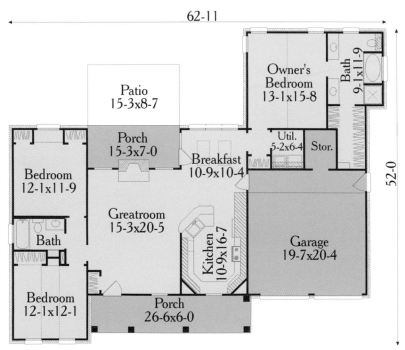

Patio
15-3x8-7

Porch
15-3x7-0

Bedroom
12-1x11-9

Bath

Bedroom
12-1x12-1

Greatroom
15-3x20-5

Kitchen
10-9x16-7

Breakfast
10-9x10-4

Owner's
Bedroom
13-1x15-8

Bath
9-1x11-9

Util.
5-2x6-4

Stor.

Garage
19-7x20-4

Porch
26-6x6-0

62-11

52-0

Design 9609
Auburn

© Larry James

Living area 1,606 sq. ft.
Total 2,339 sq. ft.

Southern Country Style 181

Design 9614
Wakefield
© Larry James

Living area 2,202 sq. ft.
Total 2,979 sq. ft.

182 Southern Country Style

Design 9616
Newcastle
© Larry James

Living area 1,685 sq. ft.
Total 2,533 sq. ft.

Southern Country Style 183

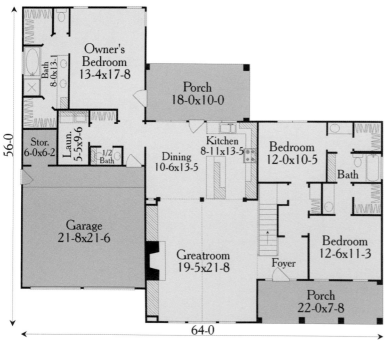

Owner's Bedroom 13-4x17-8

Bath 8-0x13-1

Porch 18-0x10-0

Stor. 6-0x6-2

Laun. 5-5x9-6

1/2 Bath

Kitchen 8-11x13-5

Dining 10-6x13-5

Bedroom 12-0x10-5

Bath

Garage 21-8x21-6

Greatroom 19-5x21-8

Foyer

Bedroom 12-6x11-3

Porch 22-0x7-8

56-0

64-0

Future 21-8x20-9

Design 9617
Broadhaven

© Larry James

Living area 1,925 sq. ft.
Total 2,799 sq. ft.

184 Southern Country Style

Carport
22-3x22-0

Porch
19-5x8-0

Storage
12-6x3-4

Owner's
Bedroom
15-8x18-7

Laun.
5-1x8-0

Bedroom
12-6x10-6

Dining
9-9x13-0

Kitchen
9-8x13-0

Bath

Bath
15-8x14-5

Bedroom
12-6x10-6

Greatroom
19-5x18-0

Foyer

Porch
22-0x7-8

57-8

58-0

Design 9618
Forest Hill
© Larry James

Living area 1,756 sq. ft.
Total 2,618 sq. ft.

Southern Country Style 185

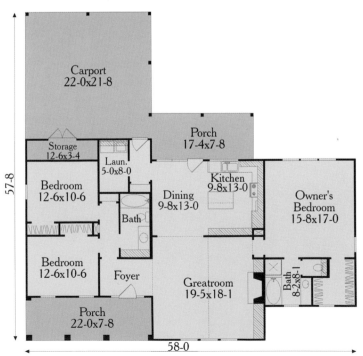

Carport
22-0x21-8

Storage
12-6x3-4

Laun.
5-0x8-0

Porch
17-4x7-8

Bedroom
12-6x10-6

Bath

Dining
9-8x13-0

Kitchen
9-8x13-0

Owner's
Bedroom
15-8x17-0

Bedroom
12-6x10-6

Foyer

Greatroom
19-5x18-1

Bath
8-2x8-1

Porch
22-0x7-8

57-8

58-0

Design 9619
The Laurens
© Larry James

Living area 1,625 sq. ft.
Total 2,474 sq. ft.

186 Southern Country Style

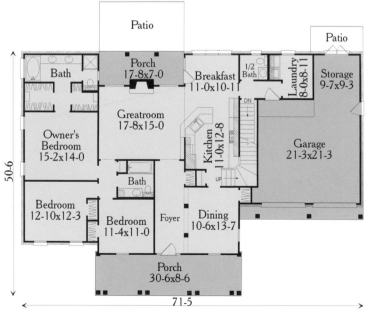

Patio

Bath

Porch
17-8x7-0

Breakfast
11-0x10-11

1/2
Bath

Laundry
8-0x8-11

Patio

Storage
9-7x9-3

Owner's
Bedroom
15-2x14-0

Greatroom
17-8x15-0

Kitchen
11-0x12-8

DN

UP

Garage
21-3x21-3

50-6

Bedroom
12-10x12-3

Bath

Bedroom
11-4x11-0

Foyer

Dining
10-6x13-7

Porch
30-6x8-6

71-5

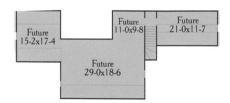

Future
15-2x17-4

Future
11-0x9-8

Future
21-0x11-7

Future
29-0x18-6

Design 9707
Williamson
© Larry James

Living area 1,997 sq. ft.
Total 2,970 sq. ft.

Southern Country Style 187

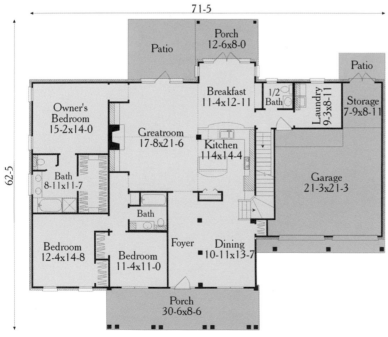

71-5

Patio

Porch
12-6x8-0

Patio

Breakfast
11-4x12-11

1/2
Bath

Laundry
9-3x8-11

Storage
7-9x8-11

Owner's
Bedroom
15-2x14-0

Greatroom
17-8x21-6

Kitchen
114x14-4

Bath
8-11x11-7

Garage
21-3x21-3

Bath

62-5

Bedroom
12-4x14-8

Bedroom
11-4x11-0

Foyer

Dining
10-11x13-7

Porch
30-6x8-6

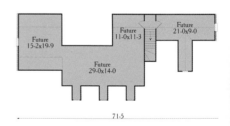

Future
15-2x19-9

Future
11-0x11-3

Future
21-0x9-0

Future
29-0x14-0

71-5

Design 9708
Southport
© Larry James

Living area 2,225 sq. ft.
Total 3,154 sq. ft.

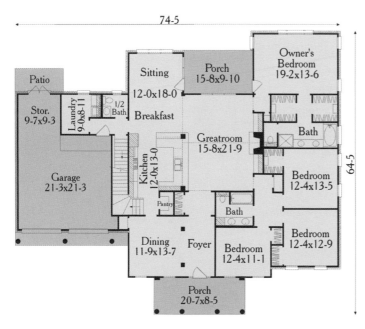

74-5

Patio

Stor.
9-7x9-3

Laundry
9-0x8-11

1/2
Bath

Sitting
12-0x18-0

Breakfast

Porch
15-8x9-10

Owner's
Bedroom
19-2x13-6

Kitchen
12-0x13-0

Greatroom
15-8x21-9

Bath

Garage
21-3x21-3

Pantry

Bath

Bedroom
12-4x13-5

64-5

Dining
11-9x13-7

Foyer

Bedroom
12-4x11-1

Bedroom
12-4x12-9

Porch
20-7x8-5

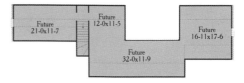

Future
21-0x11-7

Future
12-0x11-5

Future
16-11x17-6

Future
32-0x11-9

Design 9708
Southport
© Larry James

Living area 2,225 sq. ft.
Total 3,154 sq. ft.

Southern Country Style 189

26-0

Bath

Covered Deck

Master Bedroom
15-5x13-8

Stor.

Kitchen
11-7x11-8

Dining
11-7x12-9

Carport
10-0x20-0

72-0

Greatroom
15-5x12-9

UP

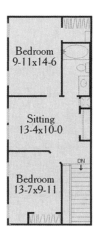

Bedroom
9-11x14-6

Sitting
13-4x10-0

DN

Bedroom
13-7x9-11

Design 9710
Harborside
© Larry James

Living area 1,587 sq. ft.
Total 2,176 sq. ft.

Porch
16-0x8-0

190 Southern Country Style

26-0

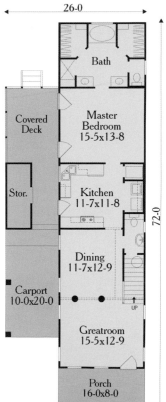

Bath

Covered
Deck

Master
Bedroom
15-5x13-8

Stor.

Kitchen
11-7x11-8

Bedroom
9-11x14-6

72-0

Sitting
13-4x10-0

Dining
11-7x12-9

Carport
10-0x20-0

Bedroom
13-7x9-11

DN

UP

Greatroom
15-5x12-9

Porch
16-0x8-0

Design 9712
The Harborside
© Larry James

Living area 1,587 sq. ft.
Total 2,176 sq. ft.

Southern Country Style 191

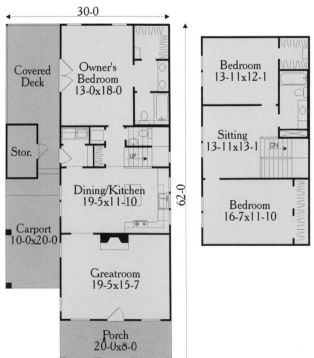

30-0

Covered
Deck

Owner's
Bedroom
13-0x18-0

Stor.

UP

Dining/Kitchen
19-5x11-10

Carport
10-0x20-0

62-0

Greatroom
19-5x15-7

Porch
20-0x8-0

Bedroom
13-11x12-1

Sitting
13-11x13-1

DN

Bedroom
16-7x11-10

Design 9714
Point Clair
© Larry James

Living area 1,778 sq. ft.
Total 2,418 sq. ft.

192 Southern Country Style

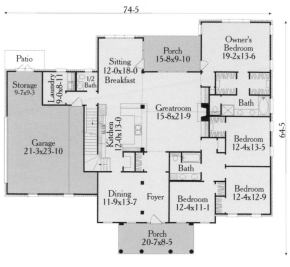

Design 9716
Hillsboro
© Larry James

Living area 2,635 sq. ft.
Total 3,634 sq. ft.

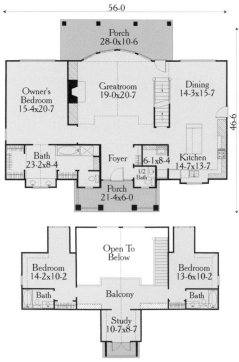

Design 9718
Hickory II
© Larry James

Living area 2,613 sq. ft.
Total 3,022 sq. ft.

Floor plan labels:

56-0

Porch
28-0x10-6

Owner's
Bedroom
15-4x20-7

Greatroom
19-0x20-7

Dining
14-3x15-7

46-6

Bath
23-2x8-4

Foyer

6-1x8-4

1/2 Bath

Kitchen
14-7x13-7

Porch
21-4x6-0

Open To Below

Bedroom
14-2x10-2

Bedroom
13-6x10-2

Bath

Balcony

Bath

Study
10-7x8-7

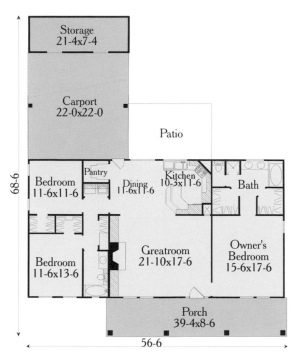

Design 9719
Hartwick

© Larry James

Living area 1,679 sq. ft.
Total 2,674 sq. ft.

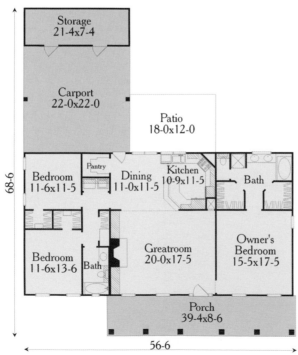

Design 9720
Mason
© Larry James

Living area 1,679 sq. ft.
Total 2,674 sq. ft.

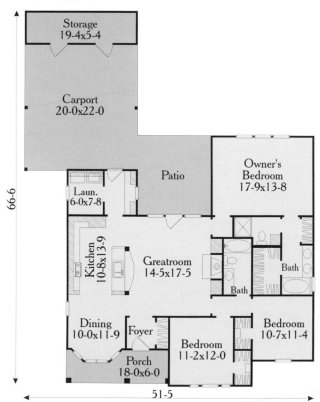

Storage
19-4x5-4

Carport
20-0x22-0

66-6

Laun.
6-0x7-8

Patio

Owner's
Bedroom
17-9x13-8

Kitchen
10-8x13-9

Greatroom
14-5x17-5

Bath

Bath

Dining
10-0x11-9

Foyer

Bedroom
11-2x12-0

Bedroom
10-7x11-4

Porch
18-0x6-0

51-5

Design 9721
Somerset
© Larry James

Living area 1,539 sq. ft.
Total 2,194 sq. ft.

Southern Country Style 197

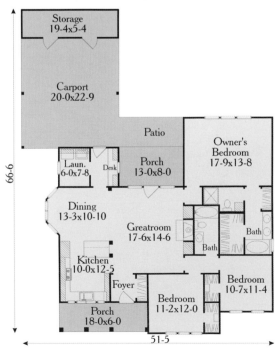

Design 9722
Taylor
© Larry James

Living area 1,543 sq. ft.
Total 2,302 sq. ft.

Storage
20-3x6-2

3 Bay Garage
20-3x30-1

Owner's
Bedroom
16-1x17-9

Porch
19-9x7-0

Morning Area
15-0x14-0

Bath

Greatroom
20-8x19-6

Breakfast
15-0x12-2

Laundry
12-0x7-10

Bedroom
11-7x13-2

Bath

1/2
Bath

Bedroom
12-10x12-1

Foyer

Dining
11-10x14-6

Kitchen
13-9x12-0

Bedroom
11-10x12-0

Porch
32-0x6-0

76-2

83-0

Design 9723
Savannah
© Larry James

Living area 2,925 sq. ft.
Total 4,111 sq. ft.

Southern Country Style 199

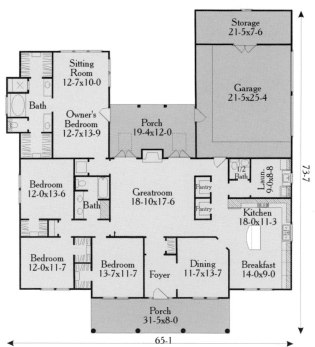

Storage
21-5x7-6

Sitting
Room
12-7x10-0

Bath

Owner's
Bedroom
12-7x13-9

Porch
19-4x12-0

Garage
21-5x25-4

Bedroom
12-0x13-6

Bath

Greatroom
18-10x17-6

Pantry

Pantry

1/2
Bath

Laun.
9-0x8-8

Kitchen
18-0x11-3

Bedroom
12-0x11-7

Bedroom
13-7x11-7

Foyer

Dining
11-7x13-7

Breakfast
14-0x9-0

Porch
31-5x8-0

73-7

65-1

**Design 9724
Longmeadow**
© Larry James

Living area 2,465 sq. ft.
Total 2,689 sq. ft.

200 Southern Country Style

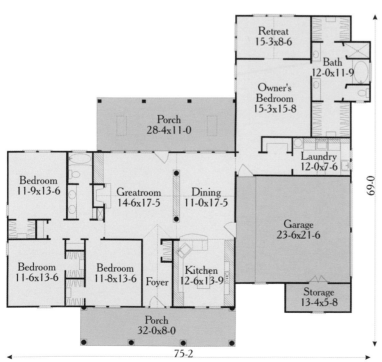

Design 9801
Lakeview
© Larry James

Living area 2,369 sq. ft.
Total 3,540 sq. ft.

Southern Country Style 201

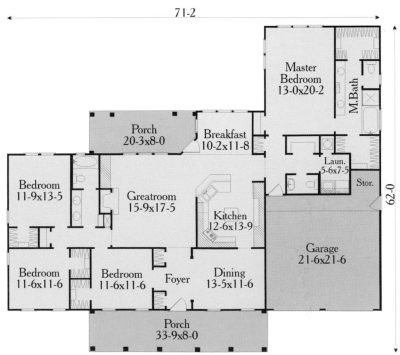

71-2

62-0

Master Bedroom
13-0x20-2

M.Bath

Porch
20-3x8-0

Breakfast
10-2x11-8

Laun.
5-6x7-5

Stor.

Bedroom
11-9x13-5

Greatroom
15-9x17-5

Kitchen
12-6x13-9

Bedroom
11-6x11-6

Bedroom
11-6x11-6

Foyer

Dining
13-5x11-6

Garage
21-6x21-6

Porch
33-9x8-0

**Design 9802
Bordlands**

© Larry James

Living area 2,267 sq. ft.
Total 3,182 sq. ft.

202 Southern Country Style

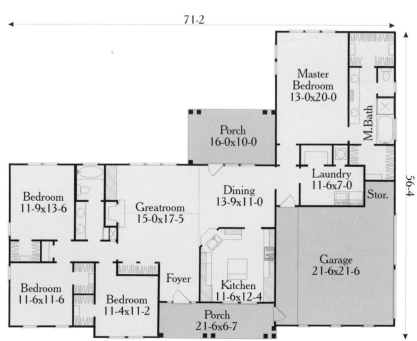

71-2

Master
Bedroom
13-0x20-0

Porch
16-0x10-0

M.Bath

Laundry
11-6x7-0

Stor.

56-4

Bedroom
11-9x13-6

Greatroom
15-0x17-5

Dining
13-9x11-0

Garage
21-6x21-6

Bedroom
11-6x11-6

Bedroom
11-4x11-2

Foyer

Kitchen
11-6x12-4

Porch
21-6x6-7

Design 9803
Dovehill
© Larry James

Living area 2,093 sq. ft.
Total 2,906 sq. ft.

Southern Country Style 203

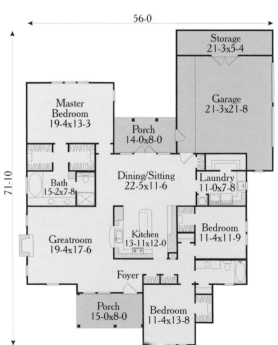

Design 9804
Cambridge
© Larry James

Living area 2,053 sq. ft.
Total 2,922 sq. ft.

Floor plan labels:

56-0

71-10

Storage
21-3x5-4

Garage
21-3x21-8

Master
Bedroom
19-4x13-3

Porch
14-0x8-0

Bath
15-2x7-8

Dining/Sitting
22-5x11-6

Laundry
11-0x7-8

Greatroom
19-4x17-6

Kitchen
13-11x12-0

Bedroom
11-4x11-9

Foyer

Porch
15-0x8-0

Bedroom
11-4x13-8

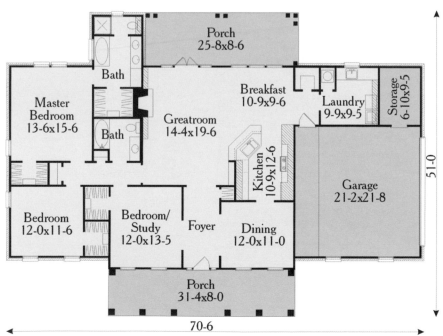

Design 9805
Kenwood

© Larry James

Living area 1,867 sq. ft.
Total 2,923 sq. ft.

Porch
25-8x8-6

Bath

Master
Bedroom
13-6x15-6

Bath

Greatroom
14-4x19-6

Breakfast
10-9x9-6

Laundry
9-9x9-5

Storage
6-10x9-5

Kitchen
10-9x12-6

Garage
21-2x21-8

Bedroom
12-0x11-6

Bedroom/
Study
12-0x13-5

Foyer

Dining
12-0x11-0

Porch
31-4x8-0

70-6

51-0

Southern Country Style 205

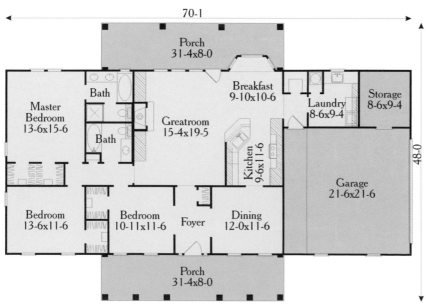

Porch
31-4x8-0

Master Bedroom
13-6x15-6

Bath

Bath

Greatroom
15-4x19-5

Breakfast
9-10x10-6

Laundry
8-6x9-4

Storage
8-6x9-4

Kitchen
9-6x11-6

Garage
21-6x21-6

Bedroom
13-6x11-6

Bedroom
10-11x11-6

Foyer

Dining
12-0x11-6

Porch
31-4x8-0

70-1

48-0

Design 9806
Borestone

© Larry James

Living area 1,688 sq. ft.
Total 2,763 sq. ft.

Photo © Mark Englund / HomeStyles

Floor plan labels:

68-0

Storage
8-6x8-10

Laundry
7-6x8-10

Breakfast
11-0x11-6

Porch
19-7x13-0

Bath
15-2x5-6

Garage
21-7x21-8

Kitchen
11-0x12-0

Greatroom
17-5x15-0

Master
Bedroom
15-2x14-0

Bath

56-6

Dining
11-0x13-6

Foyer

Bedroom
11-3x11-0

Bedroom
12-9x12-2

Porch
30-6x8-6

Design 9807
Weststone
© Larry James

Living area 1,894 sq. ft.
Total 2,993 sq. ft.

Southern Country Style 207

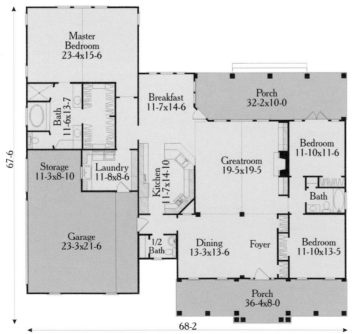

Master
Bedroom
23-4x15-6

Bath
11-6x13-7

Breakfast
11-7x14-6

Porch
32-2x10-0

Storage
11-3x8-10

Laundry
11-8x8-6

Kitchen
11-7x14-10

Greatroom
19-5x19-5

Bedroom
11-10x11-6

Bath

Garage
23-3x21-6

1/2
Bath

Dining
13-3x13-6

Foyer

Bedroom
11-10x13-5

Porch
36-4x8-0

67-6

68-2

Design 9808
Burghfield
© Larry James

Living area 2,424 sq. ft.
Total 3,677 sq. ft.

208 Southern Country Style

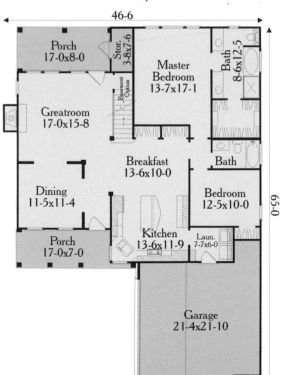

Porch
17-0x8-0

Stor.
3-8x7-6

Master
Bedroom
13-7x17-1

Bath
8-6x12-5

Greatroom
17-0x15-8

Basement Option

Dining
11-5x11-4

Breakfast
13-6x10-0

Bath

Bedroom
12-5x10-0

Porch
17-0x7-0

Kitchen
13-6x11-9

Laun.
7-7x6-0

Garage
21-4x21-10

46-6

65-0

Bedroom
16-4x15-4

Bath
9-0x6-0

Design 9809
Abronhill

© Larry James

Living area 1,983 sq. ft.
Total 2,763 sq. ft.

Southern Country Style 209

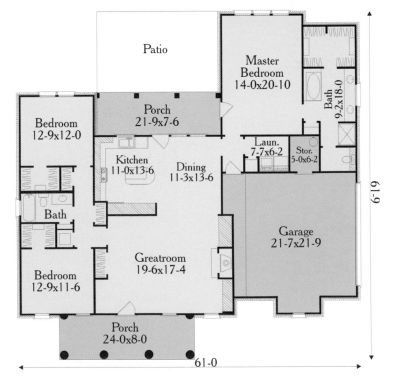

Patio

Master
Bedroom
14-0x20-10

Bath
9-2x18-0

Porch
21-9x7-6

Bedroom
12-9x12-0

Kitchen
11-0x13-6

Dining
11-3x13-6

Laun.
7-7x6-2

Stor.
5-0x6-2

Bath

Greatroom
19-6x17-4

Garage
21-7x21-9

Bedroom
12-9x11-6

Porch
24-0x8-0

61-0

61-9

Design 9810
Abbotstone
© Larry James

Living area 1,979 sq. ft.
Total 2,918 sq. ft.

Design 9811
Woodbury
© Larry James

Living area 1,973 sq. ft.
Total 3,004 sq. ft.

Photo © Mark Englund / HomeStyles

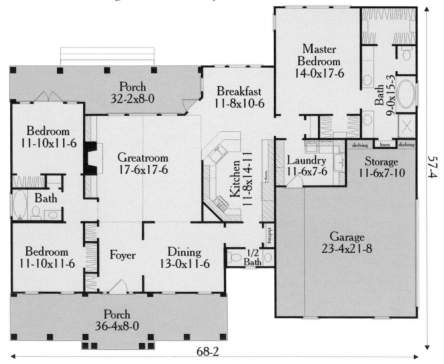

Porch
32-2x8-0

Breakfast
11-8x10-6

Master Bedroom
14-0x17-6

Bath
9-0x15-3

Bedroom
11-10x11-6

Greatroom
17-6x17-6

Kitchen
11-8x14-11

Bath

Laundry
11-6x7-6

shelving linen shelving

Storage
11-6x7-10

Bedroom
11-10x11-6

Foyer

Dining
13-0x11-6

1/2 Bath

Garage
23-4x21-8

Porch
36-4x8-0

68-2

57-4

Design 9812
Brownstone
© Larry James

Living area 2,046 sq. ft.
Total 3,196 sq. ft.

212 Southern Country Style

Photo © Mark Englund / HomeStyles

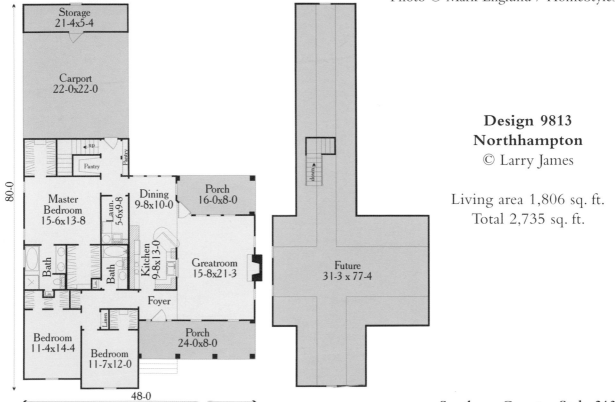

Storage
21-4x5-4

Carport
22-0x22-0

Master
Bedroom
15-6x13-8

Pantry

Laun.
5-6x9-8

Pantry

Dining
9-8x10-0

Porch
16-0x8-0

Bath

Bath

Kitchen
9-8x13-0

Greatroom
15-8x21-3

Foyer

Bedroom
11-4x14-4

Linen

Bedroom
11-7x12-0

Porch
24-0x8-0

80-0

48-0

down

Future
31-3 x 77-4

**Design 9813
Northhampton**
© Larry James

Living area 1,806 sq. ft.
Total 2,735 sq. ft.

Southern Country Style 213

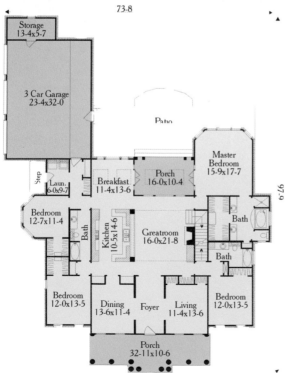

73-8

Storage
13-4x5-7

3 Car Garage
23-4x32-0

Patio

Step

Laun.
6-0x9-7

Breakfast
11-4x13-6

Porch
16-0x10-4

Master
Bedroom
15-9x17-7

97-6

Bedroom
12-7x11-4

Bath

Kitchen
10-5x14-6

Greatroom
16-0x21-8

Bath

Bath

Bedroom
12-0x13-5

Dining
13-6x11-4

Foyer

Living
11-4x13-6

Bedroom
12-0x13-5

Porch
32-11x10-6

Future
9-9x12-4

Future
9-9x12-0

Future
19-10x31-4

Design 9814
Brightstone
© Larry James

Living area 2,863 sq. ft.
Total 4,248 sq. ft.

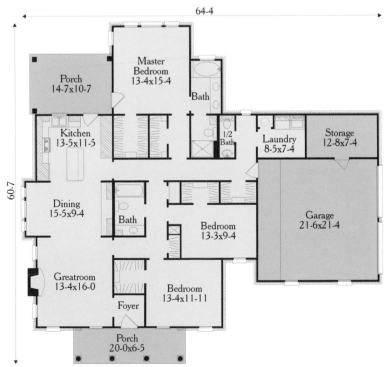

Design 9815
Easton
© Larry James

Living area 1,854 sq. ft.
Total 2,750 sq. ft.

Southern Country Style 215

Storage
17-4x5-8

Garage
20-4x21-4

56-4

Master
Bedroom
12-0x17-1

Bath

Porch
17-4x10-0

1/2
Bath

Laundry
7-4x6-3

Bedroom
11-4x10-0

Bath

Greatroom
17-4x17-4

Pantry

Kitchen/
Breakfast
11-4x20-5

61-4

Bedroom
11-4x11-4

Bedroom
11-3x10-1

Foyer

Dining
11-3x13-4

Porch
31-0x8-0

**Design 9816
Angelbrook**

© Larry James

Living area 1,997 sq. ft.
Total 2,988 sq. ft.

Design 9817
Crosley
© Larry James

Living area 1,955 sq. ft.
Total 2,946 sq. ft.

Storage
17-4x5-8

Garage
20-4x21-4

Porch
17-4x10-0

Master
Bedroom
17-4x13-6

56-4

67-4

Laundry
7-4x6-3

1/2 Bath

Pantry

Greatroom
17-4x17-4

Bath

Bath

Kitchen/
Breakfast
13-3x20-5

Dining
11-3x13-4

Foyer

Bedroom
11-3x10-1

Bedroom
11-4x11-4

Porch
31-0x8-0

Southern Country Style 217

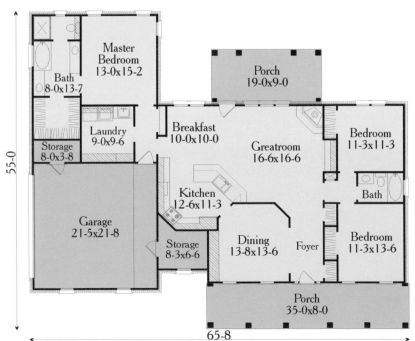

Design 9818
Loftwood

© Larry James

Living area 1,836 sq. ft.
Total 2,893 sq. ft.

218 Southern Country Style

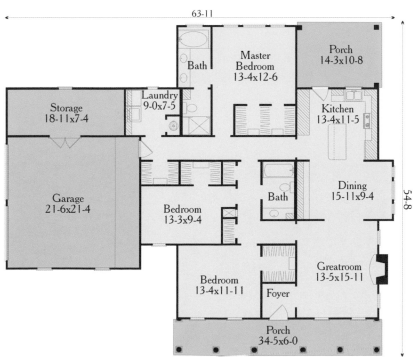

63-11

Storage
18-11x7-4

Laundry
9-0x7-5

Bath

Master
Bedroom
13-4x12-6

Porch
14-3x10-8

Kitchen
13-4x11-5

Garage
21-6x21-4

Bedroom
13-3x9-4

Bath

Dining
15-11x9-4

54-8

Bedroom
13-4x11-11

Foyer

Greatroom
13-5x15-11

Porch
34-5x6-0

Design 9819
Glennfield
© Larry James

Living area 1,675 sq. ft.
Total 2,663 sq. ft.

Southern Country Style 219

Storage
19-6x8-6

Garage
21-10x21-2

Patio
23-9x21-0

Laundry
9-8x9-3

Bath

Kitchen
11-0x16-0

Dining
12-9x16-0

Master
Bedroom
17-6x13-6

Bedroom
13-8x11-7

Bedroom
12-9x11-3

Foyer

Living Room
15-1x13-6

M.Bath
11-8x11-7

Planter Box

Stoop

Planter Box

66-0

65-0

**Design 9820
Crestridge**

© Larry James

Living area 1,800 sq. ft.
Total 2,563 sq. ft.

Design 9821
Rockford
© Larry James

Living area 1,702 sq. ft.
Total 2,487 sq. ft.

Southern Country Style 221

Storage
21-6x11-0

Garage
21-6x25-6

17-7

Laun.
9-0x8-7

1/2
Bath

Kitchen
18-0x11-6

Breakfast
14-0x9-0

Dining
11-6x13-6

Foyer

Porch
19-2x12-0

Greatroom
19-1x17-5

Bath

Bedroom
11-6x13-6

Master
Bedroom/
Sitting
Room
12-9x23-8

M.Bath
10-4x13-6

Hy/
Ac

Bedroom
12-0x13-6

Bedroom
12-0x11-7

Porch
31-5x8-0

66-1

Design 9822
Wisterwood
© Larry James

Living area 2,555 sq. ft.
Total 3,901 sq. ft.

222 Southern Country Style

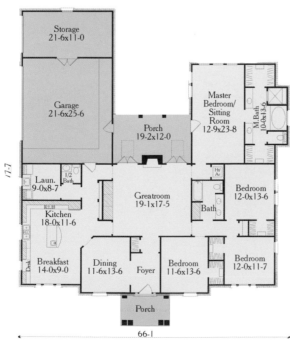

Storage
21-6x11-0

Garage
21-6x25-6

17-7

Laun.
9-0x8-7

1/2
Bath

Porch
19-2x12-0

Master
Bedroom/
Sitting
Room
12-9x23-8

M.Bath
10-0x13-6

Hw/
Ac

Greatroom
19-1x17-5

Bath

Bedroom
12-0x13-6

Kitchen
18-0x11-6

Breakfast
14-0x9-0

Dining
11-6x13-6

Foyer

Bedroom
11-6x13-6

Bedroom
12-0x11-7

Desk

Porch

66-1

Design 9823
Whindon
© Larry James

Living area 2,585 sq. ft.
Total 3,743 sq. ft.

Southern Country Style 223

**Design 9901
Brixworth**

© Larry James

Living area 2,669 sq. ft.
Total 3,488 sq. ft.

Walk-in Closet

M.Bath

Master Bedroom
17-10x15-6

Porch
13-0x10-0

Breakfast
11-5x14-0

Greatroom
17-3x19-6

Bedroom
15-6x11-6

Storage
8-2x9-10

Laun.
7-5x9-10

1/2 Bath

Kitchen
11-5x12-0

Bath

Garage
21-0x26-0

Dining
11-5x15-2

Foyer

Bedroom
11-5x13-6

Bedroom
11-7x13-6

72-4

70-6

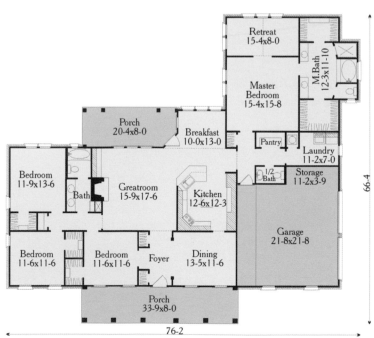

Retreat
15-4x8-0

Master
Bedroom
15-4x15-8

M.Bath
12-3x11-10

Porch
20-4x8-0

Breakfast
10-0x13-0

Pantry

Laundry
11-2x7-0

Bedroom
11-9x13-6

Bath

Greatroom
15-9x17-6

Kitchen
12-6x12-3

1/2
Bath

Storage
11-2x3-9

Bedroom
11-6x11-6

Bedroom
11-6x11-6

Foyer

Dining
13-5x11-6

Garage
21-8x21-8

Porch
33-9x8-0

66-4

76-2

Design 9902
Hartfield
© Larry James

Living area 2,506 sq. ft.
Total 3,496 sq. ft.

Southern Country Style 225

PLANTATIONS

This beautiful estate house takes its inspiration from the plantation houses of the Old South. Today's version offers modern living comfort while retaining the important characteristic of the traditional style, for example, the inviting porch sheltered by a hipped roof. The white pillars and second-floor balcony railing stand in sharp contrast to the elegant brick facade. The 3,272-square-foot design features a classic floor plan, with the rooms for daily activities on the ground floor and four bedrooms on the second story.

Design HomeStyle
J-8673
© Larry James & Associates, Inc.

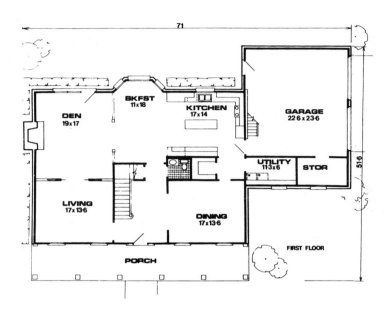

71

DEN
19 x 17

BKFST
11 x 18

KITCHEN
17 x 14

GARAGE
22 6 x 23 6

51 6

UTILITY
11 3 x 6

STOR

LIVING
17 x 13 6

DINING
17 x 13 6

FIRST FLOOR

PORCH

BR
14 9 x 12

BR
13 6 x 11 6

MBR
17 x 17

BR
14 6 x 12

BR

FOYER
BELOW

BALCONY

Photo © Mark Englund / HomeStyles

The high portico typical of southern estate houses distinguishes this imposing house. Three dormer windows rising from the steep roof further emphasize the symmetry of the facade. With its 2,888 square feet of living area distributed over two full floors, the interior is dominated by an open floor plan. High ceilings underline the generosity of the various rooms' proportions.

Design HomeStyle
E–2800
© Breland & Farmer, Designers, Inc.

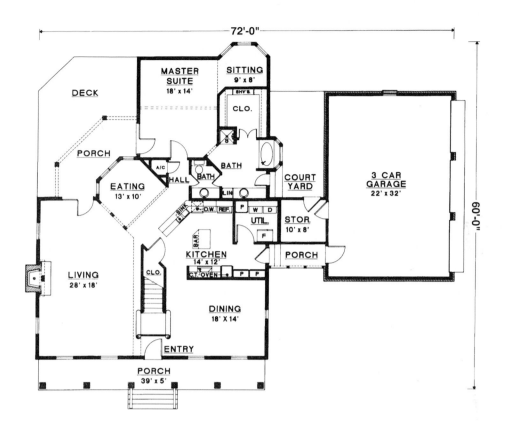

72'-0"

DECK

MASTER
SUITE
18' x 14'

SITTING
9' x 8'

SHV'S.

CLO.

PORCH

A/C

HALL

BATH

BATH

CLO.

COURT
YARD

3 CAR
GARAGE
22' x 32'

60'-0"

EATING
13' x 10'

SINK

D.W. REF.

LIN.

UTIL.

P   W   D

F

STOR.
10' x 8'

BAR

KITCHEN
14' x 12'

PORCH

LIVING
28' x 18'

CLO.

CT. OVEN

P   P

DINING
18' X 14'

ENTRY

PORCH
39' x 5'

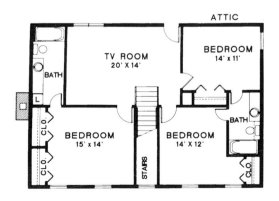

ATTIC

TV ROOM
20' X 14'

BEDROOM
14' x 11'

BATH

L

CLO.

CLO.

BEDROOM
15' x 14'

STAIRS

BEDROOM
14' X 12'

BATH

CLO.

Drawing from the famous ante-bellum tradition, this new design possesses all the charm of a southern estate house. The imposing columns support a hipped roof, while the balcony rests like a throne above the front entry. High windows with shutters provide contrast to the elegant white stucco facade. This house offers a total living area of 3,308 square feet distribute over two stories and a classically designed floor plan.

**Design HomeStyle
E-3301**
© Breland & Farmer, Designers, Inc.

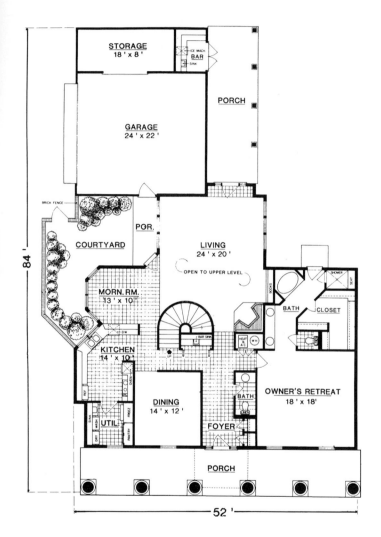

STORAGE
18' x 8'

BAR

PORCH

GARAGE
24' x 22'

BRICK FENCE

POR.

COURTYARD

LIVING
24' x 20'

OPEN TO UPPER LEVEL

SHOWER

SEAT

BATH

CLOSET

MORN. RM.
13' x 10'

HEAT & A.C.

W.H.

KITCHEN
14' x 10'

DINING
14' x 12'

BATH

OWNER'S RETREAT
18' x 18'

UTIL.

PANTRY

FOYER

PORCH

84'

52'

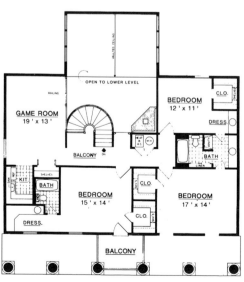

VAULTED CEILING

OPEN TO LOWER LEVEL

GAME ROOM
19' x 13'

BEDROOM
12' x 11'

CLO.

DRESS

RAILING

HEAT & A.C.

BATH

LINEN

BALCONY

DN

KIT.

SHELVES

BATH

BEDROOM
15' x 14'

CLO.

CLO.

BEDROOM
17' x 14'

DRESS.

BALCONY

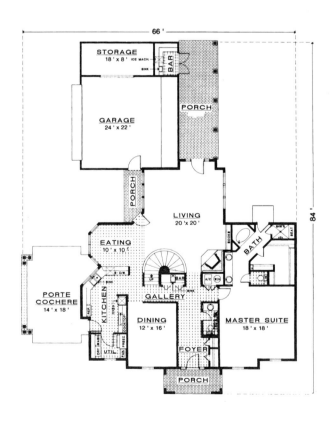

STORAGE
18' x 8'   ICE MACH.

BAR   SINK

PORCH

GARAGE
24' x 22'

PORCH

LIVING
20' x 20'

BATH

EATING
10' x 10'

PORTE COCHERE
14' x 18'

KITCHEN

GALLERY

DINING
12' x 16'

MASTER SUITE
18' x 18'

FOYER

PORCH

66'

84'

UPPER LIVING
OPEN TO LOWER LEVEL

HANDRAIL

HANDRAIL

GAME ROOM
13' x 19'

BEDROOM
11' x 12'

BALCONY

HALL

BATH

LINEN

SHELVES

KITCHEN
8' x 6'

BATH

SHELVES

BEDROOM
16' x 15'

BEDROOM
17' x 14'

DRESS.

LIN

BALCONY
6' x 14'

Design HomeStyle
E-3302
© Breland & Farmer, Designers, Inc.

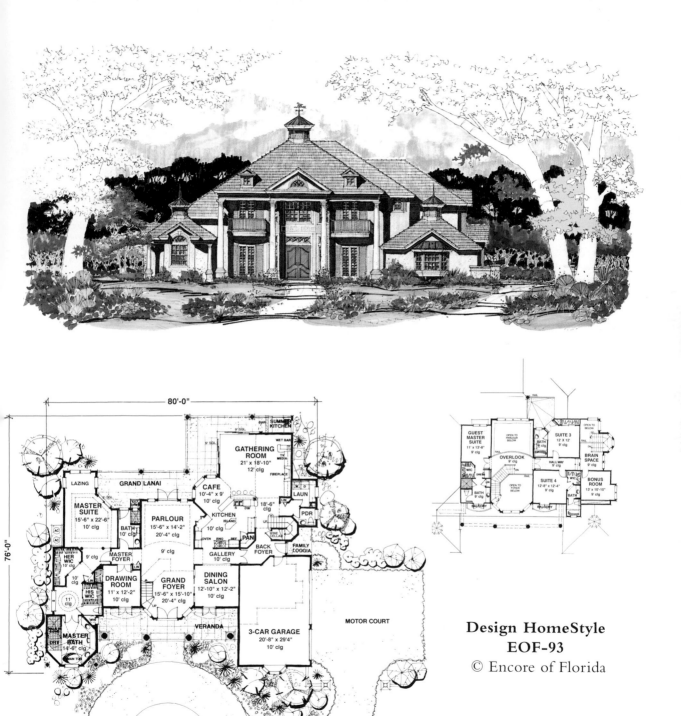

Design HomeStyle
EOF-93
© Encore of Florida

Floor plan labels:

80'-0"
76'-0"

SUMMER KITCHEN
BAR
9' SGL
WET BAR
GATHERING ROOM
21' x 18'-10"
12' clg
TV MEDIA
FIREPLACE
LAZING
GRAND LANAI
CAFE
10'-4" x 9'
10' clg
LAUN
W D
MASTER SUITE
15'-6" x 22'-6"
10' clg
PARLOUR
15'-6" x 14'-2"
20'-4" clg
KITCHEN
10' clg
ISLAND
18'-6"
PDR
BATH
10' clg
OVEN RNG REF
DW
PAN
WINE CELLAR
FAMILY LOGGIA
HER WIC
10' clg
MASTER FOYER
9' clg
GALLERY
10' clg
BACK FOYER
HIS WIC
9' clg
DRAWING ROOM
11' x 12'-2"
10' clg
GRAND FOYER
15'-6" x 15'-10"
20'-4" clg
DINING SALON
12'-10" x 12'-2"
10' clg
11' clg
MASTER BATH
14'-6"
DRY
CLEAN TUB
VERANDA
3-CAR GARAGE
20'-8" x 29'4"
10' clg
MOTOR COURT

Second floor:

GUEST MASTER SUITE
11' x 13'-8"
9' clg
OPEN TO PARLOUR BELOW
SUITE 3
12' X 12'
BATH
OPEN TO FOYER BELOW
WIC
OVERLOOK
9' clg
HALLWAY
9' clg
BRAIN SPACE
BATH
9' clg
OPEN TO FOYER BELOW
SUITE 4
12'-8" x 12'-4"
9' clg
BATH
BONUS ROOM
13' x 9'-10"
9' clg
WIC
BALCONY
BALCONY
RAIL

Photo © Mark Englund / HomeStyles

With its two full stories, this typical southern manor house offers a proud 2,606 square feet of living space. The generous balcony is the hallmark of the exterior. The kitchen and living room form a discrete area, and four bedrooms make this design ideal for the large family. The large master suite includes an extravagant bathroom with his and hers walk-in closets.

**Design HomeStyle
E-2604**
© Breland & Farmer Designers, Inc.

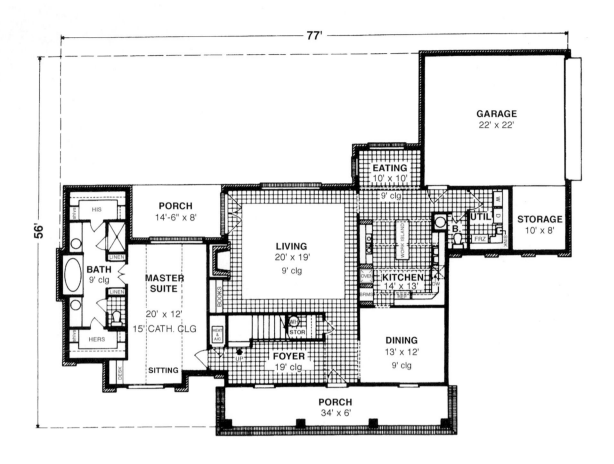

77'

56'

GARAGE
22' x 22'

EATING
10' x 10'
9' clg

PORCH
14'-6" x 8'

UTIL

STORAGE
10' x 8'

HIS

BATH
9' clg

LINEN

LINEN

LIVING
20' x 19'
9' clg

WORK ISLAND

KITCHEN
14' x 13'

OVEN

BRMS

REF

DW

MASTER
SUITE

20' x 12'
15' CATH. CLG

HERS

BOOKS

HEAT
& A/C

UP

W.I.
STOR

FOYER
19' clg

DINING
13' x 12'
9' clg

DESK

SITTING

PORCH
34' x 6'

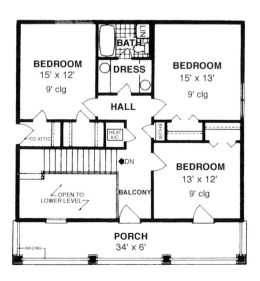

BEDROOM
15' x 12'
9' clg

BATH

LIN

DRESS

BEDROOM
15' x 13'
9' clg

HALL

TO ATTIC

HEAT
A/C

STAIRS

DN

BEDROOM
13' x 12'
9' clg

OPEN TO
LOWER LEVEL

BALCONY

RAILING

PORCH
34' x 6'

Photo © Mark Englund / HomeStyles

The entrance area of this imposing southern estate house is reminiscent of a Greek temple. Four large columns and the white stucco gable are proportional to the elaborately designed door, while the color and form of the shutters lend the finishing touch to the exterior.

**Design HomeStyle
C-8334**
© Corley Plan Service, Inc.

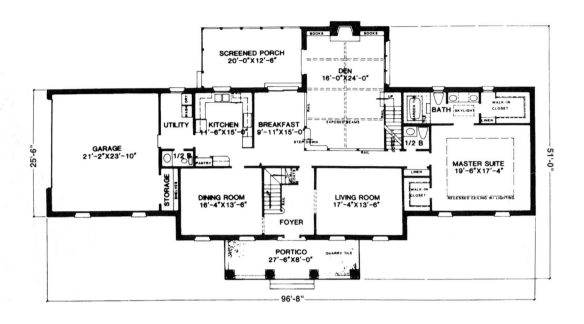

SCREENED PORCH
20'-0"X12'-6"

DEN
16'-0"X24'-0"

BOOKS   BOOKS

UTILITY

KITCHEN
11'-6"X15'-0"

BREAKFAST
9'-11"X15'-0"

RAIL

EXPOSED BEAMS

STEP DOWN

RAIL

UP

1/2 B

GARDEN TUB

BATH   SKYLIGHT

WALK-IN CLOSET

LINEN

GARAGE
21'-2"X23'-10"

STORAGE

1/2 B

PANTRY

SHELVES

MASTER SUITE
19'-6"X17'-4"

RECESSED CEILING W/ LIGHTING

DINING ROOM
16'-4"X13'-6"

RAIL

COATS

FOYER

LIVING ROOM
17'-4"X13'-6"

LINEN

WALK-IN CLOSET

PORTICO
27'-6"X8'-0"

QUARRY TILE

25'-6"

51'-0"

96'-8"

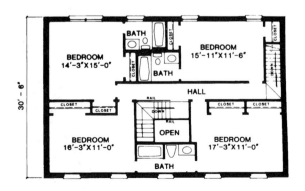

BEDROOM
14'-3"X15'-0"

BATH

CLOSET

CLOSET

BATH

BEDROOM
15'-11"X11'-6"

CLOSET

DOWN

HALL

CLOSET   CLOSET

CLOSET   CLOSET

RAIL

DOWN

RAIL

30'-6"

BEDROOM
16'-3"X11'-0"

OPEN

BEDROOM
17'-3"X11'-0"

BATH

With 3,122 square feet of living area, this house ideally combines classical style elements stemming from the colonial period with modern comfort. Particularly impressive is the design of the hipped roof and the broad covered porch, as well as the stuccoed gable with its lovely window directly above the front door. A generously arranged floor plan lends elegance to the interior of the house. To either side of the entrance are the dining room and the living room. A spacious kitchen features a breakfast area with glazed bay, which can also be used as a seating area. The adjacent family room has a beautiful bay which rises through two stories, in the middle of which is a fireplace with chimney. The house has five bedrooms and three and a half baths.

Design HomeStyle
APS-2518
© Atlanta Plan Source, Inc.

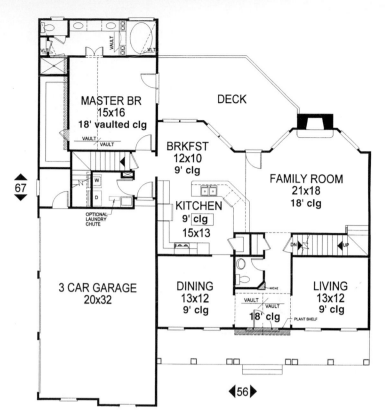

MASTER BR
15x16
18' vaulted clg
VAULT VAULT

DECK

BRKFST
12x10
9' clg

FAMILY ROOM
21x18
18' clg

67

OPTIONAL
LAUNDRY
CHUTE

KITCHEN
9' clg
15x13

3 CAR GARAGE
20x32

DINING
13x12
9' clg

VAULT VAULT

18' clg

LIVING
13x12
9' clg

PLANT SHELF

56

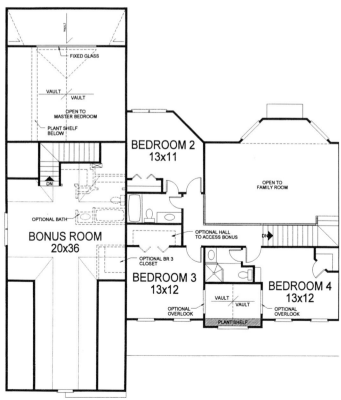

FIXED GLASS

VAULT VAULT

OPEN TO
MASTER BEDROOM

PLANT SHELF
BELOW

BEDROOM 2
13x11

OPEN TO
FAMILY ROOM

DN

OPTIONAL BATH

OPTIONAL HALL
TO ACCESS BONUS

DN

BONUS ROOM
20x36

OPTIONAL BR 3
CLOSET

BEDROOM 3
13x12

VAULT VAULT

BEDROOM 4
13x12

OPTIONAL
OVERLOOK

PLANT SHELF

OPTIONAL
OVERLOOK

Inspired by the Greek Revival, the designers Breland & Farmer have created this 3,316-square-foot house as a modern variation on the traditional mode. The extravagant entry boasting a portico supported by decorative columns and the use of elegant arched windows make this estate house an attraction. The generous use of glass is one of the dominant characteristics of the design, and it is further emphasized by the open construction. The imaginative lines are continued on the interior. A broadly curving stairway, for example, suggests exclusive design to the viewer. To the rear of the house is a lovely terrace, sheltered on three sides and open to the garden.

**Design HomeStyle
E–2704**
© Breland & Farmer Designers, Inc..

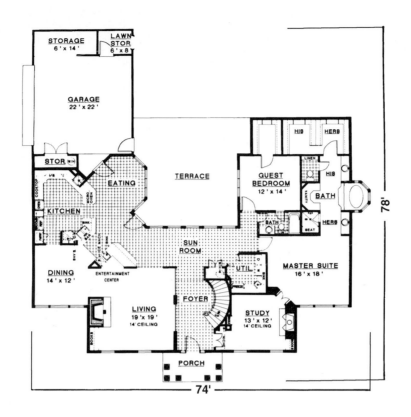

STORAGE
6' x 14'

LAWN
STOR.
6' x 8'

GARAGE
22' x 22'

STOR. (W/H)

EATING

TERRACE

HIS

HERS

GUEST
BEDROOM
12' x 14'

LINEN

HIS

BATH

STOR.

KITCHEN

MICRO
OVEN

COOKTOP

BATH

HERS

SEAT

VANITY

DINING
14' x 12'

ENTERTAINMENT
CENTER

SUN
ROOM

MASTER SUITE
16' x 18'

UTIL

FOYER

LIVING
19' x 19'
14' CEILING

STUDY
13' x 12'
14' CEILING

PORCH

74'

78'

HANDRAIL

VERANDA

BEDROOM
14' x 15'

BALCONY

BOOKS

BEDROOM
14' x 13'

BATH

HANDRAIL

BATH

Photo © Photographic Resources

Characteristic for this house are the elegant brick facade, the white stucco door and window frames that beautifully compliment the latticed windows, and the portico before the front entry. The three dormer windows that rise from the hipped roof impart an air of stateliness to the house. Based on Georgian design, this home features a living area of 3,834 square feet and a symmetrical floor plan encompassing two full stories.

**Design HomeStyle
L–836–MBC**
© Larry W. Garnett & Associates, Inc.

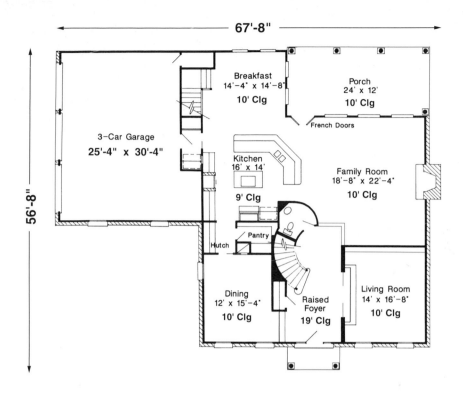

67'-8"

56'-8"

3-Car Garage
25'-4" x 30'-4"

Breakfast
14'-4" x 14'-8"
10' Clg

Porch
24' x 12'
10' Clg

French Doors

Kitchen
16' x 14'
9' Clg

Family Room
18'-8" x 22'-4"
10' Clg

Hutch

Pantry

Dining
12' x 15'-4"
10' Clg

Raised
Foyer
19' Clg

Living Room
14' x 16'-8"
10' Clg

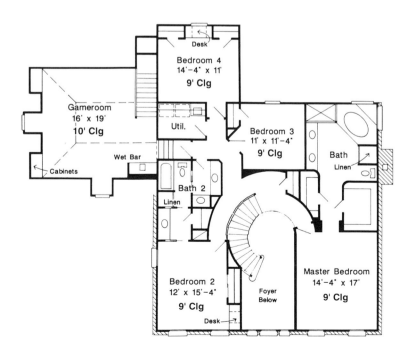

Desk

Bedroom 4
14'-4" x 11'
9' Clg

Gameroom
16' x 19'
10' Clg

Util.

Bedroom 3
11' x 11'-4"
9' Clg

Bath

Linen

Wet Bar

Cabinets

Bath 2

Linen

Bedroom 2
12' x 15'-4"
9' Clg

Foyer
Below

Master Bedroom
14'-4" x 17'
9' Clg

Desk

Photo © Mark Englund / HomeStyles

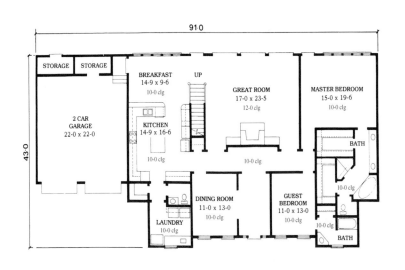

**Design HomeStyle
V-2985**
© Historical Replications Inc.

This one-story design in traditional southern style offers a total living area of 4,083 square feet. The offset roofs and the bright covered porch give the exterior its particular flair.

Design HomeStyle
E-2403
© Breland & Farmer
Designers, Inc.

Photo © Mark Englund / HomeStyles

The broad porch and balcony of this lovely southern estate house suggest pleasant hours spent in the open air. The arched windows on the ground floor are also among the characteristic elements of the style, and their rounded form is picked up by the dormer in the roof. The house offers a total of 3,008 square feet of living space, with the ground floor designated for daily living, and the master suite located in a separate wing. On the second floor are three bedrooms, two full baths and a playroom.

**Design HomeStyle
J-9420**
© Larry James & Associates, Inc.

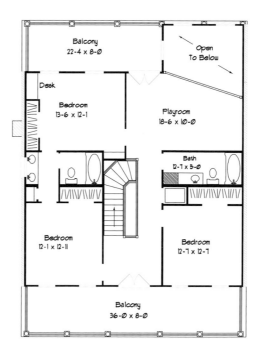

57-6

61-0

Master
Bedroom
13-1 x 16-1

M.Bath
7-10x12-2

Porch
22-4 x 8-0

Breakfast
12-7 x 11-6

Util.
6-4x7-9

Greatroom
21-6 x 17-4

Kitchen
12-4 13-4

Garage
21-3 x 23-1

Bath
8-5x5-2

Dining
12-4 x 15-6

Study
12-1 x 10-1

Foyer
6-0 x 16-3

Storage
11-6 x 3-9

Porch
36-0 x 8-0

Balcony
22-4 x 8-0

Open
To Below

Desk

Bedroom
13-6 x 12-1

Playroom
18-6 x 10-0

Bath
12-7 x 5-0

Bedroom
12-1 x 12-11

Bedroom
12-7 x 12-7

Balcony
36-0 x 8-0

Plantations 249

This building in the Georgian tradition offers a total living area of 4,204 square feet. Designed by William Poole, the house draws upon historic models and features a rethinking of all the essential elements of style. The result is an ideal combination of traditional elements and modern comfort. The gracious foyer is dominated by an imposing staircase. To either side of the foyer are the living room with fireplace and the formal dining room. The great room opens into the generously proportioned kitchen area that also has an outdoor entrance. The "Providence" features four bedrooms and three baths.

Design Providence
by William Poole

Ground floor 2,988 sq. ft.
Second floor 1,216 sq. ft.
Total 4,204 sq. ft.

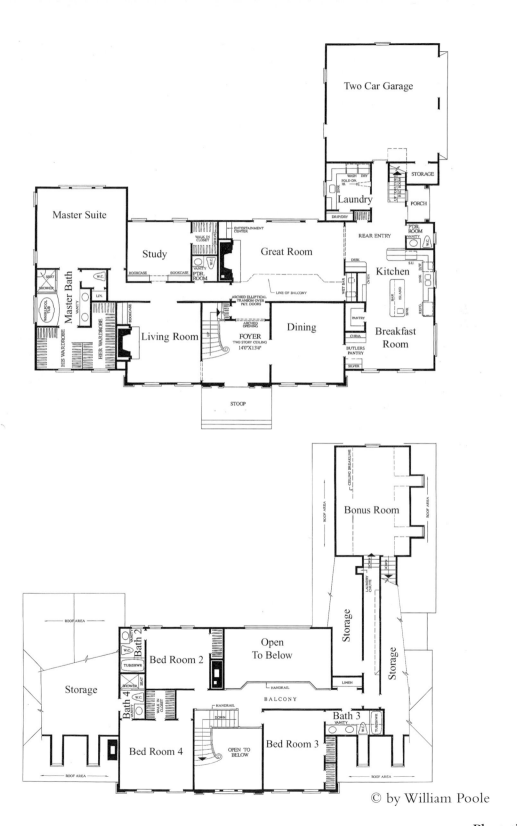

Two Car Garage

Master Suite

Study

WALK IN CLOSET

ENTERTAINMENT CENTER

Great Room

Laundry

WASH DRY

FOLD DN.

SINK

DRIP/DRY

STORAGE

REC ROOM

UP TO STUDIES

PORCH

REAR ENTRY

P'DR. ROOM

VANITY

W.C.

Master Bath

SEAT

SHOWER

VANITY

WHIRLPOOL TUB

W.C.

LIN.

BOOKCASE

BOOKCASE

VANITY

P'DR. ROOM

W.C.

LINE OF BALCONY

DESK

WET BAR

OVEN

Kitchen

S.U.

BAR

ISLAND

SINK

D/W

REFG.

HIS WARDROBE

HER WARDROBE

BOOKCASE

Living Room

ARCHED OPENING

FOYER

TWO STORY CEILING

14'0"X13'4"

ARCHED ELLIPTICAL TRANSOM OVER PKT. DOORS

Dining

PANTRY

CHINA

Breakfast Room

BUTLERS PANTRY

SILVER

STOOP

CEILING BREAKLINE

ROOF AREA

Bonus Room

ROOF AREA

ROOF AREA

LAUNDRY CHUTE

DOWN

UP

Storage

Storage

Bath 2

VANITY

W.C.

TUB/SHWR

Bed Room 2

Open To Below

LINEN

Storage

ROOF AREA

Storage

Bath 4

SHOWER

SEAT

W.C.

VANITY

WALK IN CLOSET

HANDRAIL

BALCONY

DOWN

OPEN TO BELOW

Bed Room 4

HANDRAIL

Bed Room 3

Bath 3

VANITY

W.C.

TUB/SHWR

ROOF AREA

© by William Poole

Plantations 251

This imposing estate house is from the drawing board of William Poole, who is known in the United States and abroad for his authentic southern houses. The "Ashley" represents a feudal building, the likes of which can only be found today in rare, historical areas. Taking its inspiration from the architecture of the late 18th century, the design, with a total living area of 4,488 square feet, offers the charm of days gone by with the functionality and modern conveniences of today. As can be expected of an estate of this class, the generous array of rooms includes a library and a study for the owner.

Design Ashley
by William Poole

Ground floor 2,967 sq. ft.
Second floor 1,521 sq. ft.
Total 4,488 sq. ft.

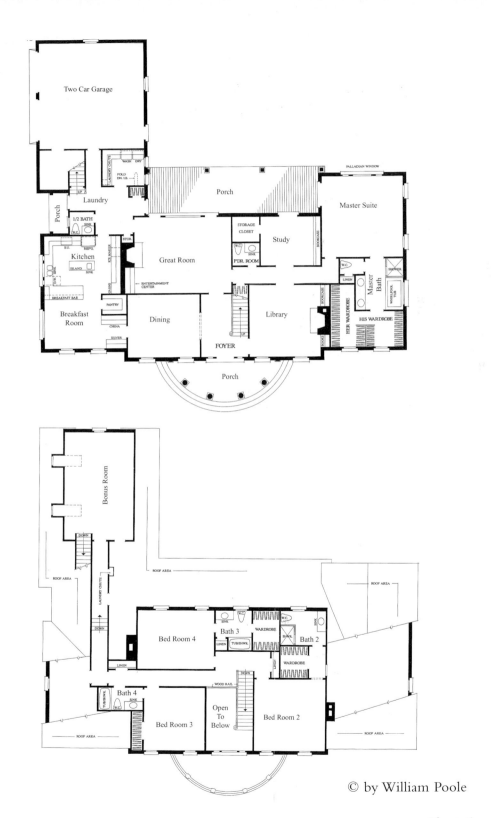

Two Car Garage

LAUNDRY CHUTE

WASH DRY

FOLD DN. T.B.

Laundry

Porch

1/2 BATH
SINK
W.C.

Kitchen
S.U.
REFG.
ISLAND
SINK
D.W.
SINK

Breakfast Bar

Breakfast Room

PANTRY

CHINA

SILVER

ICE MAKER
SINK
STOR.

OVENS

Great Room

ENTERTAINMENT CENTER

Dining

FOYER
UP

Porch

STORAGE CLOSET
W.C.
P'DR. ROOM

Study

BOOKCASE

Library

BOOKCASE

BOOKCASE

Porch

PALLADIAN WINDOW

Master Suite

W.C.
LINEN

HER WARDROBE

HIS WARDROBE

Master Bath

SHOWER

WHIRLPOOL TUB

Bonus Room

DOWN

ROOF AREA

LAUNDRY CHUTE

DOWN

ROOF AREA

ROOF AREA

ROOF AREA

SINK
W.C.

Bed Room 4

Bath 3

LINEN
TUB/SHWR.

WARDROBE

W.C.
SHWR.
Bath 2

SINK

WARDROBE

LINEN

LINEN

Bath 4
TUB/SHWR.
W.C.
SINK

Bed Room 3

WOOD RAIL

Open To Below

DOWN

Bed Room 2

ROOF AREA

ROOF AREA

© by William Poole

TRADITIONAL STYLE

Photo © Mark Englund / HomeStyles

With its 4,852 square feet of living area, this country estate house offers an unsurpassable exclusive design. The exterior is covered with an elegant brick facade that provides an ideal contrast to the stucco trim. The long face of the building is optically divided by the recessed gable design, and a broad covered porch offers an attractive place to relax. The interior provides spaces devoted to both formal and familial life.

**Design HomeStyle
FB-5478-Herm**
© Frank Betz Associates, Inc.

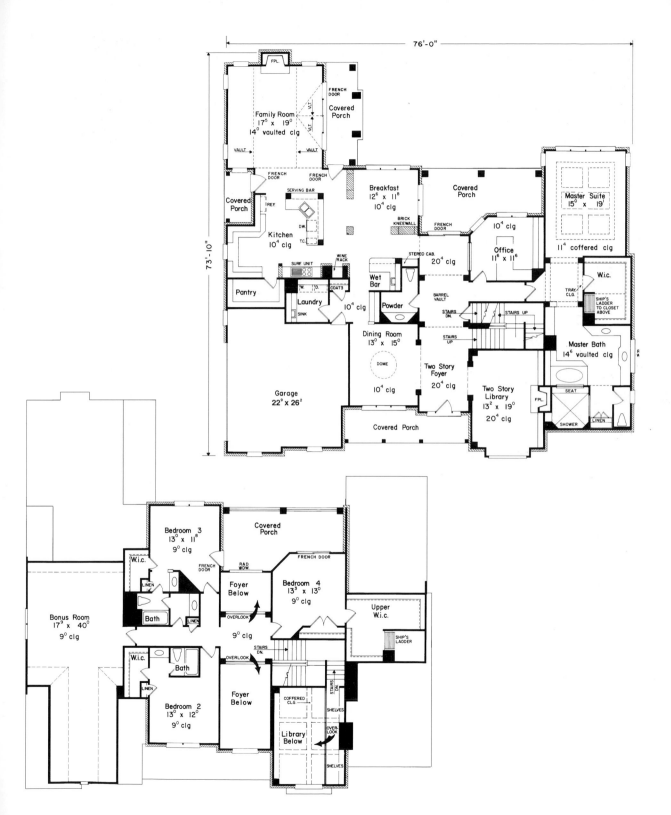

76'-0"

73'-10"

FPL

Family Room
17⁵ x 19⁰
14⁰ vaulted clg

VLT
VLT
VLT
VAULT
VAULT

FRENCH
DOOR

Covered
Porch

FRENCH
DOOR
FRENCH
DOOR

Covered
Porch

REF.

SERVING BAR

Kitchen
10⁴ clg

D.W.
T.C.

Breakfast
12⁶ x 11⁸
10⁴ clg

BRICK
KNEEWALL

Covered
Porch

FRENCH
DOOR

10⁴ clg

STEREO CAB.

20⁴ clg

Office
11⁶ x 11⁶

Master Suite
15⁰ x 19¹

11⁴ coffered clg

W.i.c.

TRAY
CLG.

SHIP'S
LADDER
TO CLOSET
ABOVE

Pantry

WINE
RACK

SURF UNIT

Laundry
10⁴ clg

W. I.D.
SINK
COATS

Wet
Bar

Powder

BARREL
VAULT

STAIRS
DN.
STAIRS UP
STAIRS
UP

Master Bath
14⁶ vaulted clg

R/W

Garage
22⁹ x 26²

Dining Room
13⁰ x 15⁰

DOME

10⁴ clg

Two Story
Foyer
20⁴ clg

Two Story
Library
13² x 19⁰
20⁴ clg

FPL

SEAT

SHOWER
LINEN

Covered Porch

Bonus Room
17⁹ x 40⁰
9⁰ clg

W.i.c.

LINEN

Bath

Bedroom 3
13⁰ x 11⁸
9⁰ clg

FRENCH
DOOR

RAD.
WDW.

Foyer
Below

9⁰ clg

OVERLOOK

Covered
Porch

FRENCH DOOR

Bedroom 4
13³ x 13⁰
9⁰ clg

Upper
W.i.c.

SHIP'S
LADDER

W.i.c.

LINEN

Bath

Bedroom 2
13⁰ x 12⁰
9⁰ clg

Foyer
Below

OVERLOOK

STAIRS
DN.

COFFERED
CLG.

SHELVES

STAIRS
DN.

OVER-
LOOK

Library
Below

OVER-
LOOK

SHELVES

Traditional Style 257

The nostalgic note of this traditional-style house owes its charm to the tasteful combination of various architectural forms and materials. Natural stone, plaster, and stucco are united in complete harmony with the beautiful windows. The form and color of the entry are picked up in the adjacent windows with shutters. The same elegance that marks the exterior is also found on the interior, where 3,115 square feet of living space is distributed over two floors.

Design HomeStyle
DD-2952
© Danze & Davis Architects, Inc.

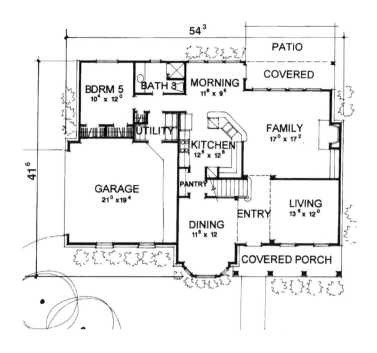

54³

PATIO

COVERED

BDRM 5
10⁴ x 12⁰

BATH 3

MORNING
11⁸ x 9⁶

FAMILY
17⁰ x 17²

41⁶

UTILITY

KITCHEN
12⁶ x 12⁸

GARAGE
21⁰ x 19⁴

PANTRY

LIVING
13⁶ x 12⁰

DINING
11⁸ x 12

ENTRY

COVERED PORCH

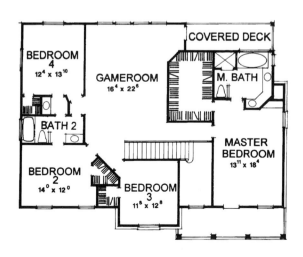

BEDROOM 4
12⁴ x 13¹⁰

GAMEROOM
16⁴ x 22⁶

COVERED DECK

M. BATH

BATH 2

BEDROOM 2
14⁰ x 12⁰

BEDROOM 3
11⁸ x 12⁸

MASTER BEDROOM
13¹¹ x 18⁴

Traditional Style 259

This estate house is characterized by numerous details, many of which become apparent to the viewer only after careful examination. The symmetrical organization of the windows lends the exterior a harmonious atmosphere. Light-colored stucco decorations on the gables underline the elegance of the design. The living area of 3,035 square feet is distributed over two full stories.

**Design HomeStyle
DD–3000–B**
© Danze & Davis Architects, Inc.

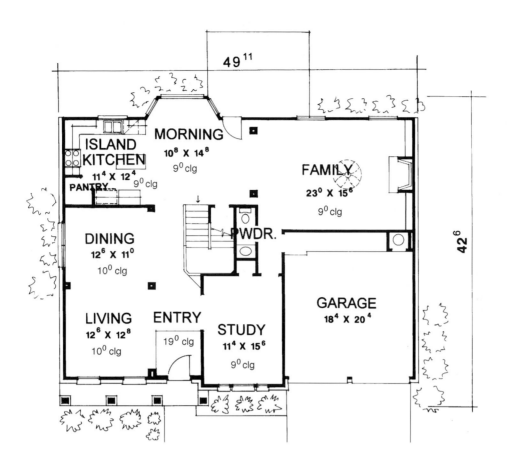

49¹¹

42⁶

ISLAND KITCHEN
11⁴ X 12⁴
9⁰ clg

PANTRY

MORNING
10⁸ X 14⁸
9⁰ clg

FAMILY
23⁰ X 15⁶
9⁰ clg

DINING
12⁶ X 11⁰
10⁰ clg

PWDR.

LIVING
12⁶ X 12⁸
10⁰ clg

ENTRY
19⁰ clg

STUDY
11⁴ X 15⁶
9⁰ clg

GARAGE
18⁴ X 20⁴

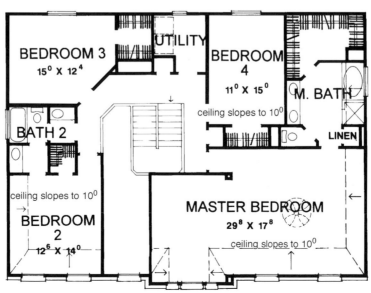

BEDROOM 3
15⁰ X 12⁴

UTILITY

BEDROOM 4
11⁰ X 15⁰
ceiling slopes to 10⁰

M. BATH

BATH 2

LINEN

ceiling slopes to 10⁰

BEDROOM 2
12⁶ X 14⁰

MASTER BEDROOM
29⁸ X 17⁸
ceiling slopes to 10⁰

Traditional Style 261

Photo © Mark Englund / HomeStyles

This traditionally styled two-story house in light-colored brick features an elegant hipped roof. The centrally located gable relaxes the lines of the front facade, and the arched window sets an exclusive accent. The total living area of 2,968 square feet is distributed equally over both stories of the house.

**Design HomeStyle
DD-2968**
© Danze & Davis Architects, Inc.

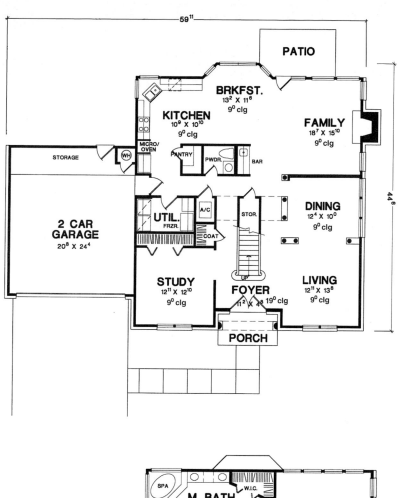

59¹¹

44⁸

PATIO

BRKFST.
13² X 11⁸
9⁰ clg

KITCHEN
10⁹ X 10¹⁰
9⁰ clg

FAMILY
18⁷ X 15¹⁰
9⁰ clg

MICRO/OVEN

STORAGE

WH

PANTRY

PWDR.

BAR

2 CAR
GARAGE
20⁸ X 24⁴

UTIL.
FRZR.

A/C

STOR.

DINING
12⁴ X 10⁰
9⁰ clg

COAT

UP

STUDY
12¹¹ X 12¹⁰
9⁰ clg

FOYER
11² X 4⁶ 19⁰ clg

LIVING
12¹¹ X 13⁸
9⁰ clg

PORCH

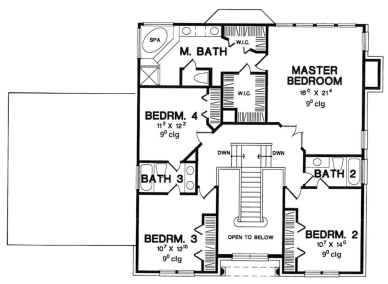

SPA

M. BATH

W.I.C.

MASTER
BEDROOM
16⁰ X 21⁴
9⁰ clg

BEDRM. 4
11² X 12²
9⁰ clg

W.I.C.

BATH 3

DWN   DWN

BATH 2

BEDRM. 3
10⁷ X 12¹⁰
9⁰ clg

OPEN TO BELOW

BEDRM. 2
10⁷ X 14⁰
9⁰ clg

Traditional Style 263

The unusual window design and imposing entry of this manor house anticipate the elegance of the interior. From the high-ceilinged foyer, an elaborate stairway rises in a curve to the second floor. To the left of the entry is a study, and on the opposite side a formal living room through which one proceeds into the dining room. The family room is accessible from the kitchen and breakfast room area, which together form a discrete unit in the house. On the second floor are four bedrooms, including a particularly luxurious master suite. The design has a total living area of 3,305 square feet.

Design HomeStyle
DD-3260
© Danze & Davis Architects, Inc.

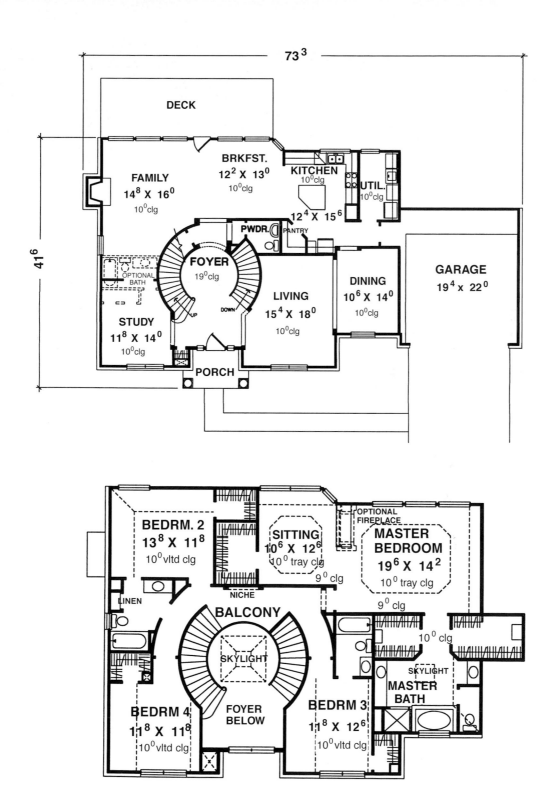

73³

DECK

FAMILY
14⁸ X 16⁰
10⁰clg

BRKFST.
12² X 13⁰
10⁰clg

KITCHEN
10⁰clg

UTIL.
10⁰clg

12⁴ X 15⁶

41⁶

OPTIONAL
BATH

FOYER
19⁰clg

PWDR.

PANTRY

GARAGE
19⁴ x 22⁰

DINING
10⁶ X 14⁰
10⁰clg

LIVING
15⁴ X 18⁰
10⁰clg

STUDY
11⁸ X 14⁰
10⁰clg

UP

DOWN

PORCH

BEDRM. 2
13⁸ X 11⁸
10⁰ vltd clg

SITTING
10⁶ X 12⁶
10⁰ tray clg

9⁰ clg

OPTIONAL
FIREPLACE

MASTER
BEDROOM
19⁶ X 14²
10⁰ tray clg

9⁰ clg

LINEN

NICHE

BALCONY

SKYLIGHT

10⁰ clg

SKYLIGHT

MASTER
BATH

BEDRM 4
11⁸ X 11⁸
10⁰ vltd clg

FOYER
BELOW

BEDRM 3
11⁸ X 12⁶
10⁰ vltd clg

Traditional Style 265

The elaborate wooden shingle facade of this rustic design is impressive. White window frames, gable trim, and the striking columns in front of the covered entry area provide for rich contrasts. The design offers a total living area of 2,883 square feet, generously distributed over two stories.

Design HomeStyle
L-222
© Larry W. Garnett Associates, Inc.

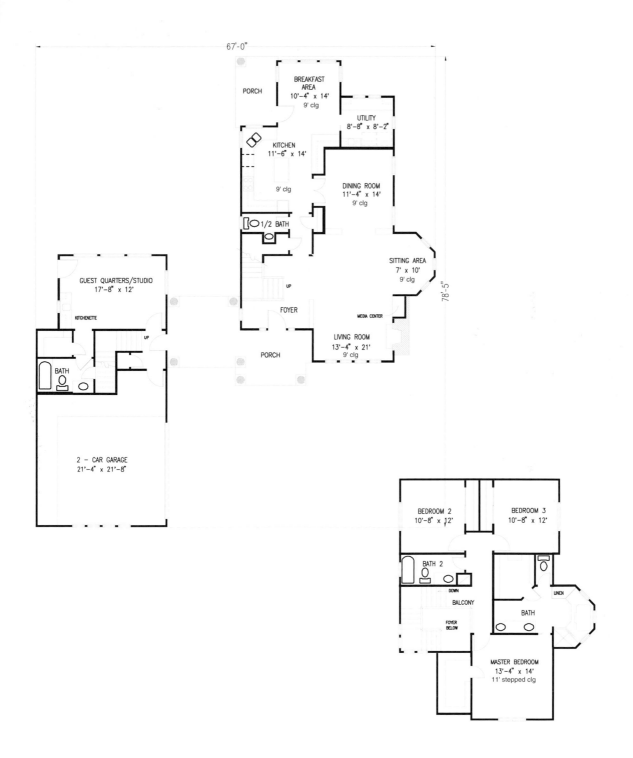

67'-0"

PORCH

BREAKFAST
AREA
10'-4" x 14'
9' clg

UTILITY
8'-8" x 8'-2"

KITCHEN
11'-6" x 14'

9' clg

DINING ROOM
11'-4" x 14'
9' clg

1/2 BATH

SITTING AREA
7' x 10'
9' clg

GUEST QUARTERS/STUDIO
17'-8" x 12'

KITCHENETTE

FOYER

MEDIA CENTER

UP

UP

BATH

PORCH

LIVING ROOM
13'-4" x 21'
9' clg

78'-5"

2 - CAR GARAGE
21'-4" x 21'-8"

BEDROOM 2
10'-8" x 12'

BEDROOM 3
10'-8" x 12'

BATH 2

DOWN

BALCONY

FOYER
BELOW

LINEN

BATH

MASTER BEDROOM
13'-4" x 14'
11' stepped clg

Traditional Style 267

Photo © Estate Creations, Inc.

This European-style house stands out particularly through its elaborate windows. The front facade has an impressive entry area, whose high window elements provide natural light to the two-story foyer inside. The white stucco trim of the cornices emphasizes the clear lines of the design and stands in beautiful contrast to the elegant brick facade. The total living area of the two full floors amounts to 3,397 square feet.

**Design HomeStyle
KLF-924**
© Estate Creations, Inc.

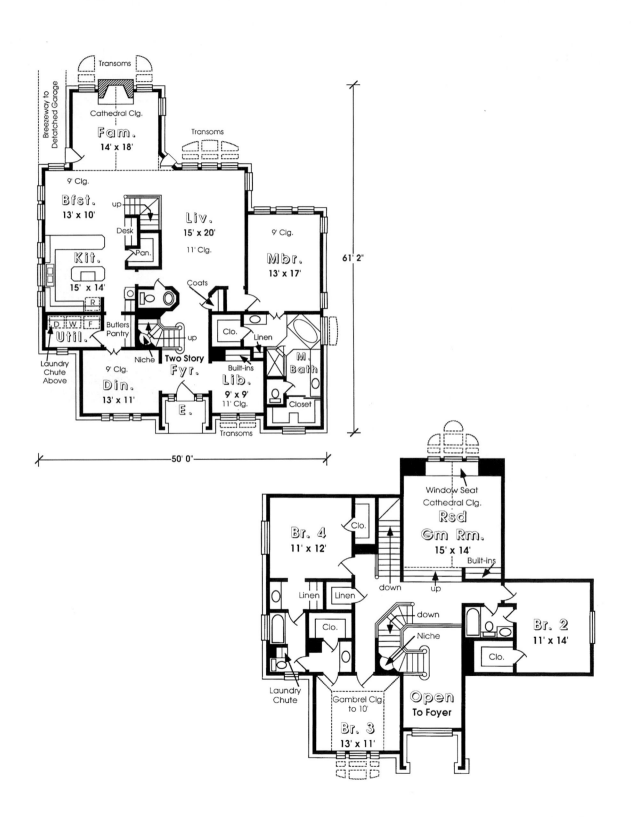

Transoms

Breezeway to Detached Garage

Cathedral Clg.

Fam.
14' x 18'

Transoms

9' Clg.

Bfst.
13' x 10'

up

Desk

Liv.
15' x 20'

11' Clg.

9' Clg.

Mbr.
13' x 17'

Kit.
15' x 14'

Pan.

Coats

R

D. W. F.

Butlers Pantry

Util.

Niche

Two Story
Fyr.

Clo.

Linen

**M.
Bath**

Laundry Chute Above

9' Clg.

Din.
13' x 11'

E.

Built-ins

Lib.
9' x 9'
11' Clg.

Closet

Transoms

61' 2"

50' 0"

Window Seat
Cathedral Clg.

Br. 4
11' x 12'

Clo.

**Rsd
Gm Rm.**
15' x 14'

Built-ins

Linen

Linen

Clo.

down

up

down

Br. 2
11' x 14'

Niche

Clo.

Laundry Chute

Gambrel Clg to 10'

**Open
To Foyer**

Br. 3
13' x 11'

Photo © Mark Englund / HomeStyles

The unusual floor plan of this nobly designed traditional house has particular flair. Within its 3,738 square feet of living area distributed over two stories, it offers a master suite with bath, a study, a formal living room, an open kitchen with breakfast nook, and a family room with fireplace on the first floor. On the second floor are three additional bedrooms, with a large area for further expansion above the garage.

Design HomeStyle
KLF-9228
© Estate Creations, Inc.

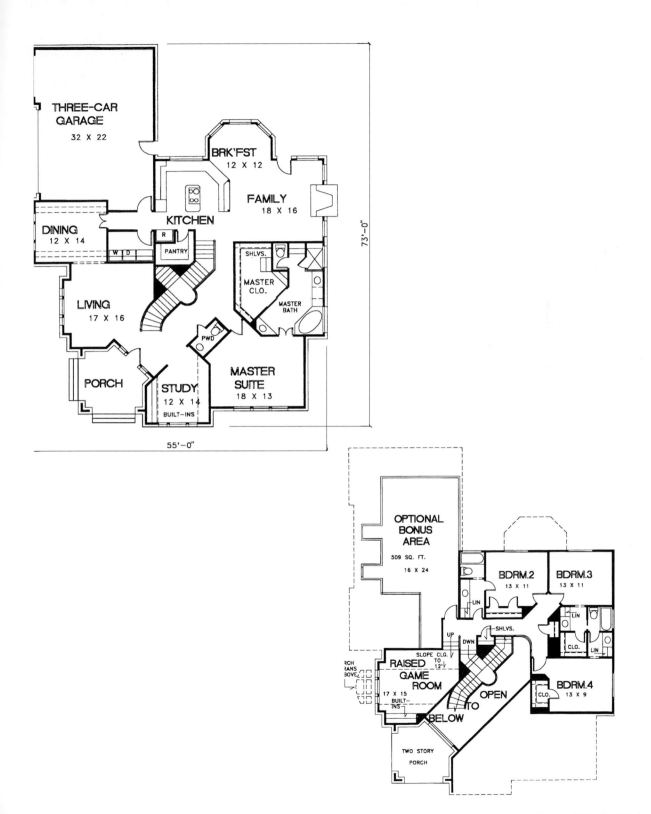

THREE-CAR
GARAGE
32 X 22

BRK'FST
12 X 12

FAMILY
18 X 16

KITCHEN

R

DINING
12 X 14

W D

PANTRY

SHLVS.

MASTER
CLO.

MASTER
BATH

LIVING
17 X 16

PWD

PORCH

STUDY
12 X 14
BUILT-INS

MASTER
SUITE
18 X 13

73'-0"

55'-0"

OPTIONAL
BONUS
AREA

509 SQ. FT.

16 X 24

BDRM.2
13 X 11

BDRM.3
13 X 11

LIN

UP

DWN

SHLVS.

LIN

CLO.

LIN

SLOPE CLG.
TO
12'

RAISED
GAME
ROOM
17 X 15
BUILT-
INS

OPEN
TO
BELOW

BDRM.4
13 X 9

CLO.

RCH
RANS
BOVE

TWO STORY
PORCH

Traditional Style 271

The offset hipped roof construction sets the tone of this two-story design. The simple facade is additionally accented by the bay windows flanking the entry. A generously proportioned floor plan distributes the 3,324-square-foot living area over two full stories. To the right and left of the foyer are the study and the formal living room. The kitchen is located on the garden side of the house, and opens to a bright breakfast room with large windows. The kitchen also allows direct access to the dining room. A sweeping staircase leads to the second story with its four bedrooms.

**Design HomeStyle
H–1413–1**
© LifeStyle HomeDesign

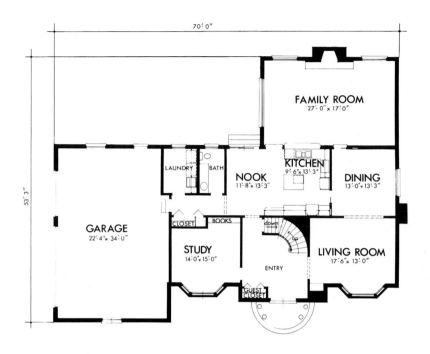

70' 0"

53' 3"

FAMILY ROOM
27' 0" x 17' 0"

LAUNDRY

BATH

KITCHEN
9' 6" x 13' 3"

NOOK
11' 8" x 13' 3"

DINING
13' 0" x 13' 3"

GARAGE
22' 4" x 34' 0"

CLOSET

BOOKS

down

up

LIVING ROOM
17' 6" x 13' 0"

STUDY
14' 0" x 15' 0"

ENTRY

GUEST CLOSET

47' 3"

31' 8"

WALK-IN CLOSET

BATH

BATH

BATH

CLOSET

BEDROOM
14' 2" x 13' 2"

CLOSET

HALL

down

BEDROOM
14' 0" x 16' 10"

BEDROOM
14' 6" x 10' 3"

CLOSET

BEDROOM
14' 2" x 13' 2"

CLOSET

Traditional Style 273

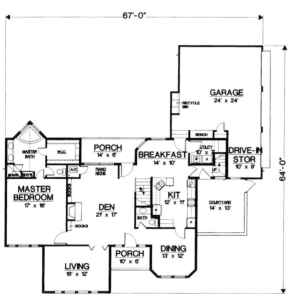

Floor plan labels (main floor):

- GARAGE 24' x 24'
- RECYCLE BIN
- BENCH
- PORCH 14' x 6'
- BREAKFAST 14' x 10'
- UTILITY 10' x
- DRIVE-IN STOR 10' x 9'
- MASTER BATH
- W.I.C.
- A/C
- PIANO NICHE
- MASTER BEDROOM 17' x 16'
- DEN 21' x 17'
- KIT 12' x 11'
- BATH
- COURTYARD 14' x 13'
- BOOKS
- LIVING 18' x 12'
- PORCH 10' x 6'
- DINING 13' x 12'

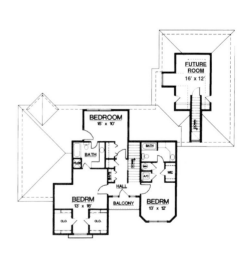

Floor plan labels (upper floor):

- FUTURE ROOM 16' x 12'
- BEDROOM 15' x 10'
- BATH
- FLUE
- BATH
- A/C
- WIC
- HALL
- BEDRM 13' x 18'
- BALCONY
- BEDRM 13' x 12'
- CLO.

Dimensions: 67'-0" (width), 64'-0" (height)

Design HomeStyle
E-2705
© Breland & Farmer, Designers, Inc.

274 Traditional Style

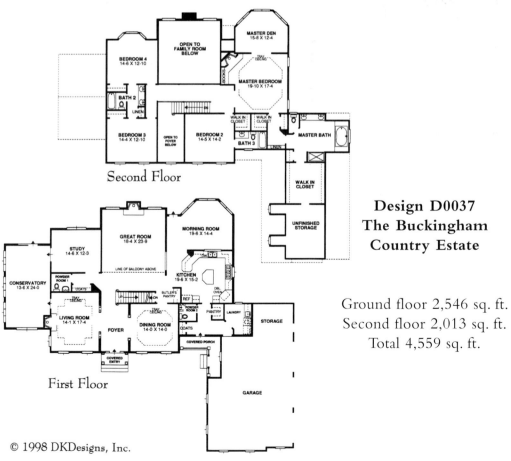

Second Floor

BEDROOM 4
14-6 X 12-10

OPEN TO
FAMILY ROOM
BELOW

MASTER DEN
15-8 X 12-4

BATH 2

LINEN

MASTER BEDROOM
19-10 X 17-4

TRAY
CEILING

BEDROOM 3
14-4 X 12-10

OPEN TO
FOYER
BELOW

BEDROOM 2
14-5 X 14-2

WALK IN
CLOSET

WALK IN
CLOSET

BATH 3

LINEN

MASTER BATH

WALK IN
CLOSET

UNFINISHED
STORAGE

First Floor

GREAT ROOM
18-4 X 23-9

MORNING ROOM
19-6 X 14-4

STUDY
14-6 X 12-3

LINE OF BALCONY ABOVE

KITCHEN
19-6 X 15-2

CONSERVATORY
13-6 X 24-0

POWDER
ROOM 1

COATS

BUTLERS
PANTRY

REF

DBL.
OVENS

TRAY
CEILING

POWDER
ROOM 2

PANTRY

LAUNDRY

STORAGE

LIVING ROOM
14-1 X 17-4

FOYER

DINING ROOM
14-0 X 14-0

TRAY
CEILING

COATS

COVERED PORCH

COVERED
ENTRY

GARAGE

Design D0037
The Buckingham
Country Estate

Ground floor 2,546 sq. ft.
Second floor 2,013 sq. ft.
Total 4,559 sq. ft.

Photo © Caddhomes

A Greek Revival-style portico gives character to the elegant entry area of this stately mansion. The interior features generous windows in the high foyer, which receives a plenitude of natural light. The house offers a total living area of 3,268 square feet distributed evenly over two stories.

**Design HomeStyle
CH-350-A**
© Caddhomes

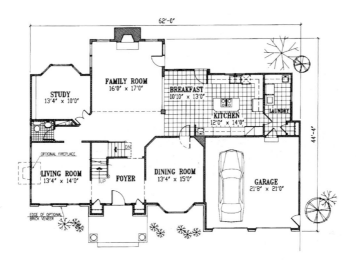

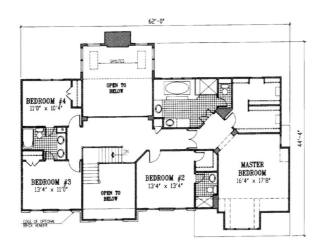

Traditional Style 277

Photo © Mark Englund / HomeStyles

The many details of the front view of this estate house attract the attention of onlookers. The striking tower design, the high and imposing entry area, and the recessed porch, together with the playful stucco decorations, create a harmonious overall impression. With 3,137 square feet of living area distributed over two stories, the floor plan offers a comprehensive array of rooms, with additional space available above the garage. The ground floor features formal dining and living rooms, as well as a two-story family room with fireplace. The well thought-out and spacious country kitchen and master suite merit special mention in the design.

Design HomeStyle
FB-5551-Shel
© Frank Betz Associates, Inc.

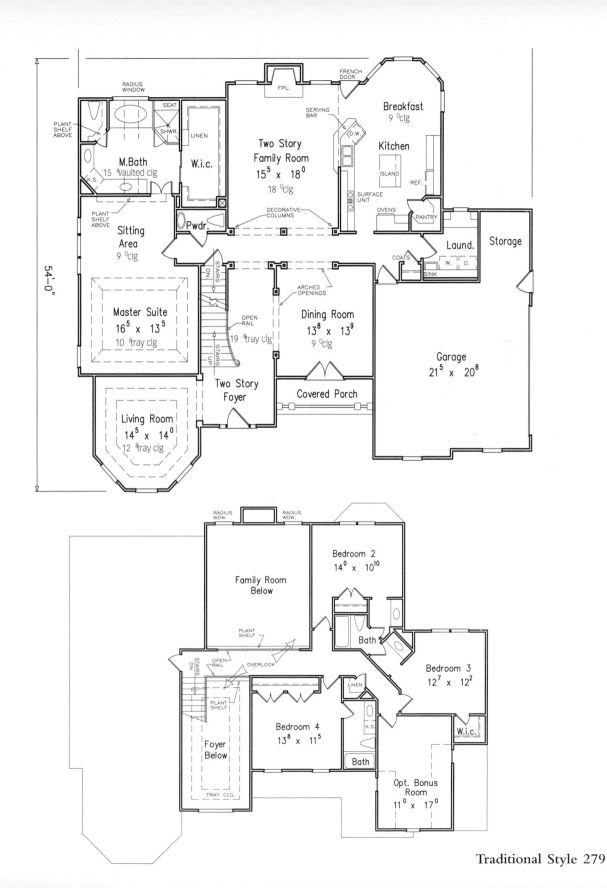

RADIUS
WINDOW

PLANT
SHELF
ABOVE

SEAT

SHWR.

LINEN

M.Bath
15 vaulted clg

W.i.c.

K.S.

PLANT
SHELF
ABOVE

Sitting
Area
9 ^{0}Clg

Pwdr.

FPL.

FRENCH
DOOR

SERVING
BAR

D.W.

Two Story
Family Room
15^5 x 18^0
18 ^{0}Clg

Breakfast
9 ^{0}Clg

Kitchen

ISLAND

REF.

SURFACE
UNIT

DECORATIVE
COLUMNS

OVENS

PANTRY

Laund.

Storage

COATS

W.   D.

SINK

STAIRS
DN

OPEN
RAIL

STAIRS
UP

ARCHED
OPENINGS

19 ^{8}tray clg

Dining Room
13^8 x 13^9
9 ^{0}Clg

Master Suite
16^5 x 13^5
10 ^{6}tray clg

Garage
21^5 x 20^8

Two Story
Foyer

Covered Porch

Living Room
14^5 x 14^0
12 ^{8}tray clg

54'-0"

RADIUS
WDW.

RADIUS
WDW.

Family Room
Below

Bedroom 2
14^0 x 10^{10}

PLANT
SHELF

Bath

STAIRS
DN

OPEN-
RAIL

OVERLOOK

PLANT
SHELF

LINEN

Bedroom 3
12^7 x 12^2

Foyer
Below

Bedroom 4
13^8 x 11^5

K.S.

W.i.c.

Bath

TRAY CLG.

Opt. Bonus
Room
11^0 x 17^0

Traditional Style 279

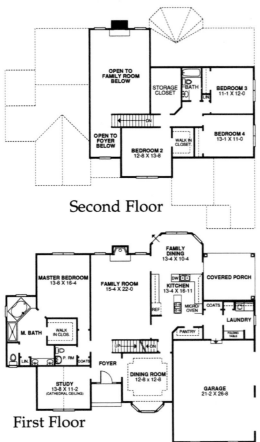

Second Floor

OPEN TO FAMILY ROOM BELOW

STORAGE CLOSET

BATH

BEDROOM 3
11-1 X 12-0

OPEN TO FOYER BELOW

BEDROOM 2
12-8 x 13-8

WALK IN CLOSET

BEDROOM 4
13-1 X 11-0

First Floor

MASTER BEDROOM
13-8 X 16-4

FAMILY ROOM
15-4 X 22-0

FAMILY DINING
13-4 X 10-4

KITCHEN
13-4 X 16-11

COVERED PORCH

M. BATH

WALK IN CLOS.

DW

MICRO OVEN

REF

COATS

LAUNDRY

P. RM

COATS

PANTRY

FOLDING TABLE

FOYER

DINING ROOM
12-8 x 12-8

LIN.

STUDY
13-8 X 11-2
(CATHEDRAL CEILING)

GARAGE
21-2 X 26-8

© 1998 DKDesigns, Inc.

Design D0001
The Avalon
Country Manor

Ground floor 1,914 sq. ft.
Second floor 800 sq. ft.
Total 2,714 sq. ft.

BEDROOM 4
13-0 x 10-6

BATH

MASTER DEN
10-0 x 11-6

WALK IN CLOSET

BEDROOM 3
11-0 x 12-5

SKYLIGHT

WALK IN CLOSET

LIN.

M. BATH

BEDROOM 2
13-0 x 15-3

DN

MASTER SUITE
13-0 x 19-3

OPEN TO BELOW

ATTIC STORAGE

Second Floor

Design D0002
The Durham
Country Manor

Ground floor 1,337 sq. ft.
Second floor 1,389 sq. ft.
Total 2,726 sq. ft.

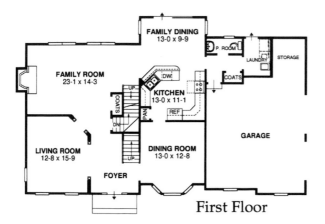

FAMILY DINING
13-0 x 9-9

P. ROOM

LAUNDRY

STORAGE

FAMILY ROOM
23-1 x 14-3

DW.

COATS

UP

COATS

KITCHEN
13-0 x 11-1

PAN.

REF.

DN

GARAGE

LIVING ROOM
12-8 x 15-9

UP

DINING ROOM
13-0 x 12-8

FOYER

First Floor

MASTER DEN
10-1 X 11-2
(CATHDERAL CEILING)

BEDROOM 4
10-1 x 11-2

BEDROOM 3
12-7 x 11-2

BATH

MASTER SUITE
13-3 X 22-10
(CATHDERAL CEILING)

WALK IN CLOSET

DN

BEDROOM 2
12-8 x 12-3

MASTER BATH

Second Floor

Design D0003
The Sheffield
Traditional

Ground floor 1,499 sq. ft.
Second floor 1,223 sq. ft.
Total 2,732 sq. ft.

POWDER ROOM

KITCHEN
10-8 x 16-10

OPT SKYLIGHT OPT SKYLIGHT

FAMILY ROOM
19-3 X 15-6

COATS

KEEPING ROOM
12-0 x 13-6
(CATHEDRAL CEILING)

DN

BUTLER'S PANTRY

REF

PANTRY

COATS

LAUNDRY

LIVING ROOM
13-11 x 18-6

UP

DINING ROOM
12-9 x 14-2 + BAY

FOYER

GARAGE
21-4 x 21-4

First Floor

© 1998 DKDesigns, Inc.

282 Traditional Style

Second Floor

MASTER DEN
10-1 X 11-2
(CATHDERAL CEILING)

BEDROOM 4
10-1 x 11-2

BEDROOM 3
12-7 x 11-2

BATH

WALK IN CLOSET

DN

MASTER SUITE
13-3 X 22-10
(CATHDERAL CEILING)

MASTER BATH

BEDROOM 2
12-8 x 12-3

First Floor

POWDER ROOM

KITCHEN
10-8 x 16-10

FAMILY ROOM
19-3 X 15-6

COATS

KEEPING ROOM
12-0 x 13-6
(CATHEDRAL CEILING)

DN

BUTLER'S PANTRY

REF

PANTRY

LAUNDRY

COATS

LIVING ROOM
13-11 x 18-6

UP

DINING ROOM
12-9 x 14-2 + BAY

FOYER

GARAGE
21-4 x 21-4

**Design D0004
The Sheffield
Federal**

Ground floor 1,499 sq. ft.
Second floor 1,223 sq. ft.
Total 2,732 sq. ft.

© 1998 DKDesigns, Inc.

MASTER DEN
10-1 X 11-2
(CATHDERAL CEILING)

BEDROOM 4
10-1 x 11-2

BEDROOM 3
12-7 x 11-2

BATH

DN

WALK IN CLOSET

MASTER SUITE
13-3 X 22-10
(CATHDERAL CEILING)

MASTER BATH

BEDROOM 2
12-8 x 12-3

Second Floor

**Design D0005
The Sheffield
Farmhouse**

Ground floor 1,499 sq. ft.
Second floor 1,223 sq. ft.
Total 2,732 sq. ft.

POWDER ROOM

KITCHEN
10-8 x 16-10

OPT SKYLIGHT   OPT SKYLIGHT

FAMILY ROOM
19-3 X 15-6

COATS

KEEPING ROOM
12-0 x 13-6
(CATHEDRAL CEILING)

DN   BUTLER'S PANTRY   REF   PANTRY

COATS   **LAUNDRY**

LIVING ROOM
13-11 x 18-6

UP

FOYER

DINING ROOM
12-9 x 14-2 + BAY

GARAGE
21-4 x 21-4

First Floor

Second Floor

MASTER DEN
10-1 X 11-2
(CATHDERAL CEILING)

BEDROOM 4
10-1 x 11-2

BEDROOM 3
12-7 x 11-2

BATH

MASTER SUITE
13-3 X 22-10
(CATHDERAL CEILING)

WALK IN CLOSET

DN

MASTER BATH

BEDROOM 2
12-8 x 12-3

**Design D0006
The Sheffield
Country Manor**

Ground floor 1,499 sq. ft.
Second floor 1,223 sq. ft.
Total 2,732 sq. ft.

First Floor

FAMILY ROOM
19-3 X 15-6

POWDER ROOM

KITCHEN
10-8 x 16-10

OPT. SKYLIGHT

OPT. SKYLIGHT

DW

KEEPING ROOM
12-0 x 13-6
(CATHEDRAL CEILING)

DN

BUTLER'S PANTRY

REF

PANTRY

COATS

LAUNDRY

LIVING ROOM
13-11 x 18-6

DINING ROOM
12-9 x 14-2 + BAY

UP

FOYER

GARAGE
21-4 x 21-4

© 1998 DKDesigns, Inc.

Second Floor

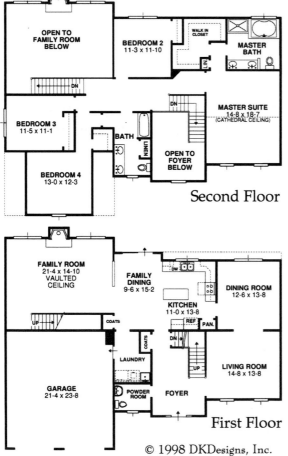

OPEN TO
FAMILY ROOM
BELOW

DN

BEDROOM 2
11-3 x 11-10

WALK IN
CLOSET

LIN

MASTER
BATH

BEDROOM 3
11-5 x 11-1

BATH

DN

MASTER SUITE
14-8 x 18-7
(CATHEDRAL CEILING)

LINEN

BEDROOM 4
13-0 x 12-3

OPEN TO
FOYER
BELOW

Second Floor

First Floor

FAMILY ROOM
21-4 x 14-10
VAULTED
CEILING

FAMILY
DINING
9-6 x 15-2

DINING ROOM
12-6 x 13-8

DW

KITCHEN
11-0 x 13-8

UP

COATS

REF   PAN.

COATS

DN

LAUNDRY

UP

LIVING ROOM
14-8 x 13-8

GARAGE
21-4 x 23-8

POWDER
ROOM

FOYER

First Floor

© 1998 DKDesigns, Inc.

**Design D0007
The Coventry
Traditional**

Ground floor 1,499 sq. ft.
Second floor 1,223 sq. ft.
Total 2,732 sq. ft.

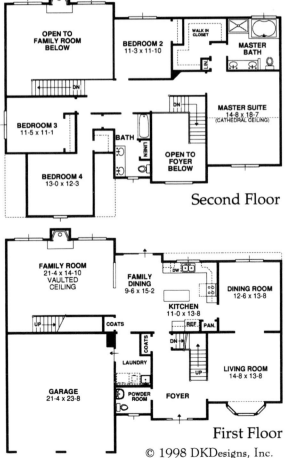

OPEN TO FAMILY ROOM BELOW

BEDROOM 2
11-3 x 11-10

WALK IN CLOSET

MASTER BATH

DN

BEDROOM 3
11-5 x 11-1

BATH

LIN

DN

MASTER SUITE
14-8 x 18-7
(CATHEDRAL CEILING)

LINEN

OPEN TO FOYER BELOW

BEDROOM 4
13-0 x 12-3

Second Floor

FAMILY ROOM
21-4 x 14-10
VAULTED CEILING

FAMILY DINING
9-6 x 15-2

DW

DINING ROOM
12-6 x 13-8

UP

COATS

KITCHEN
11-0 x 13-8

REF. PAN.

COATS

DN

UP

LIVING ROOM
14-8 x 13-8

LAUNDRY

GARAGE
21-4 x 23-8

POWDER ROOM

FOYER

First Floor

© 1998 DKDesigns, Inc.

**Design D0008
The Coventry
Federal**

Ground floor 1,499 sq. ft.
Second floor 1,223 sq. ft.
Total 2,732 sq. ft.

Traditional Style 287

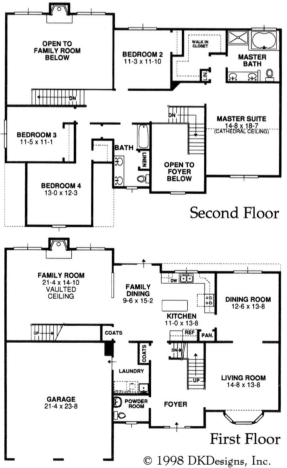

OPEN TO FAMILY ROOM BELOW

BEDROOM 2
11-3 x 11-10

WALK IN CLOSET

MASTER BATH

LIN

DN

BEDROOM 3
11-5 x 11-1

BATH

DN

MASTER SUITE
14-8 x 18-7
(CATHEDRAL CEILING)

LINEN

BEDROOM 4
13-0 x 12-3

OPEN TO FOYER BELOW

Second Floor

FAMILY ROOM
21-4 x 14-10
VAULTED CEILING

FAMILY DINING
9-6 x 15-2

DW

DINING ROOM
12-6 x 13-8

KITCHEN
11-0 x 13-8

UP

COATS

COATS

REF **PAN.**

DN

LAUNDRY

UP

LIVING ROOM
14-8 x 13-8

GARAGE
21-4 x 23-8

POWDER ROOM

FOYER

First Floor

© 1998 DKDesigns, Inc.

Design D0009
The Coventry
Farmhouse

Ground floor 1,499 sq. ft.
Second floor 1,223 sq. ft.
Total 2,732 sq. ft.

288 Traditional Style

Second Floor

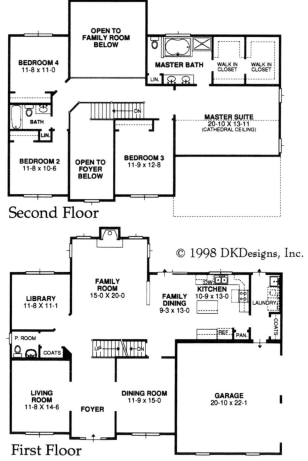

OPEN TO
FAMILY ROOM
BELOW

MASTER BATH

WALK IN
CLOSET

WALK IN
CLOSET

BEDROOM 4
11-8 x 11-0

LIN.

BATH

LIN.

MASTER SUITE
20-10 X 13-11
(CATHEDRAL CEILING)

BEDROOM 2
11-8 x 10-6

OPEN TO
FOYER
BELOW

BEDROOM 3
11-9 x 12-8

© 1998 DKDesigns, Inc.

FAMILY
ROOM
15-0 X 20-0

KITCHEN
10-9 x 13-0

FAMILY
DINING
9-3 x 13-0

LAUNDRY

LIBRARY
11-8 X 11-1

P. ROOM

COATS

REF.

PAN.

COATS

UP

DN

LIVING
ROOM
11-8 X 14-6

FOYER

DINING ROOM
11-9 x 15-0

GARAGE
20-10 x 22-1

First Floor

Design D0010
The Maison
Traditional

Ground floor 1,491 sq. ft.
Second floor 1,286 sq. ft.
Total 2,777 sq. ft.

Second Floor

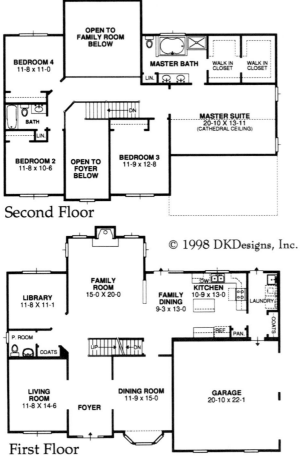

BEDROOM 4
11-8 x 11-0

OPEN TO FAMILY ROOM BELOW

MASTER BATH

WALK IN CLOSET

WALK IN CLOSET

LIN.

BATH

LIN.

BEDROOM 2
11-8 x 10-6

OPEN TO FOYER BELOW

BEDROOM 3
11-9 x 12-8

DN

MASTER SUITE
20-10 X 13-11
(CATHEDRAL CEILING)

Design D0011
The Maison
Federal

Ground floor 1,491 sq. ft.
Second floor 1,286 sq. ft.
Total 2,777 sq. ft.

© 1998 DKDesigns, Inc.

LIBRARY
11-8 X 11-1

FAMILY ROOM
15-0 X 20-0

FAMILY DINING
9-3 x 13-0

KITCHEN
10-9 x 13-0

DW

LAUNDRY

REF.

PAN.

COATS

P. ROOM

COATS

UP

DN

LIVING ROOM
11-8 X 14-6

FOYER

DINING ROOM
11-9 x 15-0

GARAGE
20-10 x 22-1

First Floor

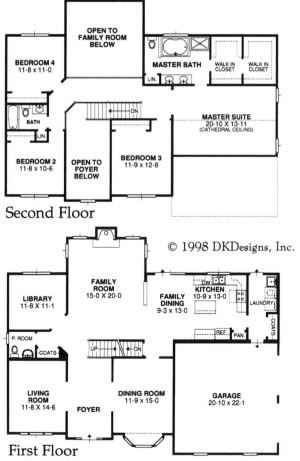

Second Floor

OPEN TO FAMILY ROOM BELOW

BEDROOM 4
11-8 x 11-0

MASTER BATH

WALK IN CLOSET

WALK IN CLOSET

LIN.

BATH

LIN.

DN

MASTER SUITE
20-10 X 13-11
(CATHEDRAL CEILING)

BEDROOM 2
11-8 x 10-6

OPEN TO FOYER BELOW

BEDROOM 3
11-9 x 12-8

© 1998 DKDesigns, Inc.

First Floor

FAMILY ROOM
15-0 X 20-0

KITCHEN
10-9 x 13-0

FAMILY DINING
9-3 x 13-0

DW

LAUNDRY

LIBRARY
11-8 X 11-1

P. ROOM

COATS

UP

DN

REF.

PAN.

COATS

LIVING ROOM
11-8 X 14-6

FOYER

DINING ROOM
11-9 x 15-0

GARAGE
20-10 x 22-1

Design D0012
The Maison
Country French

Ground floor 1,491 sq. ft.
Second floor 1,286 sq. ft.
Total 2,777 sq. ft.

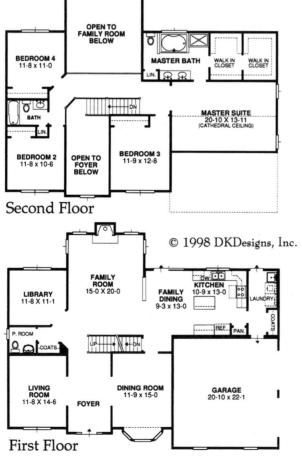

OPEN TO FAMILY ROOM BELOW

BEDROOM 4
11-8 x 11-0

MASTER BATH

WALK IN CLOSET

WALK IN CLOSET

LIN.

BATH

LIN.

MASTER SUITE
20-10 X 13-11
(CATHEDRAL CEILING)

BEDROOM 2
11-8 x 10-6

OPEN TO FOYER BELOW

BEDROOM 3
11-9 x 12-8

Second Floor

© 1998 DKDesigns, Inc.

**Design D0013
The Maison
Country Manor**

Ground floor 1,491 sq. ft.
Second floor 1,286 sq. ft.
Total 2,777 sq. ft.

LIBRARY
11-8 X 11-1

FAMILY ROOM
15-0 X 20-0

FAMILY DINING
9-3 x 13-0

KITCHEN
10-9 x 13-0

DW

LAUNDRY

P. ROOM

COATS

REF.

PAN.

COATS

UP

DN

LIVING ROOM
11-8 x 14-6

FOYER

DINING ROOM
11-9 x 15-0

GARAGE
20-10 x 22-1

First Floor

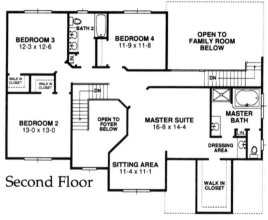

BEDROOM 3
12-3 x 12-6

BATH 2

BEDROOM 4
11-9 x 11-8

OPEN TO
FAMILY ROOM
BELOW

WALK IN
CLOSET

WALK IN
CLOSET

DN

BEDROOM 2
13-0 x 13-0

OPEN TO
FOYER
BELOW

DN

MASTER SUITE
16-8 x 14-4

MASTER
BATH

LIN

DRESSING
AREA

SITTING AREA
11-4 x 11-1

WALK IN
CLOSET

Second Floor

Design D0014
The Chateau Maison
Traditional

Ground floor 1,484 sq. ft.
Second floor 1,342 sq. ft.
Total 2,826 sq. ft.

KITCHEN
10-9 x 14-1

FAMILY
DINING
9-6 x 14-1

FAMILY ROOM
19-4 X 13-8
(CATHEDRAL
CEILING)

DINING ROOM
11-8 x 14-3

PAN.

REF

DN

COATS

UP

COATS

LAUNDRY

LIVING ROOM
13-0 x 15-1

UP

P. ROOM

FOYER

STUDY
11-4 x 10-10

GARAGE
19-4 x 21-8

First Floor

Second Floor

BEDROOM 3
12-3 x 12-6

BATH 2

BEDROOM 4
11-9 x 11-8

OPEN TO
FAMILY ROOM
BELOW

LIN.

WALK IN
CLOSET

WALK IN
CLOSET

DN

DN

BEDROOM 2
13-0 x 13-0

OPEN TO
FOYER
BELOW

MASTER SUITE
16-8 x 14-4

MASTER
BATH

LIN.

SITTING AREA
11-4 x 11-1

DRESSING
AREA

WALK IN
CLOSET

Design D0015
The Chateau Maison
Federal

Ground floor 1,484 sq. ft.
Second floor 1,342 sq. ft.
Total 2,826 sq. ft.

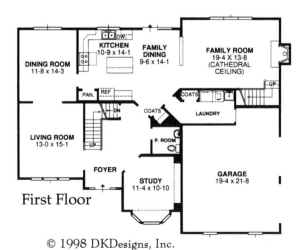

KITCHEN
10-9 x 14-1

FAMILY
DINING
9-6 x 14-1

FAMILY ROOM
19-4 X 13-8
(CATHEDRAL
CEILING)

DINING ROOM
11-8 x 14-3

PAN.

REF

DN

UP

COATS

COATS

LAUNDRY

LIVING ROOM
13-0 x 15-1

UP

P. ROOM

FOYER

STUDY
11-4 x 10-10

GARAGE
19-4 x 21-8

First Floor

© 1998 DKDesigns, Inc.

Second Floor

- **BEDROOM 3** 12-3 x 12-6
- **BATH 2**
- **BEDROOM 4** 11-9 x 11-8
- **OPEN TO FAMILY ROOM BELOW**
- **WALK IN CLOSET**
- **WALK IN CLOSET**
- **DN**
- **BEDROOM 2** 13-0 x 13-0
- **OPEN TO FOYER BELOW**
- **MASTER SUITE** 16-8 x 14-4
- **MASTER BATH**
- **DRESSING AREA**
- **SITTING AREA** 11-4 x 11-1
- **WALK IN CLOSET**

Design D0016
The Chateau Maison
Country Manor

Ground floor 1,484 sq. ft.
Second floor 1,342 sq. ft.
Total 2,826 sq. ft.

First Floor

- **KITCHEN** 10-9 x 14-1
- **FAMILY DINING** 9-6 x 14-1
- **FAMILY ROOM** 19-4 X 13-8 (CATHEDRAL CEILING)
- **DINING ROOM** 11-8 x 14-3
- **PAN.**
- **REF**
- **DN**
- **COATS**
- **COATS**
- **LAUNDRY**
- **UP**
- **LIVING ROOM** 13-0 x 15-1
- **UP**
- **P. ROOM**
- **FOYER**
- **STUDY** 11-4 x 10-10
- **GARAGE** 19-4 x 21-8

© 1998 DKDesigns, Inc.

Second Floor

WALK IN CLOSET

MASTER BATH

OPEN TO FAMILY ROOM BELOW

BEDROOM 4
11-8 x 12-11

MASTER SUITE
20-10 x 13-11

BEDROOM 3
11-9 x 12-8

OPEN TO FOYER BELOW

BEDROOM 2
11-8 x 13-10

STORAGE

First Floor

LAUNDRY

BREAKFAST AREA
9-3 x 12-10

FAMILY ROOM
15-0 x 20-0

LIBRARY
11-8 x 11-5

KITCHEN
10-9 x 12-10

COATS

PAN.

BUTLER'S PANTRY

P. ROOM

COATS

3 CAR GARAGE
20-10 x 31-8

DINING ROOM
11-9 x 14-10

FOYER

LIVING ROOM
11-8 x 14-6

Design D0017
The Astin
Country Manor

Ground floor 1,506 sq. ft.
Second floor 1,330 sq. ft.
Total 2,836 sq. ft.

© 1998 DKDesigns, Inc.

MASTER SUITE
15-8 x 17-4

WALK IN CLOSET

MASTER BATH

BATH

BEDROOM 4
11-5 x 12-11

LINEN

WALK IN CLOSET

DN

LAUNDRY

STORAGE

BEDROOM 2
12-0 x 10-8

OPEN TO FOYER BELOW

BEDROOM 3
11-9 x 10-8

Second Floor

FAMILY ROOM
15-8 x 20-11

P. ROOM

LIBRARY
12-0 x 12-11

FAMILY DINING
10-0 x 12-11

KITCHEN
10-6 x 12-11

PAN.

COATS

COATS

DN

UP

BUTLERS PANTRY

LIVING ROOM
12-0 x 16-4

UP

DINING ROOM
11-9 x 13-0

GARAGE

First Floor

Design D0018
The Devon
Country English

Ground floor 1,552 sq. ft.
Second floor 1,363 sq. ft.
Total 2,885 sq. ft.

Second Floor

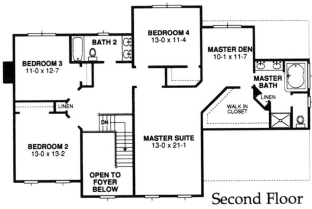

BEDROOM 4
13-0 x 11-4

BATH 2

BEDROOM 3
11-0 x 12-7

MASTER DEN
10-1 x 11-7

MASTER
BATH

LINEN

LINEN

WALK IN
CLOSET

DN

MASTER SUITE
13-0 x 21-1

BEDROOM 2
13-0 x 13-2

OPEN TO
FOYER
BELOW

**Design D0019
The Monet
Traditional**

Ground floor 1,451 sq. ft.
Second floor 1,459 sq. ft.
Total 2,910 sq. ft.

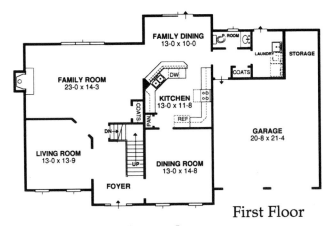

First Floor

FAMILY DINING
13-0 x 10-0

P. ROOM

LAUNDRY

STORAGE

FAMILY ROOM
23-0 x 14-3

DW

COATS

KITCHEN
13-0 x 11-8

COATS

PAN

REF

DN

GARAGE
20-8 x 21-4

LIVING ROOM
13-0 x 13-9

UP

DINING ROOM
13-0 x 14-8

FOYER

© 1998 DKDesigns, Inc.

298 Traditional Style

BEDROOM 4
13-0 x 11-4

BATH 2

BEDROOM 3
11-0 x 12-7

MASTER DEN
10-1 x 11-7

MASTER BATH

LINEN

LINEN

BEDROOM 2
13-0 x 13-2

DN

MASTER SUITE
13-0 x 21-1

WALK IN CLOSET

OPEN TO FOYER BELOW

Second Floor

Design D0020
The Monet
Federal

Ground floor 1,451 sq. ft.
Second floor 1,459 sq. ft.
Total 2,910 sq. ft.

FAMILY DINING
13-0 x 10-0

P. ROOM

LAUNDRY

STORAGE

FAMILY ROOM
23-0 x 14-3

COATS

DW

KITCHEN
13-0 x 11-8

COATS

PAN

DN

REF

GARAGE
20-8 x 21-4

LIVING ROOM
13-0 x 13-9

UP

DINING ROOM
13-0 x 14-8

FOYER

First Floor

© 1998 DKDesigns, Inc.

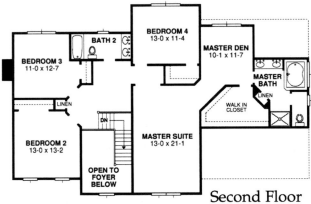

BEDROOM 4
13-0 x 11-4

BATH 2

MASTER DEN
10-1 x 11-7

BEDROOM 3
11-0 x 12-7

MASTER BATH

LINEN

LINEN

WALK IN CLOSET

DN

MASTER SUITE
13-0 x 21-1

BEDROOM 2
13-0 x 13-2

OPEN TO FOYER BELOW

Second Floor

**Design D0021
The Monet
Country Manor**

Ground floor 1,451 sq. ft.
Second floor 1,459 sq. ft.
Total 2,910 sq. ft.

FAMILY DINING
13-0 x 10-0

P. ROOM

LAUNDRY

STORAGE

FAMILY ROOM
23-0 x 14-3

COATS

DW

COATS

PAN.

KITCHEN
13-0 x 11-8

REF

DN

GARAGE
20-8 x 21-4

LIVING ROOM
13-0 x 13-9

UP

DINING ROOM
13-0 x 14-8

FOYER

First Floor

© 1998 DKDesigns, Inc.

300 Traditional Style

Second Floor

WALK IN CLOSET

MASTER BATH

LIN.

LIN.

BEDROOM 4
12-0 x 11-3

BATH

LIN.

BEDROOM 3
11-0 x 13-1

MASTER SUITE
19-9 x 15-5

BONUS ROOM
10-9 x 9-3

BEDROOM 2
11-8 x 11-0

DN.

OPEN TO FOYER BELOW

UNFINISHED STORAGE

**Design D0022
The Woodbury Grand
Farmhouse**

Ground floor 1,541 sq. ft.
Second floor 1,414 sq. ft.
Total 2,955 sq. ft.

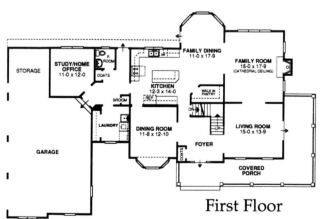

First Floor

STORAGE

STUDY/HOME OFFICE
11-0 x 12-0

COATS

BROOM

REF.

KITCHEN
12-3 x 14-0

FAMILY DINING
11-0 x 17-9

FAMILY ROOM
15-0 x 17-9
(CATHEDRAL CEILING)

WALK IN PANTRY

DN.

UP

LAUNDRY

DINING ROOM
11-8 x 12-10

LIVING ROOM
15-0 x 13-9

GARAGE

COATS

FOYER

COVERED PORCH

© 1998 DKDesigns, Inc.

WALK IN CLOSET | WALK IN CLOSET | MASTER BATH | LINEN

BEDROOM 4
11-1 x 11-0

BEDROOM 3
11-0 x 13-0

MASTER SUITE
18-5 x 13-7
(CATHEDRAL CEILING)

LIN.

BATH 2

BEDROOM 2
11-8 x 11-0

DN

OPEN TO FOYER BELOW

MASTER DEN
9-5 x 11-8

Second Floor

**Design D0023
The Woodbury
Traditional**

Ground floor 1,489 sq. ft.
Second floor 1,514 sq. ft.
Total 3,003 sq. ft.

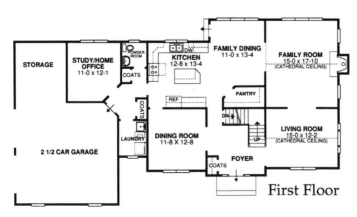

STORAGE

STUDY/HOME OFFICE
11-0 x 12-1

COATS

POWDER ROOM

KITCHEN
12-8 x 13-4

DW

FAMILY DINING
11-0 x 13-4

FAMILY ROOM
15-0 x 17-10
(CATHEDRAL CEILING)

REF

COATS

PANTRY

DN

LIVING ROOM
15-0 x 12-2
(CATHEDRAL CEILING)

DINING ROOM
11-8 X 12-8

LAUNDRY

UP

2 1/2 CAR GARAGE

FOYER

COATS

First Floor

© 1998 DKDesigns, Inc.

302 Traditional Style

WALK IN CLOSET

WALK IN CLOSET

MASTER BATH

LINEN

BEDROOM 4
11-1 x 11-0

BEDROOM 3
11-0 x 13-0

MASTER SUITE
18-5 x 13-7
(CATHEDRAL CEILING)

LIN.

BATH 2

DN

BEDROOM 2
11-8 x 11-0

MASTER DEN
9-5 x 11-8

OPEN TO FOYER BELOW

Second Floor

Design D0024
The Woodbury
Federal

Ground floor 1,489 sq. ft.
Second floor 1,514 sq. ft.
Total 3,003 sq. ft.

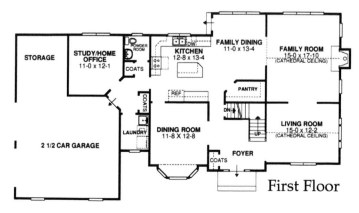

STORAGE

STUDY/HOME OFFICE
11-0 x 12-1

COATS

POWDER ROOM

DW

KITCHEN
12-8 x 13-4

FAMILY DINING
11-0 x 13-4

FAMILY ROOM
15-0 x 17-10
(CATHEDRAL CEILING)

PANTRY

REF

COATS

LAUNDRY

DINING ROOM
11-8 X 12-8

DN

LIVING ROOM
15-0 x 12-2
(CATHEDRAL CEILING)

UP

2 1/2 CAR GARAGE

FOYER

COATS

First Floor

Traditional Style 303

WALK IN CLOSET | WALK IN CLOSET | MASTER BATH | BEDROOM 4 11-1 x 11-0 | BEDROOM 3 11-0 x 13-0

LINEN

MASTER SUITE 18-5 x 13-7 (CATHEDRAL CEILING)

LIN.

BATH 2

BEDROOM 2 11-8 x 11-0

DN

OPEN TO FOYER BELOW

MASTER DEN 9-5 x 11-8

Second Floor

**Design D0025
The Woodbury
Farmhouse**

Ground floor 1,489 sq. ft.
Second floor 1,514 sq. ft.
Total 3,003 sq. ft.

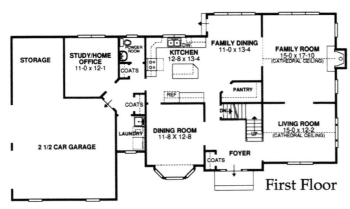

POWDER ROOM

STORAGE | STUDY/HOME OFFICE 11-0 x 12-1 | KITCHEN 12-8 x 13-4 | FAMILY DINING 11-0 x 13-4 | FAMILY ROOM 15-0 x 17-10 (CATHEDRAL CEILING)

DW

COATS

COATS

REF

PANTRY

DN

LIVING ROOM 15-0 x 12-2 (CATHEDRAL CEILING)

2 1/2 CAR GARAGE

LAUNDRY

DINING ROOM 11-8 X 12-8

UP

FOYER

COATS

First Floor

WALK IN CLOSET

WALK IN CLOSET

MASTER BATH

LINEN

BEDROOM 4
11-1 x 11-0

BEDROOM 3
11-0 x 13-0

MASTER SUITE
18-5 x 13-7
(CATHEDRAL CEILING)

LINEN

BATH 2

BEDROOM 2
11-8 x 11-0

DN

MASTER DEN
9-5 x 11-8

OPEN TO FOYER BELOW

Second Floor

Design D0026
The Woodbury
Country Manor I

Ground floor 1,489 sq. ft.
Second floor 1,514 sq. ft.
Total 3,003 sq. ft.

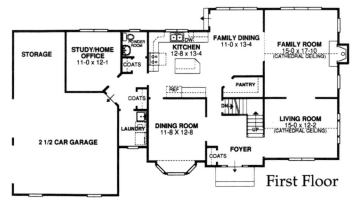

STORAGE

STUDY/HOME OFFICE
11-0 x 12-1

POWDER ROOM

KITCHEN
12-8 x 13-4

DW

FAMILY DINING
11-0 x 13-4

FAMILY ROOM
15-0 x 17-10
(CATHEDRAL CEILING)

COATS

REF

COATS

PANTRY

DN

LAUNDRY

DINING ROOM
11-8 X 12-8

UP

LIVING ROOM
15-0 x 12-2
(CATHEDRAL CEILING)

2 1/2 CAR GARAGE

FOYER

COATS

First Floor

Traditional Style 305

Design D0027
The Woodbury
Country English

Ground floor 1,489 sq. ft.
Second floor 1,514 sq. ft.
Total 3,003 sq. ft.

Second Floor

- WALK IN CLOSET
- WALK IN CLOSET
- MASTER BATH
- LINEN
- BEDROOM 4
  11-1 x 11-0
- BEDROOM 3
  11-0 x 13-0
- MASTER SUITE
  18-5 x 13-7
  (CATHEDRAL CEILING)
- LINEN
- BATH 2
- BEDROOM 2
  11-8 x 11-0
- DN
- OPEN TO FOYER BELOW
- MASTER DEN
  9-5 x 11-8

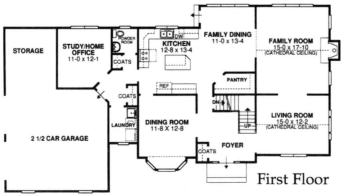

First Floor

- STORAGE
- STUDY/HOME OFFICE
  11-0 x 12-1
- POWDER ROOM
- COATS
- KITCHEN
  12-8 x 13-4
- DW
- FAMILY DINING
  11-0 x 13-4
- FAMILY ROOM
  15-0 x 17-10
  (CATHEDRAL CEILING)
- REF
- COATS
- PANTRY
- DN
- LIVING ROOM
  15-0 x 12-2
  (CATHEDRAL CEILING)
- LAUNDRY
- DINING ROOM
  11-8 X 12-8
- UP
- 2 1/2 CAR GARAGE
- COATS
- FOYER

© 1998 DKDesigns, Inc.

306 Traditional Style

Second Floor

WALK IN CLOSET

WALK IN CLOSET

MASTER BATH

LINEN

BEDROOM 4
11-1 x 11-0

BEDROOM 3
11-0 x 13-0

MASTER SUITE
18-5 x 13-7
(CATHEDRAL CEILING)

LINEN

BATH 2

BEDROOM 2
11-8 x 11-0

DN

OPEN TO
FOYER
BELOW

MASTER DEN
9-5 x 11-8

**Design D0028
The Woodbury
Country French**

Ground floor 1,489 sq. ft.
Second floor 1,514 sq. ft.
Total 3,003 sq. ft.

First Floor

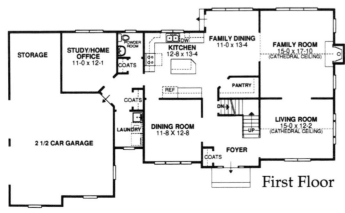

STORAGE

STUDY/HOME
OFFICE
11-0 x 12-1

POWDER ROOM

KITCHEN
12-8 x 13-4

DW

FAMILY DINING
11-0 x 13-4

FAMILY ROOM
15-0 x 17-10
(CATHEDRAL CEILING)

COATS

REF

PANTRY

COATS

DN

LAUNDRY

DINING ROOM
11-8 X 12-8

2 1/2 CAR GARAGE

LIVING ROOM
15-0 x 12-2
(CATHEDRAL CEILING)

UP

FOYER

COATS

Second Floor

BEDROOM 4
13-0 x 12-1

OPTIONAL BOOKCASES

BALCONY

OPEN TO
FAMILY ROOM
BELOW

M. BATH

WALK IN
CLOSET

BEDROOM 3
14-9 x 12-5

DN

LINEN

OPEN TO
FOYER
BELOW

MASTER
BEDROOM
13-0 x 17-1
(CATHEDRAL CEILING)

BATH

WALK IN
CLOSET

BEDROOM 2
12-0 x 11-0

First Floor

KITCHEN/BREAK
21-8 x 14-4

MICRO
OVEN

REF   PAN.

STORAGE

LAUNDRY

TWO STORY
FAMILY ROOM
20-2 X 20-0

COATS

STUDY
13-0 X 11-0

P. ROOM

COATS

DN   UP

FOYER

LIVING ROOM
13-0 X 12-5

GARAGE
21-4 x 21-8
+ STORAGE

DINING ROOM
12-0 X 13-2
+ BAY

COVERED
ENTRY

© 1998 DKDesigns, Inc.

**Design D0029
The Jefferson
Country Manor**

Ground floor 1,534 sq. ft.
Second floor 1,570 sq. ft.
Total 3,105 sq. ft.

308 Traditional Style

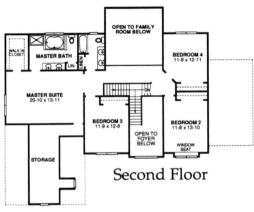

OPEN TO FAMILY ROOM BELOW

WALK IN CLOSET

MASTER BATH

LIN.

BEDROOM 4
11-8 x 12-11

MASTER SUITE
20-10 x 13-11

DN

BEDROOM 3
11-9 x 12-8

OPEN TO FOYER BELOW

BEDROOM 2
11-8 x 13-10

WINDOW SEAT

STORAGE

Second Floor

Design D0030
The Maison Grand
Country English

Ground floor 1,793 sq. ft.
Second floor 1,373 sq. ft.
Total 3,106 sq. ft.

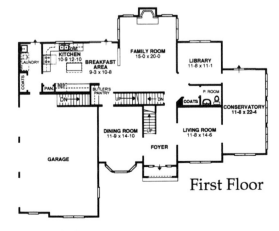

LAUNDRY

COATS

KITCHEN
10-9 12-10

BREAKFAST AREA
9-3 x 10-8

FAMILY ROOM
15-0 x 20-0

LIBRARY
11-8 x 11-1

PAN.

BUTLER'S PANTRY

DN

UP

DN

P. ROOM

COATS

CONSERVATORY
11-8 x 22-4

DINING ROOM
11-9 x 14-10

UP

LIVING ROOM
11-8 x 14-6

GARAGE

FOYER

First Floor

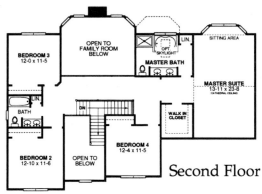

Second Floor

Floor plan labels (Second Floor):
- BEDROOM 3 12-0 x 11-5
- OPEN TO FAMILY ROOM BELOW
- LIN.
- OPT SKYLIGHT
- SITTING AREA
- MASTER BATH
- BATH
- LIN.
- MASTER SUITE 13-11 x 23-8 (CATHEDRAL CEILING)
- DN
- WALK IN CLOSET
- BEDROOM 2 12-10 x 11-6
- OPEN TO BELOW
- BEDROOM 4 12-4 x 11-5

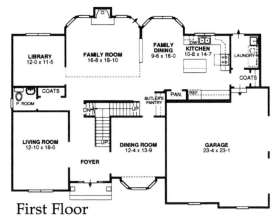

First Floor

Floor plan labels (First Floor):
- LIBRARY 12-0 x 11-5
- FAMILY ROOM 16-8 x 18-10
- FAMILY DINING 9-6 x 16-0
- KITCHEN 10-8 x 14-7
- DW
- LAUNDRY
- COATS
- COATS
- P. ROOM
- PAN.
- REF.
- BUTLER'S PANTRY
- DN
- UP
- UP
- LIVING ROOM 12-10 x 18-0
- DINING ROOM 12-4 x 13-9
- GARAGE 23-4 x 23-1
- FOYER

Design D0031
The Cambridge
Country Manor

Ground floor 1,651 sq. ft.
Second floor 1,466 sq. ft.
Total 3,117 sq. ft.

310 Traditional Style

Second Floor

BEDROOM 3
11-0 X13-1

BATH

BEDROOM 4
12-0 X 11-3

MASTER BATH

WALK IN
CLOSET

LINEN

LIN
LIN
LIN

OPEN TO
FOYER
BELOW

BEDROOM 2
11-8 X 11-0

MASTER DEN
10-9 X 9-3

MASTER SUITE
19-9 X 15-5

UNFINISHED
STORAGE

Design D0032
The Woodbury Grand
Country Manor

Ground floor 1,688 sq. ft.
Second floor 1,414 sq. ft.
Total 3,102 sq. ft.

First Floor

SKYLIGHT SKYLIGHT

FAMILY
DINING
11-0 X 17-9

FAMILY ROOM
15-0 X 17-9
(CATHEDRAL CEILING)

KITCHEN
12-8 X 14-0

DW

MICRO
OVEN

P.
ROOM

COATS

STUDY/HOME
OFFICE
11-0 X12-0

STORAGE

WALK IN
PANTRY

DN

REF.

BROOM

LIVING ROOM
15-0 X 13-9
(CATHEDRAL CEILING)

UP

DINING ROOM
11-8 X 12-10

LAUNDRY

FOYER

3 CAR GARAGE

MASTER DEN
12-0 x 8-2

WALK IN CLOSET

MASTER BATH

WALK IN CLOSET

MASTER SUITE
17-6 x 13-2

OPEN TO FAMILY ROOM BELOW

BATH

DN

DN

BEDROOM 2
11-8 x 10-8

OPEN TO FOYER BELOW

BEDROOM 3
12-1 x 14-8

BATH

LIN.

BEDROOM 4
12-1 x 11-9

Second Floor

Design D0033
The Danbury
Country Farmhouse

Ground floor 1,761 sq. ft.
Second floor 1,503 sq. ft.
Total 3,264 sq. ft.

FAMILY DINING
12-0 x 10-6

STUDY/HOME OFFICE
11-8 x 12-7

POWDER ROOM

PAN.

KITCHEN
16-5 x 11-2

FAMILY ROOM
21-3 x 14-9
(CATHEDRAL CEILING)

COATS

DN

UP

UP

LIVING ROOM
11-8 x 15-11

LAUNDRY

DINING ROOM
12-2 x 16-11

FOYER

GARAGE

First Floor

312 Traditional Style

WALK IN CLOSET **MASTER BATH** **LIN.** **BEDROOM 4** 12-9 X 11-0 **BATH** **LIN.** **BEDROOM 3** 12-9 X 11-0

LIN. **BATH**

MASTER SUITE 21-4 x 17-4

MASTER DEN 12-2 x 13-9 **OPEN TO FOYER BELOW** **BEDROOM 2** 12-10 X 11-3

Second Floor

Design D0034
The Cromwell
English Manor

Ground floor 1,665 sq. ft.
Second floor 1,672 sq. ft.
Total 3,337 sq. ft.

LAUNDRY **KITCHEN** 10-6 X 14-7 **FAMILY DINING** 9-6 x 12-4 **FAMILY ROOM** 15-0 x 21-9 **LIBRARY** 11-0 x 12-8

COATS **PANTRY** **BUTLER'S PANTRY** **P. ROOM** **COATS**

DINING ROOM 12-3 x 13-9 **FOYER** **LIVING ROOM** 12-10 x 15-9

GARAGE

First Floor

© 1998 DKDesigns, Inc.

Second Floor

Floor plan labels:
- SITTING AREA
- LINEN
- OPEN TO FAMILY ROOM BELOW
- WINDOW SEAT
- BEDROOM 3 14-0 X 11-6
- MASTER BATH
- MASTER SUITE 15-11 X 23-8 (CATHEDRAL CEILING)
- LINEN
- LINEN
- BATH 2
- BEDROOM 4 12-4 X 11-5
- DN
- OPEN TO BELOW
- BEDROOM 2 12-10 X 11-6
- WALK IN CLOSET 9-5 X 23-10
- WINDOW SEAT

Design D0035
The Ashbury
Country Manor

Ground floor 1,723 sq. ft.
Second floor 1,805 sq. ft.
Total 3,528 sq. ft.

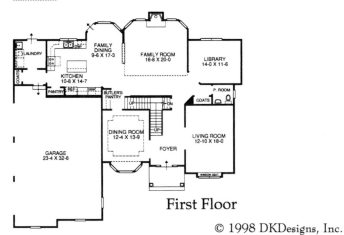

First Floor

Floor plan labels:
- LAUNDRY
- DW
- FAMILY DINING 9-6 X 17-3
- FAMILY ROOM 16-8 X 20-0
- LIBRARY 14-0 X 11-6
- COATS
- KITCHEN 10-8 X 14-7
- PANTRY
- BUTLER'S PANTRY
- DESK
- P. ROOM
- COATS
- UP
- DN
- UP
- DINING ROOM 12-4 X 13-9
- LIVING ROOM 12-10 X 18-0
- GARAGE 23-4 X 32-8
- FOYER
- WINDOW SEAT

© 1998 DKDesigns, Inc.

MASTER SUITE
15-0 x 19-5

WALK IN CLOSET

WALK IN CLOSET

BEDROOM 2
12-4 x 12-2

M. BATH

WALK IN CLOSET

LIN.

BATH

BEDROOM 5
17-8 x 14-0

BATH

BEDROOM 4
14-2 x 12-6

DN

OPEN TO BELOW

BEDROOM 3
12-4 x 11-11

STORAGE

Second Floor

FAMILY ROOM
15-0 x 22-10

FAMILY DINING
10-5 x 11-4

LIBRARY
12-4 x 12-0

LAUNDRY

COATS

KITCHEN
12-6 x 13-6

REF

BUTLER'S PANTRY

UP

DN

P. ROOM

COATS

DINING ROOM
14-3 x 14-7

UP

FOYER

LIVING ROOM
12-4 x 16-3

GARAGE

First Floor

© 1998 DKDesigns, Inc.

Design D0036
The Carrington
Country Manor

Ground floor 1,780 sq. ft.
Second floor 1,837 sq. ft.
Total 3,617 sq. ft.

An original English Tudor house was the inspiration for the design of this attractive variation. As is typical of this style, the variety of building materials used in the facade—bricks, stucco, solid wooden beams, natural stone, and wooden shingles—work together harmoniously to give the house a solid and permanent air. With a foundation measuring 78 x 30 feet, this traditional-style house requires a correspondingly large lot. The floor plan of the interior is in keeping with the classic pattern. The foyer opens into the living room and dining room, opposite each other, while the family room and an open kitchen form a unit in the back of the house. There is also a den that leads directly to the porch and is accessible from both the living room and the family room. On the second floor are five more rooms, two full baths, and an additional space above the garage.

Design 5129-Homes for Today
© Augustus Suglia, Architect

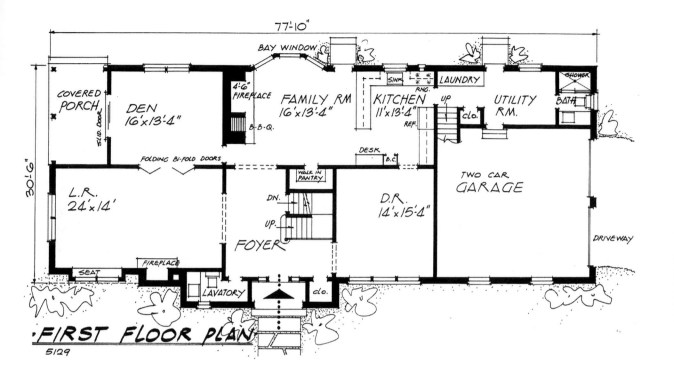

FIRST FLOOR PLAN
5129

77'-10"

BAY WINDOW

COVERED PORCH

DEN 16'x13'-4"

4'-6" FIREPLACE

B-B-Q.

FAMILY RM. 16'x13'-4"

SINK
RNG.

LAUNDRY

KITCHEN 11'x13'-4"

REF.

UP

clo.

UTILITY RM.

SHOWER

BATH

FOLDING BI-FOLD DOORS

DESK

B.C.

L.R. 24'x14'

WALK IN PANTRY

DN.

UP.

FOYER

DESK

D.R. 14'x15'-4"

TWO CAR GARAGE

30'-6"

SEAT

FIREPLACE

LAVATORY

clo.

DRIVEWAY

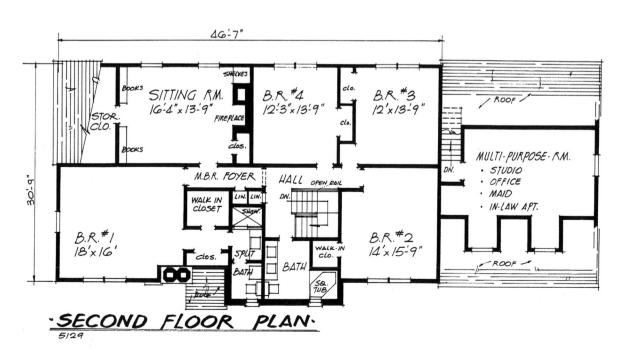

SECOND FLOOR PLAN
5129

46'-7"

BOOKS

STOR. CLO.

SITTING RM. 16'-4"x13'-9"

SHELVES

FIREPLACE

B.R. #4 12'-3"x13'-9"

clo.

clo.

B.R. #3 12'x13'-9"

ROOF

BOOKS

CLOS.

MULTI-PURPOSE RM.
• STUDIO
• OFFICE
• MAID
• IN-LAW APT.

DN.

M.B.R. FOYER

WALK IN CLOSET

LIN. LIN.

SHOW.

HALL OPEN RAIL

DN.

30'-9"

B.R. #1 18'x16'

CLOS.

SPLIT BATH

BATH

SQ. TUB

WALK IN CLO.

B.R. #2 14'x15'-9"

RIDGE

ROOF

Traditional Style 317

This Tudor-style house designed in English tradition features a variation on the hipped roof, and much of its charm is derived from the sophisticated use of various building materials. The house offers a total of 2,691 square feet of living area. The entry, which is located to the front left, leads into a two-story foyer with access to a library (left) that features a high ceiling and a door to the screened porch. To the right of the foyer is the large living room with fireplace, adjacent to the formal dining room. Toward the back yard are the kitchen, a beautiful dinette with large windows, and the family room with fireplace.

On the second floor are three generously sized bedrooms and plentiful storage space.

Design 5135–Homes for Today
© Augustus Suglia, Architect

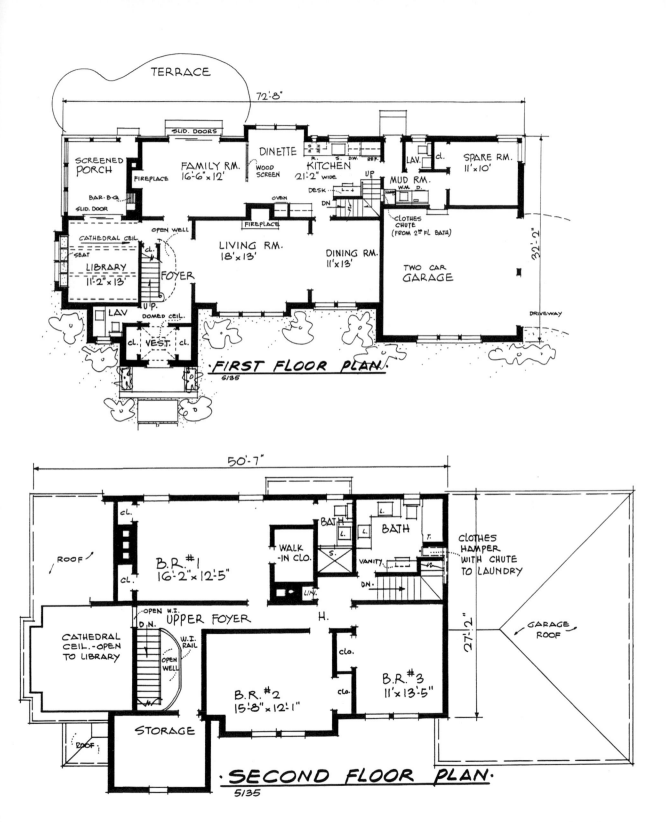

TERRACE

72'-8"

SLID. DOORS

DINETTE

KITCHEN
21'-2" WIDE

LAV.   cl.   SPARE RM.
11'×10'

SCREENED
PORCH

FAMILY RM.
16'-6"×12'

WOOD
SCREEN

FIREPLACE

R.   S.   D.W.
REF.

MUD RM.
W.M.   D.

BAR-B-Q

SLID. DOOR

OVEN

UP

DESK

DN

OPEN WELL

CLOTHES
CHUTE
(FROM 2ⁿᵈ FL BATH)

CATHEDRAL CEIL.

SEAT

LIBRARY
11'-2"×13'

cl.

FOYER

FIREPLACE

LIVING RM.
18'×13'

DINING RM.
11'×13'

TWO CAR
GARAGE

32'-2"

UP.

LAV

DOMED CEIL.

cl.   VEST.   cl.

DRIVEWAY

·FIRST FLOOR PLAN·
5135

50'-7"

cl.

B.R. #1
16'-2"×12'-5"

cl.

ROOF

WALK
-IN CLO.

BATH

L.

L.

BATH

VANITY

S.

DN.

T.

CLOTHES
HAMPER
WITH CHUTE
TO LAUNDRY

27'-2"

GARAGE
ROOF

OPEN W.I.

DN.

UPPER FOYER

H.

CATHEDRAL
CEIL.-OPEN
TO LIBRARY

W.I.
RAIL

OPEN
WELL

LIN.

clo.

B.R. #2
15'-8"×12'-1"

clo.

B.R. #3
11'×13'-5"

ROOF

STORAGE

·SECOND FLOOR PLAN·
5135

Traditional Style 319

This imposing design in the English Tudor tradition promises the finest in comfortable living environments. The two-story house is impressive in its conscious combination of building materials, including natural stone, bricks, stucco and wood. The house gives the impression of being much larger that it actually is. Two stories provide a total living area of 1,991 square feet in a classically laid-out floor plan. The 1,023-square-foot ground floor includes a large foyer, dining room, living room, study, family room with fireplace, country kitchen with eating bar, and a mud and utility room. On the second floor are four additional rooms and two baths, with the possibility of another room and bath above the two-car garage.

Design 5157–Homes for Today
© Augustus Suglia, Architect

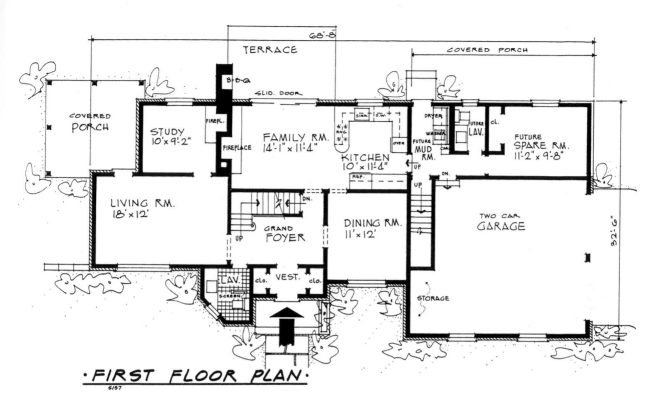

· FIRST FLOOR PLAN ·
5157

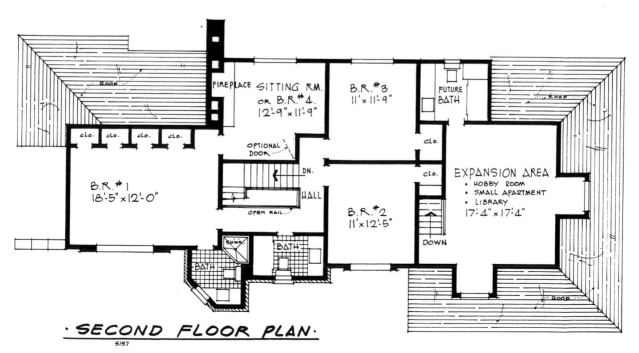

· SECOND FLOOR PLAN ·
5157

Traditional Style 321

With the "Jamison," Cadre Development presents an elegant two-story house in the colonial style. The dark red brick front is superbly accentuated by the white stucco on the gable, door and window areas. The classical lines are continued in the interior of the house. With its 984 square feet, the ground floor features a symmetrical arrangement of individual rooms. To the side of the two-story foyer is the formal living room. The kitchen with breakfast nook and the adjacent family room form a discrete area. To the left of the kitchen is the dining room. On the second floor are four bedrooms and two baths.

Design C0009-01-B Jamison
© Cadre Development

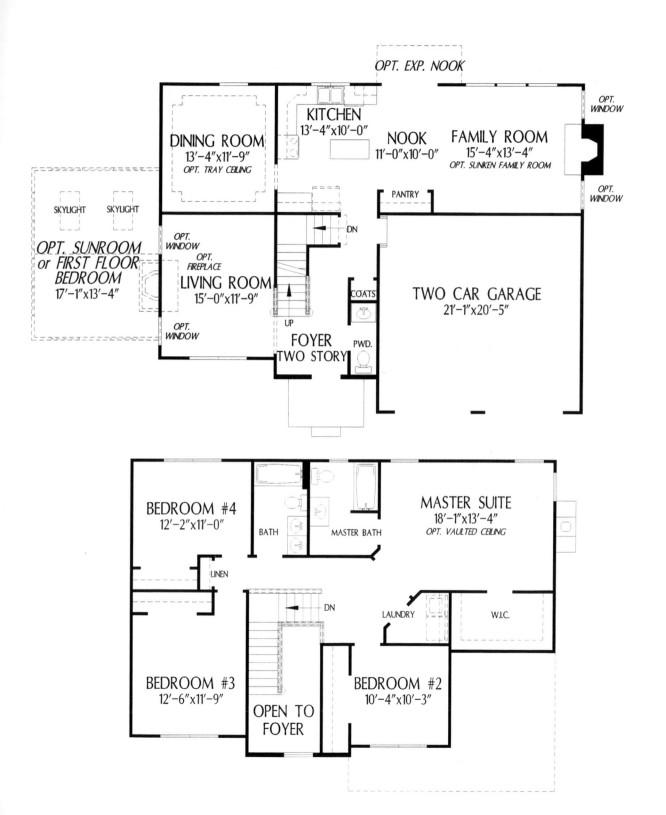

OPT. EXP. NOOK

KITCHEN
13'-4"x10'-0"

NOOK
11'-0"x10'-0"

FAMILY ROOM
15'-4"x13'-4"
OPT. SUNKEN FAMILY ROOM

OPT. WINDOW

OPT. WINDOW

DINING ROOM
13'-4"x11'-9"
OPT. TRAY CEILING

SKYLIGHT   SKYLIGHT

OPT. SUNROOM or FIRST FLOOR BEDROOM
17'-1"x13'-4"

OPT. WINDOW

OPT. FIREPLACE

LIVING ROOM
15'-0"x11'-9"

OPT. WINDOW

PANTRY

DN

COATS

TWO CAR GARAGE
21'-1"x20'-5"

UP

FOYER
TWO STORY

PWD.

BEDROOM #4
12'-2"x11'-0"

BATH

MASTER BATH

MASTER SUITE
18'-1"x13'-4"
OPT. VAULTED CEILING

LINEN

DN

LAUNDRY

W.I.C.

BEDROOM #3
12'-6"x11'-9"

OPEN TO FOYER

BEDROOM #2
10'-4"x10'-3"

Traditional Style 323

In a variation on the colonial style, the front facade of this home is finished in varicolored natural stone. Drawing on the design of the "Jamison," the "Kingston" differs in that the two-car garage features a steeper roof that attaches directly to the protruding gable element of the main house. This design sacrifices the fourth bedroom on the second floor, but two dormer windows in the garage roof offer an interesting alternative. The "Kingston" also has a wider entry area with a covered porch.

The outline of the ground floor in the "Kingston" design is identical to that of the "Jamison."

Design C0010-01-D Kingston
© Cadre Development

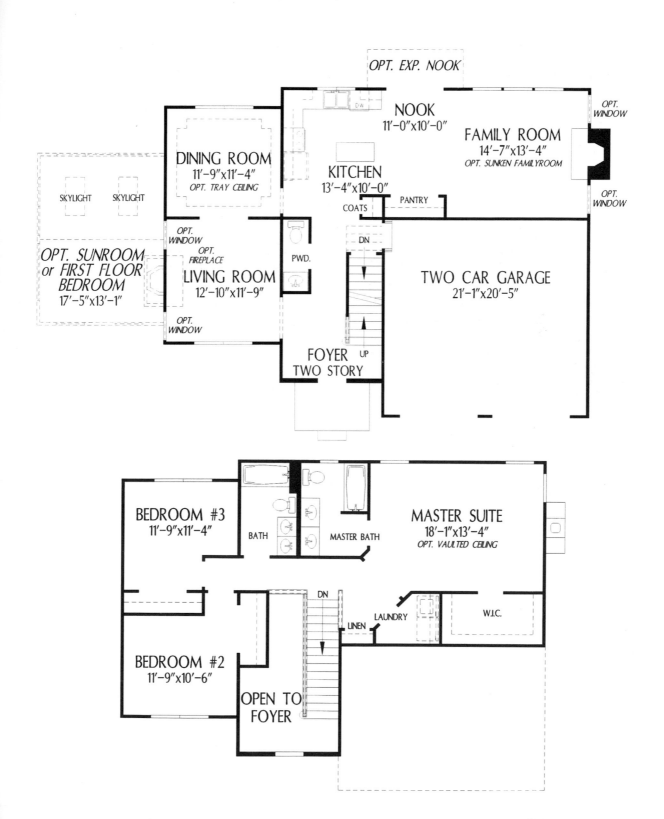

OPT. EXP. NOOK

NOOK
11'-0"x10'-0"

FAMILY ROOM
14'-7"x13'-4"
OPT. SUNKEN FAMILYROOM

OPT.
WINDOW

OPT.
WINDOW

DINING ROOM
11'-9"x11'-4"
OPT. TRAY CEILING

KITCHEN
13'-4"x10'-0"

COATS

PANTRY

SKYLIGHT   SKYLIGHT

OPT.
WINDOW

OPT.
FIREPLACE

PWD.

DN

OPT. SUNROOM
or FIRST FLOOR
BEDROOM
17'-5"x13'-1"

LIVING ROOM
12'-10"x11'-9"

TWO CAR GARAGE
21'-1"x20'-5"

OPT.
WINDOW

UP

FOYER
TWO STORY

BEDROOM #3
11'-9"x11'-4"

BATH

MASTER BATH

MASTER SUITE
18'-1"x13'-4"
OPT. VAULTED CEILING

DN

LINEN

LAUNDRY

W.I.C.

BEDROOM #2
11'-9"x10'-6"

OPEN TO
FOYER

Traditional Style 325

The "Kingston Grand" presents yet another variation in the series of colonial-style houses by Cadre Development, with a living area of 2,077 square feet. The garage has been fitted with a high gabled roof, with a window in the gable end. The foundation dimensions are the same as in the "Jamison" and "Kingston" designs. On the second floor, the floor plan has been altered slightly to make use of the increased floor area.

Design C0010-02-B
Kingston Grand
© Cadre Development

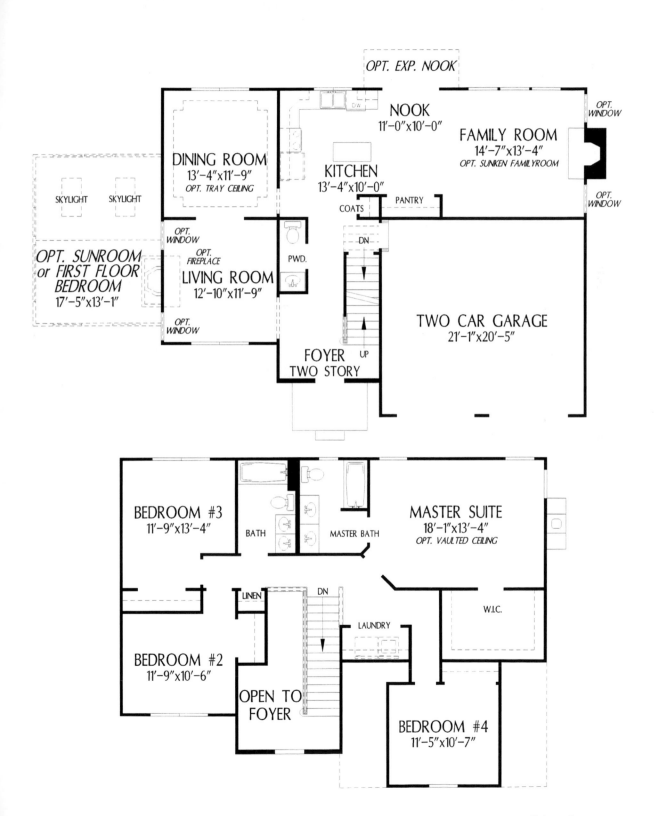

OPT. EXP. NOOK

NOOK
11'-0"x10'-0"

FAMILY ROOM
14'-7"x13'-4"
OPT. SUNKEN FAMILYROOM

OPT.
WINDOW

DINING ROOM
13'-4"x11'-9"
OPT. TRAY CEILING

KITCHEN
13'-4"x10'-0"

OPT.
WINDOW

SKYLIGHT   SKYLIGHT

PANTRY

COATS

DN

OPT. SUNROOM
or FIRST FLOOR
BEDROOM
17'-5"x13'-1"

OPT.
WINDOW

OPT.
FIREPLACE

LIVING ROOM
12'-10"x11'-9"

PWD.

TWO CAR GARAGE
21'-1"x20'-5"

OPT.
WINDOW

FOYER
TWO STORY

UP

BEDROOM #3
11'-9"x13'-4"

BATH

MASTER BATH

MASTER SUITE
18'-1"x13'-4"
OPT. VAULTED CEILING

LINEN

DN

W.I.C.

BEDROOM #2
11'-9"x10'-6"

LAUNDRY

OPEN TO
FOYER

BEDROOM #4
11'-5"x10'-7"

Traditional Style 327

With a facade entirely of wood and a tasteful entry area, this design follows the Georgian style. The symmetrical arrangement of the latticed windows and the dormers lend an elegant note to the exterior. With a living area of 1,790 square feet, the interior features a clearly designed floor plan. The 938-square-foot ground floor offers a formal living room and dining room to either side of the foyer. Between the dining room and the open kitchen with breakfast nook are a pantry and a guest bath. Four bedrooms and two full bathrooms are located on the second floor.

Design C0023-01-A Williamsburg
© Cadre Development

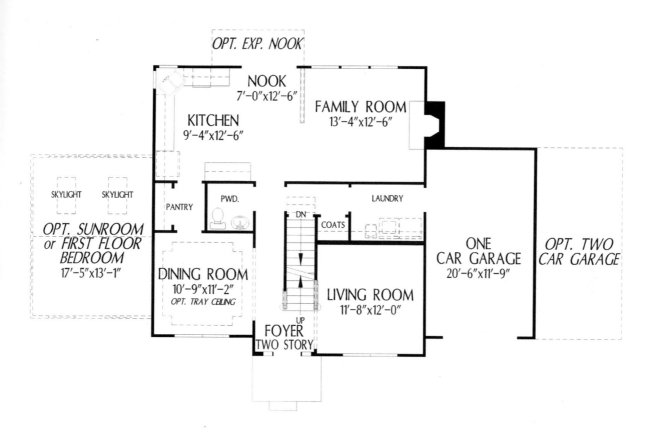

OPT. EXP. NOOK

NOOK
7'-0"x12'-6"

FAMILY ROOM
13'-4"x12'-6"

KITCHEN
9'-4"x12'-6"

SKYLIGHT   SKYLIGHT

PANTRY   PWD.   LAUNDRY

OPT. SUNROOM
or FIRST FLOOR
BEDROOM
17'-5"x13'-1"

DN   COATS

ONE
CAR GARAGE
20'-6"x11'-9"

OPT. TWO
CAR GARAGE

DINING ROOM
10'-9"x11'-2"
OPT. TRAY CEILING

LIVING ROOM
11'-8"x12'-0"

UP

FOYER
TWO STORY

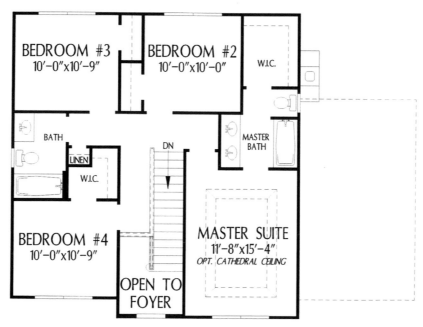

BEDROOM #3
10'-0"x10'-9"

BEDROOM #2
10'-0"x10'-0"

W.I.C.

BATH

LINEN

W.I.C.

MASTER
BATH

DN

BEDROOM #4
10'-0"x10'-9"

OPEN TO
FOYER

MASTER SUITE
11'-8"x15'-4"
OPT. CATHEDRAL CEILING

Traditional Style 329

The front view of this stately house is characterized by a wide front porch and the gable that protrudes above it. This modern version of a colonial-style house features a large two-car garage, whose doors compliment the color chosen for the porch columns, windowpanes, and the tasteful decoration of the cornice and gable. With 1,119 square feet, the ground floor offers a living room and dining room that are connected to each other, while the kitchen with breakfast nook and family room form an area of their own.

Upstairs are four bedrooms, two baths, three walk-in closets, and a laundry room spread over the 1,236-square-foot floor plan.

Design C0050-01-D
Oakmont
© Cadre Development

OPT. EXP. NOOK

DINING ROOM
13'-4"x12'-5"
OPT. TRAY CEILING

NOOK
10'-11"x9'-9"

OPT. WINDOW

FAMILY ROOM
13'-4"x15'-0"
OPT. SUNKEN FAMILYROOM

DW

KITCHEN
13'-4"x10'-0"

PANTRY

OPT. WINDOW

DN

SKYLIGHT   SKYLIGHT

OPT. WINDOW

OPT. FIREPLACE

PWD.

OPT. SUNROOM or FIRST FLOOR BEDROOM
17'-5"x13'-1"

LIVING ROOM
15'-10"x15'-1"

OPT. WINDOW

TWO CAR GARAGE
20'-5"x21'-1"

FOYER
TWO STORY

UP

MASTER BATH

W.I.C.

BATH

LINEN

BEDROOM #3
10'-0"x11'-6"

BEDROOM #2
13'-8"x10'-0"

LINEN

LINEN

DN

LAUNDRY

W.I.C.   W.I.C.

MASTER SUITE
17'-8"x15'-1"
OPT. TRAY CEILING

BEDROOM #4
11'-4"x11'-9"

OPEN TO FOYER

Traditional Style 331

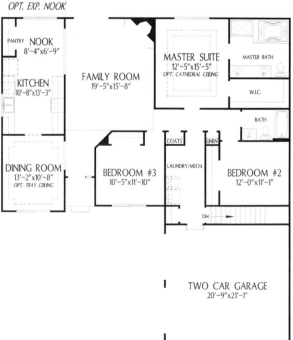

The "Raleigh" by Cadre Development features a one-story L-shaped design. The gables facing the street side have a red brick facade, in contrast to the wood clapboard siding on the rest of the house. The 1,707-square-foot floor plan is clearly organized, with a dining room, family/living room, kitchen with pantry and breakfast nook, a master suite, and two additional bedrooms.

Design C0052-01-B
Raleigh
© Cadre Development

332 Traditional Style

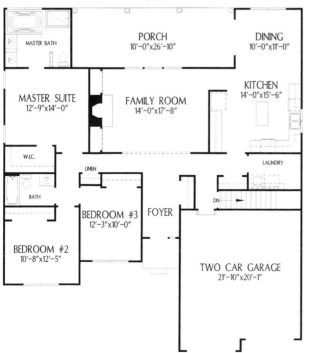

MASTER BATH

PORCH
10'-0"x26'-10"

DINING
10'-0"x11'-0"

MASTER SUITE
12'-9"x14'-0"

FAMILY ROOM
14'-0"x17'-8"

KITCHEN
14'-0"x15'-6"

W.I.C.

LINEN

LAUNDRY

BATH

BEDROOM #3
12'-3"x10'-0"

FOYER

DN

BEDROOM #2
10'-8"x12'-5"

TWO CAR GARAGE
21'-10"x20'-1"

The front view of this one-story design presents an elegant one-story stucco facade graced with contrasting shutters on the side facing toward the street. The floor plan of the "Hamilton" includes three bedrooms, a large family/living room, and a dining room.

Design C0062-01-C
Hamilton
© Cadre Development

Traditional Style 333

Red shutters set a cheerful accent to the white wooden paneling on the facade of this two-story house. The large protruding gable provides space for a library on the ground floor and an additional bedroom on the second. The 1,116-square-foot ground floor features a generous room arrangement. The two-story foyer opens onto the formal living room, while the adjacent dining room has access to the discreet unit consisting of the kitchen with breakfast nook and family room with fireplace. The second floor, with 1,066 square feet, includes a master bedroom with walk-in closet and deluxe bath. Three additional bedrooms share a second full bath.

Design C0057-01-A
Stapleton II
© Cadre Development

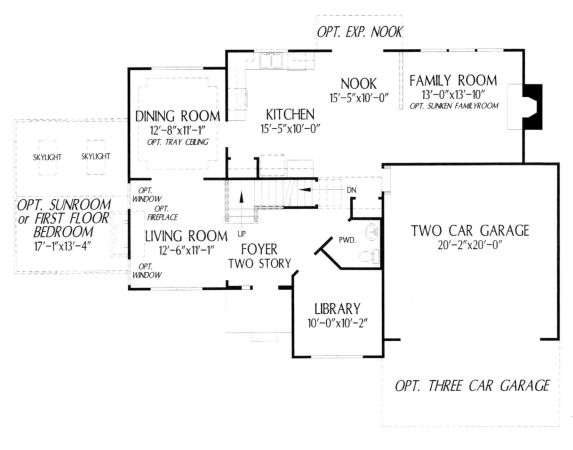

OPT. EXP. NOOK

NOOK
15'-5"x10'-0"

FAMILY ROOM
13'-0"x13'-10"
OPT. SUNKEN FAMILYROOM

DINING ROOM
12'-8"x11'-1"
OPT. TRAY CEILING

KITCHEN
15'-5"x10'-0"

SKYLIGHT   SKYLIGHT

OPT. SUNROOM
or FIRST FLOOR
BEDROOM
17'-1"x13'-4"

OPT. WINDOW

OPT. FIREPLACE

LIVING ROOM
12'-6"x11'-1"

OPT. WINDOW

DN

UP

FOYER
TWO STORY

PWD.

TWO CAR GARAGE
20'-2"x20'-0"

LIBRARY
10'-0"x10'-2"

OPT. THREE CAR GARAGE

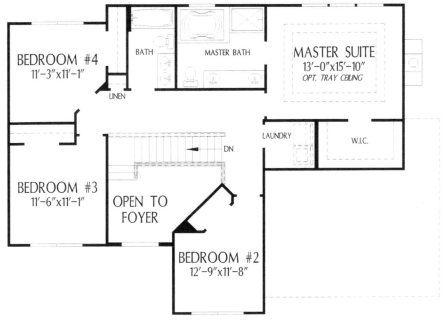

BEDROOM #4
11'-3"x11'-1"

BATH

MASTER BATH

MASTER SUITE
13'-0"x15'-10"
OPT. TRAY CEILING

LINEN

DN

BEDROOM #3
11'-6"x11'-1"

LAUNDRY

W.I.C.

OPEN TO
FOYER

BEDROOM #2
12'-9"x11'-8"

Traditional Style 335

VICTORIAN

STYLE

This design features a profusion of stylistically appropriate Victorian details. A circular porch surrounds the striking tower element with its hipped roof. The protruding gable element is graced with large latticed windows, and the white wood paneling makes a strong contrast to the varigated brick facade. The interior is dominated by the large living room with fireplace in the center of the house. The kitchen is placed between the dining room and breakfast room, while the master bedroom with deluxe bath completes the ground floor. On the second floor are three bedrooms, a game room and two full baths. The total living area of the house comprises 3,347 square feet.

Design HomeStyle
L–3347
© Larry W. Garnett & Associates, Inc.

UTIL

D W

BRKFST
11'-4" x 14'-8"
9'-0" CLG

PORCH

MASTER
BEDROOM
15'-4" x 17'-0"
9'-0" CLG

HALF
BATH

PANTRY

FRENCH DOOR

FRENCH DOOR

2-WAY FIREPLACE

LIN

UP

KITCH
11' x 13'
9'-0" CLG

GALLERY

RAISED
FOYER
8'-0" CLG

LIVING
25'-0" x 14'-4"
9'-0" CLG

BATH
9'-0" CLG

DINING
14'-4" x 11'-0"
9'-0" CLG

VERANDA

54'-0"

53'-0"

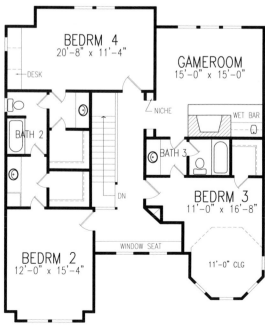

BEDRM 4
20'-8" x 11'-4"

GAMEROOM
15'-0" x 15'-0"

DESK

NICHE

WET BAR

BATH 2

BATH 3

DN

BEDRM 3
11'-0" x 16'-8"

BEDRM 2
12'-0" x 15'-4"

WINDOW SEAT

11'-0" CLG

Victorian Style 339

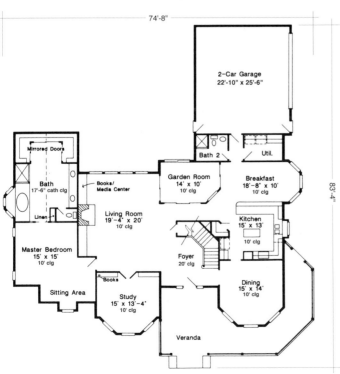

74'-8"

83'-4"

2-Car Garage
22'-10" x 25'-6"

Bath 2

Util.

Garden Room
14' x 10'
10' clg

Breakfast
18'-8" x 10'
10' clg

Mirrored Doors

Bath
17'-6" cath clg

Books/
Media Center

Living Room
19'-4" x 20'
10' clg

Kitchen
15' x 13'
10' clg

Linen

Master Bedroom
15' x 15'
10' clg

Books

Foyer
20' clg

Sitting Area

Study
15' x 13'-4"
10' clg

Dining
15' x 14'
10' clg

Veranda

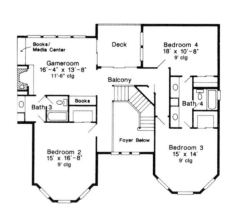

Books/
Media Center

Deck

Bedroom 4
18' x 10'-8"
9' clg

Gameroom
16'-4" x 13'-8"
11'-6" clg

Balcony

Bath 3

Books

Bath 4

Bedroom 2
15' x 16'-8"
9' clg

Foyer Below

Bedroom 3
15' x 14'
9' clg

Design HomeStyle
L-954-VC
© Larry W. Garnett & Associates,
Inc.

340 Victorian Style

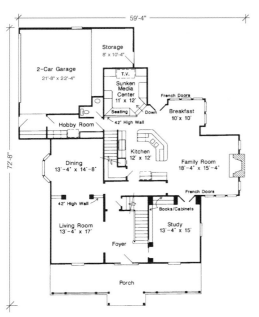

59'-4"

72'-8"

2-Car Garage
21'-8" x 22'-4"

Storage
8' x 10'-4"

T.V.

Sunken
Media
Center
11' x 12'

French Doors

Seating

Down

Breakfast
10' x 10'

Hobby Room

42" High Wall

Kitchen
12' x 12'

Dining
13'-4" x 14'-8"

Family Room
18'-4" x 15'-4"

42" High Wall

Books/Cabinets

French Doors

Living Room
13'-4" x 17'

Foyer

Study
13'-4" x 15'

Porch

Bedroom 2
13'-4" x 12'-4"

Bath 2

Util.

Deck

Bedroom 3
13'-4" x 12'-4"

Up To Optional
3rd Floor

French Doors

Bath 3

Down

Master Bedroom
18'-4" x 15'-4"

Marble
Pedestal

Books/Cabinets

Down

Dressing
Table

Bedroom 4
13'-4" x 12'-8"

Foyer
Below

Bath

Gazebo Clg.
At Tub

Exercise Room
11'-4" x 8'

Linen

Seat

Seat

Design HomeStyle
L-841-VSC
© Larry W. Garnett & Associates, Inc.

Victorian Style 341

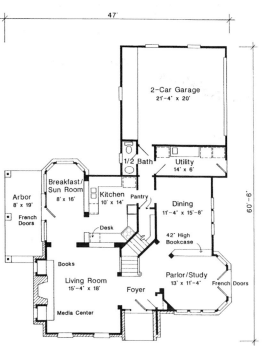

Design HomeStyle
L-720-CSB

© Larry W. Garnett &
Associates, Inc.

342 Victorian Style

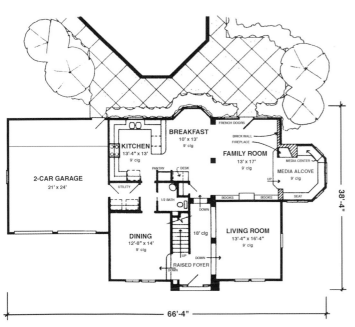

Floor plan labels (first floor):

- 2-CAR GARAGE 21' x 24'
- KITCHEN 13'-4" x 13' 9' clg
- BREAKFAST 10' x 13' 9' clg
- FAMILY ROOM 13' x 17' 9' clg
- FRENCH DOORS
- BRICK WALL
- FIREPLACE
- MEDIA CENTER
- MEDIA ALCOVE 9' clg
- PANTRY
- DESK
- UTILITY
- 1/2 BATH
- BOOKS
- BOOKS
- SEAT
- UP
- DOWN
- DINING 12'-8" x 14' 9' clg
- 18' clg
- LIVING ROOM 13'-4" x 16'-4" 9' clg
- UP
- DOWN
- DOWN
- RAISED FOYER
- 66'-4"
- 38'-4"

Floor plan labels (second floor):

- BEDROOM 3 12'-8" x 11' 9' clg
- BEDROOM 2 11'-8" x 11' 9' clg
- WIC
- BATH 1 9' clg
- SEAT 12' clg
- LINEN
- BATH 2
- LINEN
- DOWN
- BALCONY
- FOYER BELOW
- BEDROOM 4 12'-8" x 10' 9' clg
- MASTER BEDROOM 14' x 16' 9' clg
- SITTING AREA 9' x 7'-4"
- LINEN

Design HomeStyle
L-649-HB
© Larry W. Garnett & Associates, Inc.

Victorian Style 343

With its 2,454-square-foot floor plan, this exclusive estate house presents itself in homage to the Victorian epoch. The essential stylistic features of the age are lovingly replicated in numerous details. The rounded, wrap-around porch and imposing protruding tower element, which serves as a den or guest room on the ground floor and as a sitting area within the master suite on the second floor, indicate from the first glance that this is a home of the highest class. The beautifully designed windows and the restrained trim on the cornices reflect the elegance of the interior design.

Design HomeStyle
AX-1310
© Jerold Axelrod & Associates, P.C.

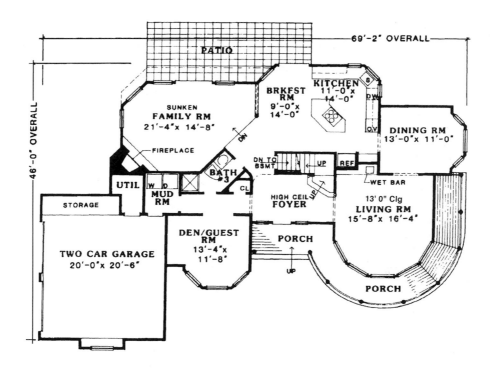

PATIO

69'-2" OVERALL

46'-0" OVERALL

KITCHEN
11'-0" x
14'-0"

BRKFST
RM
9'-0" x
14'-0"

SUNKEN
FAMILY RM
21'-4" x 14'-8"

DINING RM
13'-0" x 11'-0"

FIREPLACE

DN TO
BSMT

UP

REF

WET BAR

BATH
#3

CL

HIGH CEIL.
FOYER

13'-0" Clg
LIVING RM
15'-8" x 16'-4"

UTIL

W D

MUD
RM

STORAGE

DEN/GUEST
RM
13'-4" x
11'-8"

PORCH

UP

TWO CAR GARAGE
20'-0" x 20'-6"

PORCH

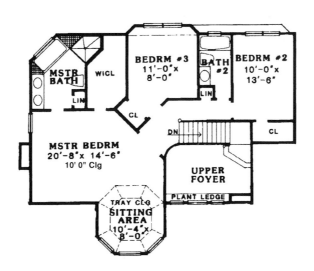

MSTR
BATH

WICL

BEDRM #3
11'-0" x
8'-0"

BATH
#2

BEDRM #2
10'-0" x
13'-6"

LIN

LIN

CL

DN

MSTR BEDRM
20'-8" x 14'-6"
10'-0" Clg

UPPER
FOYER

CL

TRAY CLG
SITTING
AREA
10'-4" x
8'-0"

PLANT LEDGE

Victorian Style 345

Photo © Mark Englund

The nostalgic atmosphere of this country house is clearly inspired by the Victorian tradition. The house offers a living area of 2,748 square feet distributed over two stories. The beautiful tower element rising from the broad, covered porch serves as a parlor on the ground floor of the house, and behind the bay window is the dining room. On the second floor are three spacious bedrooms and two baths.

**Design HomeStyle
V-2440**
© Historical Replications, Inc.

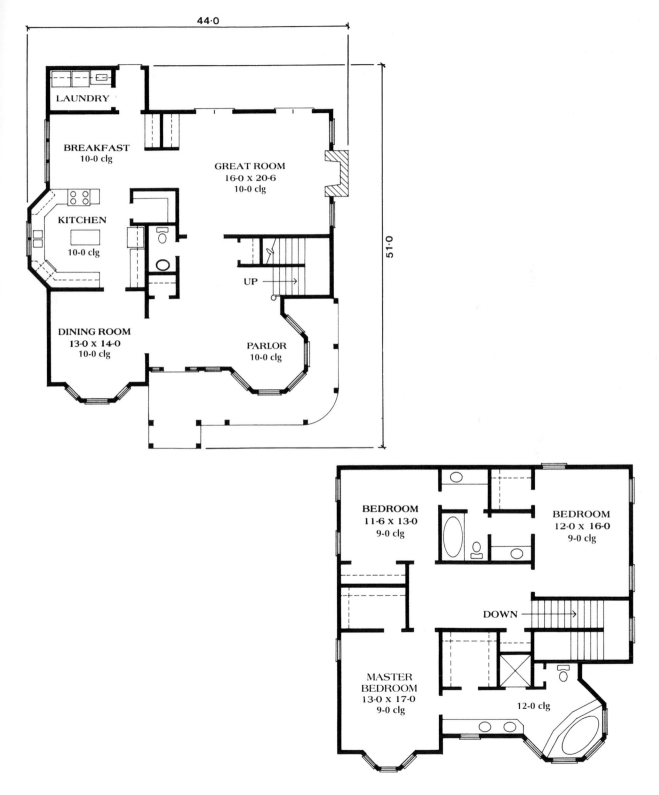

44·0

LAUNDRY

BREAKFAST
10-0 clg

GREAT ROOM
16-0 x 20-6
10-0 clg

51-0

KITCHEN

10-0 clg

UP

DINING ROOM
13-0 x 14-0
10-0 clg

PARLOR
10-0 clg

BEDROOM
11-6 x 13-0
9-0 clg

BEDROOM
12-0 x 16-0
9-0 clg

DOWN

MASTER
BEDROOM
13-0 x 17-0
9-0 clg

12-0 clg

Victorian Style 347

An imposing farmhouse design, this house offers a total floor plan of 2,438 square feet distributed over two full stories. The playful exterior of the design borrows much from the Victorian style.

Design HomeStyle
L-438-VSB
© Larry W. Garnett & Associates, Inc.

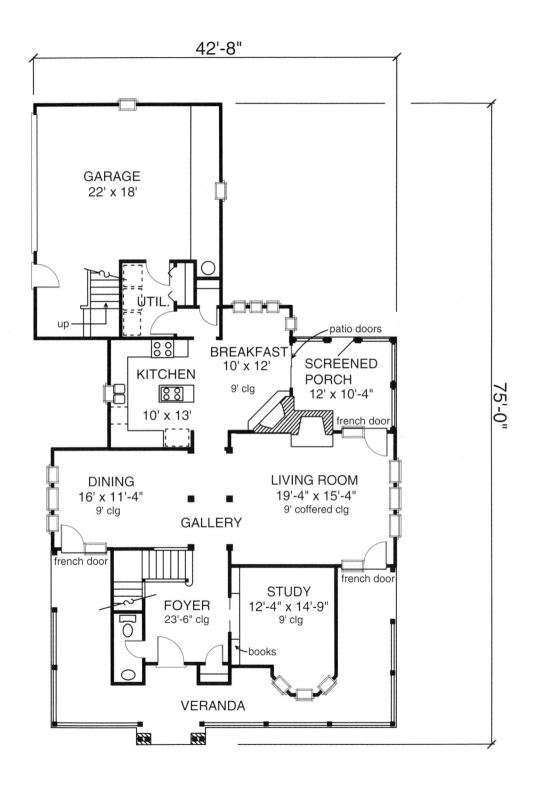

42'-8"

75'-0"

GARAGE
22' x 18'

up

UTIL.

KITCHEN
10' x 13'

BREAKFAST
10' x 12'
9' clg

patio doors

SCREENED
PORCH
12' x 10'-4"

french door

DINING
16' x 11'-4"
9' clg

LIVING ROOM
19'-4" x 15'-4"
9' coffered clg

GALLERY

french door

french door

FOYER
23'-6" clg

STUDY
12'-4" x 14'-9"
9' clg

books

VERANDA

Victorian Style 349

This charming country house design presents all the essential stylistic features characteristic of the romantic Victorian era. Fans of nostalgic architecture will treasure its 2,406-square-foot design. Offset roofs, gables, and bay windows give the house its special character. The rear of the house also features a broad covered porch, reflecting the imaginative, open and inviting floor plan on the ground and second floors.

Design HomeStyle
L-408-VB
© Larry W. Garnett & Associates, Inc.

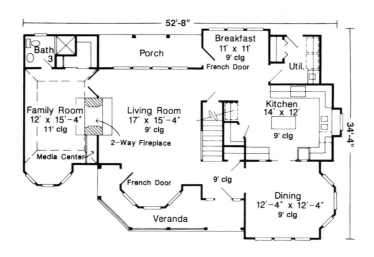

Victorian Style 351

The harmonious impression made by this stately country design is produced by the uniform use of wooden shingles on the facade. The porch with balcony and the light-colored window frames form a beautiful contrast to the shingles. The striking tower, which serves as a study on the ground floor and as a comfortable sitting area on the second floor, lends the design a nostalgic touch. The elegance of the exterior of this 4,129-square-foot house reflects the well-designed floor plan of the interior. The ground floor is devoted exclusively to active daily life, while four or five bedrooms are located on the second story.

**Design HomeStyle
L023-HD**
© Larry W. Garnett & Associates, Inc.

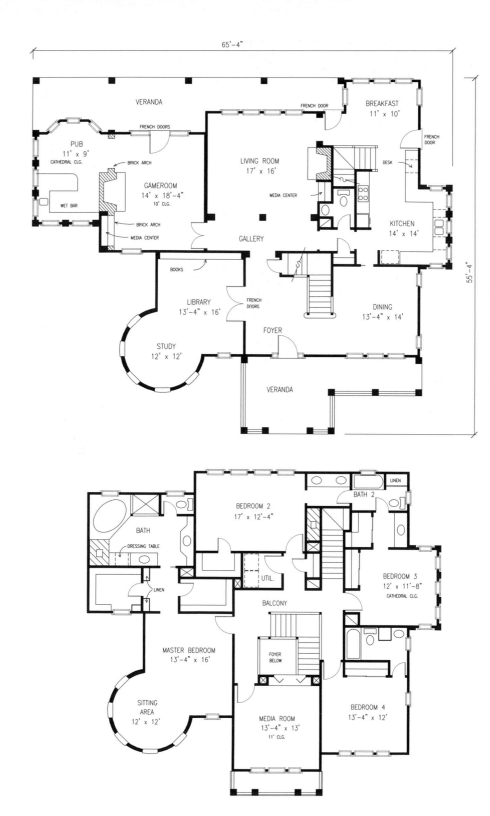

VERANDA

FRENCH DOOR

BREAKFAST
11' x 10'

FRENCH DOORS

FRENCH
DOOR

PUB
11' x 9'
CATHEDRAL CLG.

BRICK ARCH

LIVING ROOM
17' x 16'

DESK

WET BAR

GAMEROOM
14' x 18'-4"
10' CLG.

MEDIA CENTER

KITCHEN
14' x 14'

BRICK ARCH

MEDIA CENTER

GALLERY

BOOKS

LIBRARY
13'-4" x 16'

FRENCH
DOORS

DINING
13'-4" x 14'

FOYER

STUDY
12' x 12'

VERANDA

BEDROOM 2
17' x 12'-4"

BATH 2

LINEN

BATH

DRESSING TABLE

LINEN

UTIL.

BEDROOM 3
12' x 11'-8"
CATHEDRAL CLG.

BALCONY

MASTER BEDROOM
13'-4" x 16'

FOYER
BELOW

SITTING
AREA
12' x 12'

MEDIA ROOM
13'-4" x 13'
11' CLG.

BEDROOM 4
13'-4" x 12'

65'-4"

55'-4"

Victorian Style 353

The playful treatment of forms and accessories that characterizes the Victorian style gives this house its unmistakable flair. The obligatory tower element and roof designs, the broad covered porches, the richly detailed railings and gables, and last but not least, the elaborate design of the facade with shingles and clapboards are a necessary part of an original Victorian house. This successful design contains a total of 1,938 square feet distributed over two stories, and can be built with either three or four bedrooms.

Design 5162–Homes for Today
© Augustus Suglia, Architect

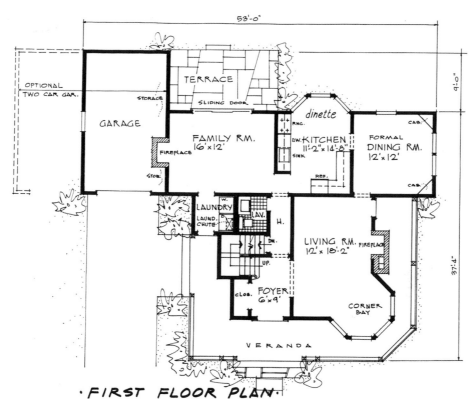

53'-0"

9'-0"

OPTIONAL
TWO CAR GAR.

TERRACE

STORAGE

SLIDING DOOR

GARAGE

dinette

RNG.

CAB.

FAMILY RM.
16'x12'

FIREPLACE

DW. KITCHEN
11'-2"x14'-8"

FORMAL
DINING RM.
12'x12'

SINK

STOR.

REF.

CAB.

37'-4"

LAUNDRY

W.

LAV.

D.

LAUND.
CHUTE

H.

LIVING RM.
12'x18'-2"

FIREPLACE

DN.

UP.

CLOS.

FOYER
6'x9'

CORNER
BAY

VERANDA

·FIRST FLOOR PLAN·

B.R.#2
12'x12'

CLO.

B.R.#4
10'-6"x10'-8"

CLO.

B.R.#3
12'x12'

CLO.

LIN.

HALL

·ALTERNATE 4 BED RM. PLAN·

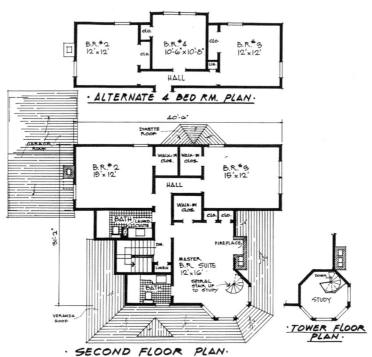

40'-6"

DINETTE
ROOF

GARAGE
ROOF

WALK-IN
CLOS.

WALK-IN
CLOS.

B.R.#2
15'x12'

HALL

B.R.#3
15'x12'

31'-2"

WALK-IN
CLOS.

CLO.

CLO.

FIREPLACE

BATH

LAUND.
CHUTE

DN.

LINEN

MASTER
B.R. SUITE
12'x16'

SPIRAL
STAIR UP
TO STUDY

DOWN

BATH

STUDY

VERANDA
ROOF

·SECOND FLOOR PLAN·

·TOWER FLOOR
PLAN·

Victorian Style 355

This design, closely based on Victorian models, is ideally suited to a narrow lot. This modern variation also includes a garage for automobiles. The interplay among wooden paneling, bricks, and shingles is interesting and directs the viewer's attention to the beautifully designed arched window frames. The path to the house, beneath a richly decorated entry porch, leads past the two-car garage. The bright foyer allows a bier into the spacious great room with its high vaulted ceiling. The kitchen with a breakfast room in the bay has direct access to the dining room and a laundry room. The second floor features three bedrooms and two baths, and allows an unobstructed view into the great room below.

Design 5175–Homes for Today
© Augustus Suglia, Architect

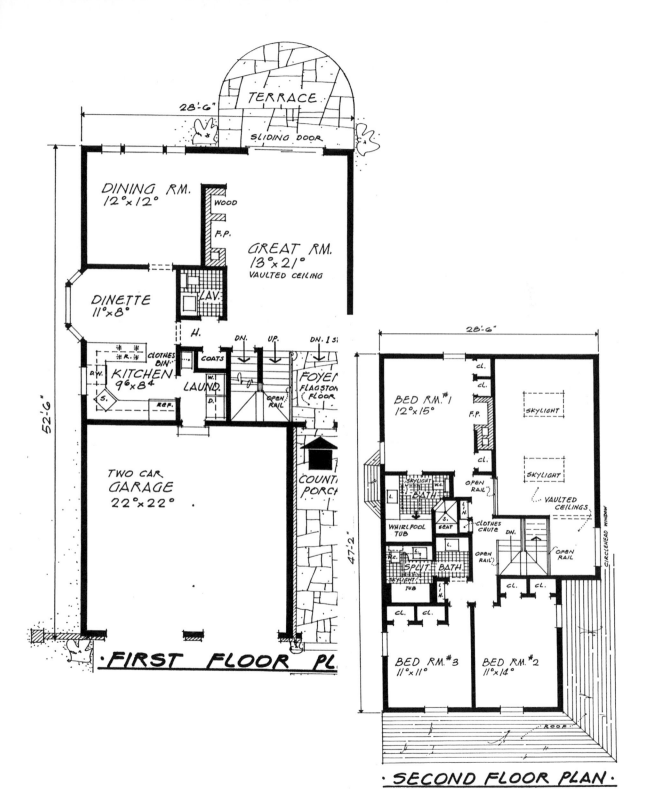

TERRACE

SLIDING DOOR

28'-6"

DINING RM.
12°x12°

WOOD

F.P.

GREAT RM.
13°x21°
VAULTED CEILING

DINETTE
11°x8°

LAV.

52'-6"

H.

CLOTHES
BIN

COATS

DN.   UP.   DN. 1 St

KITCHEN
9°x8⁴

D.W.

LAUND.

OPEN
RAIL

FOYER
FLAGSTONE
FLOOR

REF.

TWO CAR
GARAGE
22°x22°

COUNTRY
PORCH

·FIRST FLOOR PL

28'-6"

cl.
cl.

BED RM.#1
12°x15°

F.P.

SKYLIGHT

47'-2"

cl.

SKYLIGHT

BATH

W.C.

OPEN
RAIL

VAULTED
CEILINGS

WHIRLPOOL
TUB

SEAT

CLOTHES
CHUTE

DN.

OPEN
RAIL

W.C.

SPLIT BATH

OPEN
RAIL

CIRCLEHEAD WINDOW

SKYLIGHT
TUB

cl.
cl.

cl.   cl.

cl.   cl.

BED RM.#3
11°x11°

BED RM.#2
11°x14°

ROOF

·SECOND FLOOR PLAN·

Victorian Style 357

An exemplary model of the elaborate architecture of Victorian houses, this design offers the entire spectrum of historically accurate forms and follows the authentic model down to the last detail. A wide stairway dominates the generously proportioned foyer, while the parlor to the side of the foyer features a window seat. The formal dining room allows access to the kitchen through a butler's pantry. Toward the garden, the great room with fireplace features high, wide French doors that open onto the terrace. The master bedroom on the second floor of the house also has a fireplace, an adjacent dressing room with built-in closets, and an exclusive bath with whirlpool and shower. The two additional bedrooms share a large full bath.

Design 5180-Homes for Today
© Augustus Suglia, Architect

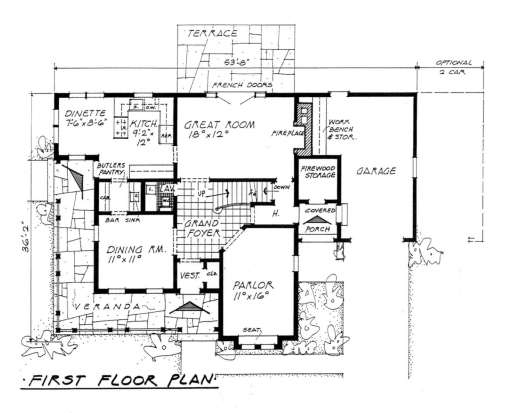

FIRST FLOOR PLAN

TERRACE

53'-8"

FRENCH DOORS

OPTIONAL 2 CAR

DINETTE 7'-6" x 8'-6"

KITCH. 9'-2" x 12°

GREAT ROOM 18° x 12°

WORK BENCH & STOR.

FIREPLACE

BUTLERS PANTRY

FIREWOOD STORAGE

GARAGE

CAB.

LAV.

UP

DOWN

BAR SINK

H.

COVERED PORCH

36'-2"

DINING RM. 11° x 11°

GRAND FOYER

VEST.

CLO.

PARLOR 11° x 16°

VERANDA

SEAT

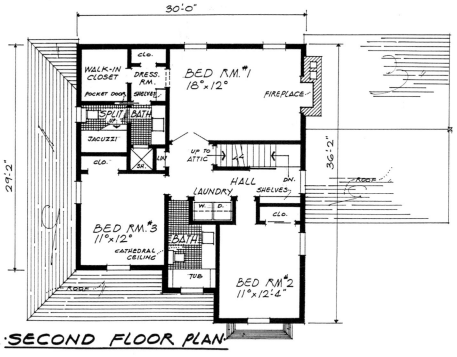

SECOND FLOOR PLAN

30'-0"

CLO.

WALK-IN CLOSET

DRESS. RM.

BED RM. #1 18° x 12°

FIREPLACE

POCKET DOOR

SHELVES

SPLIT BATH

UP

JACUZZI

CLO.

SH.

LIN.

UP TO ATTIC

36'-2"

29'-2"

HALL

DN.

ROOF

LAUNDRY

SHELVES

W. D.

CLO.

BED RM. #3 11° x 12°

BATH

CATHEDRAL CEILING

TUB

BED RM. #2 11° x 12'-4"

ROOF

With this house, the leading designer of Victorian-style architecture has succeeded in retaining the important elements of a typically imaginative Victorian exterior without any loss of modern comfort. Among the impressive details is the wrap-around porch and an imposing tower element that serves as a foyer on the ground floor and as an exclusive bath on the second floor. The 1,134-square-foot ground floor features an ideal floor plan. The elaborate stairs in the circular foyer immediately suggest the overriding elegance of the house. Bordered by the wrap-around porch, the parlor with fireplace is situated on the left side of the house. The centrally located kitchen allows access to the dining room as well as the family room with fireplace. Sliding glass doors lead from there to the garden terrace. On the upper floor, in addition to the master suite with deluxe bath, are three further bedrooms that share a full bath.

Design 5190-Homes for Today
© Augustus Suglia, Architect

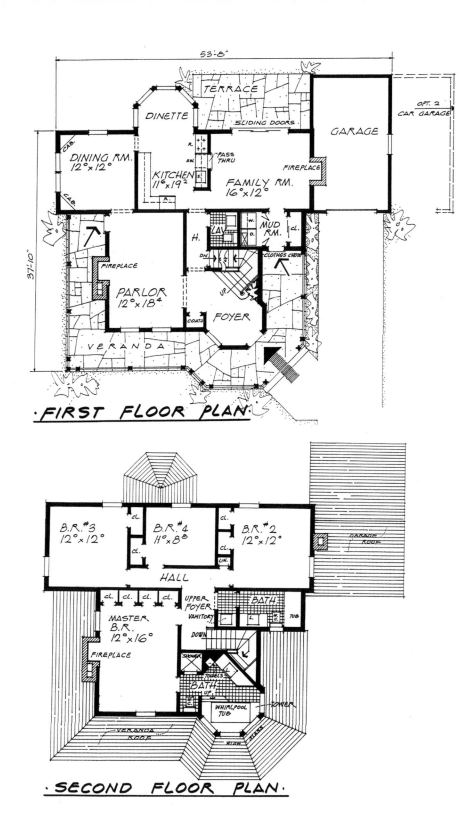

·FIRST FLOOR PLAN·

53'-8"

TERRACE

DINETTE

SLIDING DOORS

GARAGE

OPT. 2 CAR GARAGE

DINING RM. 12°×12°

CAB.

KITCHEN 11⁶×19²

PASS THRU

R.

AW.

FAMILY RM. 16°×12°

FIREPLACE

37'-10"

CAB.

R.

W.

D.

LAV.

MUD RM.

cl.

H.

CLOTHES CHUTE

FIREPLACE

PARLOR 12°×18⁴

DN.

UP.

FOYER

COATS

VERANDA

·SECOND FLOOR PLAN·

B.R. #3 12°×12°

cl.

B.R. #4 11°×8⁸

cl.

B.R. #2 12°×12°

GARAGE ROOF

cl.

cl.

LIN.

HALL

cl. cl. cl. cl.

UPPER FOYER

BATH

VANITORY

L.

TUB

MASTER B.R. 12°×16°

DOWN

FIREPLACE

SHOWER

BATH

TOWELS

W.C.

UP

WHIRLPOOL TUB

TOWER

VERANDA ROOF

HIGH ROOF

Victorian Style 361

The nostalgic impression created by this country house derives from the arched window frames that combine with the broad porch into a harmonious ensemble. The gable decorations and elaborately turned posts and railing of the entry porch are clear references to Victorian influence on the design. The interior of the house is modern and comfortable. On the right side of the house is the daily living area with dining room, kitchen with snack bar and a striking glass bay for a breakfast area. The great room with vaulted ceiling and fireplace forms the center of the house. Adjacent to it is the master suite with deluxe bath. On the second floor are three large bedrooms and two full baths.

Design 5200–Homes for Today
© Augustus Suglia, Architect

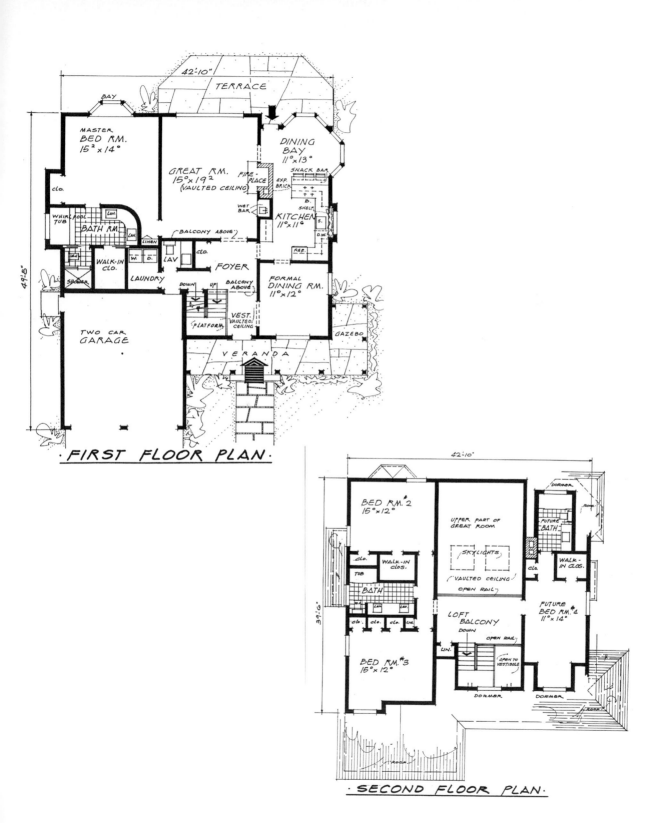

· FIRST FLOOR PLAN ·

· SECOND FLOOR PLAN ·

Victorian Style 363

A large, beautifully designed window graces the central dormer gable of this stately country house. The Victorian influence continues with the richly decorated porch, and the restrained gable decoration sets a further accent. Many large windows adorn the classical wooden exterior, allowing the relatively open interior to be flooded with light. On the 1,615-square-foot ground floor are the dining room, kitchen with breakfast room, and in the center, the two-story great room with direct access to a garden terrace. The great room also opens onto the study with its own fireplace. The master suite, located to the front of the house, features a large bath with double sinks, a shower, whirlpool and separate toilet. A walk-in closet and other built-in closets are included in the design. The stairs to the second floor open onto a loft that allows a free view into the foyer and the great room lying opposite. Two further bedrooms, each with generous closet space, and a full bath are located here.

Design 5201-Homes for Today
© Augustus Suglia, Architect

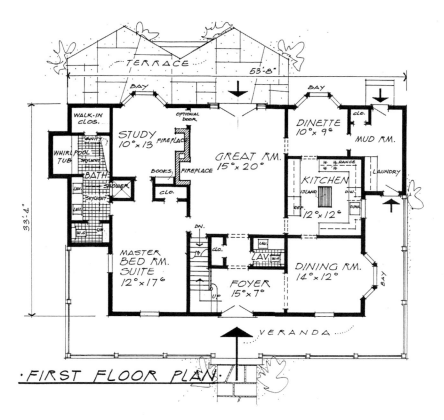

Labels in First Floor Plan:

TERRACE

53'-8"

BAY · BAY

WALK-IN CLOS.

STUDY 10°×13

OPTIONAL DOOR

CLO.

DINETTE 10°×9°

MUD RM.

VANITY

WHIRLPOOL TUB

SKYLIGHT

BATH

SHOWER

SKYLIGHT

LAV.

LAV.

W.C.

L/H

GREAT RM. 15°×20°

BOOKS. FIREPLACE

FIREPLACE

CLO.

RANGE

KITCHEN

ISLAND

REF.

D.W.

12°×12°

LAUNDRY

33'-4"

MASTER BED RM. SUITE 12°×17⁶

DN.

CLO.

UP

LAV.

LAV.

FOYER 15°×7°

DINING RM. 14°×12°

BAY

VERANDA

·FIRST FLOOR PLAN·

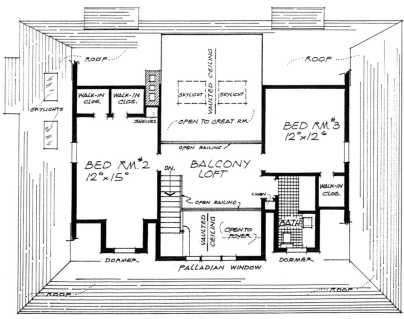

Labels in Second Floor Plan:

ROOF · ROOF

SKYLIGHTS

WALK-IN CLOS. · WALK-IN CLOS.

SHELVES

VAULTED CEILING

SKYLIGHT · SKYLIGHT

OPEN TO GREAT RM.

OPEN RAILING

BED RM. #3 12°×12⁶

BED RM. #2 12°×15°

DN.

BALCONY LOFT

OPEN RAILING

LINEN

WALK-IN CLOS.

VAULTED CEILING

OPEN TO FOYER

BATH

DORMER

PALLADIAN WINDOW

DORMER

ROOF · ROOF

·SECOND FLOOR PLAN·

The spectacular tower element lends a special character to this country house. Together with the elaborate design of the facade, the tower is an attractive eye-catcher. This Victorian design distinguishes itself from traditional country houses with its unusual window design and the restrained color of the wood paneling and shingles. With its 1,421 square feet of living space, the ground floor features a large country kitchen with access to a mud and utility room toward the garden terrace, and a generously designed living area with the two-story great room, and the dining room. To the rear of the house is the master bedroom with bath and walk-in closet. The tower stairs lead to the second floor with two bedrooms and a full bath.

Design 5202–Homes for Today
© Augustus Suglia, Architect

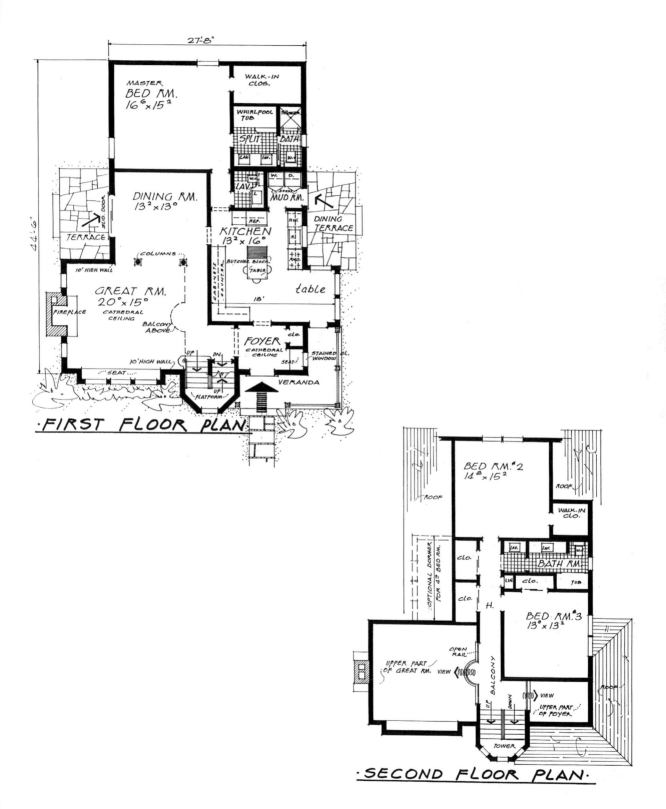

·FIRST FLOOR PLAN·

27'-8"

44'-6"

MASTER
BED RM.
16⁶×15²

WALK-IN
CLOS.

WHIRLPOOL
TUB

SHOWER

SPLIT

BATH

LAV.

LAV.

W.

W.C.

LAV.

L.

W. D.

DOOR

MUD RM.

DINING RM.
13²×13⁰

REF.

KITCHEN
13²×16⁰

AW.

DINING
TERRACE

TERRACE

SKID DOOR

COLUMNS

CABINETS COUNTER

BUTCHER BLOCK
TABLE

table

TRASH
RM.

10' HIGH WALL

GREAT RM.
20⁰×15⁰
CATHEDRAL
CEILING

BALCONY
ABOVE

18'

FIREPLACE

clo.

FOYER
CATHEDRAL
CEILING

STAINED GL.
WINDOW

10' HIGH WALL

UP

DN

SEAT

SEAT

UP
PLATFORM

VERANDA

·SECOND FLOOR PLAN·

BED RM.#2
14⁸×15²

ROOF

ROOF

WALK-IN
CLO.

OPTIONAL DORMER
FOR 4ᵗʰ BED RM.

clo.

LAV.

LAV.

W.

BATH RM

clo.

LIN

clo.

TUB

H.

UPPER PART
OF GREAT RM.

OPEN
RAIL

VIEW

BED RM.#3
13⁰×13²

UP BALCONY

DOWN

VIEW

UPPER PART
OF FOYER

VIEW

ROOF

TOWER

Victorian Style 367

FARMHOUSES

Photo © Mark Englund / HomeStyles

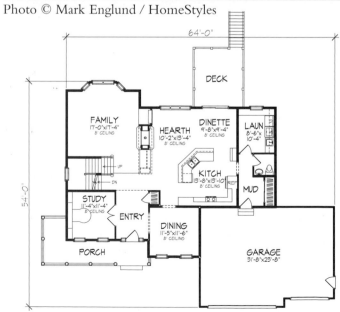

64'-0"

DECK

FAMILY
17'-0"x17'-4"
8' CEILING

HEARTH
10'-2"x13'-4"
8' CEILING

DINETTE
9'-8"x9'-4"
8' CEILING

LAUN
8'-6"x
10'-4"

54'-0"

KITCH
13'-8"x13'-10"
8' CEILING

MUD

STUDY
11'-4"x11'-4"
8' CEILING

ENTRY

DINING
11'-5"x11'-6"
8' CEILING

GARAGE
31'-8"x23'-8"

PORCH

MASTER
SUITE
15'-6"x17'-0"
TRAY

MSTR
BATH

BDRM 2
11'-4"x11'-0"
8' CEILING

W.I.C.

HALL

BATH

DN   RAILING

BDRM 4
11'-4"x11'-6"
8' CEILING

OPEN TO
BELOW

BDRM 3
11'-5"x11'-4"
8' CEILING

Design HomeStyle
L-97800-HB
© LifeStyle HomeDesign

370 Farmhouses

Photo © Mark Englund / HomeStyles

Design HomeStyle
LS-97841-RE
© Lifestyle HomeDesign

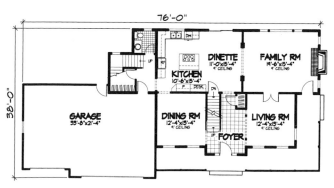

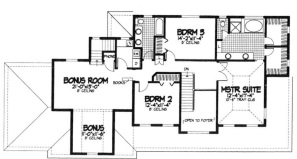

The porch that stretches across the front of this house provides an interesting frame for the symmetrically arranged windows, and the white posts and railing are a beautiful contrast to the wooden facade. With a total living area of 3,142 square feet, this design is ideal for larger families. The floor pan includes four bedrooms, but an additional room designated in the plans as a game room can be remodeled according to desire. One of the highlights of this home is the generous country kitchen, designed to be the heart of family life.

**Design HomeStyle
DD-3098-C**
© Danze & Davis Architects, Inc.

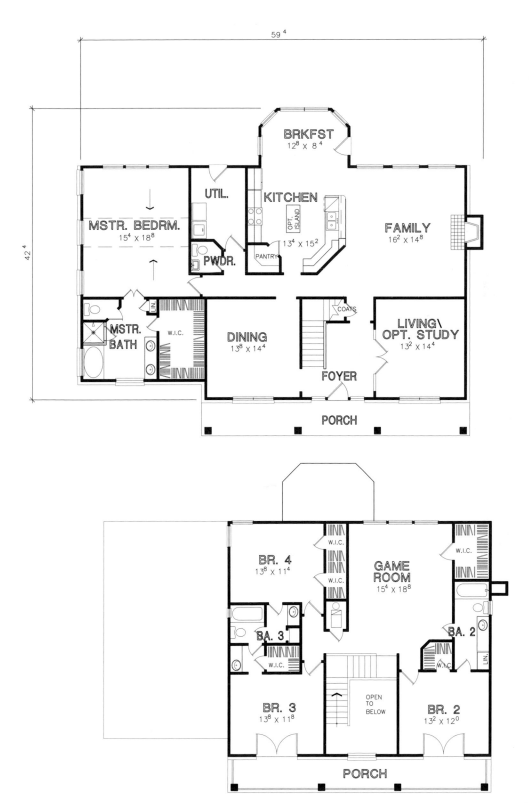

59⁴

42⁴

BRKFST
12⁸ X 8⁴

UTIL.

KITCHEN
13⁴ X 15²

OPT. ISLAND

MSTR. BEDRM.
15⁴ X 18⁸

FAMILY
16² X 14⁸

PWDR.

PANTRY

LIN.

W.I.C.

MSTR. BATH

DINING
13⁸ X 14⁴

COATS

LIVING\ OPT. STUDY
13² X 14⁴

FOYER

PORCH

BR. 4
13⁸ X 11⁴

W.I.C.

GAME ROOM
15⁴ X 18⁸

W.I.C.

W.I.C.

BA. 3

BA. 2

W.I.C.

LIN.

BR. 3
13⁸ X 11⁸

OPEN TO BELOW

BR. 2
13² X 12⁰

PORCH

Farmhouses 373

The special features of this nostalgic farm-house design are the wrap-around porch and the numerous sun decks. The rich use of windows in the front suggests a bright, well-lit interior. The floor plan on the ground floor is devoted exclusively to daily life, while the second floor offers four bedrooms and three full baths.

**Design HomeStyle
DD-2757**
© Danze & Davis Architects, Inc.

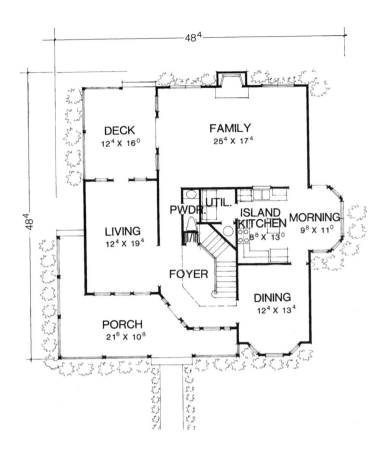

48⁴

48⁴

DECK
12⁴ X 16⁰

FAMILY
25⁴ X 17⁴

PWDR.

UTIL.

ISLAND
KITCHEN
8⁸ X 13⁰

MORNING
9⁸ X 11⁰

LIVING
12⁴ X 19⁴

FOYER

DINING
12⁴ X 13⁴

PORCH
21⁶ X 10⁸

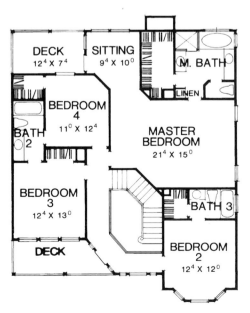

DECK
12⁴ X 7⁴

SITTING
9⁴ X 10⁰

M. BATH

BEDROOM
4
11⁰ X 12⁴

LINEN

BATH
2

MASTER
BEDROOM
21⁴ X 15⁰

BEDROOM
3
12⁴ X 13⁰

BATH 3

DECK

BEDROOM
2
12⁴ X 12⁰

Farmhouses 375

The large front windows and a wrap-around vernal supported on posts distinguish the exterior of this lovely two-story farmhouse design. The total living area of 2,578 square feet is distributed over both stories. On the ground floor are the dining room, a formal living room, a country kitchen with breakfast area, a family room with fireplace, a utility room, and a master suite with its own bath and walk-in closet. On the second floor are two bedrooms and a full bath. The plan offers an additional large space above the two-car garage that could be finished as a hobby room or additional bedroom.

**Design HomeStyle
DD-2127**
© Danze & Davis Architects, Inc.

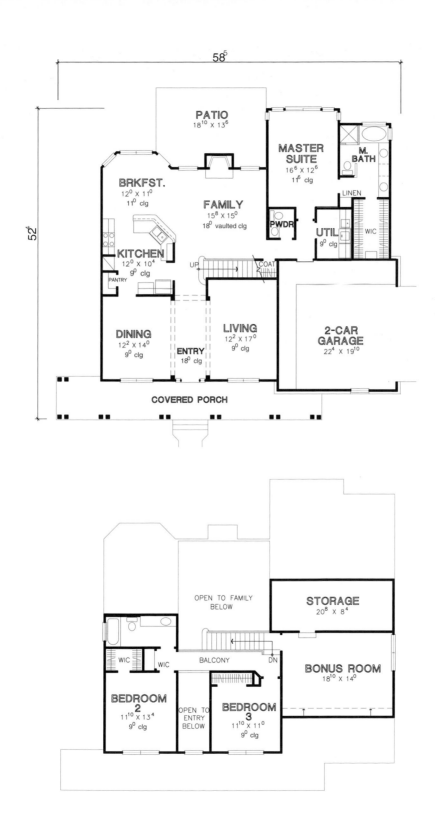

58⁵

52⁴

PATIO
18¹⁰ X 13⁶

MASTER SUITE
16⁶ X 12⁶
11⁶ clg

M. BATH

LINEN

BRKFST.
12⁰ X 11⁰
11⁰ clg

FAMILY
15⁸ X 15⁰
18⁰ vaulted clg

PWDR

UTIL
9⁰ clg

WIC

KITCHEN
12⁰ X 10⁴
9⁰ clg

PANTRY

UP

COAT

DINING
12² X 14⁰
9⁰ clg

ENTRY
18⁰ clg

LIVING
12² X 17⁰
9⁰ clg

2-CAR GARAGE
22⁴ X 19¹⁰

COVERED PORCH

OPEN TO FAMILY BELOW

STORAGE
20⁸ X 8⁴

WIC

WIC

BALCONY

DN

BONUS ROOM
18¹⁰ X 14⁰

BEDROOM 2
11¹⁰ X 13⁴
9⁰ clg

OPEN TO ENTRY BELOW

BEDROOM 3
11¹⁰ X 11⁰
9⁰ clg

Farmhouses 377

Photo © Mark Englund / HomeStyles

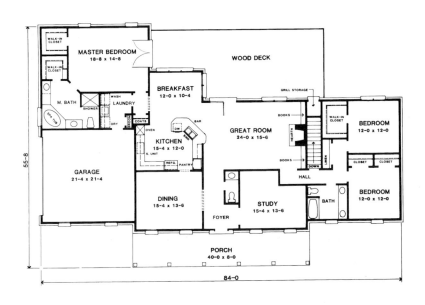

This country-style design offers 2,485 square feet of living area on a single story.

**Design HomeStyle
C-9525**
© Corley Plan Services, Inc.

Photo © Mark Englund / HomeStyles

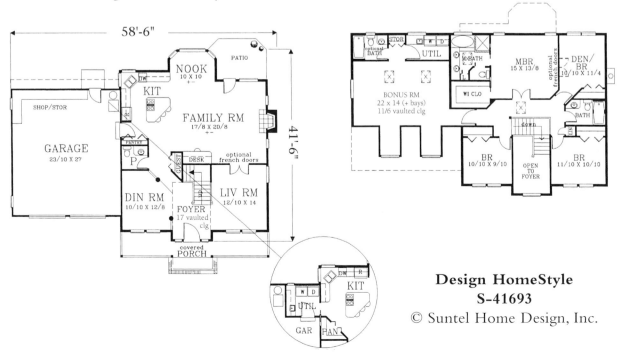

58'-6"

NOOK
10 X 10
+ -

PATIO

KIT

DW

FAMILY RM
17/8 X 20/8
+ -

41'-6"

SHOP/STOR

GARAGE
23/10 X 27

PANTRY

GUEST

DESK

optional
french doors

P

DIN RM
10/10 X 12/8

FOYER
17 vaulted
clg

LIV RM
12/10 X 14

covered
PORCH

DW   R
W D

KIT

UTIL

GAR   PAN

STOR   W D

optional
BATH

UTIL

M BATH

BONUS RM
22 x 14 (+ bays)
11/6 vaulted clg

WI CLO

MBR
15 X 13/8

DEN/
BR
10/10 X 11/4

optional french doors

BATH

BR
10/10 X 9/10

down

OPEN
TO
FOYER

LIN

BR
11/10 X 10/10

**Design HomeStyle
S-41693**

© Suntel Home Design, Inc.

Farmhouses 379

A distinctive feature of this impressive farmhouse-style design is its wide, wrap-around porch, which is typical for this architectural style. Above the wide front door is a beautifully decorated gable with an elegant arched window. The floor plan of the 3,014-square-foothouse is clearly organized. Situated at the rear of the house, both the breakfast room and the master suite feature bay windows. In addition, the exclusive master bath is very comfortably fitted with a whirlpool, a shower, double sinks and two walk-in closets.

Design HomeStyle
AX-95335
© Jerold Axelrod & Associates, Inc.

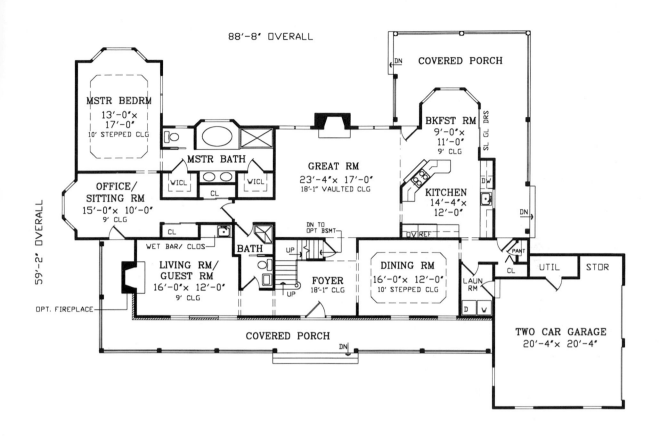

88'-8" OVERALL

59'-2" OVERALL

COVERED PORCH

DN

MSTR BEDRM
13'-0" x
17'-0"
10' STEPPED CLG

BKFST RM
9'-0" x
11'-0"
9' CLG

SL GL DRS

MSTR BATH

WICL

CL

WICL

GREAT RM
23'-4" x 17'-0"
18'-1" VAULTED CLG

KITCHEN
14'-4" x
12'-0"

DW

OFFICE/
SITTING RM
15'-0" x 10'-0"
9' CLG

DN

CL

WET BAR/ CLOS

BATH

UP

DN TO
OPT BSMT

UP

DV REF

PANT

CL

UTIL

STOR

LIVING RM/
GUEST RM
16'-0" x 12'-0"
9' CLG

FOYER
18'-1" CLG

DINING RM
16'-0" x 12'-0"
10' STEPPED CLG

LAUN
RM

OPT. FIREPLACE

D W

TWO CAR GARAGE
20'-4" x 20'-4"

COVERED PORCH

DN

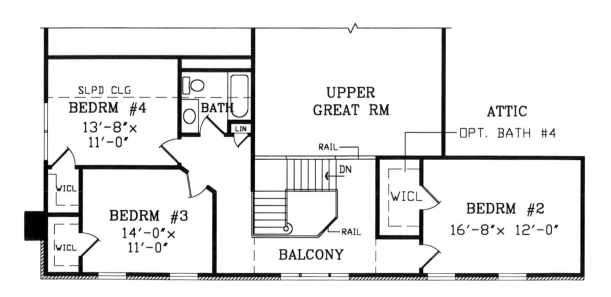

SLPD CLG

BEDRM #4
13'-8" x
11'-0"

BATH

LIN

UPPER
GREAT RM

ATTIC

OPT. BATH #4

RAIL

WICL

DN

WICL

BEDRM #3
14'-0" x
11'-0"

RAIL

BEDRM #2
16'-8" x 12'-0"

WICL

BALCONY

Photo © Mark Englund / HomeStyles

The striking feature of this country house is its large front porch, made especially charming by the fine detail work on the posts. With a living area of 3,153 square feet distributed over two stories, including four bedrooms and spacious living areas, this design is well-suited for a large family.

Design HomeStyle
E-3103
© Breland & Farmer Designers, Inc..

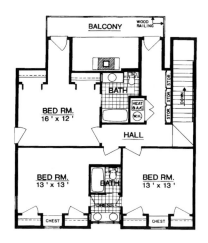

This classical farmhouse design with its living area of 3,102 square feet offers even large families plenty of space. The charm of the exterior derives from the wrap-around porch, whose architecturally fitting white railing and posts are in complete harmony with the numerous latticed windows and elaborate gable decoration.

Design HomeStyle
DD-3102
© Danze & Davis Architects, Inc.

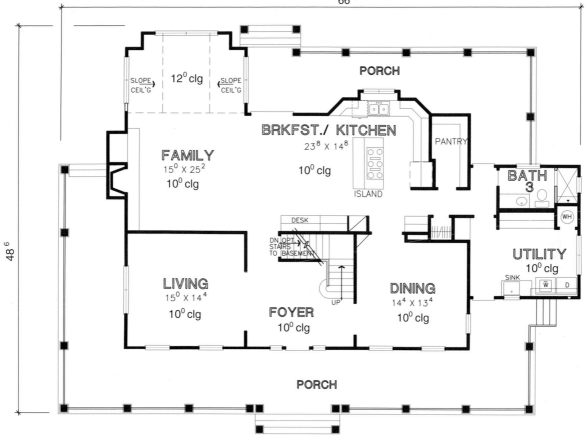

66⁴

48⁶

SLOPE CEIL'G → 12⁰ clg ← SLOPE CEIL'G

PORCH

FAMILY
15⁰ X 25²
10⁰ clg

BRKFST./ KITCHEN
23⁸ X 14⁸
10⁰ clg

PANTRY

ISLAND

BATH 3

UTILITY
10⁰ clg

WH

SINK W D

DESK

DN OPT. STAIRS TO BASEMENT

UP

LIVING
15⁰ X 14⁴
10⁰ clg

FOYER
10⁰ clg

DINING
14⁴ X 13⁴
10⁰ clg

PORCH

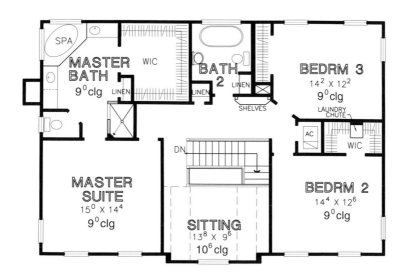

SPA

MASTER BATH
9⁰ clg

WIC

LINEN

BATH 2

LINEN

LINEN

SHELVES

BEDRM 3
14² X 12²
9⁰ clg

LAUNDRY CHUTE

AC

WIC

DN

MASTER SUITE
15⁰ X 14⁴
9⁰ clg

SITTING
13⁸ X 9⁶
10⁶ clg

BEDRM 2
14⁴ X 12⁶
9⁰ clg

Farmhouses 385

Photo © Mark Englund / HomeStyle

With its elegant brick facade, light latticed windows and contrasting shutters, this stately country house of 3,046 square feet makes an ideal home for a large family. The entry to the wrap-around porch acts as a frame for the beautifully designed front doorway.

**Design HomeStyle
C-9630**
© Corley Plan Service, Inc.

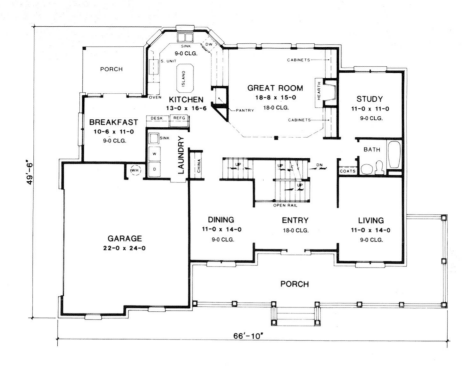

PORCH

KITCHEN
13-0 x 16-6

9-0 CLG.

SINK

S. UNIT

ISLAND

OVEN

GREAT ROOM
18-8 x 15-0
18-0 CLG.

CABINETS

HEARTH

CABINETS

PANTRY

STUDY
11-0 x 11-0
9-0 CLG.

BREAKFAST
10-6 x 11-0
9-0 CLG.

DESK   REFG

SINK

W

D

(WH)

LAUNDRY

CHINA

BATH

COATS

UP   UP   DN

OPEN RAIL

DINING
11-0 x 14-0
9-0 CLG.

ENTRY
18-0 CLG.

LIVING
11-0 x 14-0
9-0 CLG.

GARAGE
22-0 x 24-0

PORCH

49'-6"

66'-10"

COVERED
DECK

MASTER
BEDROOM
13-0 x 19-2
9-0 CLG.

GREAT ROOM
(below)

PLANT
SHELF

BEDROOM
11-0 x 12-0

SITTING
AREA

OPEN RAIL

CLOSET

BALCONY

SLOPE CLG.

LINEN

STOR

CLOSET

SLOPE CLG.

BATH

CLOSET

SPA
TUB

BATH
12-0 CLG.

SHOWER

SLOPE CLG.

LINEN

BEDROOM
11-0 x 13-6
10-0 CLG.

SLOPE CLG.

OPEN RAIL

ENTRY
(below)

SLOPE CLG.

BEDROOM
11-0 x 12-0
10-0 CLG.

KNEE
SPACE

BATH

CLOSET

Farmhouses 387

Photo © Mark Englund / HomeStyles

This imposing farmhouse offers every imaginable modern comfort. The exterior of the
design incorporates the essential historical
characteristics of the style. The center point of
the wide covered porch that wraps around the
house is a stately protruding gable with an
elegant arched window. This house offers
3,373 square feet of living space distributed
over two full stories.

**Design HomeStyle
AX-89304**
© Jerold Axelrod & Associates, P.C.

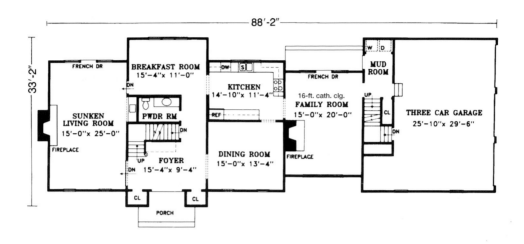

88'-2"

33'-2"

FRENCH DR

BREAKFAST ROOM
15'-4"x 11'-0"

DN

SUNKEN LIVING ROOM
15'-0"x 25'-0"

FIREPLACE

PWDR RM

DN

UP FOYER
DN 15'-4"x 9'-4"

CL

CL

PORCH

KITCHEN
14'-10"x 11'-4"

DW S

REF

DINING ROOM
15'-0"x 13'-4"

FRENCH DR

16-ft. cath. clg.
FAMILY ROOM
15'-0"x 20'-0"

FIREPLACE

W D

MUD ROOM

UP

CL

DN

THREE CAR GARAGE
25'-10"x 29'-6"

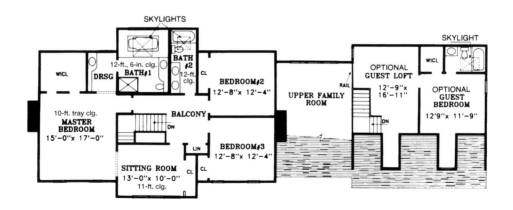

SKYLIGHTS

WICL

DRSG

BATH#1

12-ft., 6-in. clg.

BATH #2
12-ft. clg.

CL

BEDROOM#2
12'-8"x 12'-4"

10-ft. tray clg.
MASTER BEDROOM
15'-0"x 17'-0"

BALCONY

DN

LIN

BEDROOM#3
12'-8"x 12'-4"

SITTING ROOM
13'-0"x 10'-0"
11-ft. clg.

CL CL

UPPER FAMILY ROOM

RAIL

SKYLIGHT

WICL

OPTIONAL GUEST LOFT
12'-9"x 16'-11"

DN

OPTIONAL GUEST BEDROOM
12'9"x 11'-9"

This farmhouse, which stands on a slight hill, features a broad covered, wrap-around porch, whose elaborate details make it a work of art. The two-story house offers a total living area of 2,565 square feet and an array of spacious rooms designed to meet the needs of even a large family.

Design HomeStyle J-86134
© Larry James & Associates, Inc.

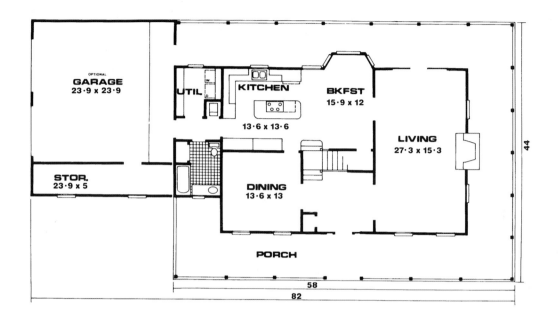

OPTIONAL
GARAGE
23·9 x 23·9

UTIL

KITCHEN
13·6 x 13·6

BKFST
15·9 x 12

LIVING
27·3 x 15·3

44

STOR.
23·9 x 5

DINING
13·6 x 13

PORCH

58

82

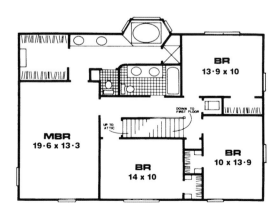

BR
13·9 x 10

MBR
19·6 x 13·3

DOWN TO
FIRST FLOOR

UP TO
ATTIC

BR
14 x 10

BR
10 x 13·9

Farmhouses 391

Photo © Mark Englund HomeStyles

This modern variation on a country farm-house offers a living area of 2,834 square feet distributed over two stories. The covered porch leads directly to the foyer, which is flanked by a dining room and living room. From the large kitchen one has access to a large pantry and to the laundry room. The highlight of the design is without doubt the centrally located, two-story family room with fireplace. On the second floor, in addition to the comfortable master suite with bath, are three further bedrooms and two full baths.

Design HomeStyle
FB-5010-Mary
© Frank Betz Associates, Inc.

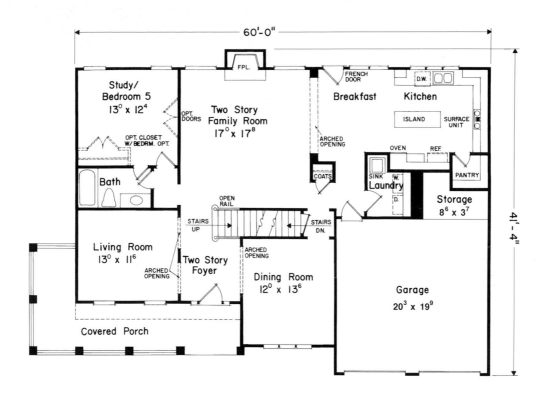

60'-0"

Study/
Bedroom 5
13⁰ x 12⁴

OPT.
DOORS

OPT. CLOSET
W/ BEDRM. OPT.

Bath

FPL.

Two Story
Family Room
17⁰ x 17⁸

ARCHED
OPENING

COATS

FRENCH
DOOR

D.W.

Breakfast

Kitchen

ISLAND

SURFACE
UNIT

OVEN

REF.

SINK

W.

Laundry

D.

PANTRY

Storage
8⁶ x 3⁷

OPEN
RAIL

STAIRS
UP

STAIRS
DN.

Living Room
13⁰ x 11⁶

ARCHED
OPENING

Two Story
Foyer

ARCHED
OPENING

Dining Room
12⁰ x 13⁶

Garage
20³ x 19⁹

Covered Porch

41'-4"

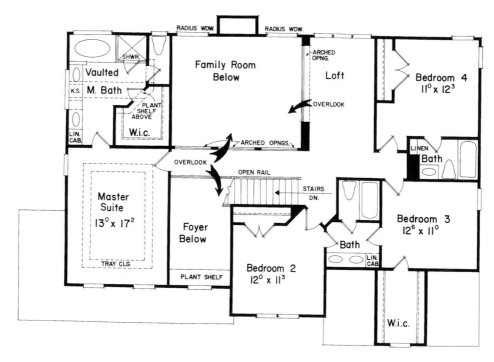

RADIUS WDW.

RADIUS WDW.

SHWR.

Vaulted

K.S.

M. Bath

PLANT
SHELF
ABOVE

W.i.c.

LIN.
CAB.

Family Room
Below

ARCHED
OPNG.

Loft

OVERLOOK

Bedroom 4
11⁰ x 12³

ARCHED OPNGS.

OVERLOOK

LINEN

Bath

Master
Suite
13⁰ x 17²

TRAY CLG.

OPEN RAIL

STAIRS
DN.

Foyer
Below

Bath

Bedroom 3
12⁶ x 11⁰

PLANT SHELF

Bedroom 2
12⁰ x 11³

LIN.
CAB.

W.i.c.

Farmhouses 393

The "Edgewood Trail" presents a combination of an authentic farmhouse of earlier times with the comforts of modern living. With its wide wrap-around front porch, horizontal paneling and a parapet on the metal roof, the design reflects classical elements of farmhouse style. The interior of the house, however, bears no trace of the simplicity associated with former times. High ceilings, large windows and bays give the interior a bright and friendly atmosphere. To the right of the centrally located grand room are the country kitchen and dining room. A parlor at the front of the house is available for formal occasions. The house features four bedrooms, two-and-a-half baths, and a two-car garage.

Design 6667
Edgewood Trail
© Sater Design

Living area 3,183 sq. ft.
Total 4,182 sq. ft.

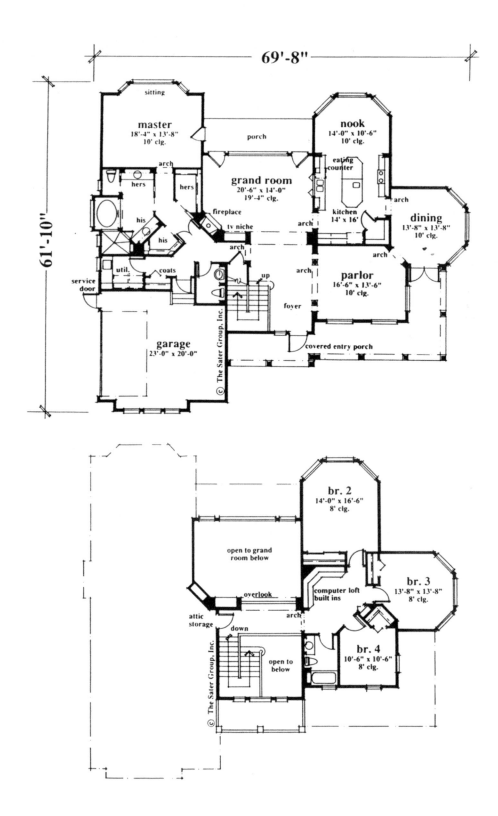

sitting

master
18'-4" x 13'-8"
10' clg.

porch

nook
14'-0" x 10'-6"
10' clg.

arch

hers

hers

his

his

grand room
20'-6" x 14'-0"
19'-4" clg.

fireplace

tv niche

arch

eating
counter

kitchen
14' x 16'

dining
13'-8" x 13'-8"
10' clg.

arch

arch

arch

arch

util.

coats

service
door

up

arch

foyer

parlor
16'-6" x 13'-6"
10' clg.

garage
23'-0" x 20'-0"

covered entry porch

© The Sater Group, Inc.

br. 2
14'-0" x 16'-6"
8' clg.

open to grand
room below

overlook

computer loft
built ins

br. 3
13'-8" x 13'-8"
8' clg.

attic
storage

down

arch

open to
below

br. 4
10'-6" x 10'-6"
8' clg.

© The Sater Group, Inc.

69'-8"

61'-10"

Farmhouses 395

This beautiful design is distinguished with a wide wrap-around porch and a center gable with a lovely arched window. The house has three chimneys, two of which stand on either gable end of the main house. The 2,932-square-foot interior offers a clearly arranged floor plan. On the ground floor, the large country kitchen and open family room form a discrete unit. The large master suite is fitted with a comfortable private bath.

Design HomeStyle
L–934–VSB
© Larry W. Garnett & Associates, Inc.

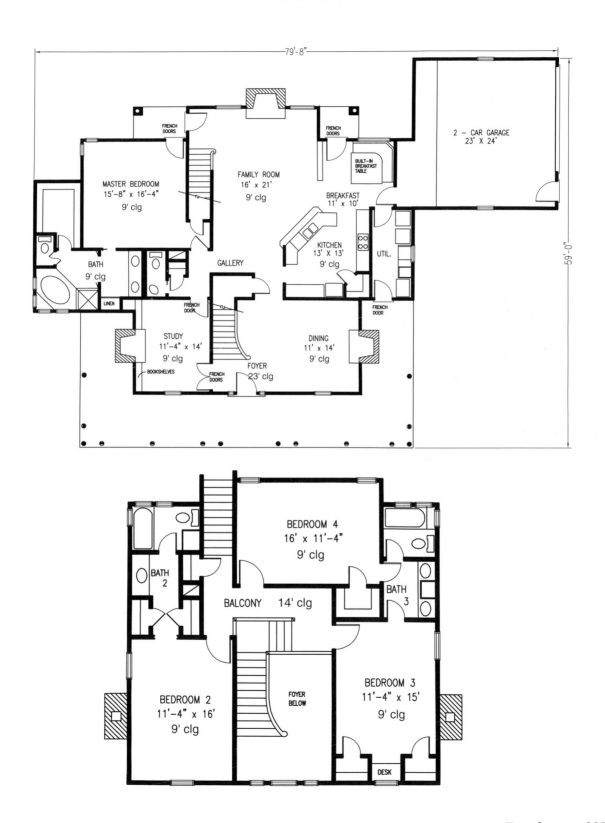

79'-8"

FRENCH DOORS

FRENCH DOORS

2 – CAR GARAGE
23' X 24'

MASTER BEDROOM
15'-8" x 16'-4"
9' clg

FAMILY ROOM
16' x 21'
9' clg

BUILT-IN
BREAKFAST
TABLE

BREAKFAST
11' x 10'

BATH
9' clg

GALLERY

KITCHEN
13' x 13'
9' clg

UTIL.

LINEN

FRENCH
DOOR

FRENCH
DOOR

STUDY
11'-4" x 14'
9' clg

DINING
11' x 14'
9' clg

BOOKSHELVES

FRENCH
DOORS

FOYER
23' clg

59'-0"

BATH
2

BEDROOM 4
16' x 11'-4"
9' clg

BATH
3

BALCONY   14' clg

BEDROOM 2
11'-4" x 16'
9' clg

FOYER
BELOW

BEDROOM 3
11'-4" x 15'
9' clg

DESK

Farmhouses 397

Photo © Kershner Communications

This traditional farmhouse offers a living area of 2,464 square feet. Typical for this architectural style is the wide, covered, wrap-around porch. The straight lines that characterize the exterior are continued on the inside of the house. The floor plans of the ground floor and second story are characterized by architectural symmetry.

Design HomeStyle
H 3711
© LifeStyle HomeDesign

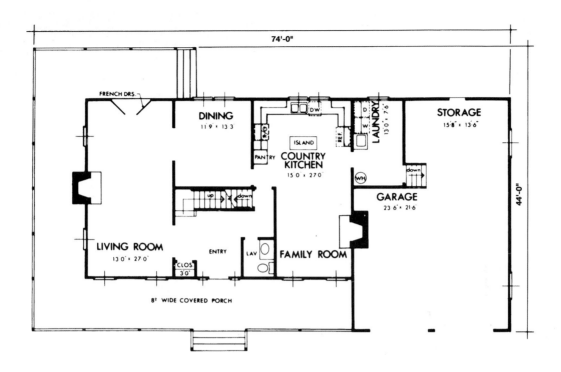

FRENCH DRS.

DINING
11·9 × 13·3

COUNTRY
KITCHEN
15·0 × 27·0

ISLAND

PANTRY

DW

LAUNDRY
13·0 × 7·6

STORAGE
15·8 × 13·6

REF.

WH

GARAGE
23·6 × 21·6

down

LIVING ROOM
13·0 × 27·0

ENTRY

LAV

FAMILY ROOM

up   down

CLOS.
3·0

8' WIDE COVERED PORCH

74'-0"

44'-0"

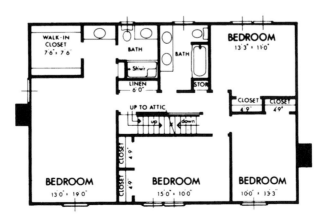

WALK-IN
CLOSET
7·6 × 7·6

BATH

BATH

BEDROOM
13·3 × 11·0

Sh'w'r

LINEN
6·0

STOR.

CLOSET
4·9

CLOSET
4·9

UP TO ATTIC

up   down

CLOSET
4·9

CLOSET
4·9

BEDROOM
13·0 × 19·0

BEDROOM
15·0 × 10·0

BEDROOM
10·0 × 13·3

Farmhouses 399

The wrap-around porch of the "Homestead" is not only an extraordinary eye-catcher, but also invites one to spend time relaxing in the fresh air. This magnificent family home with four bedrooms succeeds in combining nostalgic charm with modern comfort. The detailed floor plan deserves special attention. From the centrally placed foyer, the living room is situated to the left. From there, one passes through a wet bar into the great room with fireplace, which leads into the kitchen with breakfast room and adjacent dining room. In a separate section of the house is the master suite with comfortable bath. On the second floor are three further bedrooms that share two full baths, and an additional large space above the master suite and garage that can be finished to suit the needs of the owners.

Design Homestead
by William Poole

Ground floor 1,913 sq. ft.
Second floor 996 sq. ft.
Total 2,909 sq. ft

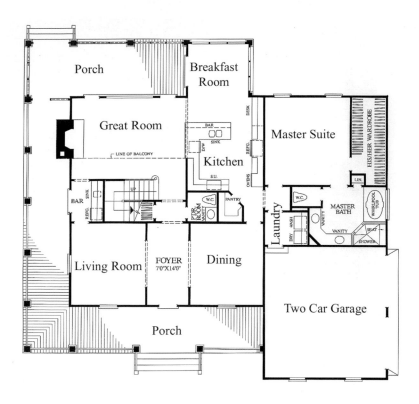

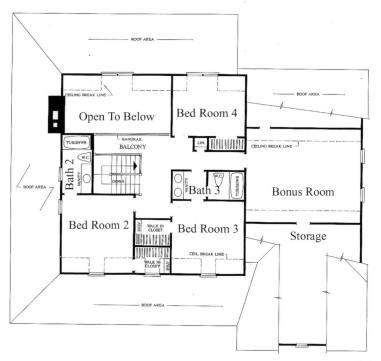

© by William Poole

Three large dormers decorate the gable roof of this beautiful country house design. The wrap-around porch completes the image of an authentic farmhouse. The white post and railing of the porch effectively accent the rustic wooden facade and harmonize perfectly with the white latticed windows. The gables of the dormers are roofed with fine wooden shingles. With a living area of 1,991 square feet, the house is designed for a family with a yen for a nostalgic atmosphere. The 1,141-square-footground floor features a large country kitchen with dinette, a family room with an external fireplace, and the formal area comprised of a living room and a dining room. The 850-square-foot second floor contains three bedrooms and two baths, with a large area for expansion located above the two-car garage.

Design 5155–Homes for Today
© Augustus Suglia, Architect

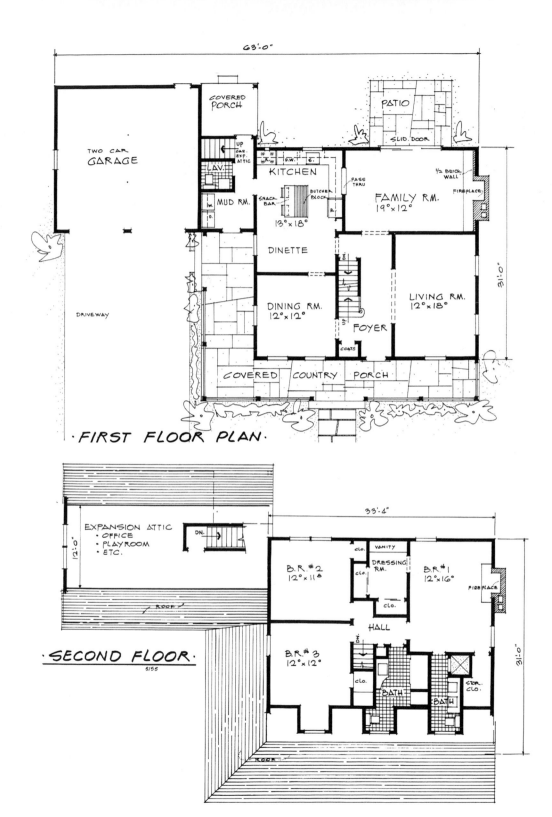

63'-0"

COVERED PORCH

TWO CAR GARAGE

PATIO

SLID. DOOR

UP GAR. EXP. ATTIC

KITCHEN

D.W.

FAMILY RM.
19°×12°

½ BRICK WALL

PASS THRU

FIREPLACE

LAV.

MUD RM.

SNACK BAR

BUTCHER BLOCK

13°×18°

DINETTE

31'-0"

DRIVEWAY

DINING RM.
12°×12°

FOYER

COATS

LIVING RM.
12°×18°

COVERED   COUNTRY   PORCH

FIRST FLOOR PLAN

EXPANSION ATTIC
• OFFICE
• PLAYROOM
• ETC.

DN.

33'-4"

12'-0"

ROOF

CLO.

VANITY

B.R. #2
12°×11⁸

CLO.

DRESSING RM.

B.R. #1
12°×16°

FIREPLACE

CLO.

SECOND FLOOR

5/55

HALL

B.R. #3
12°×12°

DN.

CLO.

BATH

BATH

STOR. CLO.

31'-0"

ROOF

The highlight of this striking design is clearly the widow's walk rising from the roof. It not only imparts a special note to the house—the tower can also be entered and used. A typical wrap-around porch is the perfect addition to the simple elegance of the main body of the house. The classical wooden facade is enhanced by the latticed windows and brightly painted shutters. The ground floor, with a living area of 992 square feet, contains a dining room and a living room with fireplace to either side of the foyer, a country kitchen with a dinette in a well-lighted bay, and a family room also with a fireplace, and with direct access to the terrace. Beneath the roof of the two-car garage is the mud room with entrances to the garage, the dinette, and the porch. The large square second floor features a master suite with two walk-in closets and a fireplace, two additional bedrooms, as well as a winding staircase into the glassed-in widow's walk.

Design 5174–Homes for Today
© Augustus Suglia, Architect

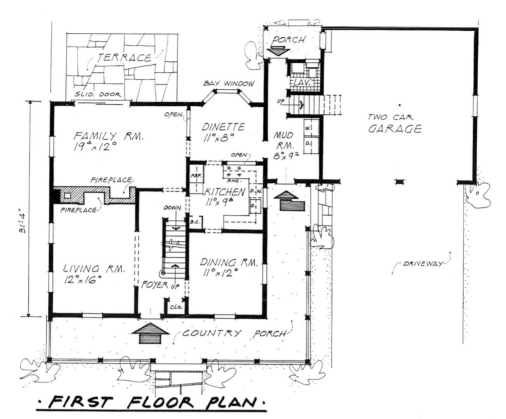

·FIRST FLOOR PLAN·

·SECOND FLOOR PLAN·

·TOWER PLAN·

·ALT. PLAN IF TOWER IS ELIMINATED·

For many fans of country house designs, this stately farmhouse is the essence of a country-style house. Three dormers jutting from the roof and the protective, wrap-around porch lend this home the charm of days gone by. In planning the 1,916-square-foothouse, the designer might have worked according to the motto "exterior nostalgic—interior, highly modern." The foyer offers entry into the formal dining room and, beyond the stairs, into the centrally located two-story great room. Large French doors lead onto the terrace, and skylights provide additional natural light. A large country kitchen with dinette in a bay window has direct access to the mud room and a pantry. The left side of the ground floor is devoted to the master suite with deluxe bath and dressing room. On the second floor are two additional bedrooms and a full bath. The loft allows a view into the great room below.

Design 5187-Homes for Today
© Augustus Suglia, Architect

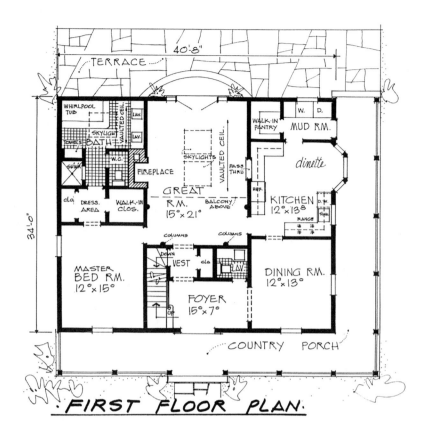

40'-8"

TERRACE

34'-0"

WHIRLPOOL TUB

LAV.

LAV.

SKYLIGHT

VAULTED CEIL.

TOWELS

BATH

W.C.

SH'WR

cl.

DRESS. AREA

WALK-IN CLOS.

FIREPLACE

SKYLIGHTS

VAULTED CEIL.

GREAT RM.
15° x 21°

BALCONY ABOVE

PASS THRU

WALK-IN PANTRY

W. | D.

MUD RM.

dinette

KITCHEN
12° x 13⁸

REF.

D.W.

SINK

RANGE

MASTER BED RM.
12° x 15°

DOWN

VEST.

cl.

LAV.

COLUMNS

COLUMNS

DINING RM.
12° x 13°

FOYER
15° x 7°

UP

COUNTRY   PORCH

· FIRST FLOOR PLAN ·

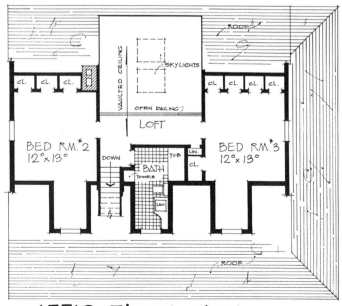

ROOF

cl. | cl. | cl.

VAULTED CEILING

SKYLIGHTS

cl. | cl. | cl. | cl.

OPEN RAILING

LOFT

BED RM.#2
12° x 13°

DOWN

BATH

TUB

LIN.

cl.

TOWELS

LAV.

BED RM.#3
12° x 13°

ROOF

ROOF

· ATTIC FLOOR PLAN ·

The architect has provided two variations for the exterior of this home; personal taste can determine whether one prefers the classical or the modern solution. The room arrangement is identical in either case. The centrally located entrance leads into the foyer, which is flanked by a dining room and a living room. The large country kitchen features a snack bar in the center. The family room has a fireplace and sliding glass doors that open onto the terrace. On the second floor are the master suite with bath, built-in closets, and walk-in closets, and two further bedrooms that share a full bath. In the attic above the two-car garage is sufficient place for a hobby room or a guest room.

Design 5194-Homes for Today
© Augustus Suglia, Architect

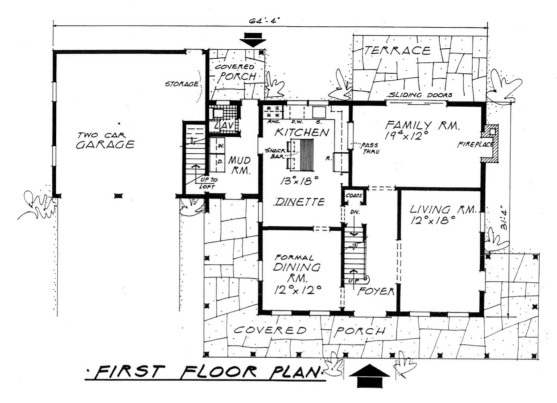

·FIRST FLOOR PLAN·

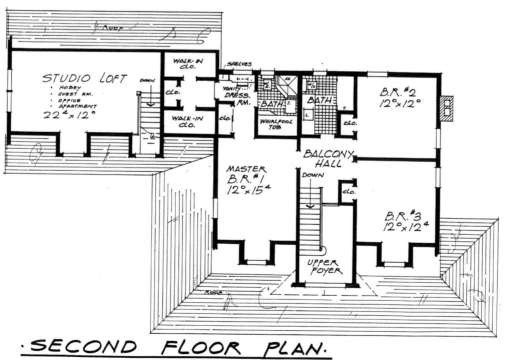

·SECOND FLOOR PLAN·

The three dormers give this farmhouse design an individual note. The small hipped roofs form an interesting contrast to the gabled roof of the main body of the house. The broad, wrap-around porch shelters the house on three sides, and provides three entrances to the house. The centrally placed main entrance leads into the foyer. To the left is the dining room, which adjoins the dinette with bay window and the open country kitchen. The two-story great room is adjacent to a small den. The master suite with bath and walk-in closet is also located on the ground floor. On the second story are two well-lit bedrooms and a full bath. From the gallery one looks down into the open great room. Two skylights provide for natural light and underline the generously open room arrangement.

Design 5195–Homes for Today
© Augustus Suglia, Architect

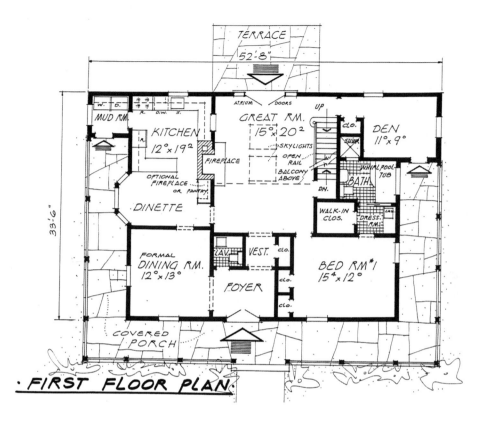

TERRACE
52'-8"

MUD RM.

W. D.
R. D.W. S.

KITCHEN
12⁰×19²

OPTIONAL
FIREPLACE
OR PANTRY

FIREPLACE

DINETTE

FORMAL
DINING RM.
12⁰×13⁰

ATRIUM DOORS

GREAT RM.
15⁰×20²

SKYLIGHTS

OPEN
RAIL

BALCONY
ABOVE

DN.

UP

CLO.

SH'WR

W.I.C.

BATH

WHIRLPOOL
TUB

DEN
11⁰×9⁰

LAV.

WALK-IN
CLOS.

DRESS.
RM.

LAV. VEST. CLO.

FOYER

CLO.

CLO.

BED RM #1
15⁴×12⁰

COVERED
PORCH

33'-6"

·FIRST FLOOR PLAN·

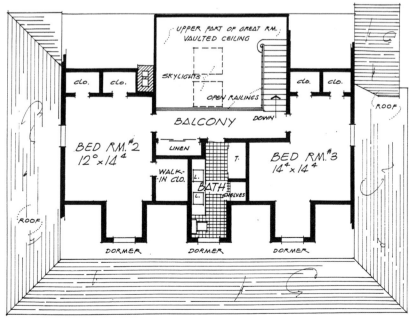

ROOF

CLO. CLO.

BED RM.#2
12⁰×14⁴

WALK-
IN CLO.

UPPER PART OF GREAT RM.
VAULTED CEILING

SKYLIGHTS

OPEN RAILINGS

BALCONY

LINEN

BATH

L.

L.

DOWN

CLO. CLO.

ROOF

T.

SHELVES

BED RM.#3
14⁴×14⁴

ROOF

DORMER

DORMER

DORMER

·SECOND FLOOR PLAN·

Although the front of this house has the appearance of a delicate country cottage, behind the facade is a generous 2,239 square feet of living space. Its balanced floor plan makes it a favorite home for families. The symmetrical design is continued through the wood-shingled dormers. The artistically worked porch and the elegant front doorway provide further accents. Inside, to the front of the house are the master suite with bath and walk-in closet and the great room with fireplace. Behind the great room are the dining room and the kitchen with a dinette and a pantry.

The second floor features two spacious bedrooms, both with walk-in closets. Above the two-car garage are 226 additional square feet for expansion, accessible by a separate staircase.

Design 5204-Homes for Today
© Augustus Suglia, Architect

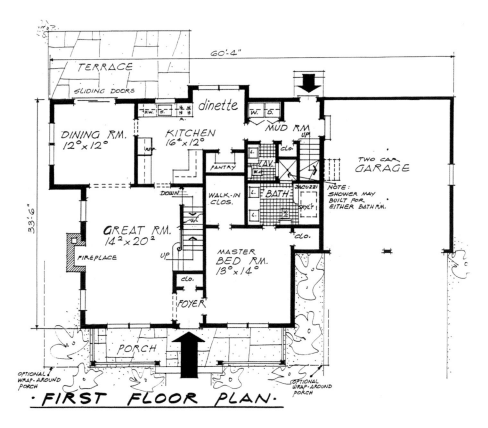

TERRACE

SLIDING DOORS

60'-4"

dinette

DINING RM.
12⁰ × 12⁰

KITCHEN
16⁴ × 12⁰

MUD RM.

UP

TWO CAR
GARAGE

REF.

PANTRY

LAV.
W.C.

clo.

NOTE:
SHOWER MAY
BUILT FOR
EITHER BATH RM.

WALK-IN
CLOS.

BATH

DOWN

JACUZZI

SKY'LT.

clo.

33'-6"

GREAT RM.
14² × 20²

wl

UP

MASTER
BED RM.
13⁰ × 14⁰

FIREPLACE

clo.

FOYER

PORCH

OPTIONAL
WRAP-AROUND
PORCH

OPTIONAL
WRAP-AROUND
PORCH

·FIRST FLOOR PLAN·

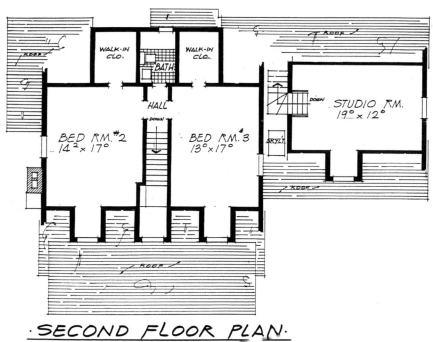

ROOF

ROOF

WALK-IN
CLO.

BATH

WALK-IN
CLO.

ROOF

STUDIO RM.
19⁰ × 12⁰

HALL

DOWN

UP

DOWN

BED RM. #2
14² × 17⁰

DOWN

BED RM. #3
13⁰ × 17⁰

SKY'LT

ROOF

ROOF

·SECOND FLOOR PLAN·

This rustic farmhouse design is distinguished by a ground-floor facade of natural stone. The central gable of the main body of the house with its large, beautifully designed windows underlines the harmonious impression of the front. The roof of the three-car garage is ornamented with a cupola. The clear lines are also evident in the roof of the wrap-around porch. On the interior, an elegant curved stairway leads from the imposing foyer to the second story. The formal dining room offers access through a butler's pantry to the large country kitchen with a dinette in a large-windowed bay. To the left of the kitchen is an exercise room, to the right a large, two-story great room with fireplace. The master suite with bath and walk-in closet are on the right side of the ground floor. Three bedrooms and a full bath are on the second floor.

Design 5205-Homes for Today
© Augustus Suglia, Architect

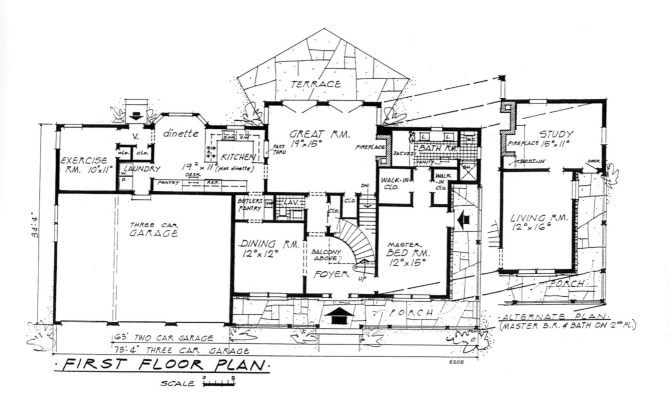

FIRST FLOOR PLAN

EXERCISE RM. 10'x11'

dinette

V.

clo. clo.

LAUNDRY

KITCHEN

19²x11' (plus dinette)

DESK

PANTRY REF.

SINK D.W.

PASS THRU

THREE CAR GARAGE

BUTLERS PANTRY

SINK

LAV.

DINING RM. 12'x12'

BALCONY ABOVE

FOYER

UP

CLO.

CLO.

TERRACE

GREAT RM. 19'x15'

FIREPLACE

JACUZZI

BATH RM.

L. L.

VANITY

SH.

W.

DN.

WALK-IN CLO.

WALK-IN CLO.

MASTER BED RM. 12'x15'

STUDY

FIREPLACE 15'x11'

BUILT-IN

DOOR

LIVING RM. 12'x16'

PORCH

ALTERNATE PLAN
(MASTER B.R. & BATH ON 2ⁿᵈ FL.)

PORCH

34'4"

63' TWO CAR GARAGE
73'-4" THREE CAR GARAGE

5205

SCALE 0 1 5

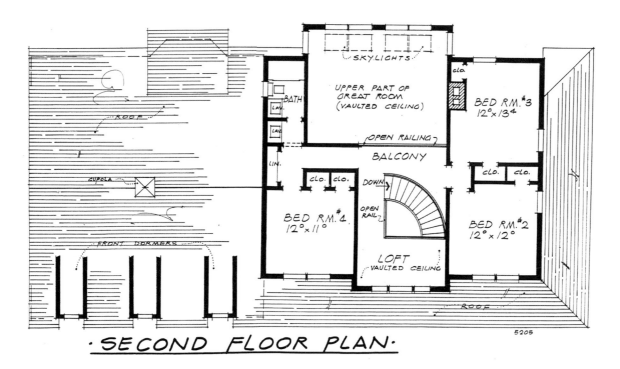

SECOND FLOOR PLAN

ROOF

CUPOLA

FRONT DORMERS

SKYLIGHTS

UPPER PART OF GREAT ROOM (VAULTED CEILING)

OPEN RAILING

BALCONY

BATH

LAV.

LAV.

LIN.

CLO. CLO.

BED RM. #4 12'x11'

DOWN

OPEN RAIL

LOFT VAULTED CEILING

clo

BED RM. #3 12'x13'⁴

CLO. CLO.

BED RM. #2 12'x12'

ROOF

5205

The rustic appearance of this house derives form the natural stone facing of the gable and the chimney, which forms an excellent contrast to the wood-covered facade. Adjacent to the kitchen is an inviting covered porch. With a living area of approximately 534 square feet on the ground floor and a selection of rooms including a living room with fireplace, a dining room, a bedroom, kitchen, and bath, the house is suitable for a young couple or a single person. The attic offers space for two rooms and a bath, with sufficient light provided by the windows on the gable ends.

Design 5126-Homes for Today
© Augustus Suglia, Architect

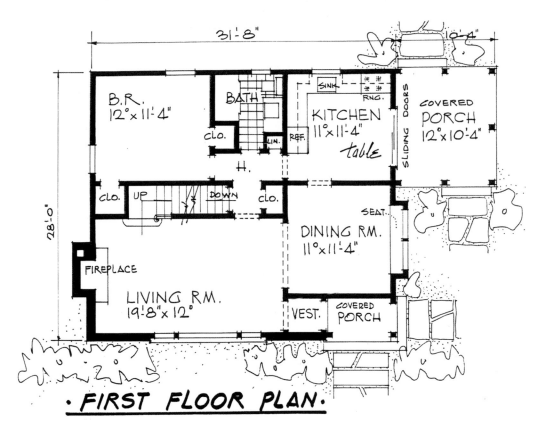

31'-8"

10'-4"

28'-0"

B.R.
12'×11'-4"

BATH

CLO.

KITCHEN
11'×11'-4"
table

SINK
RNG.

REF.

LIN.

H.

SLIDING DOORS

COVERED
PORCH
12'×10'-4"

CLO.

UP

DOWN

CLO.

FIREPLACE

LIVING RM.
19'-8"×12'

SEAT.

DINING RM.
11'×11'-4"

VEST.

COVERED
PORCH

·FIRST FLOOR PLAN·

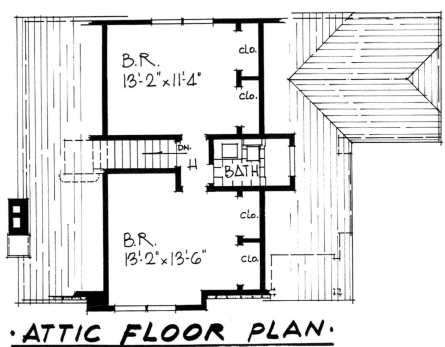

B.R.
13'-2"×11'-4"

CLO.

CLO.

DN.

H.

BATH

CLO.

CLO.

B.R.
13'-2"×13'-6"

CLO.

CLO.

·ATTIC FLOOR PLAN·

COUNTRY STYLE

Photo © Mark Englund / HomeStyles

The exterior of this 3,236-square-foot house, designed by architect Frank Betz, makes clear at a glance that this is a home of superior class. The detailed stucco decorations contrasting with the elegant brick facade and the tasteful design of the windows reflect the exclusiveness of the interior design. Among the highlights of the creative floor plan are the spacious kitchen on the ground floor and the palatial master suite on the second, complete with its own fireplace.

Design HomeStyle
FB-5477-Carm
© Frank Betz Associates, Inc.

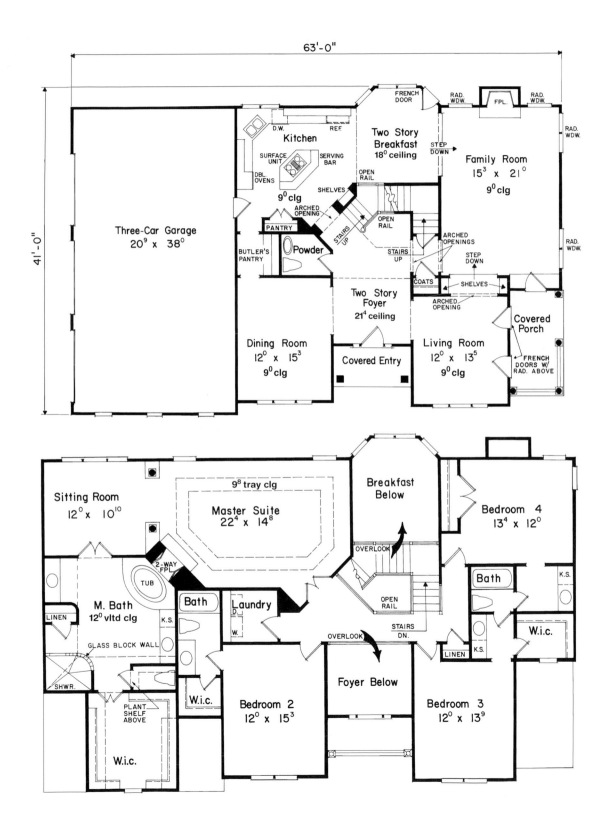

Three-Car Garage
20^9 x 38^0

63'-0"

41'-0"

Kitchen
SURFACE UNIT
DBL. OVENS
SERVING BAR
9^0 clg
D.W.
REF.
SHELVES
ARCHED OPENING

FRENCH DOOR

Two Story Breakfast
18^0 ceiling
OPEN RAIL
STEP DOWN

RAD. WDW.
FPL.
RAD. WDW.
RAD. WDW.

Family Room
15^3 x 21^0
9^0 clg

RAD. WDW.

PANTRY
BUTLER'S PANTRY
Powder
STAIRS UP
OPEN RAIL
STAIRS UP
ARCHED OPENINGS
STEP DOWN

COATS
SHELVES
ARCHED OPENING

Covered Porch

Dining Room
12^0 x 15^3
9^0 clg

Two Story Foyer
21^4 ceiling

Covered Entry

Living Room
12^0 x 13^5
9^0 clg

FRENCH DOORS W/ RAD. ABOVE

Sitting Room
12^0 x 10^{10}

9^8 tray clg

Master Suite
22^4 x 14^8

Breakfast Below

OVERLOOK

Bedroom 4
13^4 x 12^0

2-WAY FPL.
TUB
Bath
Laundry
D.
W.

Bath
K.S.

M. Bath
12^0 vltd clg
LINEN
K.S.

GLASS BLOCK WALL

SHWR.
PLANT SHELF ABOVE

OPEN RAIL
STAIRS DN.

W.i.c.

LINEN
K.S.

W.i.c.

Bedroom 2
12^0 x 15^3

OVERLOOK

Foyer Below

Bedroom 3
12^0 x 13^9

Country Style 421

Photo © Mark Englund / HomeStyles

This design by Frank Betz is truly a dream house. With an elegant stucco facade, elaborate window design, and imposing entrance, this home has the charm of a small castle, and provides a total of 4,055 square feet of living area distributed over two full stories. The interior continues the pattern of attention to detail. High ceilings of striking design make every room an experience.

Design HomeStyle
FB-5446–Elam
© Frank Betz Associates, Inc.

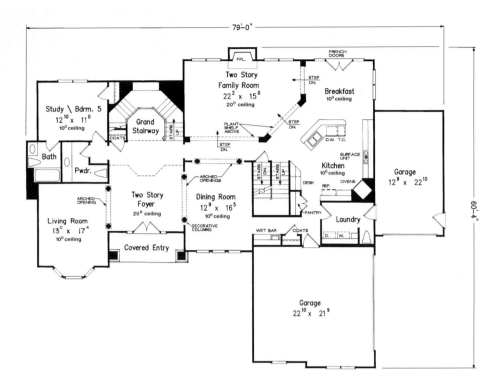

Two Story Family Room
22^2 x 15^0
20^0 ceiling

FPL.

FRENCH DOORS

STEP DN.

Breakfast
10^0 ceiling

Study \ Bdrm. 5
12^{10} x 11^0
10^0 ceiling

Grand Stairway

STAIRS UP

COATS

PLANT SHELF ABOVE

STEP DN.

STEP DN.

D.W. T.C.

SURFACE UNIT

Bath

Pwdr.

ARCHED OPENINGS

Kitchen
10^0 ceiling

Garage
12^9 x 22^{10}

ARCHED OPENING

Two Story Foyer
20^8 ceiling

Dining Room
12^9 x 16^5
10^0 ceiling

STAIRS

STAIRS

DESK

REF.

OVENS

Living Room
13^0 x 17^4
10^0 ceiling

DECORATIVE COLUMNS

PANTRY

Laundry

D. W.

Covered Entry

WET BAR

COATS

Garage
22^{10} x 21^9

79'-0"

60'-4"

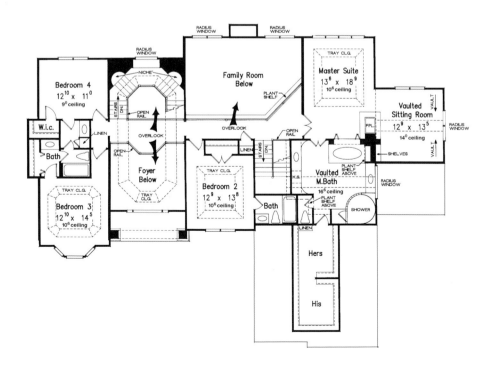

RADIUS WINDOW

RADIUS WINDOW

RADIUS WINDOW

TRAY CLG.

Bedroom 4
12^{10} x 11^0
9^0 ceiling

NICHE

Family Room Below

Master Suite
13^6 x 18^9
10^6 ceiling

PLANT SHELF

Vaulted Sitting Room
12^9 x 13^5
14^0 ceiling

VAULT

VAULT

RADIUS WINDOW

STAIRS DN.

OPEN RAIL

OVERLOOK

OVERLOOK

OPEN RAIL

FPL.

W.i.c.

LINEN

SHELVES

Bath

OPEN RAIL

Foyer Below

LINEN

STAIRS DN.

PLANT SHELF ABOVE

RADIUS WINDOW

TRAY CLG.

TRAY CLG.

Bedroom 2
12^9 x 13^8
10^6 ceiling

K.S.

Vaulted M.Bath
16^6 ceiling

Bedroom 3
12^{10} x 14^5
10^6 ceiling

TRAY CLG.

Bath

LINEN

PLANT SHELF ABOVE

SHOWER

RADIUS WINDOW

Hers

His

Country Style 423

Photo © Mark Englund / HomeStyles

The classical exterior of this European-influenced colonial-style house impresses the viewer with its white stucco facade, clearly accented by the dark shutters. The imaginative gable design and beautifully arranged windows lend elegance to the front of the house. The 2,835-square-foot living area is generously apportioned over two stories, including four bedrooms on the second floor.

Design HomeStyle
FB-5364-Deer
© Frank Betz Associates, Inc.

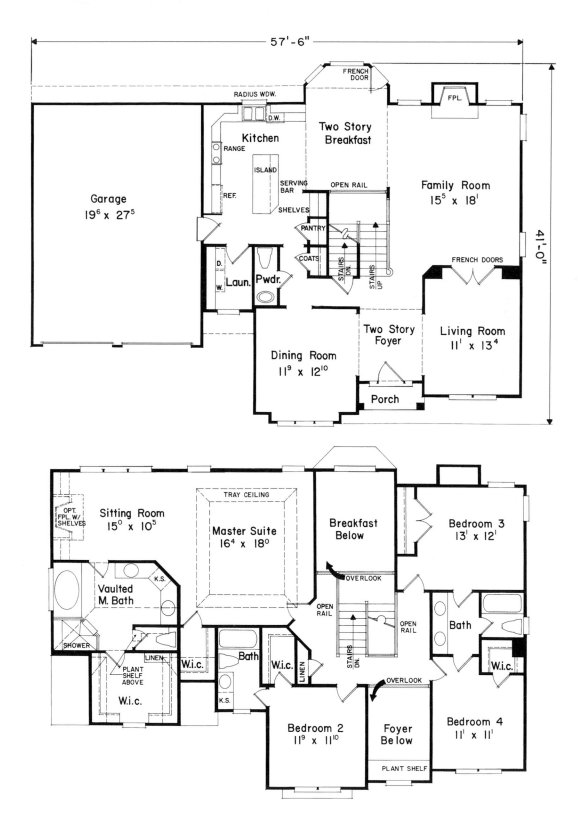

Garage
19⁶ x 27⁵

Kitchen

RADIUS WDW.

D.W.

RANGE

ISLAND

REF.

SERVING BAR

SHELVES

PANTRY

COATS

D.

W.

Laun. **Pwdr.**

FRENCH DOOR

Two Story Breakfast

OPEN RAIL

STAIRS DN.

STAIRS UP

FPL.

Family Room
15⁵ x 18¹

FRENCH DOORS

Dining Room
11⁹ x 12¹⁰

Two Story Foyer

Porch

Living Room
11¹ x 13⁴

57'-6"

41'-0"

OPT. FPL. W/ SHELVES

Sitting Room
15⁰ x 10⁵

TRAY CEILING

Master Suite
16⁴ x 18⁰

Breakfast Below

Bedroom 3
13¹ x 12¹

Vaulted M. Bath

K.S.

SHOWER

PLANT SHELF ABOVE

LINEN

W.i.c.

W.i.c.

Bath

W.i.c.

LINEN

K.S.

OVERLOOK

OPEN RAIL

STAIRS DN.

OPEN RAIL

Bath

W.i.c.

Bedroom 2
11⁹ x 11¹⁰

Foyer Below

OVERLOOK

PLANT SHELF

Bedroom 4
11¹ x 11¹

Country Style 425

Photo © Mark Englund / HomeStyles

An original combination of materials plays an important role in the exterior appearance of this house. Together with the elaborately designed gables, the facade gives this 3,691-square-foot design much of its special character. Imaginative lines are also evident in the floor plan for the interior of the house. The large country kitchen—the center of family life—and the stellar design of the master suite on the ground floor deserve special mention.

Design HomeStyle
FB-5345-Jern
© Frank Betz Associates, Inc.

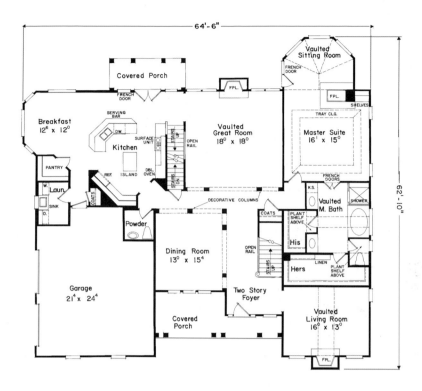

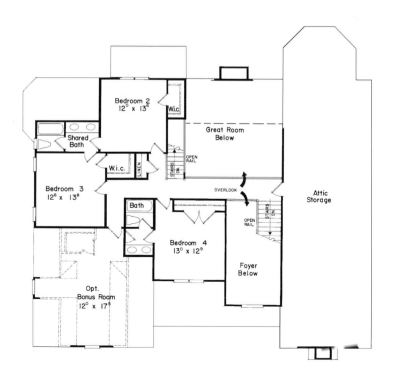

Country Style 427

Photo © Phillip Mueller

Fans of rustic design will appreciate this home. This stately 3,120-square-foot wooden house was built entirely with natural materials. Its shingled facade and beautifully designed windows underline the charm of this variation on the country style. A wrap-around porch, deck and screened porch offer ample opportunities to enjoy the open air. The natural stone chimney further emphasizes the solidity of the construction.

**Design HomeStyle
FI-3120**
© Framed Ideas

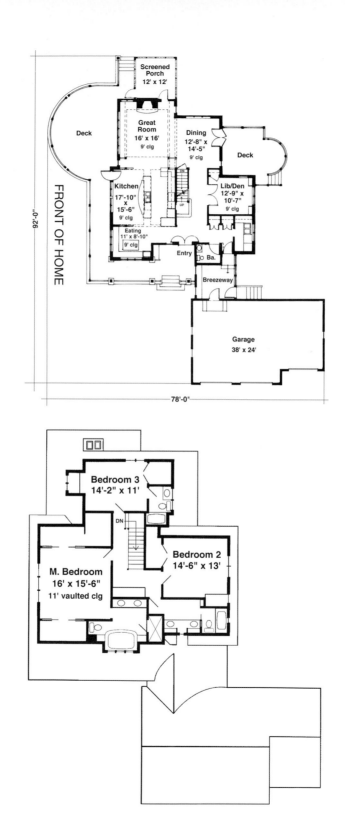

Screened Porch
12' x 12'

Deck

Great Room
16' x 16'
9' clg

Dining
12'-8" x 14'-5"
9' clg

Deck

Kitchen
17'-10" x 15'-6"
9' clg

DN

UP

Lib/Den
12'-9" x 10'-7"
9' clg

Eating
11' x 8'-10"
9' clg

Entry

Ba.

Breezeway

Garage
38' x 24'

FRONT OF HOME

92'-0"

78'-0"

Bedroom 3
14'-2" x 11'

DN

Bedroom 2
14'-6" x 13'

M. Bedroom
16' x 15'-6"
11' vaulted clg

Country Style 429

Photo © Mark Englund / HomeStyles

Characteristic of this European-looking house is the staggered gable construction. The elegant stucco trim is prominant against the light stucco facade. The interior of the 2,763-sq.-ft- house features a dining room and a formal living room to either side of the open, two-story foyer. The family room with fireplace, generous kitchen, and well-lit breakfast area form a discreet living area. On the second floor are four bedrooms, three full baths, and a laundry area.

Design HomeStyle
FB-5027-Olym
© Frank Betz Associates, Inc.

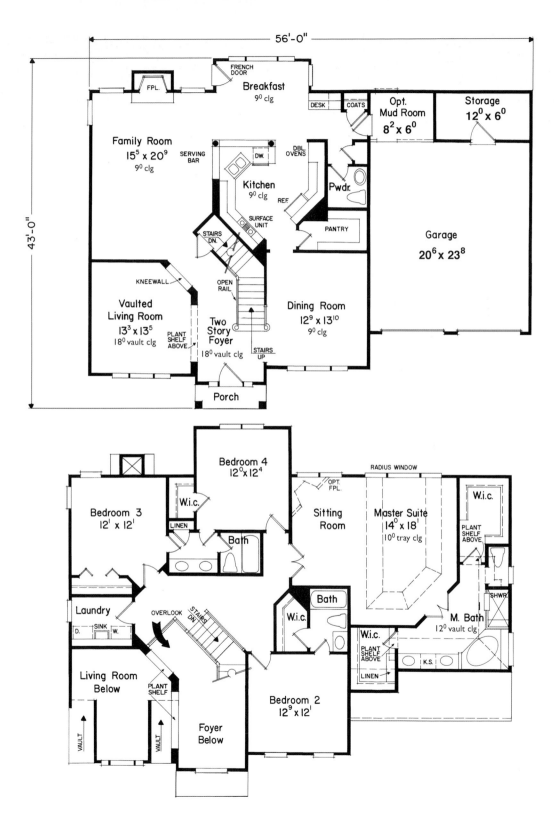

56'-0"

43'-0"

Family Room
15⁵ x 20⁹
9⁰ clg

FPL.

FRENCH DOOR

Breakfast
9⁰ clg

DESK

COATS

Opt. Mud Room
8² x 6⁰

Storage
12⁰ x 6⁰

SERVING BAR

DW.

DBL. OVENS

Kitchen
9⁰ clg

REF

Pwdr.

Garage
20⁶ x 23⁸

SURFACE UNIT

STAIRS DN.

OPEN RAIL

KNEEWALL

Vaulted Living Room
13³ x 13⁵
18⁰ vault clg

PLANT SHELF ABOVE

PANTRY

Dining Room
12⁹ x 13¹⁰
9⁰ clg

Two Story Foyer
18⁰ vault clg

STAIRS UP

Porch

Bedroom 4
12⁰ x 12⁴

W.i.c.

LINEN

Bath

RADIUS WINDOW

OPT. FPL.

Sitting Room

Master Suite
14⁰ x 18¹
10⁰ tray clg

W.i.c.

PLANT SHELF ABOVE

Bedroom 3
12¹ x 12¹

Laundry

D. | SINK | W.

OVERLOOK

STAIRS DN.

Bath

W.i.c.

W.i.c.

PLANT SHELF ABOVE

LINEN

SHWR.

M. Bath
12⁰ vault clg

K.S.

Living Room Below

PLANT SHELF

VAULT

VAULT

Foyer Below

Bedroom 2
12⁹ x 12¹

Country Style 431

Photo © Mark Englund / HomeStyles

The exterior of this appealing house features a staggered gable design. Against the elegant stucco facade, the detailed trim stands out optimally. With 2,883 square feet, the interior offers dining and living rooms, a two-story family room, and a large country kitchen with breakfast area on the ground floor. The master suite with a luxurious bath and large walk-in closet and three additional bedrooms occupy the second floor.

**Design HomeStyle
FB-5049-Ever**
© Frank Betz Associates, Inc.

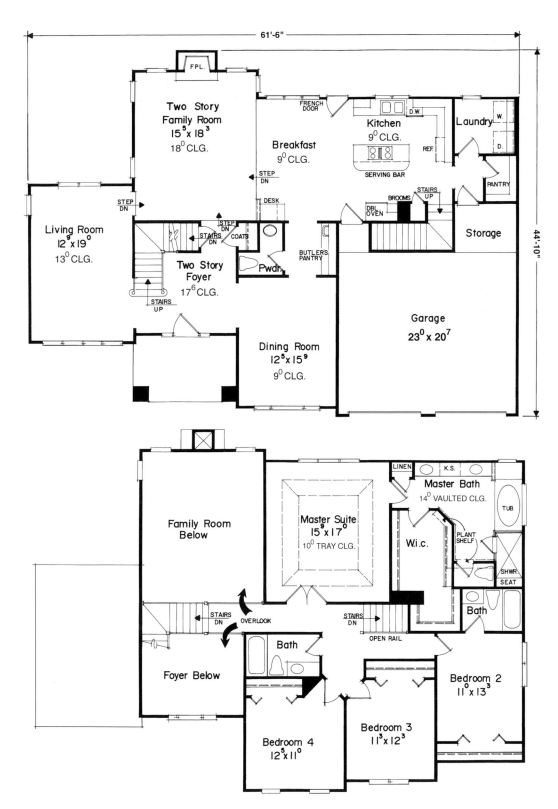

61'-6"

44'-10"

Two Story Family Room
15^5 x 18^3
18^0 CLG.

FPL.

FRENCH DOOR

Kitchen
9^0 CLG.

D.W.

Laundry

W.

Breakfast
9^0 CLG.

REF.

SERVING BAR

D.

STEP DN

PANTRY

STEP DN

DESK

BROOMS

STAIRS UP

Living Room
12^9 x 19^0
13^0 CLG.

STEP DN

DBL OVEN

STAIRS DN

COATS

Pwdr.

Storage

Two Story Foyer
17^6 CLG.

BUTLER'S PANTRY

STAIRS UP

Dining Room
12^5 x 15^9
9^0 CLG.

Garage
23^0 x 20^7

LINEN

K.S.

Master Bath
14^0 VAULTED CLG.

TUB

Family Room Below

Master Suite
15^9 x 17^0
10^0 TRAY CLG.

Wic.

PLANT SHELF

SHWR

SEAT

STAIRS DN

OVERLOOK

STAIRS DN

Bath

OPEN RAIL

Bath

Foyer Below

Bath

Bedroom 2
11^0 x 13^3

Bedroom 4
12^5 x 11^0

Bedroom 3
11^3 x 12^3

Country Style 433

Photo Mark Englund / HomeStyles

This bungalow offers comfortable living on a single level. The light stucco facade provides a distinctive backdrop for the dark red shutters and is crowned by a well-designed hipped roof. The entry area features arched windows that suggest the luxury of the interior. At the center of the house is the large living room with fireplace, with direct access to the garden porch. Particular attention is due the private bath that forms a part of the master suite.

**Design HomeStyle
E-2302**
© Breland & Farmer Designers, Inc.

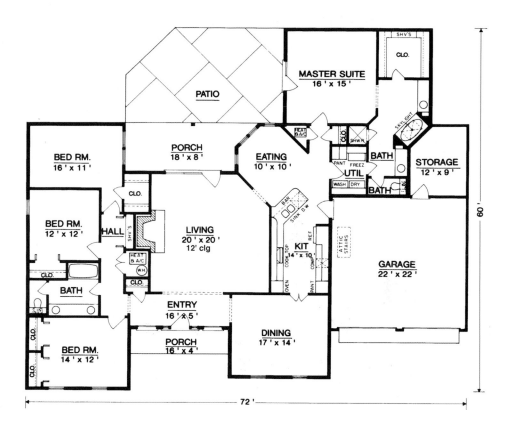

MASTER SUITE
16' x 15'

SHV'S

CLO.

PATIO

PORCH
18' x 8'

EATING
10' x 10'

BED RM.
16' x 11'

HEAT
B A/C

CLO.

SHW'R

BATH

STORAGE
12' x 9'

CLO.

PANT

FREEZ

UTIL

BED RM.
12' x 12'

HALL

SHV'S

LIVING
20' x 20'
12' clg

BAR

SINK D W

WASH

DRY

BATH

CLO.

KIT
14' x 10'

REF

ATTIC STAIRS

HEAT
B A/C

COOK TOP

GARAGE
22' x 22'

CLO.

WH

BATH

CLO.

OVEN

PANT

LIN

BED RM.
14' x 12'

CLO.

CLO.

ENTRY
16' x 5'

PORCH
16' x 4'

DINING
17' x 14'

60'

72'

FURR

MIRROR

LINEN

SINK

DRAWERS

FURR

CULTURED
MARBLE

MIRROR

SINK

DRAWERS

FURR

MIRROR

LINEN

SINK

DRAWER

Country Style 435

Photo © Mark Englund / HomeStyles

This design stretches over a total living area of 3,210 square feet, distributed over two stories. On the ground floor are a living room and dining room toward the front of the house, while the large family room and adjacent kitchen form a discreet area. The master suite includes a private bath. On the second floor are two bedrooms, two full baths, and a large game room.

Design HomeStyle
DD-3245
© Danze & Davis Architects, Inc.

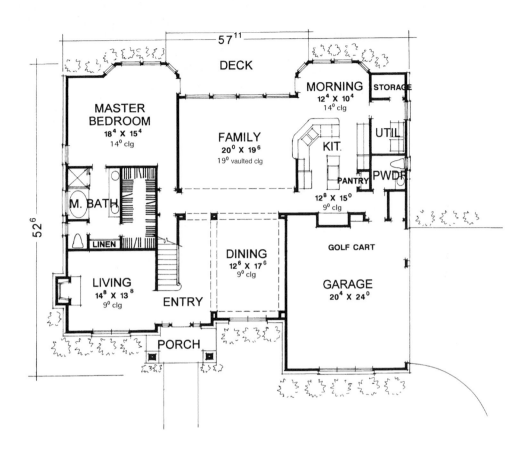

57¹¹

DECK

MASTER
BEDROOM
18⁴ X 15⁴
14⁰ clg

MORNING
12⁴ X 10⁴
14⁰ clg

STORAGE

FAMILY
20⁰ X 19⁶
19⁰ vaulted clg

KIT.

UTIL

52⁶

M. BATH

PANTRY

PWDR.

12⁸ X 15⁰
9⁰ clg

LINEN

DINING
12⁶ X 17⁶
9⁰ clg

GOLF CART

LIVING
14⁸ X 13⁸
9⁰ clg

ENTRY

GARAGE
20⁴ X 24⁰

PORCH

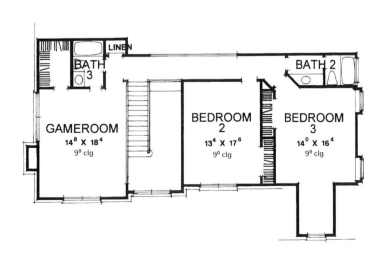

BATH
3

LINEN

BATH 2

GAMEROOM
14⁸ X 18⁴
9⁰ clg

BEDROOM
2
13⁴ X 17⁶
9⁰ clg

BEDROOM
3
14⁰ X 16⁴
9⁰ clg

Country Style 437

Photo © Mark Englund / HomeStyles

Tasteful gable architecture graces this hipped-roof design. The windows are framed in white stucco trim, and together with the shutters make an attractive contrast to the brick facade. The interior of the house, with 2,954 square feet of living area distributed over two stories, is equally detailed and offers a comprehensive array of rooms. On the ground floor are the dining room, study, and master suite with bath. The two-story family room with fireplace adjoins the large kitchen with a breakfast nook in the bay. On the second floor are three additional bedrooms and two full baths.

**Design HomeStyle
APS-2911**
© Atlanta Plan Source, Inc.

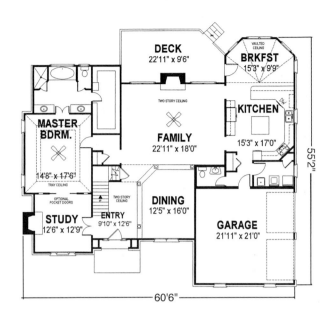

DECK
22'11" x 9'6"

BRKFST
15'3" x 9'9"

VAULTED CEILING

TWO STORY CEILING

KITCHEN
15'3" x 17'0"

MASTER BDRM.
14'8" x 17'6"
TRAY CEILING

FAMILY
22'11" x 18'0"

OPTIONAL POCKET DOORS

TWO STORY CEILING

DINING
12'5" x 16'0"

STUDY
12'6" x 12'9"

ENTRY
9'10" x 12'6"

GARAGE
21'11" x 21'0"

55'2"

60'6"

OPEN BELOW

BEDRM 4
13'0" x 11'6"

OPEN BELOW

BEDRM 2
12'5" x 12'5"

PLANT SHELF

BEDRM 3
11'3" x 17'1"

Country Style 439

Photo © Mark Englund / HomeStyles

This lovely country-style house offers 2,598 square feet of living area distributed over two stories. The sophisticated floor plan features generously proportioned rooms. The gables and protruding elements serve to interrupt the long lines of the building, and its light-colored wooden facade harmonizes beautifully with the black roof. Colored shutters provide a restrained accent. There is a terrace at the front of the house, and a sun deck on the side facing the yard.

**Design HomeStyle
AX-1310**
© Jerold Axelrod & Associates, P.C.

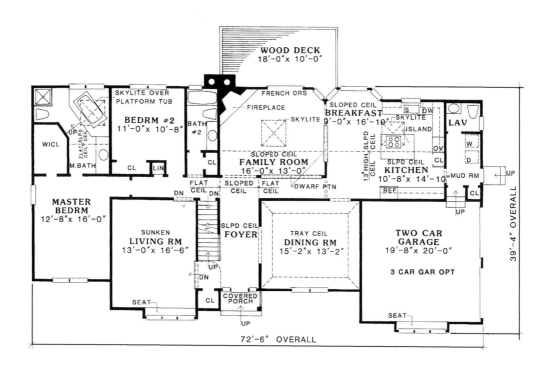

WOOD DECK
18'-0"x 10'-0"

SKYLITE OVER
PLATFORM TUB

BEDRM #2
11'-0"x 10'-8"

FRENCH DRS

SLOPED CEIL

BREAKFAST
9'-0"x 16'-10"

FIREPLACE

SKYLITE

SKYLITE

ISLAND

LAV

BATH
#2

WICL

M.BATH

SLOPED CEIL
FAMILY ROOM
16'-0"x 13'-0"

CL

CL

LIN

OV

CL

SLPD CEIL
KITCHEN
10'-8"x 14'-10"

MUD RM

W

D

CL

13°HIGH SLPD CEIL

BEE

**MASTER
BEDRM**
12'-8"x 16'-0"

FLAT
CEIL

SLOPED
CEIL

FLAT
CEIL

DWARF PTN

DN

DN

SLPD CEIL
FOYER

UP

**SUNKEN
LIVING RM**
13'-0"x 16'-6"

TRAY CEIL
DINING RM
15'-2"x 13'-2"

**TWO CAR
GARAGE**
19'-8"x 20'-0"

UP

DN

3 CAR GAR OPT

39'-4" OVERALL

SEAT

CL

**COVERED
PORCH**

UP

SEAT

72'-6" OVERALL

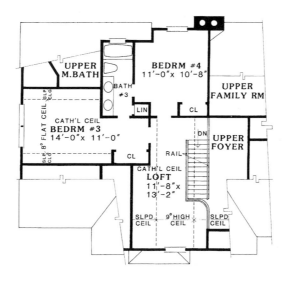

UPPER
M.BATH

BEDRM #4
11'-0"x 10'-8"

BATH
#3

UPPER
FAMILY RM

CATH'L CEIL
BEDRM #3
14'-0"x 11'-0"

LIN

CL

FLAT CEIL

SLP CLG

SLP 8° CLG

CL

RAIL

DN

**UPPER
FOYER**

CATH'L CEIL
LOFT
11'-8"x
13'-2"

SLPD
CEIL

9° HIGH
CEIL

SLPD
CEIL

Country Style 441

Photo © Mark Englund / HomeStyles

Characteristic of this European-inspired country house are the two gable constructions with their beautiful windows on the front of the house. The partial use of brick provides an interesting contrast to the wooden facade. The elegant stucco trim on the gables reinforces the clear lines of the style. The two stories of the house offer a total living area of 2,980 square feet.

**Design HomeStyle
L-982-SB**
© Larry W. Garnett & Associates, Inc.

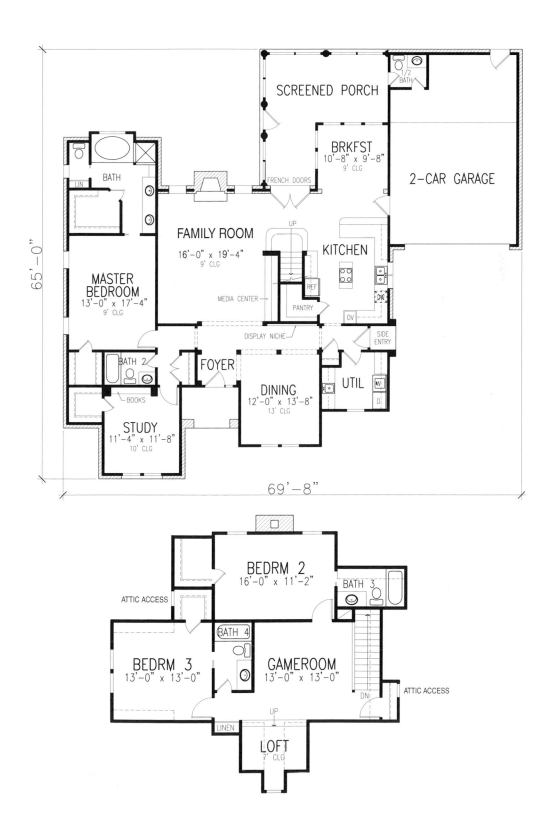

SCREENED PORCH

1/2 BATH

BATH

LIN

BRKFST
10'-8" x 9'-8"
9' CLG

2-CAR GARAGE

FRENCH DOORS

FAMILY ROOM
16'-0" x 19'-4"
9' CLG

UP

KITCHEN

MASTER
BEDROOM
13'-0" x 17'-4"
9' CLG

MEDIA CENTER

REF

PANTRY

OV

SIDE
ENTRY

DISPLAY NICHE

BATH 2

FOYER

DINING
12'-0" x 13'-8"
13' CLG

UTIL

W

D

BOOKS

STUDY
11'-4" x 11'-8"
10' CLG

65'-0"

69'-8"

BEDRM 2
16'-0" x 11'-2"

BATH 3

ATTIC ACCESS

BATH 4

BEDRM 3
13'-0" x 13'-0"

GAMEROOM
13'-0" x 13'-0"

ATTIC ACCESS

DN

LINEN

UP

LOFT
7' CLG

Country Style 443

Photo © Mark Englund / HomeStyles

This house offers a well thought-out floor plan with 3,177 square feet of living space. The large, high-ceilinged foyer features an elegant curved stairway that typifies the sophistication of the interior design. To the left of the foyer is a formal living room with fireplace, followed by the dining room, which leads to the kitchen with morning room. The center of the house is the open family room, or game room. The master suite at the front of the house features an exclusive bath.

Design HomeStyle
L-3177
© Larry W. Garnett & Associates, Inc.

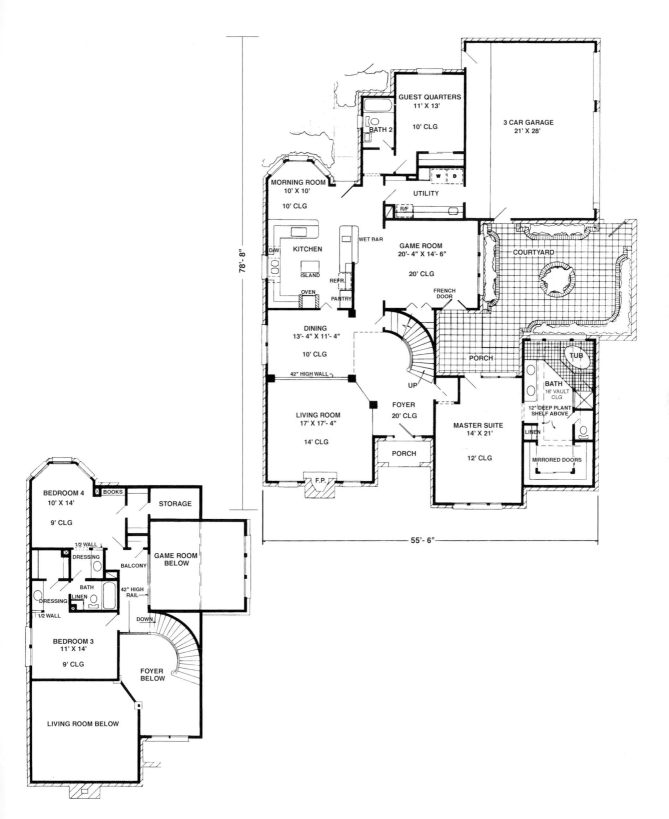

GUEST QUARTERS
11' X 13'

10' CLG

BATH 2

3 CAR GARAGE
21' X 28'

MORNING ROOM
10' X 10'

10' CLG

UTILITY

W D

R/F

WET BAR

KITCHEN

GAME ROOM
20'- 4" X 14'- 6"

20' CLG

COURTYARD

ISLAND

OVEN

REFR.

PANTRY

FRENCH
DOOR

PORCH

DINING
13'- 4" X 11'- 4"

10' CLG

DW

42" HIGH WALL

LIVING ROOM
17' X 17'- 4"

14' CLG

FOYER
20' CLG

UP

MASTER SUITE
14' X 21'

12' CLG

TUB

BATH
16' VAULT
CLG

12" DEEP PLANT
SHELF ABOVE

LINEN

MIRRORED DOORS

PORCH

F.P.

78'- 8"

55'- 6"

BEDROOM 4
10' X 14'

9' CLG

BOOKS

STORAGE

1/2 WALL

DRESSING

BALCONY

GAME ROOM
BELOW

BATH

LINEN

42" HIGH
RAIL

DRESSING

1/2 WALL

DOWN

BEDROOM 3
11' X 14'

9' CLG

FOYER
BELOW

LIVING ROOM BELOW

Country Style 445

Photo © Mark Englund / HomeStyles

This colonial-style house with European flair distinguishes itself through its elegant brick facade. The sophisticated design features offset gable elements. A wide front door with side windows that allow natural light to enter the foyer graces the center of the house. The design provides 4,129 square feet of living space distributed over two stories.

Design HomeStyle
L–131–MBD
© Larry W. Garnett & Associates, Inc.

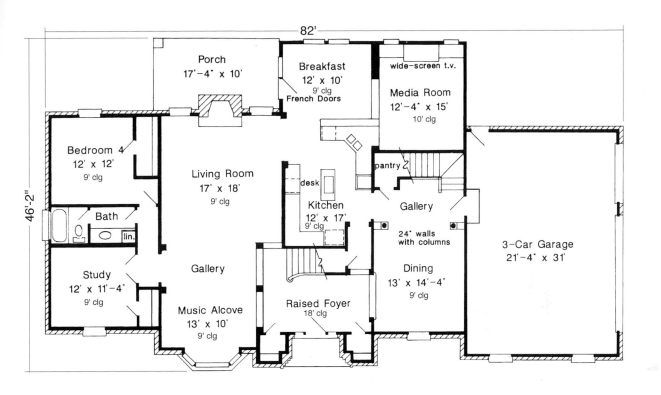

82'

46'-2"

Porch
17'-4" x 10'

Breakfast
12' x 10'
9' clg
French Doors

wide-screen t.v.

Media Room
12'-4" x 15'
10' clg

Bedroom 4
12' x 12'
9' clg

Living Room
17' x 18'
9' clg

desk

pantry

Bath

lin.

Kitchen
12' x 17'
9' clg

Gallery

Study
12' x 11'-4"
9' clg

Gallery

24" walls
with columns

3-Car Garage
21'-4" x 31'

Music Alcove
13' x 10'
9' clg

Raised Foyer
18' clg

Dining
13' x 14'-4"
9' clg

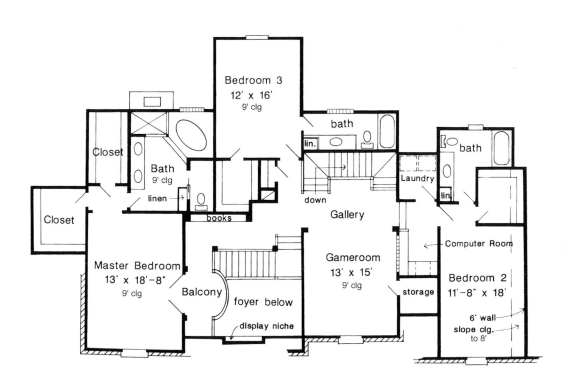

Bedroom 3
12' x 16'
9' clg

Closet

bath

lin.

bath

Bath
9' clg

Laundry

lin.

linen

Closet

books

down

Gallery

Computer Room

Master Bedroom
13' x 18'-8"
9' clg

Balcony

foyer below

Gameroom
13' x 15'
9' clg

storage

Bedroom 2
11'-8" x 18'

display niche

6' wall
slope clg.
to 8'

Country Style 447

Photo © Mark Englund / HomeStyles

Floor plan labels:

68'-0"

73'-8"

Transoms

Slope Clg. to 11'-1"
MASTER
15'-0" x 17'-0"

Gambrel Clg. to 11'-1"
FAMILY
22'-0" x 14'-0"

9'-1" Clg.
BRKFST.
8'-0" x 15'-0"

PORCH
4 x 4 Skylite

PORCH

Slope Clg. to 11'-1"

Transoms

Transoms

Slope Clg. to 11'-1"
BEDROOM 2
15'-0" x 13'-0"

MSTR. BATH
Slope Clg. to 11'-1"

P.

Snack Bar

9'-1" Clg.
KITCHEN
16'-0" x 14'-0"

11'-1" Clg.

Built-ins

Flush Tile Fireplace

LIVING
21'-0" x 16'-0"

Built-ins

Plants Above

Linen

CLO.

UP

13'-1" Clg.
FOYER

Chest

CLO.

PWDR.

Coffer Clg. to 10'-1"
DINING
12'-0" x 14'-0"

PORCH

Bookshelves

Coffer Clg. to 11'-1"
STUDY
14'-4" x 16'-0"

Built-ins

9'-1" Clg.
BEDROOM 3
13'-0" x 12'-0"

Linen

CLO.

GOLF CART
7'-0" x 7'-0"

UTIL.
W/D

Transom

TWO CAR GARAGE
21'-0" x 21'-0"

This one-story house stands out for its offset roof and gable design. The stone-clad bay underscores the elegance of the design. The 2,737-square-foot floor plan is rich in detail, including varied ceiling treatments and generous storage space.

**Design HomeStyle
KLF-9710**
© Estate Creations, Inc.

448 Country Style

Photo © Mark Englund / HomeStyles

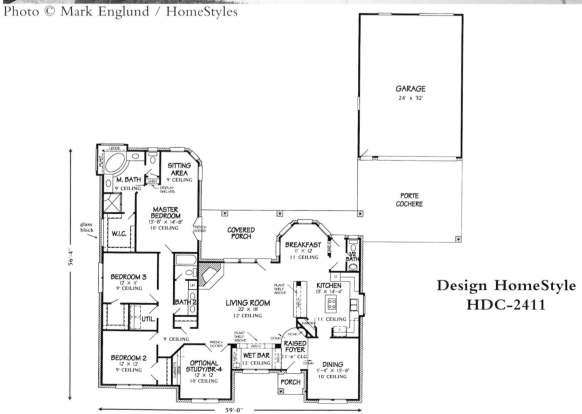

GARAGE
24' x 32'

PORTE
COCHERE

**Design HomeStyle
HDC-2411**

SITTING
AREA
9' CEILING
DISPLAY
SHELVES

M. BATH
9' CEILING

LINEN

LEDGE

PLANT

MASTER
BEDROOM
13'-8" X 14'-8"
10' CEILING

FRENCH
DOORS

COVERED
PORCH

BREAKFAST
11' X 12'
11' CEILING

1/2
BATH

W.I.C.

glass
block

KITCHEN
13' X 14'-4"
11' CEILING

BEDROOM 3
12' X 11'
9' CEILING

BATH 2

LIN

PLANT
SHELF
ABOVE

NICHE

UTIL.

9' CEILING

FRENCH
DOORS

LIVING ROOM
22' X 18'
12' CEILING

PLANT
SHELF
ABOVE

PANTRY

NICHE

DOWN

BEDROOM 2
12' X 12'
9' CEILING

OPTIONAL
STUDY/BR-4
12' X 12'
10' CEILING

WET BAR
12' CEILING

RAISED
FOYER
11'-6" CLG.

DOWN

DINING
11'-4" X 13'-8"
10' CEILING

PORCH

56'-4"

59'-0"

Country Style 449

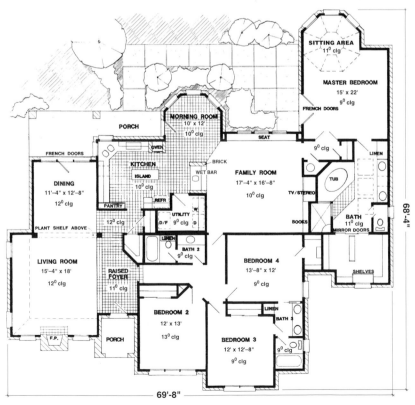

SITTING AREA
11^0 clg

MASTER BEDROOM
15' x 22'
9^0 clg

FRENCH DOORS

PORCH

MORNING ROOM
10' x 12'
10^0 clg

SEAT

9^0 clg

LINEN

FRENCH DOORS

DINING
11'-4" x 12'-8"
12^0 clg

KITCHEN

OVEN

ISLAND
10^0 clg

BRICK

WET BAR

FAMILY ROOM
17'-4" x 16'-8"
10^0 clg

TUB

TV/STEREO

PANTRY

REFR.

PLANT SHELF ABOVE

12^0 clg

UTILITY

D/F 9^0 clg D

W

BOOKS

BATH
11^0 clg
MIRROR DOORS

LIVING ROOM
15'-4" x 18'
12^0 clg

LINEN

BATH 2
9^0 clg

RAISED FOYER
11^0 clg

BEDROOM 4
13'-8" x 12'
9^0 clg

SHELVES

$68'-4"$

BEDROOM 2
12' x 13'
13^0 clg

LINEN

BATH 3

F.P.

PORCH

BEDROOM 3
12' x 12'-8"
9^0 clg

9^0 clg

$69'-8"$

**Design HomeStyle
L-2885**
© Larry W. Garnett
Associates, Inc.

450 Country Style

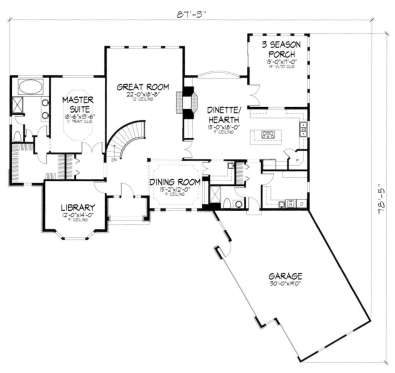

3 SEASON PORCH
15'-0"x17'-0"
14' VLTD CLG

GREAT ROOM
22'-0"x18'-8"
12' CEILING

MASTER SUITE
18'-6"x13'-6"
11' TRAY CLG

DINETTE/ HEARTH
15'-0"x18'-0"
9' CEILING

DINING ROOM
15'-2"x12'-0"
9' CEILING

LIBRARY
12'-0"x14'-0"
9' CEILING

DN

GARAGE
30'-0"x19'-0"

87'-3"

78'-5"

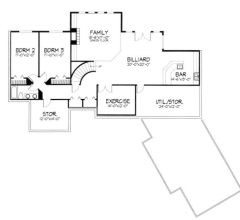

FAMILY
18'-6"x17'-0"
SUNKEN FLOOR

BDRM 2
11'-0"x12'-0"

BDRM 3
11'-10"x11'-0"

BILLIARD
20'-0"x20'-0"

BAR
14'-6"x15'-0"

EXERCISE
14'-0"x12'-0"

UTIL/STOR.
24'-0"x12'-0"

STOR.
12'-0"x14'-0"

Design HomeStyle
L-96846-KL
© Larry W. Garnett & Associates, Inc.

Country Style 451

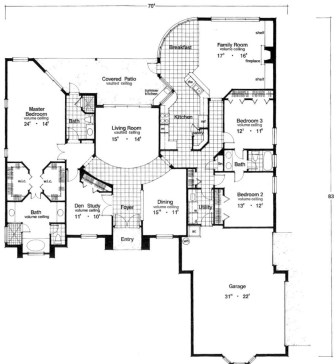

The sophisticated 2,931-square-foot floor plan of this design offers comfortable living on a single level. A spacious master suite and two additional bedrooms are included.

Design HomeStyle
HDS-99-178
© James Zirkel
Home Design Services, Inc.

PORCH

SEAT

MORNING
9'-2" x 9'-10"
10' CLG.
9' CLG.

UTIL

D W

LINEN

TILE

BATH

FAMILY
15'-0" x 19'-4"
10' CLG.

9' CLG.

KITCHEN

OV

DW

PAN

REF

DINING
14'-8" x 11'-4"
9' CLG.

MASTER
BEDROOM
14'-4" x 18'-4"
10' CLG.

9' CLG.

BEDRM 2
11'-4" x 12'-4"
9' CLG.

BATH 3

BATH 2

DN

DN

DN

FOYER

BEDRM 3
11'-4" x 10'-8"
9' CLG.

LIVING
15'-4" x 18'-0"
12' CLG.

PORCH

BEDRM 4
11'-4" x 12'-0"
10' CLG.

FP

53'-2"

69'-4"

**Design HomeStyle
L-2602-c**

© Larry W. Garnett
Associates, Inc.

Country Style 453

The "Thistlewood," with a stately living area of 3,549 square feet, is clearly a European-inspired design. The exterior features a mixture of building materials including natural stone and wooden paneling. Numerous arched windows and the imaginative interplay of form and color indicate an extraordinary house even at first glance. In addition to a formal dining room and living room, the first floor includes a great room with adjacent kitchen and two bedrooms. The master suite features a private bath and walk-in closets. Two additional bedrooms are on the second floor, while the additional space above the garage can be finished to accommodate a number of different purposes.

Design Thistlewood
by William Poole

Ground floor 2,568 sq. ft.
Second floor 981 sq. ft.
Total 3,549 sq. ft.

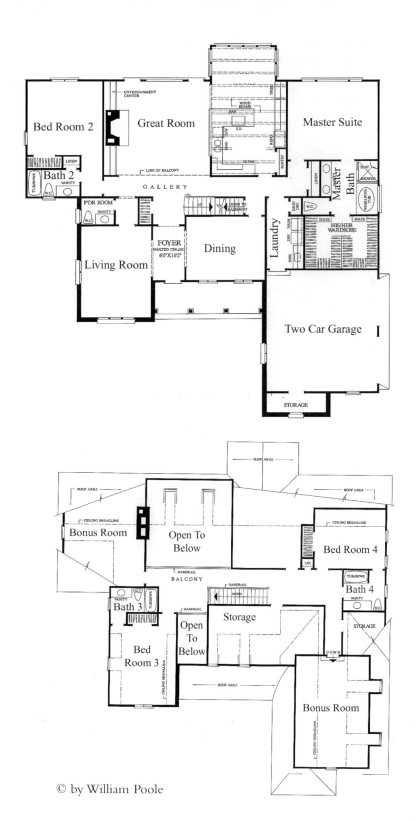

Bed Room 2

Great Room

Master Suite

ENTERTAINMENT CENTER

WOOD BEAMS

BAR

S.U.

LINEN

GREENS

PANTRY

Bath 2

TUB/SHWR

W.C.

VANITY

LINE OF BALCONY

G A L L E R Y

SEAT

SHOWER

Master Bath

LINEN

WHIRLPOOL TUB

PDR ROOM

W.C.

VANITY

DN

DOWN TO BASEMENT

DRIP/DRY

W.C.

SHLVS

SHLVS

Living Room

FOYER
VAULTED CEILING
6'0"X10'2"

Dining

Laundry

SINK

DRY WASH

HIS/HER WARDROBE

Two Car Garage

STORAGE

ROOF AREA

ROOF AREA

ROOF AREA

CEILING BREAKLINE

CEILING BREAKLINE

Bonus Room

Open To Below

Bed Room 4

LIN.

TUB/SHWR

Bath 4

VANITY

W.C.

HANDRAIL

BALCONY

HANDRAIL

DOWN

Bath 3

W.C.

VANITY

TUB/SHWR

STORAGE

HANDRAIL

Open To Below

Storage

Bed Room 3

CEILING BREAKLINE

Open To Below

ROOF AREA

DOWN

Bonus Room

CEILING BREAKLINE

© by William Poole

Country Style 455

62^{11}

COVERED DECK

FAMILY
17^8 X 17^0

MORNING
10^0 X 11^0

MASTER
BEDROOM
14^4 X 19^0

LIVING
16^8 X 15^4

KITCHEN
14^0 X 12^0

UTILITY

57^{10}

LINEN

PANTRY

M. BATH

BATH
2

FOYER

DINING
12^0 X 13^8

GARAGE
21^0 X 22^8

BEDROOM 2
12^4 X 14^0

PORCH

PLAN 2891
DANZE & DAVIS ARCHITECTS, INC
AUSTIN, TEXAS   (512) 343-0714

BATH
4

BEDROOM
3
14^2 X 13^8

BATH
3

BEDROOM
4
12^0 X 13^0

BONUS
13^0 X 23^0

Design HomeStyle
DD-2891
© Danze & Davis Architects, Inc.

456 Country Style

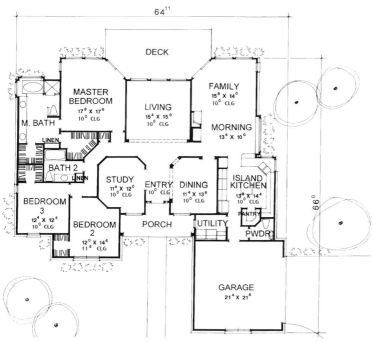

This attractive country-style house design makes a bold impression with its high hipped roof, a generously glazed entry area, and beautiful arched windows. The original floor plan of the interior offers pleasant surprises and encompasses a living area of 2,396 square feet.

Design HomeStyle
DD-2372
© Danze & Davis Architects, Inc.

Country Style 457

Photo © Mark Englund / HomeStyles

The high gable element that optically inter-
rupts the length of the building characterizes
the front of this design. The house offers 2,338
square feet of living area, with an open floor
plan on the first floor. The kitchen is centrally
located between the dining room and the
breakfast area, while the adjacent living room
is open in design and includes a large fireplace.
In addition to the master suite with large
private bath, the ground floor also features a
study. On the second floor are two bedrooms
and a large playroom.

**Design HomeStyle
DD-2338**
© Danze & Davis Architects, Inc.

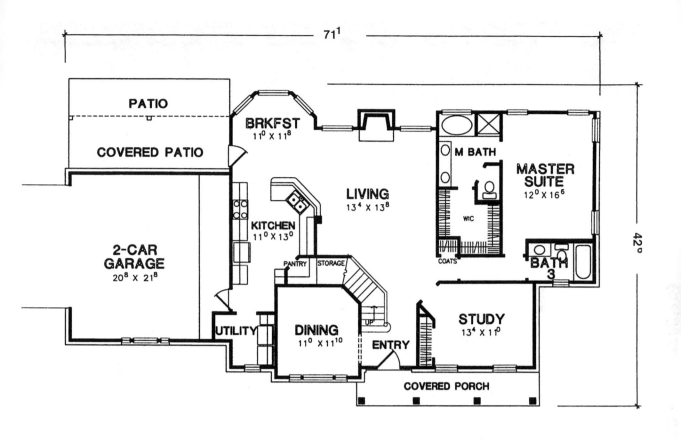

71¹

42⁰

PATIO

COVERED PATIO

BRKFST
11⁰ X 11⁸

2-CAR
GARAGE
20⁸ X 21⁸

KITCHEN
11⁰ X 13⁰

LIVING
13⁴ X 13⁸

M BATH

WIC

MASTER
SUITE
12⁰ X 16⁶

COATS

BATH
3

PANTRY   STORAGE

UTILITY

DINING
11⁰ X 11¹⁰

UP

ENTRY

STUDY
13⁴ X 11⁰

COVERED PORCH

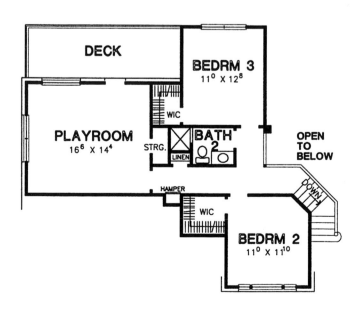

DECK

BEDRM 3
11⁰ X 12⁸

WIC

PLAYROOM
16⁶ X 14⁴

STRG.

BATH
2

LINEN

OPEN
TO
BELOW

HAMPER

WIC

DOWN

BEDRM 2
11⁰ X 11¹⁰

Country Style 459

Photo © Mark Englund / HomeStyles

With a grandiose 4,815 square feet of living area, this dream house offers a large selection of room distributed over two full stories. The elegant front entrance leads into an exclusive open foyer, from which a broad curved stair–way leads to the upper story. To the sides of the foyer are the living and dining rooms. The large family room features a fireplace and high French doors with access to the terrace.

Design HomeStyle
AX-2344
© Jerold Axelrod & Associates, Inc.

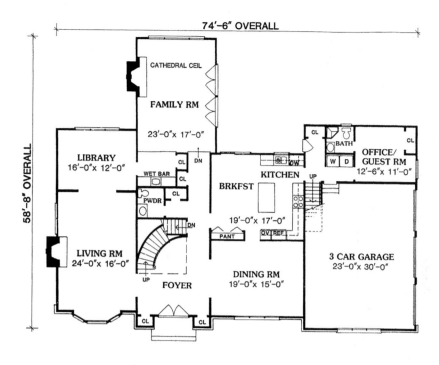

74'-6" OVERALL

58'-8" OVERALL

CATHEDRAL CEIL

FAMILY RM
23'-0"x 17'-0"

LIBRARY
16'-0"x 12'-0"

CL DN

CL

WET BAR

CL

CL

PWDR

KITCHEN

CL

BATH

W D

OFFICE/ GUEST RM
12'-6"x 11'-0"

CL

BRKFST

UP

LIVING RM
24'-0"x 16'-0"

DN

UP

FOYER

PANT

OV REF

DINING RM
19'-0"x 15'-0"

19'-0"x 17'-0"

3 CAR GARAGE
23'-0"x 30'-0"

CL

CL

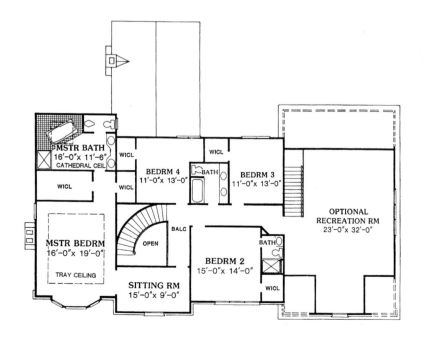

MSTR BATH
16'-0"x 11'-6"
CATHEDRAL CEIL

WICL

WICL

BEDRM 4
11'-0"x 13'-0"

BATH

BEDRM 3
11'-0"x 13'-0"

WICL

WICL

OPTIONAL RECREATION RM
23'-0"x 32'-0"

MSTR BEDRM
16'-0"x 19'-0"

TRAY CEILING

OPEN

BALC

SITTING RM
15'-0"x 9'-0"

BEDRM 2
15'-0"x 14'-0"

BATH

WICL

Country Style 461

This hipped-roof house intrigues the viewer with its gable architecture. The 3,376-square-foot house with four bedrooms is suitable for a large family. On the ground floor are the dining room, family room, a large country kitchen with breakfast nook and a sun room in the beautiful bay, a study, and a master suite with its own bath. Three additional bedrooms are on the second floor. The design includes a two-car garage.

Design HomeStyle
APS-3307
© Atlanta Plan Source, Inc.

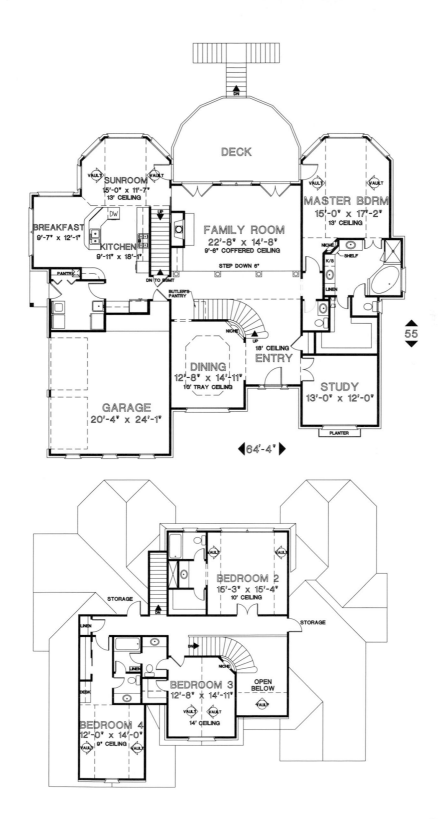

DECK

SUNROOM
15'-0" x 11'-7"
13' CEILING

VAULT   VAULT

MASTER BDRM
15'-0" x 17'-2"
13' CEILING

VAULT   VAULT

BREAKFAST
9'-7" x 12'-1"

DW

UP

FAMILY ROOM
22'-8" x 14'-8"
9'-6" COFFERED CEILING

KITCHEN
9'-11" x 18'-1"

STEP DOWN 6"

NICHE

K/S   SHELF

PANTRY

DN TO BSMT

LINEN

BUTLER'S
PANTRY

NICHE

UP

18' CEILING

ENTRY

55

DINING
12'-8" x 14'-11"
10' TRAY CEILING

STUDY
13'-0" x 12'-0"

GARAGE
20'-4" x 24'-1"

PLANTER

◀64'-4"▶

STORAGE

BEDROOM 2
15'-3" x 15'-4"
10' CEILING

VAULT   VAULT

DN

STORAGE

LINEN

LINEN

NICHE

OPEN
BELOW

DESK

BEDROOM 3
12'-8" x 14'-11"
14' CEILING

VAULT   VAULT

VAULT

BEDROOM 4
12'-0" x 14'-0"
9' CEILING

VAULT   VAULT

Country Style 463

The light stucco facade effectively contrasts with the beautiful details of this European-flavor design and immediately impresses the viewer. The staggered gable architecture, stucco-trimmed windows, arched windows and bays lend the front a distinct note of elegance. The total living area of 3,264 square feet is generously apportioned over two stories. With four bedrooms, the house is suited for a large family.

**Design HomeStyle
APS-3201**
© Atlanta Plan Source, Inc.

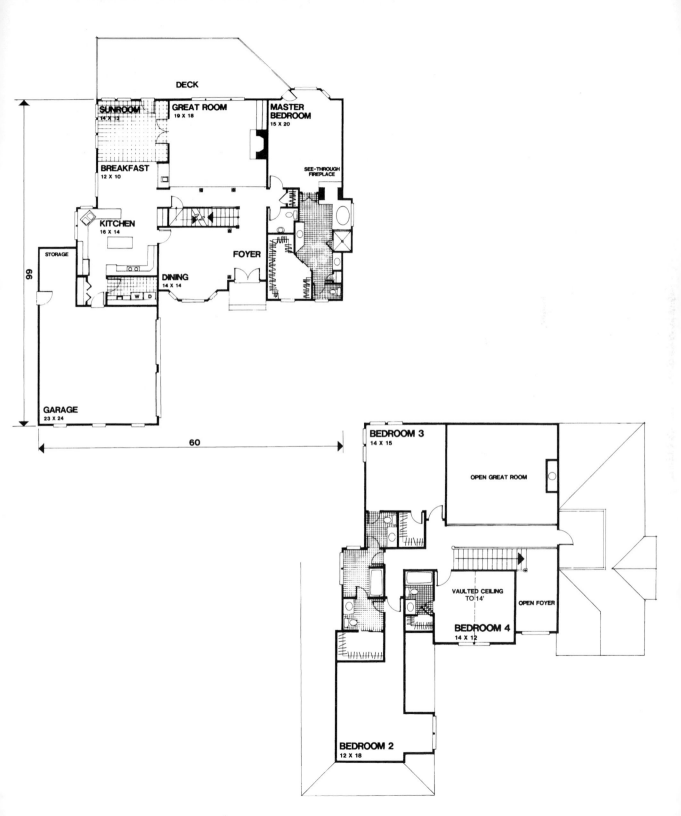

DECK

SUNROOM
14 X 13

GREAT ROOM
19 X 18

MASTER
BEDROOM
15 X 20

BREAKFAST
12 X 10

SEE-THROUGH
FIREPLACE

STORAGE

KITCHEN
16 X 14

FOYER

DINING
14 X 14

W   D

66

60

GARAGE
23 X 24

BEDROOM 3
14 X 15

OPEN GREAT ROOM

VAULTED CEILING
TO 14'

OPEN FOYER

BEDROOM 4
14 X 12

BEDROOM 2
12 X 18

Country Style 465

DECK
22'-8" x 11'-8"

FIREPLACE

TRAY CEILING

DINING
12'-0" x 12'-0"

TRAY CEILING

MSTR. SUITE
13'-4" x 12'-0"

KITCHEN

BRKFST.
9'-0" x 10'-10"

FAMILY
18'-0" x 22'-4"
14' HIGH CEILING

12'-8" x 10'-10"

TRAY CEILING

MSTR. SUITE
12'-0" x 12'-0"

STUDY
10'-4" x 9'-0"

PANTRY

STAIRS TO
BONUS ROOM

STORAGE

62'

LINEN

BEDROOM 2
11'-0" x 14'-0"

ENTRY
12' HIGH CEILING

STAIRS TO
BASEMENT

BEDROOM 3
11'-0" x 14'-0"

PORCH
12' HIGH CEILING

VAULT

VAULT

69'

GARAGE
21'-0" x 25'-6"

BONUS ROOM ABOVE
5' HIGH KNEE WALLS

This one-story country house design offers an ideal floor plan for families. The family room at the center of the house features a fireplace and offers direct access to the sun deck. The kitchen is conveniently located adjacent to the dining room, the breakfast nook, and the utility room. The unique master suite also deserves special mention.

Design HomeStyle
APS-2316
© Atlanta Plan Source, Inc.

Photo © Mark Englund / HomeStyles

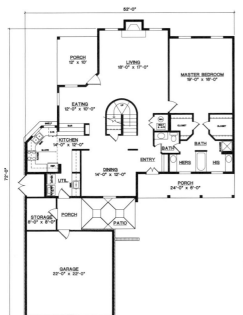

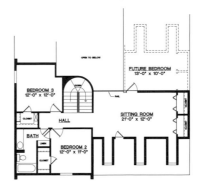

Design HomeStyle
E-2403
© Breland & Farmer, Designers, Inc.

SUNBELT

Photo © Mark Englund / HomeStyles

This house, with 2,447 square feet of living area, promises pure living pleasure on a single level. The front of the house with its inviting entry area piques one's curiosity about the interior. Upon passing through the foyer, the viewer is greeted by an incomparably striking floor plan. A broad palette of rooms is ar-ranged into formal and familial living areas.

Design HomeStyle
HDS-99-248

© James Zirkel Home Design Service, Inc.

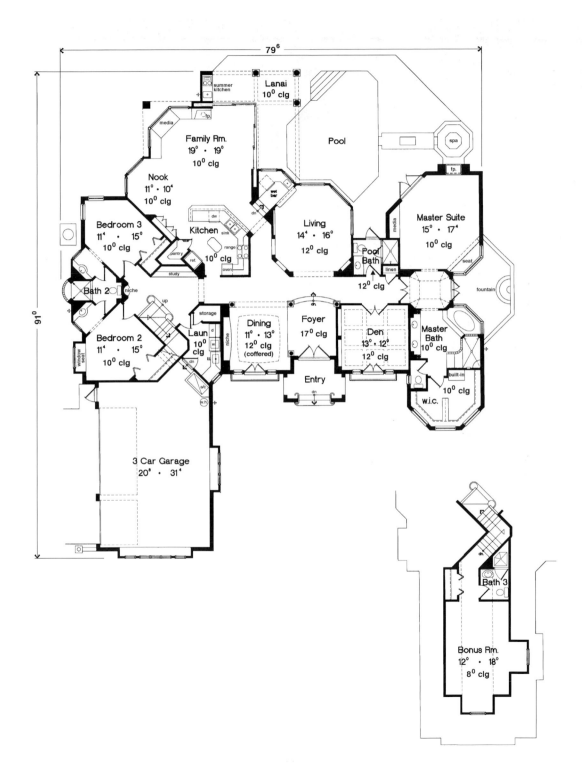

79⁶

91⁰

summer
kitchen

Lanai
10⁰ clg

fp.

media

Family Rm.
19⁰ · 19⁰
10⁰ clg

Pool

spa

fp.

Nook
11⁰ · 10⁴
10⁰ clg

wet
bar

dn

Master Suite
15⁰ · 17⁴
10⁰ clg

media

Bedroom 3
11⁴ · 15⁰
10⁰ clg

Kitchen
10⁰ clg

dw

sink

Living
14⁴ · 16⁰
12⁰ clg

pantry

range

ref.

study

oven

Pool
Bath

12⁰ clg

linen

seat

fountain

Bath 2

niche

up

storage

Laun
10⁰
clg

niche

Dining
11⁰ · 13⁰
12⁰ clg
(coffered)

Foyer
17⁰ clg

Den
13⁰ · 12⁰
12⁰ clg

Master
Bath
10⁰ clg

built-in

Bedroom 2
11⁴ · 15⁰
10⁰ clg

window
seat

dn

w
d

a/c

Entry

dn

w.i.c.

10⁰ clg

wr.h.

3 Car Garage
20⁸ · 31⁴

Bath 3

Bonus Rm.
12⁰ · 18⁰
8⁰ clg

Sunbelt 471

Photo © Mark Englund / HomeStyles

This design offers a palatial 4,092 square feet of living area distributed over two stories. The house is impressive not only in the elegant architecture of its exterior, characterized by offset roofs and dormers, but also because the same generous proportions dominate the interior. The open kitchen, formal living room and master suite all have access to the covered porch, which leads to the yard. The design of the master bath with its unsurpassed luxury deserves special mention.

Design HomeStyle
HDS-99-299
© James Zirkel Home Design Services, Inc.

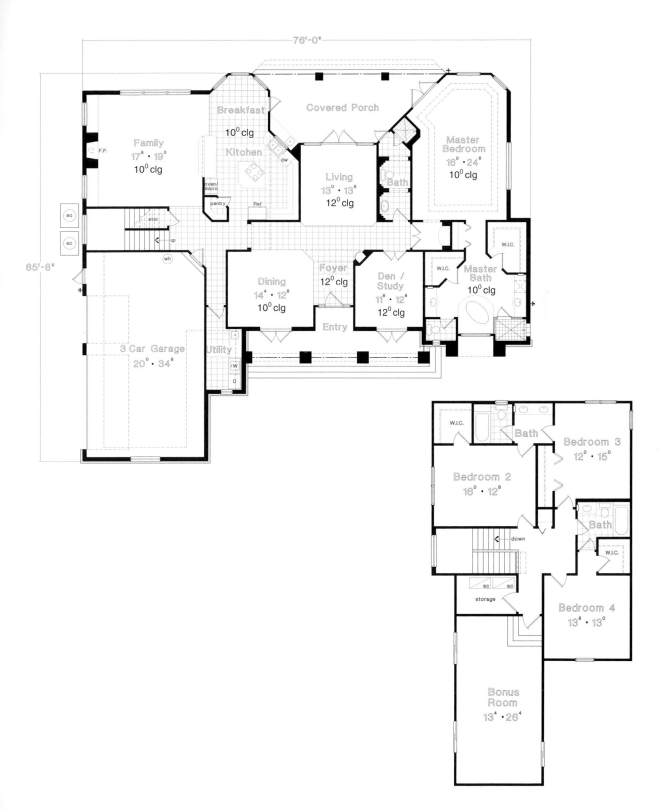

Breakfast
10^0 clg

Covered Porch

Family
$17^8 \cdot 19^0$
10^0 clg

Kitchen

Master Bedroom
$16^0 \cdot 24^8$
10^0 clg

F.P.

oven/micro

pantry

Ref

dw

Living
$13^0 \cdot 13^8$
12^0 clg

Bath

ac

ac

stor.

up

wh

Dining
$14^4 \cdot 12^8$
10^0 clg

Foyer
12^0 clg

Den / Study
$11^8 \cdot 12^8$
12^0 clg

W.I.C.

W.I.C.

Master Bath
10^0 clg

Entry

3 Car Garage
$20^0 \cdot 34^8$

Utility

W

D

76'-0"

65'-8"

Bath

W.I.C.

Bedroom 2
$16^0 \cdot 12^8$

Bedroom 3
$12^0 \cdot 15^0$

down

Bath

W.I.C.

ac   ac

storage

Bedroom 4
$13^8 \cdot 13^0$

Bonus Room
$13^4 \cdot 26^4$

Sunbelt 473

© The Sater Group Inc.

With its total living area of 4,758 square feet, this imposing building appears at first glance to be even larger than it is. The front of the house impresses the observer with its three-arched entry, flanked by two tower constructions. This striking architectural approach is continued in the interior of the house. A large foyer discreetly divides the formal living and dining rooms from the entry area. The ground floor also features a large private living area consisting of a kitchen with breakfast nook and spacious leisure room. A study with direct access to a garden veranda is adjacent to the opulent master suite with bath. On the second floor are an additional two bathrooms and three bedrooms, two of which have their own balconies.

Design 6651
Hillcrest Ridge
© Sater Design

Living area 4,758 sq. ft.
Total 6,537 sq. ft.

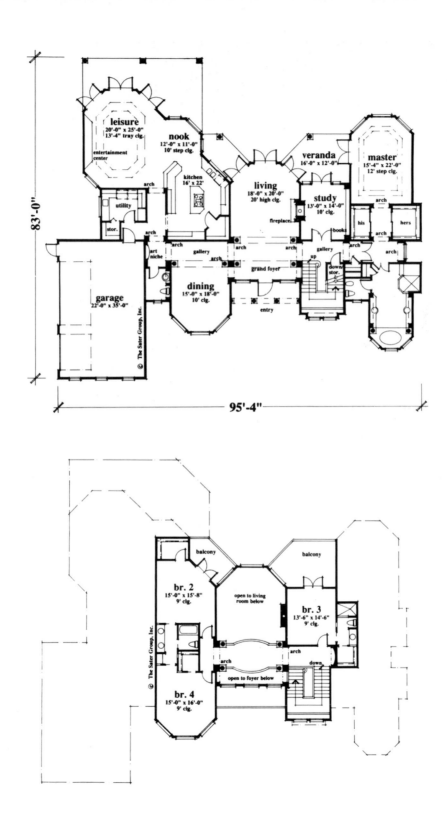

leisure
20'-0" x 25'-0"
13'-4" tray clg.

entertainment center

nook
12'-0" x 11'-0"
10' step clg.

kitchen
16' x 22'

utility

stor.

arch

arch

arch

art niche

gallery

arch

dining
15'-0" x 18'-0"
10' clg.

garage
22'-0" x 35'-0"

© The Sater Group, Inc.

living
18'-0" x 20'-0"
20' high clg.

fireplace

arch

arch

arch

grand foyer

entry

veranda
16'-0" x 12'-0"

study
13'-0" x 14'-0"
10' clg.

books

master
15'-4" x 22'-0"
12' step clg.

arch

his

hers

arch

arch

up

down

gallery

stor.

83'-0"

95'-4"

br. 2
15'-0" x 15'-8"
9' clg.

balcony

open to living
room below

br. 3
13'-6" x 14'-6"
9' clg.

br. 4
15'-0" x 16'-0"
9' clg.

arch

arch

open to foyer below

down

balcony

© The Sater Group, Inc.

Sunbelt 475

Offset roofs, gables, dormers, and the interesting interplay of window and door shapes characterize the exterior of this estate house. Inside, the 2,181-square-foot ground floor presents a carefully thought-out arrangement of rooms. The room inside the tower that is so striking from the street side serves as a formal dining room that adjoins the large kitchen with breakfast nook. These latter in turn form a unit with the adjacent grand room. In addition, the ground floor also features a study and a master suite with a comfortable bath and his-and-her walk-in closets. On the second floor are a full bath and two additional bedrooms, one with access to a deck.

**Design 6652
Elk River Lane**
© Sater Design

Living area 2,890 sq. ft.
Total 4,301 sq. ft.

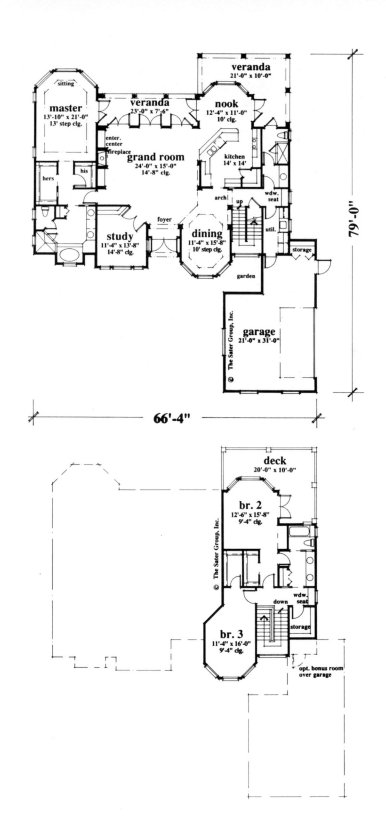

veranda
21'-0" x 10'-0"

sitting

master
13'-10" x 21'-0"
13' step clg.

veranda
23'-0" x 7'-6"

nook
12'-4" x 11'-0"
10' clg.

enter.
center
fireplace

grand room
24'-0" x 15'-0"
14'-8" clg.

kitchen
14' x 14'

his

hers

wdw.
seat

arch

up

util.

foyer

study
11'-4" x 13'-8"
14'-8" clg.

dining
11'-4" x 15'-8"
10' step clg.

storage

garden

© The Sater Group, Inc.

garage
21'-0" x 31'-0"

79'-0"

66'-4"

deck
20'-0" x 10'-0"

br. 2
12'-6" x 15'-8"
9'-4" clg.

© The Sater Group, Inc.

wdw.
seat

down

storage

br. 3
11'-4" x 16'-0"
9'-4" clg.

opt. bonus room
over garage

Sunbelt 477

The elegant facade of this two-story house by the architect Sater is characterized by a balanced application of brick and stucco. The beautifully designed gables that follow the slope of the hipped roofs combined with the use of arched windows and doors make this house especially attractive. The 2,894-square-foot ground floor exhibits a sophisticated floor plan. The living room with a cathedral ceiling stands at the center of the house. Formal rooms such as the dining room and study flank the foyer, while the kitchen with breakfast nook and the leisure room form a unit directed toward the garden. The master suite is fitted with a large walk-in closet and its own spacious bath. The design includes an additional bedroom (or guest room) and bath on both floors of the house.

Design 6653
Wentworth Trail
© Sater Design

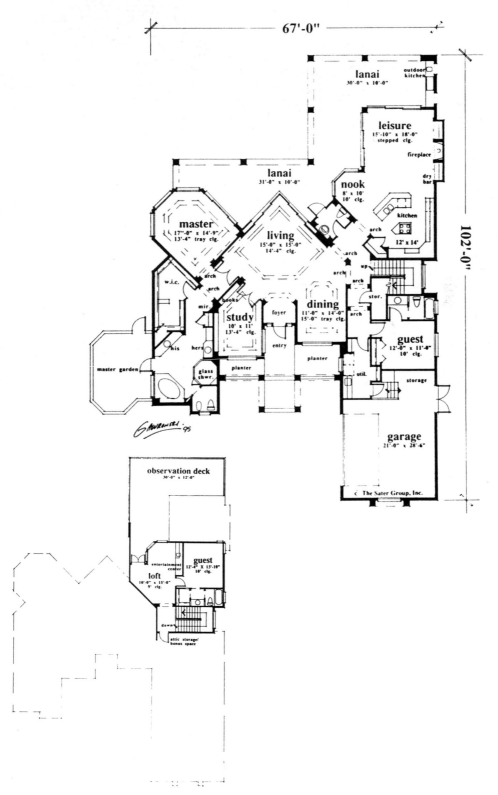

67'-0"

102'-0"

lanai
30'-0" x 10'-0"

outdoor kitchen

leisure
15'-10" x 18'-0"
stepped clg.

fireplace

dry bar

lanai
31'-0" x 10'-0"

nook
8' x 10'
10' clg.

master
17'-0" x 14'-9"
13'-4" tray clg.

living
15'-0" x 15'-0"
14'-4" clg.

arch

kitchen

12' x 14'

arch

w.i.c.

arch

arch

arch

up

stor.

mir.

nooks

arch

arch

guest
12'-0" x 11'-0"
10' clg.

his

hers

study
10' x 11'
13'-4" clg.

foyer

dining
11'-0" x 14'-0"
15'-0" tray clg.

master garden

glass shwr.

planter

entry

planter

util.

storage

garage
21'-0" x 28'-6"

Gawronski '95

c The Sater Group, Inc.

observation deck
30'-0" x 12'-0"

entertainment center

loft
10'-0" x 15'-0"
9' clg.

guest
12'-4" X 13'-10"
10' clg.

down

attic storage/
bonus space

Sunbelt 479

© The Sater Group Inc.

The two-story "Nassau Cove" by Sater Design is ideally suited to serve as a family or vacation cottage. Horizontal wooden panels, latticed windows with shutters, and the parapet on the striking metal roof lend the house a special air. The offset roofs, gables, and dormers accentuate the charm of the design. A covered entry porch and two sun decks at the rear of the house offer sufficient room for enjoying the out-of-doors. Three bedrooms and two baths are distributed on the ground floor with 1,342 square feet and the second floor with 511 square feet.

Design 6654
Nassau Cove
© Sater Design

Living area 1,853 sq. ft.
Total 4,127 sq. ft.

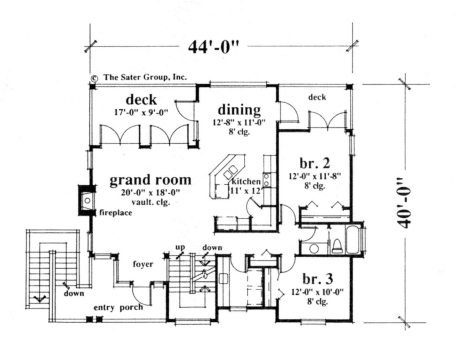

44'-0"

© The Sater Group, Inc.

deck
17'-0" x 9'-0"

dining
12'-8" x 11'-0"
8' clg.

deck

br. 2
12'-0" x 11'-8"
8' clg.

grand room
20'-0" x 18'-0"
vault. clg.

kitchen
11' x 12'

fireplace

40'-0"

up   down

foyer

down

br. 3
12'-0" x 10'-0"
8' clg.

entry porch

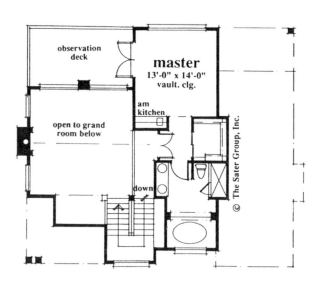

observation
deck

master
13'-0" x 14'-0"
vault. clg.

am
kitchen

open to grand
room below

© The Sater Group, Inc.

down

Sunbelt 481

© The Sater Group Inc.

An attractive alternation of stone and stucco is the hallmark of the facade of this traditional design with a living area of 4,106 square feet. The striking columns that decorate the entry emphasize the elegance of the design, and hint at the magnificent interior. The wide, inviting foyer suggests the generous room proportions and arrangement, and allows a view into the central living room with fireplace and direct access to the large back veranda. The large kitchen with a center island is adjacent to the breakfast nook and leisure room. This private area features glazing toward the garden, assuring lots of sunlight. In addition, the ground floor offers a study, a dining room, and a luxurious master suite with a comfortable bath. Three rooms and two baths are located on the second floor.

Design 6656
Stoney Creek Way
© Sater Design

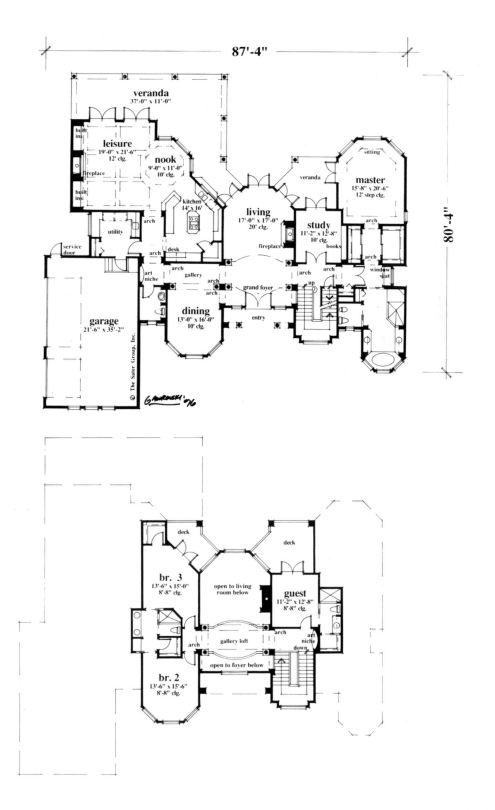

87'-4"

80'-4"

veranda
37'-0" x 11'-0"

leisure
19'-0" x 21'-6"
12' clg.

built ins

fireplace

built ins

nook
9'-0" x 11'-0"
10' clg.

kitchen
14' x 16'

arch

utility

living
17'-0" x 17'-0"
20' clg.

fireplace

study
11'-2" x 12'-8"
10' clg.

books

veranda

sitting

master
15'-8" x 20'-6"
12' step clg.

arch

arch

window seat

service door

arch

desk

arch

art niche

gallery

arch

arch

grand foyer

arch

up

arch

arch

garage
21'-6" x 35'-2"

© The Sater Group, Inc.

dining
13'-0" x 16'-0"
10' clg.

entry

GAWROWSKI '96

deck

deck

br. 3
13'-6" x 15'-0"
8'-8" clg.

open to living
room below

guest
11'-2" x 12'-8"
8'-8" clg.

arch

art niche

gallery loft

arch

down

arch

br. 2
13'-6" x 15'-6"
8'-8" clg.

open to foyer below

Sunbelt 483

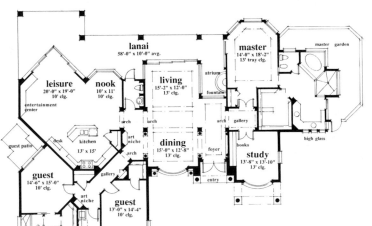

Design 6657
Biltmore Trace
© Sater Design

Living area 3,248 sq. ft.
Total 4,796 sq. ft.

This is a spectacular and inimitable house plan. From the two-story foyer, the viewer's gaze passes to the inner courtyard with fountain. The floor plan clearly organizes the living areas, and each bedroom has its own full bath.

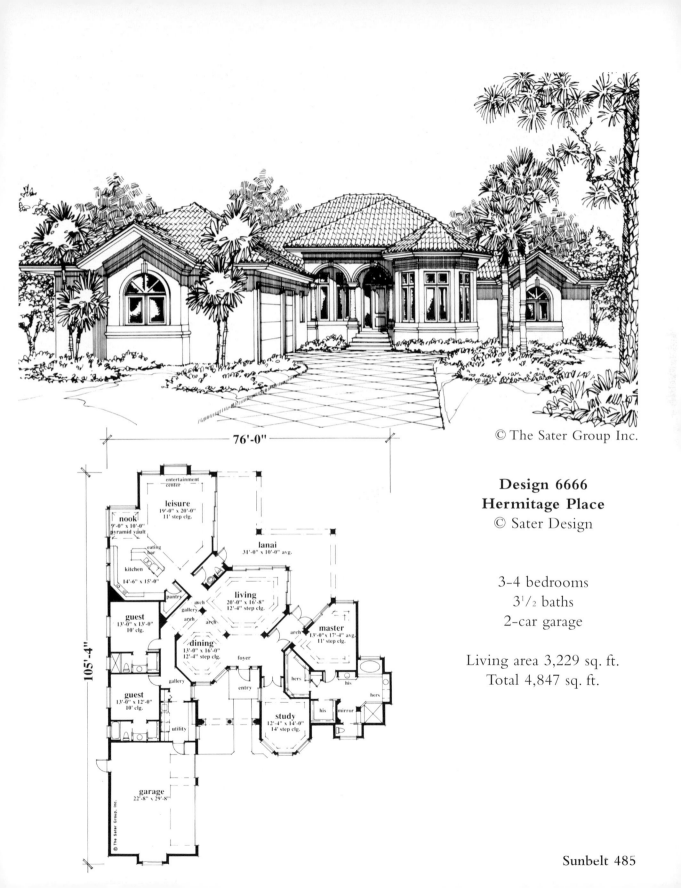

© The Sater Group Inc.

76'-0"

105'-4"

entertainment center

leisure
19'-0" x 20'-0"
11' step clg.

nook
9'-0" x 10'-0"
pyramid vault

lanai
31'-0" x 10'-0" avg.

eating bar

kitchen
14'-6" x 15'-0"

pantry

living
20'-0" x 16'-8"
12'-4" step clg.

master
13'-0" x 17'-4" avg.
11' step clg.

gallery

arch

arch   arch

arch

guest
13'-0" x 13'-0"
10' clg.

dining
13'-0" x 16'-0"
12'-4" step clg.

foyer

hers

his

guest
13'-0" x 12'-0"
10' clg.

gallery

entry

his   mirror

hers

study
12'-4" x 14'-0"
14' step clg.

utility

garage
22'-8" x 29'-8"

© The Sater Group, Inc.

Design 6666
Hermitage Place
© Sater Design

3-4 bedrooms
3½ baths
2-car garage

Living area 3,229 sq. ft.
Total 4,847 sq. ft.

Sunbelt 485

This appealing farm house design is especially suitable for young, growing families. With its horizontal wooden facade, dormers, and attractive front porch, the exterior design fits well into any neighborhood. Crossing the wide covered porch, one enters the foyer, from which one can enter either the dining room or the spacious living room through attractive archways. An arch also separates the great room from the dining room. The kitchen with its glazed breakfast nook and the great room form a private area with direct access to the garden veranda. The house has four bedrooms and a study (or fifth bedroom) over a total living area of 2,527 square feet, with 1,676 square feet on the ground floor and 851 square feet on the second. The total area of the house including the garage and storage areas is 3,394 square feet.

Design 6662
Canterbury Trail
© Sater Design

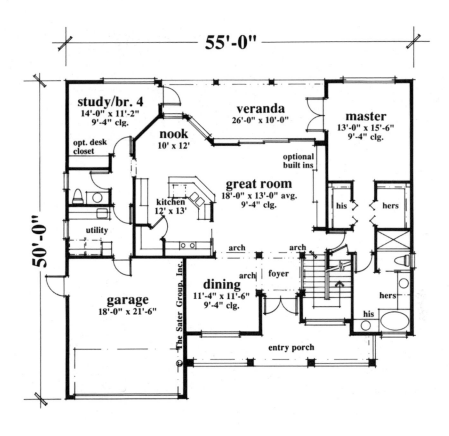

55'-0"

50'-0"

study/br. 4
14'-0" x 11'-2"
9'-4" clg.

opt. desk
closet

nook
10' x 12'

veranda
26'-0" x 10'-0"

master
13'-0" x 15'-6"
9'-4" clg.

optional
built ins

great room
18'-0" x 13'-0" avg.
9'-4" clg.

his

hers

kitchen
12' x 13'

utility

arch

arch

his

foyer

hers

arch

garage
18'-0" x 21'-6"

dining
11'-4" x 11'-6"
9'-4" clg.

hers

his

The Sater Group, Inc.

entry porch

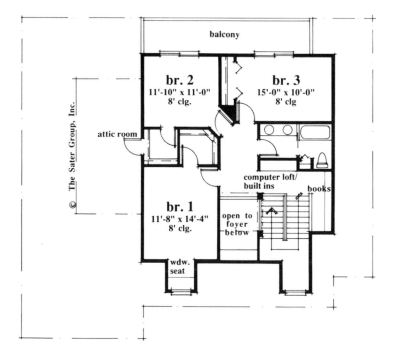

balcony

br. 2
11'-10" x 11'-0"
8' clg.

br. 3
15'-0" x 10'-0"
8' clg

attic room

computer loft/
built ins

books

br. 1
11'-8" x 14'-4"
8' clg.

open to
foyer
below

© The Sater Group, Inc.

wdw.
seat

Sunbelt 487

© The Sater Group Inc.

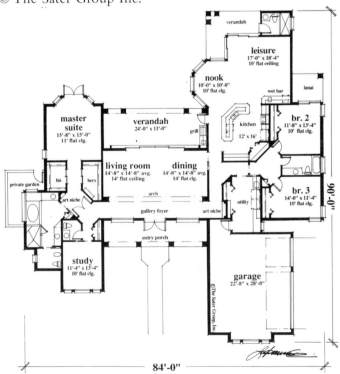

Design 6663
Queenstown Harbour Way
© Sater Design

Living area 2,977 sq. ft.
Total 4,408 sq. ft.

The elaborate building style of this house signalizes that this is a home of superior class. The high columns in front of the entrance are proportional to the large arched windows in the entry area, which hint at the elegance of the interior of the house.

© The Sater Group Inc.

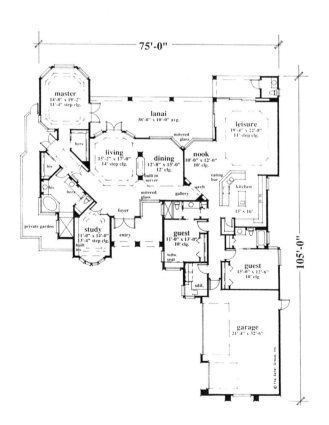

Design 6665
Royal Birkdale Lane
© Sater Design

3-4 bedrooms
3¹/₂ baths
3-car garage

Living area 3,279 sq. ft.
Total 4,785 sq. ft.

The front view of this two-story house is characterized by the clear lines of the offset hipped roofs and gables. The fine stucco work on the facade accentuates the elegance of the arched windows, while the open floor plan of the interior profits from the generous use of glass. Particularly the formal living and dining rooms, which form a cohesive unit quite distinct from the more private area to the back of the house, are bright and flooded with light. The ground floor is devoted to daily life. The kitchen with an eating bar, a breakfast nook, and leisure area are oriented toward the garden, accessible across a covered terrace. At the other end of the ground floor is the master suite with its own spacious bath and his-and-her walk-in closets. Two further rooms and another bathroom are found on the second floor.

Design 6675
Lochwood Drive
© Sater Design

Living area 3,285 sq. ft.

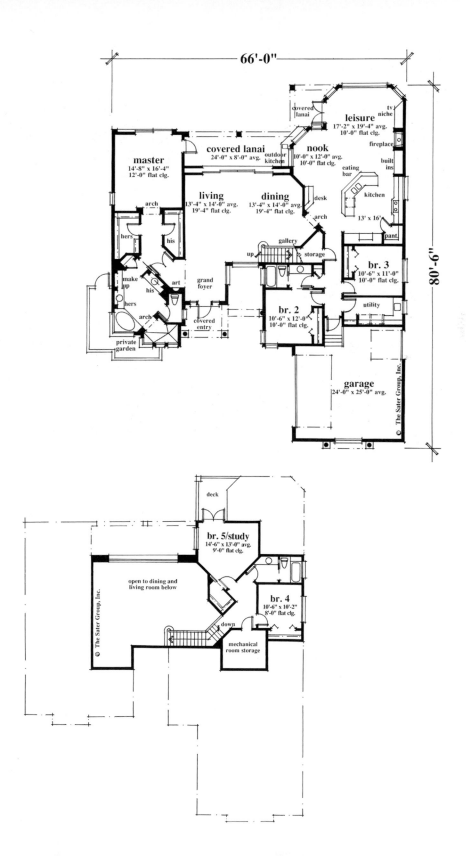

66'-0"

80'-6"

covered lanai

leisure
17'-2" x 19'-4" avg.
10'-0" flat clg.

tv niche

master
14'-8" x 16'-4"
12'-0" flat clg.

covered lanai
24'-0" x 8'-0" avg.

outdoor kitchen

nook
10'-0" x 12'-0" avg.
10'-0" flat clg.

fireplace

built ins

eating bar

arch

living
13'-4" x 14'-0" avg.
19'-4" flat clg.

dining
13'-4" x 14'-0" avg.
19'-4" flat clg.

desk

arch

kitchen
13' x 16'

hers

his

gallery

storage

pant.

make up

his

art

up

grand foyer

br. 3
10'-6" x 11'-0"
10'-0" flat clg.

hers

arch

covered entry

br. 2
10'-6" x 12'-0"
10'-0" flat clg.

utility

private garden

garage
24'-0" x 25'-0" avg.

© The Sater Group, Inc.

deck

br. 5/study
14'-6" x 13'-0" avg.
9'-0" flat clg.

open to dining and living room below

br. 4
10'-6" x 10'-2"
8'-0" flat clg.

down

© The Sater Group, Inc.

mechanical room storage

Sunbelt 491

85'-4"

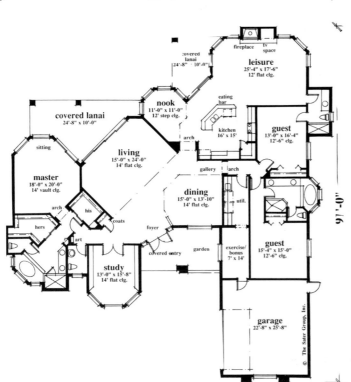

covered
lanai
24'-8" 10'-0"

leisure
25'-4" x 17'-6"
12' flat clg.

fireplace   tv
space

eating
bar

nook
11'-0" x 11'-0"
12' step clg.

kitchen
16' x 15'

guest
13'-0" x 16'-4"
12'-6" clg.

covered lanai
24'-8" x 10'-0"

sitting

living
15'-0" x 24'-0"
14' flat clg.

arch

master
18'-0" x 20'-0"
14' vault clg.

gallery   arch

dining
15'-0" x 13'-10"
14' flat clg.

his

arch

hers

coats

util.

guest
15'-4" x 15'-0"
12'-6" clg.

art

foyer

covered entry

garden

exercise/
bonus
7' x 14'

study
13'-0" x 15'-8"
14' flat clg.

91'-0"

garage
22'-8" x 25'-8"

© The Sater Group, Inc.

Design 6676
Bay Landing Drive
© Sater Design

3-4 bedrooms
3 1/2 baths
2-car garage

Living area 3,714 sq. ft.
Total 4,577 sq. ft.

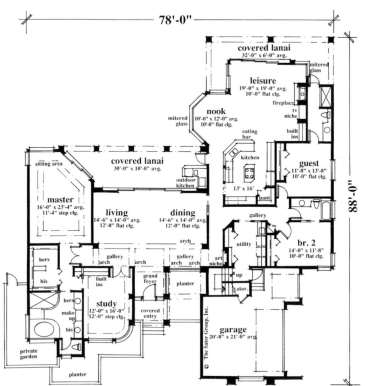

Design 6679
© Sater Design

The well-proportioned use of brick and stucco on the facade of this house allows the arched windows to stand out particularly well. Arches are also used on the interior of this spacious and beautiful home to separate the gallery from the formal living and dining rooms, located at the center of the house.

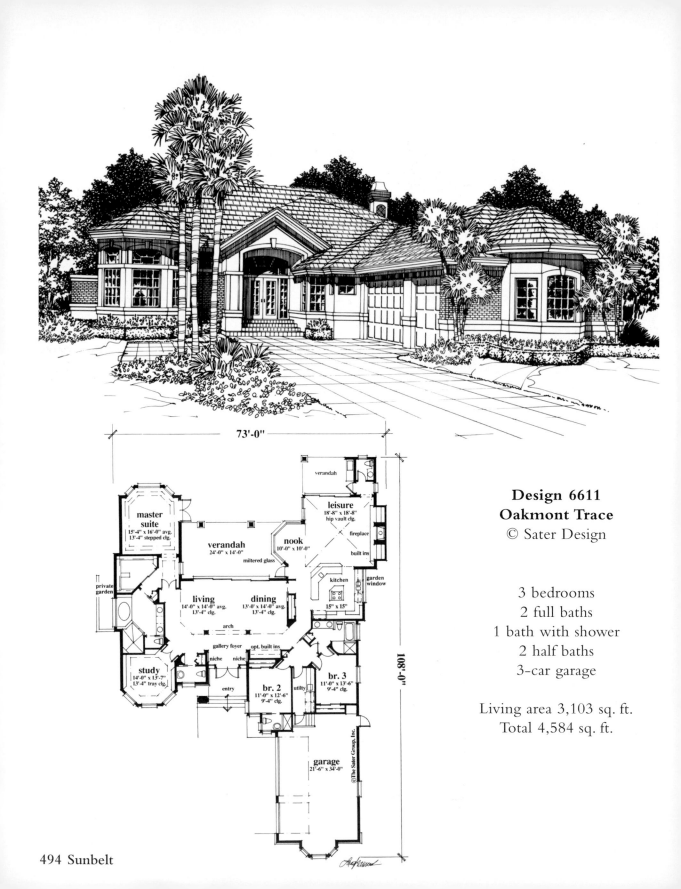

Design 6611
Oakmont Trace
© Sater Design

3 bedrooms
2 full baths
1 bath with shower
2 half baths
3-car garage

Living area 3,103 sq. ft.
Total 4,584 sq. ft.

Floor plan labels:

73'-0"
108'-0"

master suite
15'-4" x 16'-0" avg.
13'-4" stepped clg.

private garden

study
14'-0" x 13'-7"
13'-4" tray clg.

verandah
24'-0" x 14'-0"

living
14'-0" x 14'-0" avg.
13'-4" clg.

dining
13'-0" x 14'-0" avg.
13'-4" clg.

arch

gallery foyer

niche   niche

entry

opt. built ins

nook
10'-0" x 10'-0"

miltered glass

kitchen

15" x 15"

leisure
18'-8" x 18'-8"
hip vault clg.

verandah

fireplace

built ins

garden window

br. 2
11'-0" x 12'-6"
9'-4" clg.

utilty

br. 3
11'-0" x 13'-6"
9'-4" clg.

garage
21'-6" x 34'-0"

©The Sater Group, Inc.

494 Sunbelt

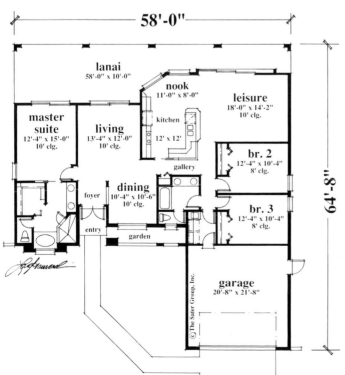

Floor Plan Labels

- **lanai** 58'-0" x 10'-0"
- **nook** 11'-0" x 8'-0"
- **leisure** 18'-0" x 14'-2" 10' clg.
- **master suite** 12'-4" x 15'-0" 10' clg.
- **living** 13'-4" x 12'-0" 10' clg.
- **kitchen** 12' x 12'
- **br. 2** 12'-4" x 10'-4" 8' clg.
- **gallery**
- **dining** 10'-4" x 10'-6" 10' clg.
- **br. 3** 12'-4" x 10'-4" 8' clg.
- **foyer**
- **entry**
- **garden**
- **garage** 20'-8" x 21'-8"

58'-0"

64'-8"

© The Sater Group, Inc.

Design 6603
La Costa Court
© Sater Design

3 bedrooms
2 baths
2-car garage

Living area 1,776 sq. ft.
Total 2,850 sq. ft.

Sunbelt 495

© The Sater Group Inc.

"Southern Hills Place" is a single-story design with atmosphere. The striking entry and large front windows indicate the generous proportions of the design from the outside. The living areas, including the kitchen, breakfast nook and adjacent dining room, feature 14-foot ceilings. The high point of the house is the centrally placed two-story living room. The second-floor gallery that leads to the two upstairs bedrooms affords a view into the living room. The master suite on the ground floor includes a luxurious bathroom with a shower, whirlpool, double sink vanity, and a separate toilet.

Design 6613
Southern Hills Place
© Sater Design

Living area 2,448 sq. ft.
Total 3,694 sq. ft.

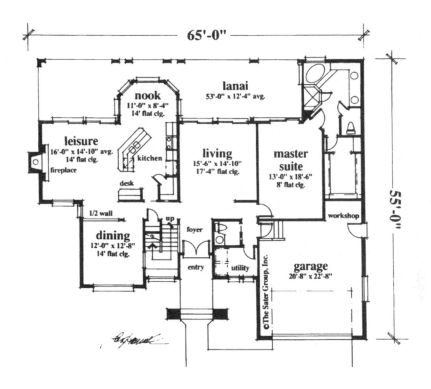

65'-0"

55'-0"

nook
11'-0" x 8'-4"
14' flat clg.

lanai
53'-0" x 12'-4" avg.

leisure
16'-0" x 14'-10" avg.
14' flat clg.

fireplace

kitchen

living
15'-6" x 14'-10"
17'-4" flat clg.

master
suite
13'-0" x 18'-6"
8' flat clg.

desk

1/2 wall

up

foyer

workshop

©The Sater Group, Inc.

dining
12'-0" x 12'-8"
14' flat clg.

entry

utility

garage
20'-8" x 22'-8"

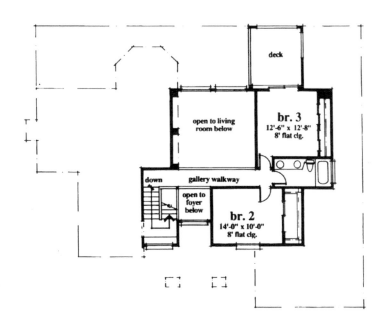

deck

open to living
room below

br. 3
12'-6" x 12'-8"
8' flat clg.

down

gallery walkway

open to foyer
below

br. 2
14'-0" x 10'-0"
8' flat clg.

Sunbelt 497

© The Sater Group Inc.

**Design 6621
Kingston Harbour**
© Sater Design

Ground floor 1,736 sq. ft.
Second floor 1,642 sq. ft.
Third floor 927 sq. ft.

Living area 2,569 sq. ft.
Total 4,305 sq. ft.

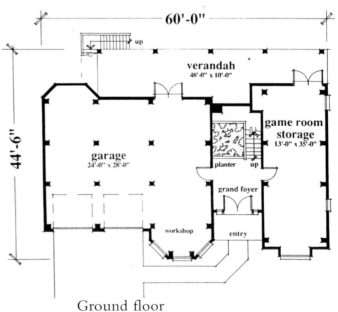

Ground floor

Second floor

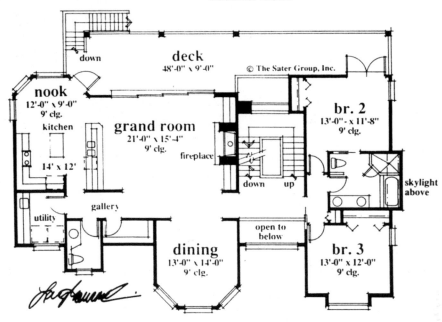

down

deck
48'-0" x 9'-0"

© The Sater Group, Inc.

nook
12'-0" x 9'-0"
9' clg.

kitchen

14' x 12'

grand room
21'-0" x 15'-4"
9' clg.

fireplace

br. 2
13'-0" - x 11'-8"
9' clg.

down   up

skylight
above

gallery

utility

dining
13'-0" x 14'-0"
9' clg.

open to
below

br. 3
13'-0" x 12'-0"
9' clg.

Third floor

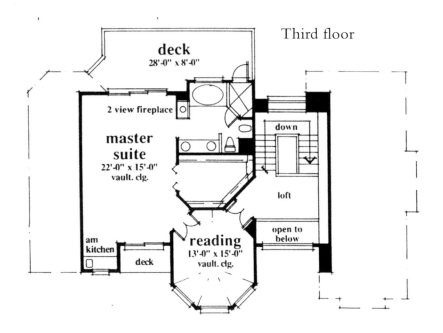

deck
28'-0" x 8'-0"

2 view fireplace

down

**master
suite**
22'-0" x 15'-0"
vault. clg.

loft

am
kitchen

deck

open to
below

reading
13'-0" x 15'-0"
vault. clg.

Sunbelt 499

© The Sater Group Inc.

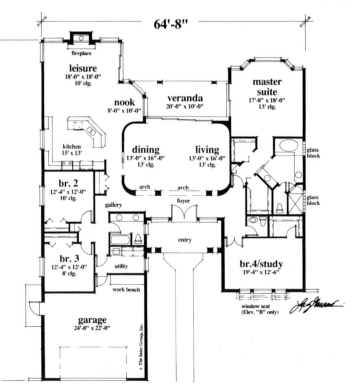

64'-8"

fireplace

leisure
18'-0" x 18'-0"
10' clg.

nook
8'-0" x 10'-0"

veranda
20'-0" x 10'-0"

**master
suite**
17'-8" x 18'-0"
13' clg.

kitchen
15' x 13'

dining
13'-0" x 16'-0"
13' clg.

living
13'-0" x 16'-0"
13' clg.

glass
block

br. 2
12'-4" x 12'-0"
10' clg.

arch

arch

glass
block

gallery

foyer

br. 3
12'-4" x 12'-0"
8' clg.

entry

utility

br.4/study
19'-4" x 12'-6"

work bench

garage
24'-8" x 22'-0"

window seat
(Elev. "B" only)

© The Sater Group, Inc.

**Design 6624
Pebble Beach Way**

© Sater Design

4 bedrooms
2^1/$_2$ baths
2-car garage

Living area 2,998 sq. ft.
Total 3,976 sq. ft.

© The Sater Group Inc.

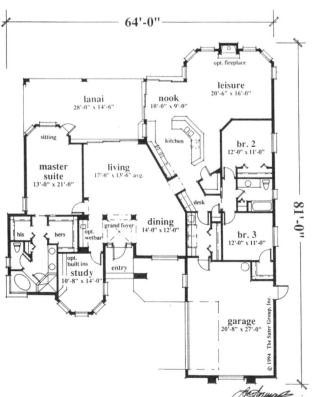

Design 6626
La Costa Trace
© Sater Design

3-4 bedrooms
2 baths
2-car garage

Living area 2,589 sq. ft.
Total 3,630 sq. ft.

Sunbelt 501

© The Sater Group Inc.

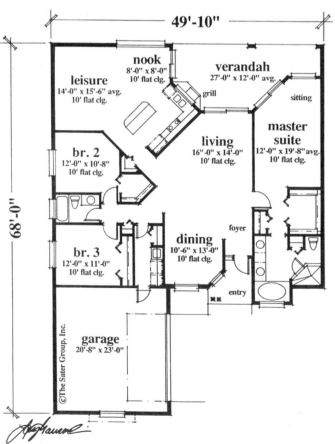

nook
8'-0" x 8'-0"
10' flat clg.

verandah
27'-0" x 12'-0" avg.

grill

sitting

leisure
14'-0" x 15'-6" avg.
10' flat clg.

master
suite
12'-0" x 19'-8" avg.
10' flat clg.

living
16"-0" x 14'-0"
10' flat clg.

br. 2
12'-0" x 10'-8"
10' flat clg.

foyer

dining
10'-6" x 13'-0"
10' flat clg.

br. 3
12'-0" x 11'-0"
10' flat clg.

entry

garage
20'-8" x 23'-0"

©The Sater Group, Inc.

49'-10"

68'-0"

Design 6630
Forest Oaks Place
© Sater Design

3 bedrooms
2 baths
2-car garage

Living area 1,953 sq. ft.
Total 2,763 sq. ft.

502 Sunbelt

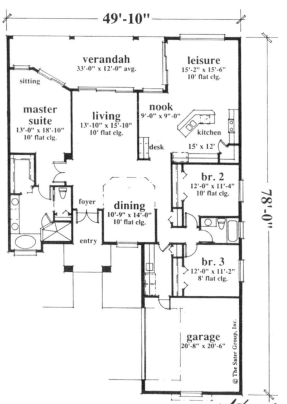

49'-10"

verandah
33'-0" x 12'-0" avg.

leisure
15'-2" x 15'-6"
10' flat clg.

sitting

master suite
13'-0" x 18'-10"
10' flat clg.

living
13'-10" x 15'-10"
10' flat clg.

nook
9'-0" x 9'-0"

kitchen

desk

15' x 12'

foyer

dining
10'-9" x 14'-0"
10' flat clg.

br. 2
12'-0" x 11'-4"
10' flat clg.

entry

br. 3
12'-0" x 11'-2"
8' flat clg.

78'-0"

© The Sater Group, Inc.

garage
20'-8" x 20'-6"

**Design 6631
Indian Wells Trace**

© Sater Design

3 bedrooms
2 baths
2-car garage

Living area 2,185 sq. ft.
Total 3,050 sq. ft.

Sunbelt 503

Photo © Mark Englund / HomeStyles

This stately house features an unconventional yet appealling floor plan and, with a living area of 3,436 square feet, offers every imaginable comfort for both the residents and their guests.

Design HomeStyle
HDS-99-300
© James Zirkel Home Design Services, Inc.

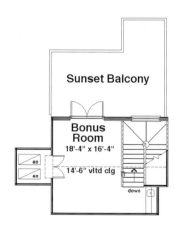

Sunset Balcony

Bonus Room
18'-4" x 16'-4"
14'-6" vltd clg
down

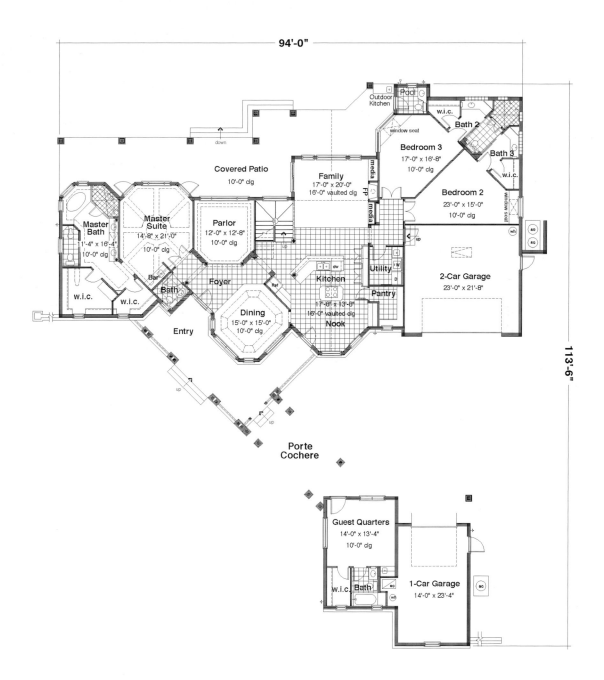

94'-0"

113'-6"

Outdoor Kitchen

Pool

window seat

w.i.c.

Bath 2

Bath 3

w.i.c.

Bedroom 3
17'-0" x 16'-8"
10'-0" clg

Covered Patio
10'-0" clg

Family
17'-0" x 20'-0"
16'-0" vaulted clg

Bedroom 2
23'-0" x 15'-0"
10'-0" clg

media

FP

media

window seat

wh

ac

ac

up

Master
Bath
11'-4" x 16'-4"
10'-0" clg

Master
Suite
14'-8" x 21'-0"
10'-0" clg

Parlor
12'-0" x 12'-8"
10'-0" clg

Utility

dw

d

2-Car Garage
23'-0" x 21'-8"

w.i.c.

w.i.c.

Bar

Bath

Foyer

Kitchen

Pantry

Ref

Dining
15'-0" x 15'-0"
10'-0" clg

Nook

Kitchen
17'-8" x 13'-8"
16'-0" vaulted clg

Entry

up

up

Porte
Cochere

Guest Quarters
14'-0" x 13'-4"
10'-0" clg

w.i.c.

Bath

wh

ac

1-Car Garage
14'-0" x 23'-4"

ac

down

Sunbelt 505

© The Sater Group Inc.

The exterior design of this 2,794-square-foot house gives the impression of being much larger than it actually is. The high, two-story entry area and playful treatment of the protruding roofs and additions lend the house a great deal of charm. The breadth and generosity of design is continued in the interior. The commanding grand room with a 19-foot ceiling imparts an overwhelming sense of spaciousness. The kitchen is located between the dining room and breakfast nook, and is separated from the grand room by an eating bar. In addition to a master suite with its own large bath and two walk-in closets, the ground floor also features a study and a second bedroom. The second floor, which offers a view into the rooms below, provides a loft and a third bedroom with full bath.

Design 6608
Torrey Pines Way
© Sater Design

Living area 2,794 sq. ft.
Total 3,978 sq. ft.

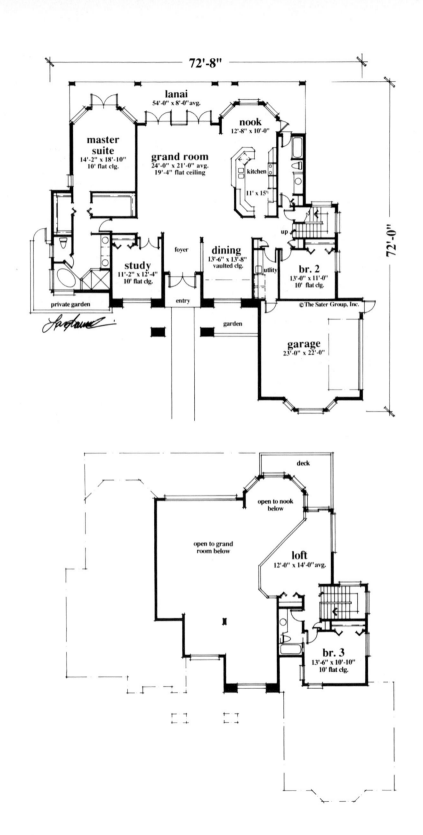

lanai
54'-0" x 8'-0" avg.

nook
12'-8" x 10'-0"

master
suite
14'-2" x 18'-10"
10' flat clg.

grand room
24'-0" x 21'-0" avg.
19'-4" flat ceiling

kitchen

11' x 15"

up

foyer

dining
13'-6" x 13'-8"
vaulted clg.

study
11'-2" x 12'-4"
10' flat clg.

utility

br. 2
13'-0" x 11'-0"
10' flat clg.

private garden

entry

©The Sater Group, Inc.

garden

garage
23'-0" x 22'-0"

72'-8"

72'-0"

deck

open to nook
below

open to grand
room below

loft
12'-0" x 14'-0" avg.

br. 3
13'-6" x 10'-10"
10' flat clg.

Sunbelt 507

© The Sater Group Inc.

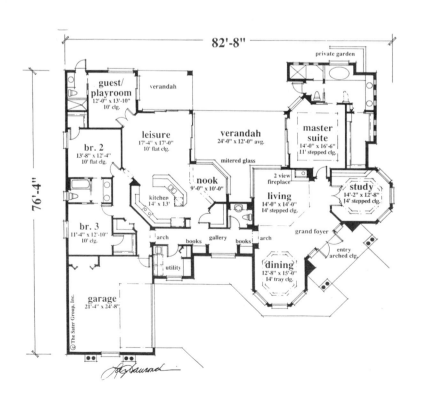

Design 6633
Royal Troon Lane
© Sater Design

4-5 bedrooms
3 1/2 baths
2-car garage

Living area 2,986 sq. ft.
Total 4,278 sq. ft.

508 Sunbelt

© The Sater Group Inc.

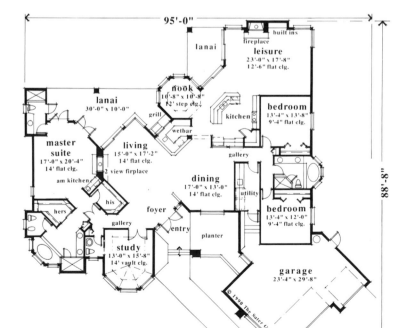

Design 6634
Innsbrook Place
© Sater Design

3-4 bedrooms
3¹/₂ baths
2-car garage

Living area 3,477 sq. ft.
Total 4,907 sq. ft.

Sunbelt 509

© The Sater Group Inc.

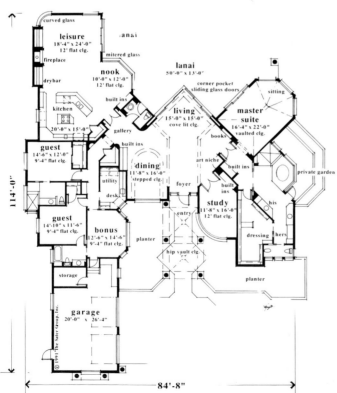

curved glass

leisure
18'-4" x 24'-0"
12' flat clg.

lanai

fireplace

drybar

nook
10'-0" x 12'-0"
12' flat clg.

mitered glass

lanai
50'-0" x 13'-0"

built ins

corner pocket
sliding glass doors

sitting

kitchen
20'-0" x 15'-0"

built ins

gallery

living
15'-0" x 15'-0"
cove lit clg.

master suite
16'-4" x 22'-0"
vaulted clg.

books

guest
14'-6" x 12'-0"
9'-4" flat clg.

built ins

dining
11'-8" x 16'-0"
stepped clg.

art niche

built ins

private garden

utility

desk

foyer

built ins

guest
14'-10" x 11'-6"
9'-4" flat clg.

entry

study
11'-8" x 16'-0"
12' flat clg.

his

bonus
12'-6" x 14'-6"
9'-4" flat clg.

planter

dressing

hers

hip vault clg.

storage

planter

114'-0"

garage
20'-0" x 26'-4"

© 1991 The Sater Group, Inc.

84'-8"

Design 6637
Vintage Trace Way
© Sater Design

3-4 bedrooms
3½ baths
2-car garage

Living area 4,186 sq. ft.
Total 5,782 sq. ft.

510 Sunbelt

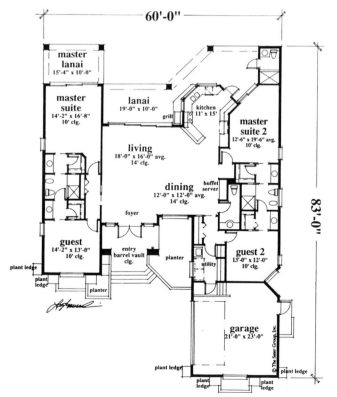

master lanai
15'-4" x 10'-0"

master suite
14'-2" x 16'-8"
10' clg.

lanai
19'-0" x 10'-0"

kitchen
11' x 15'

grill

master suite 2
12'-6" x 19'-6" avg.
10' clg.

living
18'-0" x 16'-0" avg.
14' clg.

dining
12'-0" x 12'-0" avg.
14' clg.

buffet server

foyer

guest
14'-2" x 13'-0"
10' clg.

entry
barrel vault clg.

planter

utility

guest 2
13'-0" x 12'-0"
10' clg.

plant ledge

plant ledge

planter

60'-0"

83'-0"

garage
21'-0" x 23'-0"

plant ledge

plant ledge

plant ledge

plant ledge

Design 6645
Waterford Street
© Sater Design

4 bedrooms
3½ baths
2-car garage

Living area 2,473 sq. ft.
Total 3,797 sq. ft.

Sunbelt 511

© The Sater Group Inc.

The elegance of this villa is not limited to its grand exterior with its balanced combination of brick and stuccoed gables. The well-thought-out floor plan of the interior is also a winning point. The two-story design of the "Edgewood" is ideal for a large family. The ground floor with 2,551 square feet is organized into formal and familial areas. The kitchen with a breakfast nook forms a single unit. The study and the formal dining room flank the foyer and open toward the two-story living room with fireplace and an elegant stairway that leads to the second story, which features a loft, two bedrooms and a full bath.

Design 6646
Edgewood Court
© Sater Design

Living area 3,590 sq. ft.
Total 5,385 sq. ft.

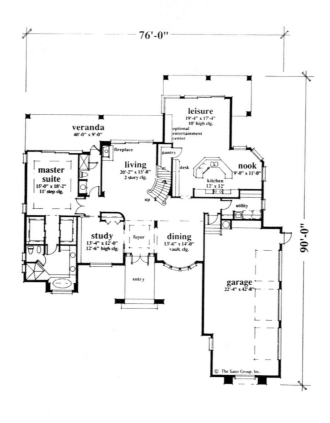

veranda
40'-0" x 9'-0"

leisure
19'-4" x 17'-4"
10' high clg.

optional
entertainment
center

fireplace

pantry

master
suite
15'-0" x 18'-2"
11' step clg.

living
20'-2" x 15'-8"
2 story clg.

desk

nook
9'-0" x 11'-0"

kitchen
12' x 12'

up

utility

study
13'-4" x 12'-0"
12'-6" high clg.

foyer

dining
13'-6" x 14'-0"
vault. clg.

entry

garage
22'-4" x 42'-8"

© The Sater Group, Inc.

76'-0"

90'-0"

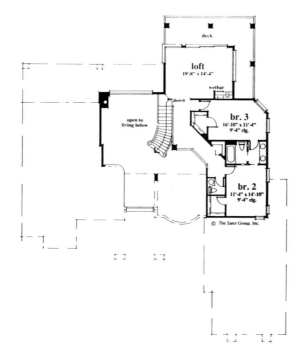

deck

loft
19'-8" x 14'-4"

wetbar

down

open to
living below

br. 3
16'-10" x 11'-4"
9'-4" clg.

br. 2
11'-4" x 14'-10"
9'-4" clg.

© The Sater Group, Inc.

Sunbelt 513

The "Cotton Creek Trace" by Sater Design presents a perfect combination of traditional elegance and contemporary design. The exterior features a balanced mixture of facades and clear lines formed by the roofs and dormers. The beautifully designed windows and an elaborate entry area lend the exterior a note of exclusiveness that is continued in the interior. From the imposing foyer, the view progresses to the formal living room, which is separated from the entry area with filigree arches. Both the luxurious master suite and a more private living area consisting of the kitchen with breakfast nook and adjoining leisure room open to the large veranda overlooking the garden. On the second floor are a study and a guest room.

Design 6650
Cotton Creek Trace
© Sater Design

Living area 3,748 sq. ft.
Total 5,593 sq. ft.

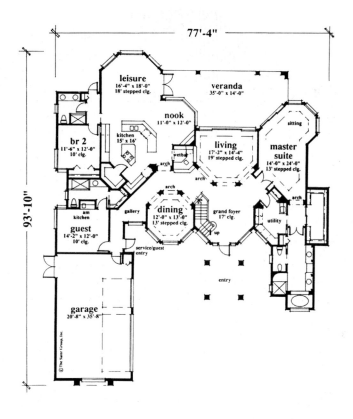

77'-4"

leisure
16'-4" x 18'-0"
18' stepped clg.

veranda
35'-0" x 14'-0"

nook
11'-0" x 12'-0"

kitchen
15' x 16'

br 2
11'-6" x 12'-0"
10' clg.

sitting

living
17'-2" x 14'-4"
19' stepped clg.

master
suite
14'-0" x 24'-0"
13' stepped clg.

wetbar

arch

arch

arch

arch

am
kitchen

gallery

dining
12'-0" x 13'-0"
13' stepped clg.

grand foyer
17' clg.

utility

guest
14'-2" x 12'-0"
10' clg.

service/guest
entry

up

entry

garage
20'-8" x 35'-8"

93'-10"

© The Sater Group, Inc.

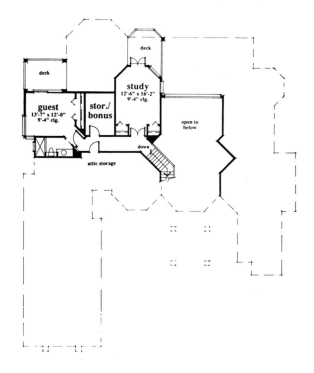

deck

deck

study
12'-6" x 16'-2"
9'-4" clg.

guest
13'-7" x 12'-0"
9'-4" clg.

stor./
bonus

open to
below

down

attic storage

Sunbelt 515

COTTAGES

This fascinating two-story cottage features a covered porch. The highlight of the design is undoubtedly the widow's walk rising from the metal roof, which is not merely a stylistic element, but is also practical and inhabitable. A garage is located under the house. Stairs lead from it to the first floor, which is designed for daily living with its spacious and bright great room, dining room and open kitchen. The first floor opens onto a large, covered porch. On the second floor are the master suite with walk-in closet, a second bedroom, and two full baths. A stairway leads up to the tower room, which features a small balcony. The "Saddle River" offers a living area of 1,620 square feet.

Design 6681
Saddle River
© Sater Design

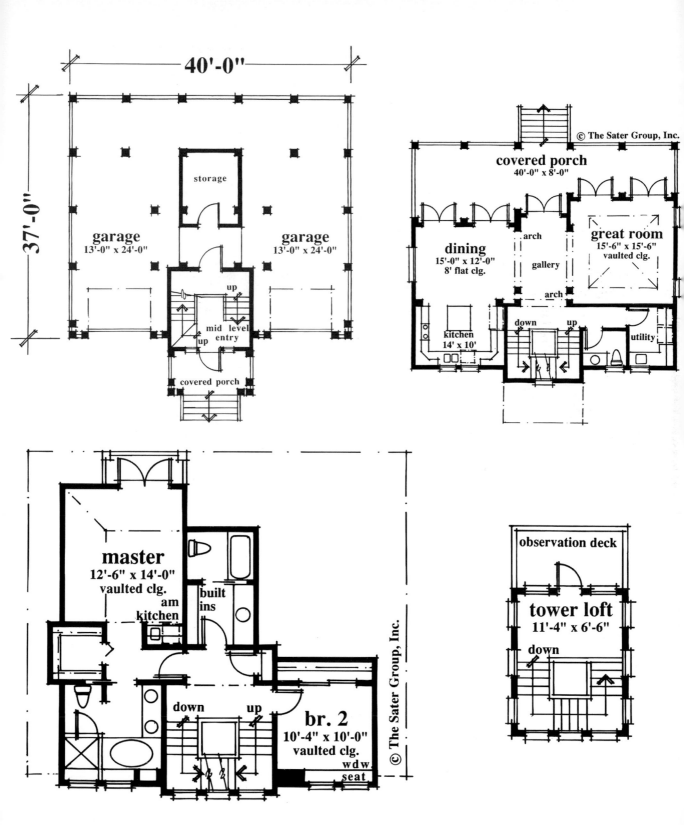

40'-0"

37'-0"

storage

garage
13'-0" x 24'-0"

garage
13'-0" x 24'-0"

up

mid level entry

up

covered porch

© The Sater Group, Inc.

covered porch
40'-0" x 8'-0"

dining
15'-0" x 12'-0"
8' flat clg.

arch

gallery

arch

great room
15'-6" x 15'-6"
vaulted clg.

down

up

kitchen
14' x 10'

utility

master
12'-6" x 14'-0"
vaulted clg.

am
kitchen

built
ins

down

up

br. 2
10'-4" x 10'-0"
vaulted clg.

wdw.
seat

© The Sater Group, Inc.

observation deck

tower loft
11'-4" x 6'-6"

down

Cottages 519

With its 2,608 square feet, this dream of a cottage offers a generous floor plan with an open design. The living room with a cathedral ceiling is surrounded on two sides by an inviting wrap–around porch. Further covered outdoor seating is offered by the entry porch and a second-floor balcony off the master bedroom at the rear of the house.

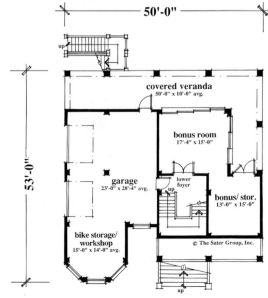

Design 6682-Seagrove Beach
© Sater Design

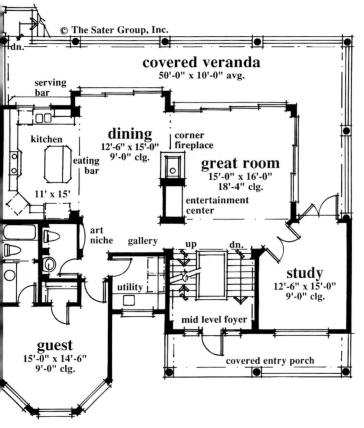

© The Sater Group, Inc.

covered veranda
50'-0" x 10'-0" avg.

dn.

serving
bar

dining
12'-6" x 15'-0"
9'-0" clg.

corner
fireplace

kitchen

eating
bar

11' x 15'

great room
15'-0" x 16'-0"
18'-4" clg.

entertainment
center

art
niche

gallery

utility

up

dn.

study
12'-6" x 15'-0"
9'-0" clg.

mid level foyer

guest
15'-0" x 14'-6"
9'-0" clg.

covered entry porch

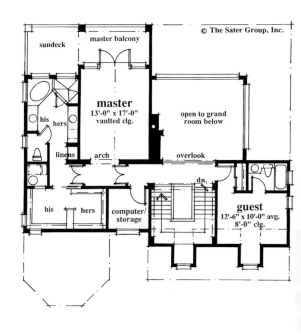

sundeck

master balcony

© The Sater Group, Inc.

his

hers

master
13'-0" x 17'-0"
vaulted clg.

open to grand
room below

linens

arch

overlook

his

hers

computer/
storage

dn.

guest
12'-6" x 10'-0" avg.
8'-0" clg.

This comfortable cottage derives its charm from the numerous striking details of the facade. The wooden shingles of the gable harmonize beautifully with the horizontal paneling on the front of the house. The metal roof sets a further stylistic accent. The rear of the house is dominated by a wrap-around porch and a second-floor balcony. At the heart of the 1,290-square-foot ground floor is the centrally located great room with fireplace. The adjacent kitchen features an eating bar and access to the formal dining room. The ground floor also houses the master suite, while two additional bedrooms on the second floor make the cottage spacious enough for most families.

Design 6683
Periwinkle Way
© Sater Design

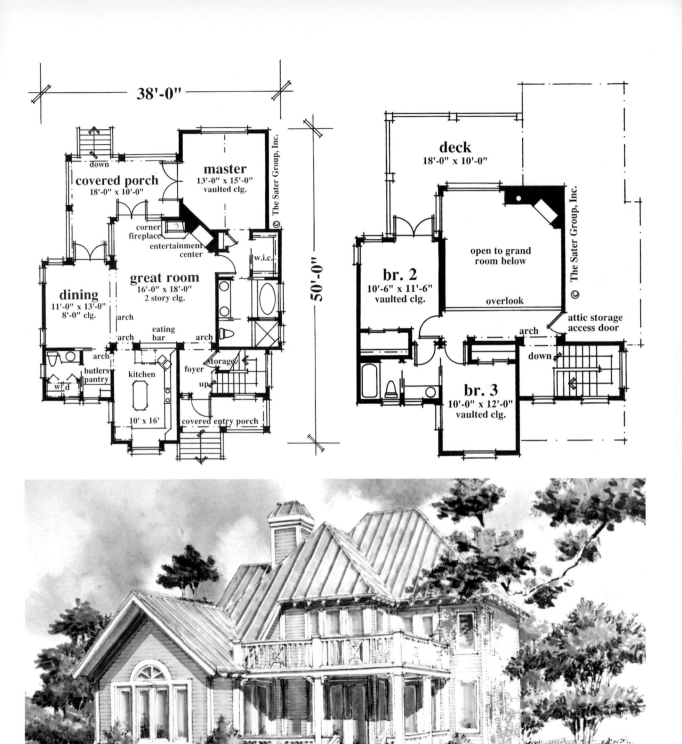

38'-0"

down

covered porch
18'-0" x 10'-0"

master
13'-0" x 15'-0"
vaulted clg.

© The Sater Group, Inc.

corner fireplace

entertainment center

w.i.c.

dining
11'-0" x 13'-0"
8'-0" clg.

great room
16'-0" x 18'-0"
2 story clg.

arch

arch

eating bar

arch

arch

storage

butlers pantry

foyer

w/d

kitchen

up

10' x 16'

covered entry porch

50'-0"

deck
18'-0" x 10'-0"

open to grand room below

© The Sater Group, Inc.

br. 2
10'-6" x 11'-6"
vaulted clg.

overlook

attic storage access door

arch

down

br. 3
10'-0" x 12'-0"
vaulted clg.

The design of this 2,465-square-foot cottage is modeled on an actual 19th-century Carribean estate, and features beautiful covered porches on both the front and rear of the house and a high-ceilinged great room.

Design 6684
Southampton Bay
© Sater Design

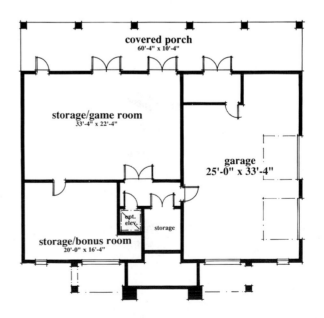

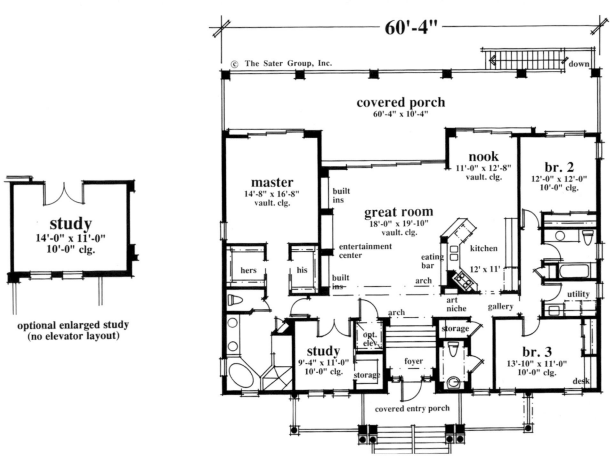

60'-4"

© The Sater Group, Inc.

down

covered porch
60'-4" x 10'-4"

master
14'-8" x 16'-8"
vault. clg.

built ins

nook
11'-0" x 12'-8"
vault. clg.

br. 2
12'-0" x 12'-0"
10'-0" clg.

great room
18'-0" x 19'-10"
vault. clg.

kitchen
12' x 11'

entertainment center

eating bar

built ins

hers

his

arch

study
14'-0" x 11'-0"
10'-0" clg.

optional enlarged study
(no elevator layout)

art niche

gallery

utility

opt. elev.

arch

study
9'-4" x 11'-0"
10'-0" clg.

storage

arch

foyer

storage

br. 3
13'-10" x 11'-0"
10'-0" clg.

desk

covered entry porch

Garden terraces, covered porches, balus-
trades and richly trimmed balconies mark
the exterior of this unique and appealing
cottage design.

Design 6685
Charleston Street
© Sater Design

Ground floor 935 sq. ft.
Second floor 1,305 sq. ft.
Third floor 1,208 sq. ft.

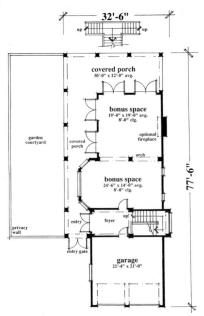

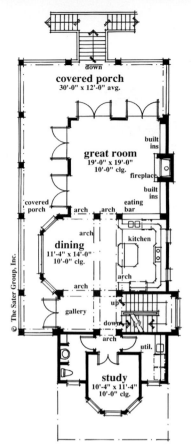

covered porch
30'-0" x 12'-0" avg.

great room
19'-0" x 19'-0"
10'-0" clg.

built ins

fireplace

built ins

covered porch

arch   arch

eating bar

arch

dining
11'-4" x 14'-0"
10'-0" clg.

arch

kitchen

arch

arch

gallery

up

down

arch

util.

study
10'-4" x 11'-4"
10'-0" clg.

© The Sater Group, Inc.

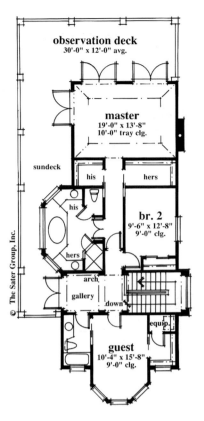

observation deck
30'-0" x 12'-0" avg.

master
19'-0" x 13'-8"
10'-0" tray clg.

sundeck

his

hers

his

br. 2
9'-6" x 12'-8"
9'-0" clg.

hers

arch

gallery

down

equip.

guest
10'-4" x 15'-8"
9'-0" clg.

© The Sater Group, Inc.

This design, inspired by the sunny Key West islands, features an effective exterior with a large covered porch and second-floor balcony. Large French windows provide the great room with natural light. Arches serve as room dividers between the kitchen and the dining room. "Shadow Lane" features three bedrooms and two full baths.

Design 6686
Shadow Lane
© Sater Design

Ground floor 1,046 sq. ft.
Second floor 638 sq. ft.
Total 1,684 sq. ft.

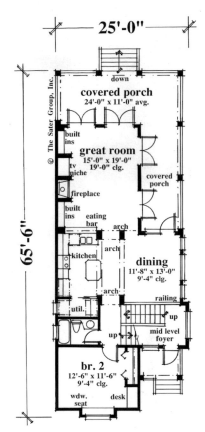

25'-0"

65'-6"

© The Sater Group, Inc.

covered porch
24'-0" x 11'-0" avg.

down

built ins

great room
15'-0" x 19'-0"
19'-0" clg.

tv niche

fireplace

covered porch

built ins

eating bar

arch

dining
11'-8" x 13'-0"
9'-4" clg.

kitchen

arch

arch

railing

util.

up

up

mid level foyer

br. 2
12'-6" x 11'-6"
9'-4" clg.

wdw. seat

desk

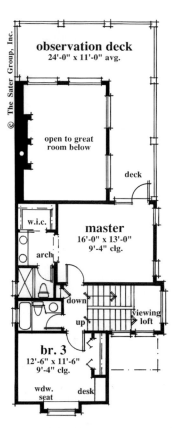

© The Sater Group, Inc.

observation deck
24'-0" x 11'-0" avg.

open to great room below

deck

w.i.c.

arch

master
16'-0" x 13'-0"
9'-4" clg.

down

up

viewing loft

br. 3
12'-6" x 11'-6"
9'-4" clg.

wdw. seat

desk

The front of this Neoclassic-Revival-style summer cottage features a beautiful glazed entrance. On the rear of the house, wide covered porches and open balconies invite relaxation. The living area of the design is 2,991 square feet.

Design 6689
Hemingway Lane
© Sater Design

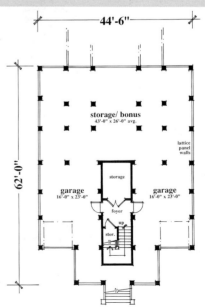

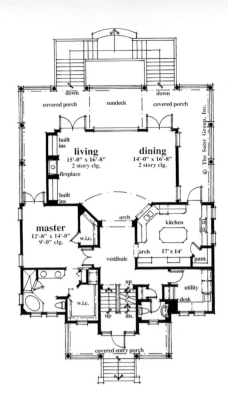

built ins

living
15'-0" x 16'-8"
2 story clg.

fireplace

built ins

dining
14'-0" x 16'-8"
2 story clg.

© The Sater Group, Inc.

down

covered porch

sundeck

down

covered porch

arch

kitchen

master
12'-8" x 14'-0"
9'-0" clg.

w.i.c.

arch

17' x 14'

pant.

vestibule

w.i.c.

up

dn.

up

utility

desk

covered entry porch

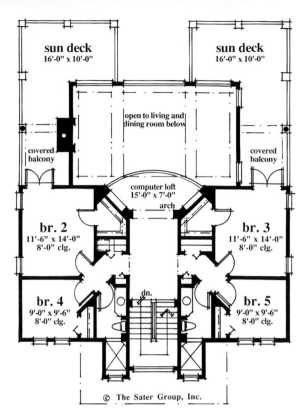

sun deck
16'-0" x 10'-0"

sun deck
16'-0" x 10'-0"

open to living and
dining room below

covered
balcony

covered
balcony

computer loft
15'-0" x 7'-0"

arch

br. 2
11'-6" x 14'-0"
8'-0" clg.

br. 3
11'-6" x 14'-0"
8'-0" clg.

br. 4
9'-0" x 9'-6"
8'-0" clg.

dn.

br. 5
9'-0" x 9'-6"
8'-0" clg.

© The Sater Group, Inc.

The "Georgetown Cove" is a charming and nostalgic two-story summer cottage. The classic paneling of the facade and the use of wooden shingles on the gable harmoniously augment the beautiful arched windows that make the back of the house so striking. They also provide sufficient light to the large great room in spite of the covered porch. The kitchen with its island and eating bar is open to the dining room. In addition to the master suite, two bedrooms, one of which has a walk-in closet, and another full bath are located on the second floor. With a living area of 1,824 square feet, the house appears larger from the outside than it actually is. It is relatively narrow, as well, at just over 27 feet wide, making this design an ideal choice for a narrow plot.

Design 6690
Georgetown Cove
© Sater Design

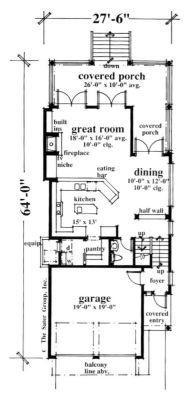

27'-6"

64'-0"

down

covered porch
26'-0" x 10'-0" avg.

built ins

great room
18'-0" x 16'-0" avg.
10'-0" clg.

fireplace

tv

niche

eating bar

covered porch

dining
10'-0" x 12'-0"
10'-0" clg.

kitchen
15' x 13'

half wall

equip.

d

w

pantry

up

up

foyer

garage
19'-0" x 19'-0"

covered entry

balcony line abv.

c The Sater Group, Inc.

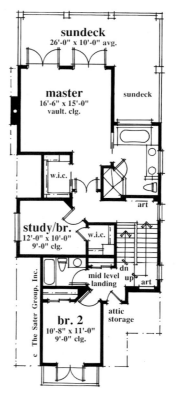

sundeck
26'-0" x 10'-0" avg.

master
16'-6" x 15'-0"
vault. clg.

sundeck

w.i.c.

art

study/br.
12'-0" x 10'-0"
9'-0" clg.

w.i.c.

dn

up

mid level landing

art

attic storage

br. 2
10'-8" x 11'-0"
9'-0" clg.

c The Sater Group, Inc.

Cottages 533

The "Nantucket Sound" summer house is distinguished by a playful treatment of form and color. The imposing entry area hints at the elegance and comfort that typify the 2,957-square-foot interior. High ceilings and large windows provide a sense of spaciousness in the living area.

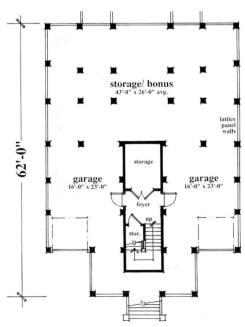

Design 6693
© Sater Design

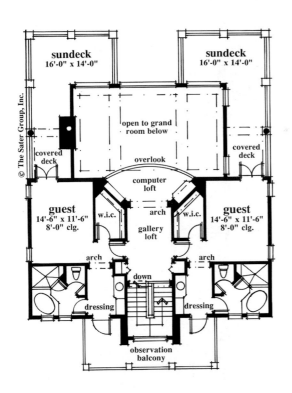

sundeck
16'-0" x 14'-0"

sundeck
16'-0" x 14'-0"

© The Sater Group, Inc.

open to grand
room below

covered
deck

covered
deck

overlook

computer
loft

guest
14'-6" x 11'-6"
8'-0" clg.

w.i.c.

arch

w.i.c.

guest
14'-6" x 11'-6"
8'-0" clg.

gallery
loft

arch

arch

down

dressing

dressing

observation
balcony

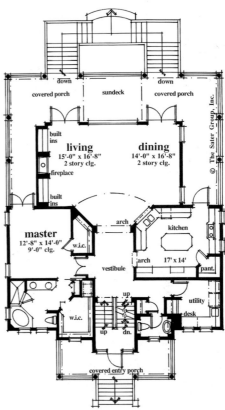

down

down

covered porch

sundeck

covered porch

built
ins

living
15'-0" x 16'-8"
2 story clg.

dining
14'-0" x 16'-8"
2 story clg.

© The Sater Group, Inc.

fireplace

built
ins

arch

kitchen

master
12'-8" x 14'-0"
9'-0" clg.

w.i.c.

17' x 14'

pant.

arch

vestibule

w.i.c.

up

utility

desk

up

dn.

up

covered entry porch

Cottages 535

With a narrow profile of 27½ feet, the "Duval Street" design is suitable even for narrow lots. The nostalgic flair of this Key West-inspired 2,120-square-foot cottage has a ground floor that features a comfortable living area composed of an open kitchen, a large great room with fireplace, and direct access to the broad covered porch. On the second floor, the master suite is fitted with a deluxe bath, a walk-in closet and high, arched French doors that open onto a private sun deck. The two additional bedrooms are located toward the front of the house and share a balcony above the garage. A study and another full bath complete the second floor.

Design 6701
Duval Street
© Sater Design

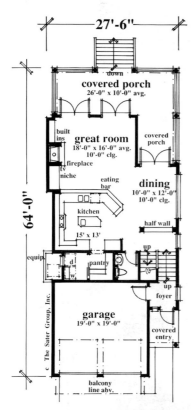

27'-6"

covered porch
26'-0" x 10'-0" avg.

down

built ins

great room
18'-0" x 16'-0" avg.
10'-0" clg.

covered porch

fireplace

tv niche

eating bar

dining
10'-0" x 12'-0"
10'-0" clg.

kitchen
15' x 13'

half wall

64'-0"

equip

d w

pantry

up

up foyer

garage
19'-0" x 19'-0"

covered entry

balcony line abv.

c The Sater Group, Inc.

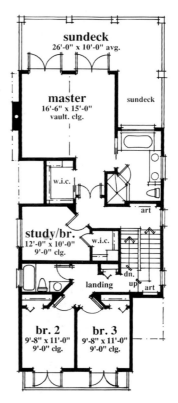

sundeck
26'-0" x 10'-0" avg.

master
16'-6" x 15'-0"
vault. clg.

sundeck

w.i.c.

art

study/br.
12'-0" x 10'-0"
9'-0" clg.

w.i.c.

dn.

up

landing

art

br. 2
9'-8" x 11'-0"
9'-0" clg.

br. 3
9'-8" x 11'-0"
9'-0" clg.

This book includes plans by the following:

American Home Plans

Atlanta Plan Source, Inc.

Breland & Farmer Designers, Inc.

Caddhomes

Cadre Design

Carini Engineerings Designs, P.C.

Columbia Design Group

Corley Plan Service, Inc.

Danze & Davis Architects, Inc.

DKDesigns

Encore of Florida

Estate Creations, Inc.

Framed Ideas

Frank Betz Associates, Inc.

Genesis Architecture and Planning

Historical Replications, Inc.

Home Design Center

Homes for Today

HomeStyles, Inc.

James Zirkel Home Design Service Inc.

Jerold Axelrod & Associates, P.C

Larry James & Associates, Inc.

Larry W. Garnett

LifeStyle HomeDesign

Michael Suglia, Architect

Nelsons Design Group

Sater Design

Stephen's Design Group

Suntel Home Designs, Inc.

William Poole Design

Completely finished blueprints and construction plans are available directly from the individual architects for all the house designs presented in this book. Further information on contacting the architects is listed below, or can be directly requested from the HomeStyles agency.
All the house designs in this book are **copyrighted** and are to be used only after purchasing the blueprints and building plans.
Transgressions will be prosecuted to the fullest extent of the law.

Augustus Suglia, A.I.A
Homes for Today
382 Church Ave.
Cedarhurst, NY   11516
Phone Number   1-516-569-4241
Fax Number   1-516-569-4241
http://www.homes4today.com
homes4today@iname.com

HomeStyles
Publishing and Marketing Inc.
213 East 4th Street
St. Paul, MN 55101
Phone Number 1-612-5000
Fax Number 1-612-602-5001
http://www.homestyles.com

DKDesigns, Inc.
CadreDevelopment
Phone Number 1-888.681.0166
www.cadredevelopment.com

The Sater Design Collection, Inc.
3461 Bonita Bay Boulevard
Suite 220
Bonita Springs, Florida 34134
Phone Number 1-800-718-PLAN

Larry James Designs
2208 Justice Street
Monroe, Louisiana 71201
Phone Number 1-318-322-5892
Fax Number 1-318-325-5538
http://www.larryjames.com
ljdesigns@larryjames.com

Internationale Infoline
concept HOME PLANS
An der Reitbahn 2
21218 Seevetal - Germany
Phone Number 49(0) 4105 555 555
www.american-dreamhomes.de
concepthomeplans@t-online.de